9分达人雅思阅读真题还原及解析 3

王毅 辜驰◎编著

2014年－2006年6套最新阅读真题

◎ 与最新题库原文一字不差！
◎ 与雅思真题题目一模一样！！
◎ 与官方标准答案完全一致！！！

2014.1.25 Wealth in A Cold Climate

2013.4.13 Antarctica - in from the cold?

2013.3.9 Tasmanian Tiger

2013.2.23 Source of Knowledge

2013.1.12 The Forgotten Forest

2012.6.9 Morse Code

2011.4.30 Internal Market, Selling the Brand Inside

2010.1.30 Living Dunes

9分达人温馨提示：
如果你在考试中恰好遇到本书收录的某篇文章，请按捺住内心的激动，细心把题答完。

商务印书馆国际有限公司

图书在版编目（CIP）数据

9分达人雅思阅读真题还原及解析.3/王毅，辜驰编著.—北京：商务印书馆国际有限公司，2014.4
ISBN 978-7-5176-0064-0

Ⅰ.①9… Ⅱ.①王… ②辜… Ⅲ.①IELTS－阅读教学－题解 Ⅳ.①H319.4-44

中国版本图书馆 CIP 数据核字(2014)第066377号

9分达人雅思阅读真题还原及解析3

商务印书馆国际有限公司出版发行
（北京市东城区史家胡同甲24号 邮编100010
电子邮箱：*cpinter@public3.bta.net.cn*）

特约编辑：吴 蓉
责任编辑：李 强 唐峰雁
封面设计：金 莎
全国新华书店经销
发行热线：（010）84921043
传真：（010）62117166
编辑部电话：（010）84921043
北京合众伟业印刷有限公司印刷
字数：400千字
开本：787×1092mm 1/16 16.5印张
2014年5月第1版第1次印刷
定价：58.00元

前 言

《9分达人系列》的出版绝非偶然。现今市面上不乏雅思阅读经典系列教材，其种类繁多，且均面临着同一个问题，即书中所收录的题目大多已过时，多数已被剑桥雅思考试委员会弃之不用，在今后的考试中也基本上不会再出现，因而这些图书远远无法满足广大考生对雅思考试最前沿信息的需求。基于上述情况，我们在对最新雅思真题精心研究和反复推敲后，结合自身经验，提笔创作了第一本《9分达人雅思阅读真题还原》。该书出版后不久便获得了广大考生的认可。不过，由于缺乏解析，该书没能为广大考生进一步解惑。众多读者在使用该教材时，纵使知道自己的答案有误，却也只知其然，而不知其所以然。因此，我们在考生和出版方的提议下为该书续写了一本解析，以满足考生对参考材料的需求，这就是现在为广大雅思考生所熟知的《9分达人雅思阅读真题还原及解析》。真题与解析的完美结合更加贴合了雅思考生的需求，并受到广大考生读者的一致好评和热情推荐。2012年夏，《9分达人雅思阅读真题还原及解析2》也经过辛勤创作与广大读者正式见面，并受到了"烤鸭"们的热烈追捧。

与时俱进、推陈出新是图书行业发展的必然要求，《9分达人系列》也理所当然地顺应了这一趋势。跟不上雅思考试的时代步伐，解决不了广大考生的最新难题，就无法真正实现服务于读者、服务于考生的终极目标和承诺。为此，我们投入了大量精力，细心筛选经典试题并加以还原、精心编著词汇和题目详解，并配以参考译文，最终创作出了迄今最新一代的《9分达人雅思阅读真题还原及解析3》。本书经过多番努力，现已正式出版，其中收录了最新的6套雅思阅读真题。《9分达人雅思阅读真题还原及解析3》不仅是我们的心血之作，更是考生进行考前冲刺复习、寻找考场体验、保持做题手感、训练解题方法和技巧、扩充核心阅读词汇、押中现场考题的宝典。

《9分达人雅思阅读真题还原及解析3》有以下几大特色：

一、最新雅思阅读真题完整收录。

为了让考生在考前调整好心态，又不失适当的训练，本书收录了2014年-2006年6套完整的最新阅读真题。这6套阅读真题与《9分达人雅思阅读真题还原及解析》和《9分达人雅思阅读真题还原及解析2》所收录的真题均不重合。考生可根据自己的实际情况选做其中的题目，然后再对照解析部分查漏补缺，巩固已有的知识和经验，加深对雅思考试考点的印象和理解。如此，考生既不会有太大的压力，又能持续保持考试状态和解题手感，让自己在第一时间把握主动权。

二、增加“词汇详解”版块。

本书在已有的“真题集”、“题目详解”和“参考译文”三个版块的基础上，又增添了“词汇详解”这一版块，为考生的词汇积累提供了极为丰富的素材。“词汇详解”中的词汇均来自对应阅读文章及题目，并按照词汇在原文及题目中的先后顺序进行排列，包含词性、释义、词源、词根词缀、“小故事”和其他拓展信息等。内容丰富多彩，读起来非常有趣，并不像单纯的词汇书那样枯燥乏味。如此一来，既有助于考生加深对文章的理解，又能够帮助考生扩充词汇量。

三、题目详解令人耳目一新；经验与技巧总结助考生事半功倍；参考译文让理解更加深刻。

首先，我们结合题目信息与原文信息，对每一道阅读题目进行了详细的讲解。内容清晰明了，细致到位，通俗易懂，让人豁然开朗。其次，解析中包含了经过反复的思量、推敲和总结的多年雅思考试经验，汇聚了最有效的解题思路、方法和技巧。相信考生在掌握好这些技巧与经验后会对考试的题型有一个更明确的概念，从而能够更好地应对现场考试。最后，我们还为每一篇阅读文章提供了精确的参考译文，以帮助考生加深理解。

四、押题宝典。

在考场中，幸运的考生或许会惊喜地发现：眼前的雅思阅读题竟然与《9分达人雅思阅读真题还原及解析3》中的题目一模一样！若真是如此，那么请“烤鸭”们先按捺住内心的激动，细心地把题答完吧！

为广大考生提供优质的图书和服务是我们最真诚的愿望，考生和读者对我们的支持、鼓励和意见也将进一步促进和推动我们的进步与提高。为了时刻跟进考生的需求和对图书的反映，我们成立了新航道雅思读者互动QQ群（群号见封底）、新航道9分达人微博（http://weibo.com/3104127681）及9分达人微信（“9分达人”二维码见封面），诚邀广大雅思考生和英语爱好者的加盟。如果您想提高自己，那就不要犹豫了，加入我们的大家庭，与志同道合者一起交流畅谈吧！如果您对我们有任何意见或建议，也请不要忘记告诉我们哦！我们会悉心对待每一位读者的意见和提议，力求不断进步，为广大考生和读者编织美好的明天！

最后，我们衷心祝愿考生取得优异的成绩！

编者

2014年5月

我的英语词汇观

My English Wordview

wordview *n.* 词汇观（该词是仿照 worldview“世界观”而造“coin”出来的词汇，用来表达一个人对于单词或单词学习及记忆的看法。）

“背单词是超级无敌宇宙霹雳巨难”是我听到的大多数考生对于背单词的抱怨。然而，回顾自己当初学习英语的过程，虽有感难意，但也不至于此，自己反而还能享受背单词的过程。于是乎，便萌生了写下这篇文章的念头，以冀广大考生能够“我坚持，我成功”，以考促学，在备考中找到乐趣，享受人生。

现在作为一名雅思培训老师回顾大学期间自己的英语学习，既走过弯路，也走过捷径。现在看来，我深深地相信一点“万事万物都有捷径，关键在于你是否能找到这个捷径。”单词学习并不难，甚至能够“过目不忘”，you may respectfully disagree。当然这要靠方法，这里我简单介绍一下我总结的 PAVE 背单词的原则和方法。PAVE 是一个符合英语语言学、心理学和英语自然习得习惯的背单词的原则和方法。

Pave 本身是一个单词，词性是动词，意思是“铺设，为……铺平道路或者安排”。我们通常用“pave the way for…”的固定搭配来表达“为……准备或铺平道路”的意思。单词学习虽然不是英语学习的全部，但是它能够很好地 pave the way for better English learning；英语学习虽然不是大学生活的全部，但是它够很好地 pave the way for future careers。不好意思，有点扯远了（I got a little bit carried away here）。总而言之，这个 wordview 和 worldview 还是有点联系的。言归正传，PAVE 在这里实际上是一个“首字母缩写词（acronym）”，每一个字母代表一个单词学习的原则。

P=Pronunciation

A=Affixes and word roots

V=Visualisation

E=Extensive reading

Pronunciation 背单词的原则在于英语是拼音语言（it uses phonological scripts in contrast to the logographic scripts used by Chinese），**背单词一定要记发音**（must associate the pronunciation of a word with its spelling），而不要像学习象形文字一样去记字形。回想我们中文的学习过程，其实就是汉字的学习过程。小学时，老师告诉我们："同学们，横着写一笔是一，回去抄写 50 遍；两笔是二，也抄写 50 遍；三笔是三，也要抄 50 遍；注意四可不是四笔，四是这样写的，回去抄写 200 遍……"这样一来，人们就自然养成了**学习中文字词就要记字形、要抄写的习惯**。这个习惯经常被人们带到学习英语的过程中（Native Language Transfer/L1 Transfer：母语迁移现象），于是我们也就不难见到大量的同学记英文单词就是抄抄抄，重点完全放在单词的拼写上。其实，英语是拼音语言，并非象形的汉字要记忆字形。对于英语，记住发音就等于记住拼写，知道拼写也应该能把发音念出来（though there may be some irregularities）。例如：isotope、Mesopotamia、affliction、melamine，大家可以直接按照一个一个的音节拼写念出它们的发音，分别就是 i.so.tope、Me.so.po.ta.mia、af.flic.tion、me.la.mine。总而言之，**记忆英文单词一定要转换思路：重点不在拼写，而在发音，并且一定要学会把英文拼写和发音联系起来**。这样一来也提高了学生对英语单词的听力认知，雅思听力的提高亦指日可待，看电影、看美剧时也不用再看字幕，其间乐趣不可言喻啊。

Affixes and word roots 的意思是"词根词缀"。其实英语和中文一样，词都是由词素（morpheme）构成。不过在中文中词素是单个的汉字，一个一个的汉字再组成词，英文中是由词根词缀组成词。所以我常把词根词缀比喻成英文中的"汉字"，**提倡记忆单词就像我们最初学习中文一样：先学"汉字"，然后学习由"汉字"组词，再由词造句**。例如：有一个中文词"高血盐"，大家肯定没有听说过，也没见过吧。那么这就是一个生词。这个词大家记一遍能记住吗？还有一个词，叫做"火肌"或"水肌"。记一遍能记住吗？最近还流行一些词，什么"我伙呆"，什么"喜大普奔"，第一次见到这些词时，只记一遍能记住吗？我相信你肯定是可以的。原因就在于这些词的汉字大家都认识。同理，如果大家都熟悉词根词缀，凡是由认识的词根词缀组成的单词，记一遍自然就能记住了。其实，很多老师都强调这一点，这里就不再赘述了。

使用 Visualisation 的原则学习单词来源于心理学中对于长期记忆的研究（long-term memory）。意思是把要记忆的单词与一个生动的场景（context）或其他已有的长期记忆的事物联系在一起，这样大脑便可以自然地运用 semantic encoding（语义编码）的记忆模式储存在记忆语言区中。

> Information can be kept alive in short-term working memory by rote repetition, or maintenance rehearsal. But to transfer something into long-term memory, you would find it much more effective to use elaborative rehearsal—a strategy that involves thinking about the material in a more meaningful way and associating it with other knowledge that is already in long-term memory. (Saul Kassin)

换句话说，就是以一个故事来记单词，每个单词配一个有趣、生动的小故事，该故事可能来源于词本身的辞源（etymological stories），也可能来源于该词经典的使用，或错误的使用而闹出的笑话（anecdotes）等。这样一来，每学习一个单词就像读一个故事。只记单词记不住，但是读故事总是会有印象，这时稍微用一点记忆力就可以“过目不忘”了。当然，也不一定非得是故事，只要有丰富的信息，而非简单的单词释义，就有很大的好处，且信息越丰富，记忆越深刻，也就越能够 associate with other knowledge，这就是 Saul Kassin 所说的 semantic encoding。一本或多本好的词汇书也就必不可少了，它对单词要有详细的讲解，例如从词根词缀上，从历年真题上，从例句上，从近义词辨析上，从一些小故事上等等。总之，信息量越丰富，单词在长期记忆区中留下的印象就越深。单词**“在于学习，不在于背诵（‘study’ rather than ‘memorise’）”**。

Extensive reading 这一原则中文叫做泛读。这里的泛读并非是要去读很多的阅读材料，而是要一次性地读很多的单词，单词的量一定要多，而且要读很多的单词书，越多越好，多多益善。也就是说泛读分为两个方面，一方面是单词的泛读，**简单来说，就是“读”或“学习”单词，而不是“记忆”单词。而且不是一天“读”30 个或 50 个词，而是一定要坚持一天“读”500–1000 个单词（如果不能保证，酌情而减也是可以的）。保证量！当然，这并不是说需要一次性就把这些单词记住，而是要首先混个眼熟**，这样可以迅速积累词根词缀的知识（因为词根词缀会反复、重复出现），而且可以产生记单词的感觉，暂且称之为“词感”，**靠遍数来征服，科学地运用艾宾浩斯（H. Ebbinghaus）记忆规律曲线多次复习**，而不是纯粹靠记忆力。当然，这个原则一定要结合前3个原则一起来利用。另一方面是单词书的泛读，**我提倡拥有多本词汇书，越多越好**。在学习过程中，当对其中一本出现厌倦感时，立刻更换另外一本词汇书，因为是“新书”，所以总是能带来新鲜的刺激，便可以继续学习下去。如果再次感到疲惫，便继续更换。虽然不够经济，但是经济和效果有时候是相矛盾的关系。或者我们可以将这种做法看成是一个trade-off，以经济来换取效果。如此一来，便可保持不停的学习，在不同词汇书的穿插阅读期间可以一遍又一遍见到熟悉的单词，这在心理学上叫做elaborative rehearsal。长此以往，单词学习必然不会再那么困难，而且不同的词汇书通常能提供单词不同侧面的信息，例如：A-Z编排的词汇书能提供释义，词根词缀的词汇书能提供关于词根词缀的知识和衍生，分类词汇书能提供扩展、联系方面的内容，故事词汇书能提供visual information或单词使用的context等。总之，通过练习，考生一定可以像大多数英文老师或native speakers一样，遇到任何一个生词，不管长短如何，意思偏僻还是熟悉，都可以“过目不忘”了。举一个实际例子吧，我在大学期间学习GRE时，也像大多数学生一样基本一个月搞定所有GRE词汇（GRE词汇可以说是又生僻、又变态，甚至有人开玩笑说大多数GRE词汇，人生中只有在考GRE时才会见到一次，以后就再也不会见到了）。当时在学习GRE期间，我买了十几本GRE词汇书，什么《红宝书》、《蓝宝书》、《黑宝书》、《巴朗词表》、《GRE逆序》、《GRE分类》、《1000精品词汇系列》等等。总之只要一有时间，我就随便拿出来一本翻翻，翻烦了就立刻换下一本调剂一下。不同的词汇书也互相补充了词汇不同方面的信息，如此下来，GRE词汇就记得非常熟练了。

综合上面的讲述，这里我给大家推荐学习雅思词汇必备的4大类词汇书：

1. 按照A-Z字母顺序编排的词汇书。

2. 按照词根词缀编排的词汇书。

3. 按照词汇类别编排的词汇书。

4. 按照考试频率或逆序编排的，或者读故事记单词类的词汇书。

这4类词汇书结合在一起，随时翻阅，甚至还可以找一本带练习的词汇书，在做题过程中记单词。因为你会发现，在单词书上记单词有时不一定能留下印象，但是做题时，题目往往会在大脑中留下深刻的印象，不论是难题还是简单题，是做错的题还是做对的题，亦或是让人纠结的题。

虽然说了这么多，但是有的同学可能还是会说："老师，不管怎样学习，我背单词总是背了就忘，背了就忘啊！"我真想对他说："恭喜你，你就是人类"。遗忘是人类的正常现象，是大脑自我保护的机制，否则我们的大脑就会被 snowed under by excessive amount of unnecessary information/memories。其实，学习就需要 reinforce and consolidate 我们所学过的知识，毕竟语言这样的东西就是 use it or lose it。所以，我坚持，我成功！

最后借鉴一下武侠术语说说词汇学习的三个境界吧！一、单词的初识阶段。看到了，记得背过，什么意思不太有印象。此乃"玉清境界"。二、单词的熟悉阶段。通过单词书的运用结合做题，看到单词已然熟知单词的释义。此乃"太清境界"。三、单词的总结阶段。遇到单词，不仅知道意思，还能够立刻回忆出曾经见过的历年考题、考法和规律。此乃"玄清境界"。第一层玉清境大多数人在第一个月即可修成，但越往后艰深困难处便显现出来。第二层太清境一般人便要再修习一两个月。第三层玄清境更是一个分水岭，资质稍微差一点的便一生停滞于此，好一些的修习两三个月或四五个月也不稀奇。然而，如若修习到第三层境界，便是有了万法的根本，可以驾驭词汇，御空而行，风驰电掣，诛灭诸般英语考试之妖魔鬼怪，震天撼地考出满分成绩也非极难之事啦！

王毅

2014 年 5 月于北京

“词汇详解”使用说明

本书是在综合了大量《9 分达人雅思阅读真题还原及解析》和《9 分达人雅思阅读真题还原及解析 2》的读者反馈之后增加了词汇详解部分，目的是为了更好地提高读者的词汇水平。

该“词汇详解”的编排特色有三：

1. 取消所有单词音标注释。

正如我在“我的英语词汇观”中所提及的认识英语作为拼音语言，其书写和发音的联系是学好英语的第一步。窃以为中国学生英语学习障碍之一就是在学习英语的初期学习了音标，这使得大量学生难以体会发音和拼写的联系。取消音标注释就是为了帮助学生认知单词与发音之间的直接关系。如果考生遇到不会读的单词，一定要尝试根据单词的拼写去读一下，例如：musicophilia 就读作 Mew.Zee.Koh.Fee.Lee.Ah，不同的发音或重音都尝试一下，哪个念起来通畅、易念或好听，哪个一般就是对的，因为英语也讲究语言发音的优美和流畅，除非自己的审美比较奇葩。

2. 每个单词都尽量增加大量的注释。

这是为了实现“我的英语词汇观”中的 Visualisation，为学生提供关于该词汇丰富的信息，帮助学生把该词与自己已有的相关信息联系到一起，以便该词能在脑海中留下深刻的印象，从而顺利地“注册”在长期记忆之中，同时帮助考生更好地了解该词的一些应用，使考生能在雅思口语、写作或生活中运用该词汇。

3. 单词按照文章及题目中出现的顺序编排。

这种编排方式并非传统的 A 到 Z 的编排方式，有助于考生在阅读每篇文章的过程中检索该文章的生词。

该“词汇详解”的使用方法有三：

1. 正常做完一套题后使用（较为推荐）。

考生把书中题目当成考前“模考”（mock test）来使用，能够比较直接地反映出考生的真实英文水平，帮助考生收集比较真实的考试数据用以制定合理的应试策略，并且能够暴露考试中可能出现的种种问题，然后在分析总结阶段再使用该词汇详解就可以帮助考生分析是否是由于词汇问题导致题目解答错误，并在此时提高并加深考生对词汇的理解，有助于英语实力的提升。

2. **做题之前先熟悉或学习所有词汇**。

通常适用于没有太多时间做模考或者无法坚持做模考、只期望把本书作为考前押题或预测使用的同学。此时该"词汇详解"或可以作为"难词表"(glossary)，读者在阅读过程中遇到不熟悉的词汇时可以在其中查找。考生也可以一次性提前熟悉文中或题目里的所有生词，这样有助于更好地记忆文章内容和题目，帮助考生更好地确定和分析正确答案。

3. **把词汇部分单独拿出来当成词汇学习书来使用**。

如果时间充裕，甚至可以把词汇部分单独拿出来当成一本词汇学习书，通过词汇的学习和相对应的雅思文章阅读来提高自己的单词和阅读实力，达到以考促学的效果。

当然，编者水平有限，希望广大读者能够多多反馈或吐槽（新浪微博：@王毅老师）。我们以为，如果读者反应良好，我们会按照这种形式出版一套全新词汇书籍，共上、中、下三册，涵盖所有雅思核心词汇，其中对每个单词都有大量讲解，从词根、词缀到词源小故事，从单词辨析到应用详解，总之信息量一定是非常大的，甚至一页中只有两三个单词，其余全是讲解，这样必能大大加深考生对单词的理解、应用和记忆。我们坚信，考生的单词量的提高绝不是老师讲出来的，而是考生辛勤学来的，**但是好的单词书和单词讲解必定能使考生事半功倍！**

王毅

2014年5月于北京

致《9分达人系列》读者

读者疑问

1. 有了《剑1-剑9》，我还需要《9分达人系列》吗？

2.《9分达人》之后又有《9分达人2》与《9分达人3》，这到底是神马节奏？你们在拍电影吗？

3. 复习中应该什么时候使出《9分达人系列》这个大招？怎样才能让花出去的钱物超所值，转化成得分？

4. 为什么每本书只有区区六七套题，是不是太坑了点？

5. 每篇文章、题目、答案都跟真实考试一模一样吗？为什么感觉有些文章看起来比官方真题中要更“肥”一些呢？难度与实际考试能一样吗？

6. 有谁可以告诉我，为什么《9分达人》（阅读系列第一本）最后一套题没！有！答！案！？

7. 为什么如此高大上的力作，纸张却像“盗版书”？

答疑解惑

1. 有了《剑1-剑9》，我还需要《9分达人系列》吗？

在回答这个问题之前，我们先来了解一下雅思考试的机制。“烤鸭”们都知道，雅思考试极为频繁，平均每月4场。这就意味着剑桥雅思考试委员会的出题速度远远跟不上试题更新的步伐，因此日理万机的委员会专家们不可能每次考试都使用新题。事实上，雅思考试有一个庞大的题库，每场考试的题目都是计算机从题库中按一定公式抽取组合而成。就好像一个养满了鱼的大池塘，每次都从里面捞出几条来让你认认这都是谁。若我们能先认识几条“熟鱼”，那肯定是“善莫大焉”。然而，考试委员会的“渔夫”们从来就没有打算将这个宽广的鱼池对外开放，只是选取了较有代表性的“老鱼”编纂而成了《剑1-剑9》，以此勉强平复广大考生对真题的渴望之情。自1996年出版以来，《剑1-

剑9》以其权威性已经成为雅思界的经典教材，那么《9分达人系列》又有什么优势呢？它凭什么敢于和这位泰山北斗叫板呢？

事实上，《9分达人系列》与《剑1-剑9》的区别就在于以下两点：

（1）时新性

无论是最早的《剑1》，还是最新的《剑9》，书中所收录的真题均为剑桥雅思考试委员会早已弃之不用的老题、旧题。其中所收录的题目远远不及它的首发日期那么新。而《9分达人系列》所收录的题目都是作者根据自身的经验所编写的，以阅读系列为例，其中《9分达人》涵盖了2011年-2007年最新的8套阅读真题，《9分达人2》收录了2012年-2006年最新7套阅读真题，现在最新的《9分达人3》则收录了2014年-2006年最新6套阅读真题，三本书所收入的真题均不重合，绝非剑桥雅思考试委员会弃之不用的老题或旧题。如此，《9分达人系列》与《剑1-剑9》，哪个更加青春活力就显而易见了。

（2）命中率

我们必须要明白的一个事实是：题目一旦被收录到《剑桥雅思真题集》系列中，雅思考试委员会便会立即将其从现行题库中剔除。换言之，《剑1-剑9》所收录的题目基本不可能在真实考试中再次出现，其命中率几乎为零。而《9分达人系列》所收录的真题仍在现行题库之中，并且自出版以来已屡次在考试中重现（具体请参见“本书所收集文章及对应考试日期一览”），其命中率可以说是剑桥系列的无穷大倍。

总结来说，作为雅思界的权威用书，《剑1-剑9》以官方的角度展示了雅思考试。考生若想全面了解雅思考试的题型、难度和出题思路，认真学习这一系列的书籍十分必要。而《9分达人系列》则更像是一招便可致命的武林秘笈，考生若想一窥雅思考试的现行题库，或想在短期内迅速提高分数，那么《9分达人系列》无疑是最佳选择了！

2.《9分达人》之后又有《9分达人2》与《9分达人3》，这到底是神马节奏？你们在拍电影吗？

正如上述所提到的：“以阅读系列为例，《9分达人》涵盖了2011年-2007年最新8套雅思阅读真题，《9分达人2》收入了2012年-2006年最新7套雅思阅读真题，现在最新的《9分达人3》则收录了2014年-2006年最新6套雅思阅读真题，三本书所收入的真题均不重合。”

“烤鸭”应该都知道，雅思考试平均每月举办4场，全年共48场，那么从2006年至今，约已举办了400多场。而《9分达人》、《9分达人2》与《9分达人3》这三本书所收录的真题均源自这 400 多场考试。它们基本都是近几年考过一次、甚至多次的雅思真题，而且也极有可能在未来的雅思考试中再次、甚至反复地出现。因此，《9 分达人》、《9 分达人 2》与《9 分达人 3》互相并不冲突，它们所收录的题目均不重合，且都有命中的可能性，就像伟大的人民卫士葫芦娃，每一位都各有所长，“合体”之后更是可以成为无敌小金刚，让各位“烤鸭”战无不胜，所向披靡。

因此，《9 分达人》、《9 分达人 2》与《9 分达人 3》的联系就在于它们所收录的题目均是真题，都有相同的可能再一次出现在真实的考试中。三者的区别则在于它们所收录的题目都是不一样的，不重复的。此外，值得一提的是，《9 分达人雅思阅读真题还原及解析 3》在原有的阅读真题、题目详解、参考译文的基础上，又增添了词汇详解版块，使得本书的内容更为丰富。

3. 复习中应该什么时候使出《9 分达人系列》这个大招？怎样才能让花出去的钱物超所值，转化成得分？

对于这个问题，小编认为应该要具体情况具体分析了。有的“烤鸭”可能会认为在考前做这一系列书最合适，因为可以把它们当作预测或押题书来使用。对于这类时间紧迫的考生来说，这样做不失为一个好办法。但是，小编想说，如果时间还算充裕，“烤鸭”们可千万不要浪费了和“葫芦娃们”在一起的幸福时光，等到考试的前一天才开始翻阅啊！小编建议这类“烤鸭”能够静下心来细细研读，从文章内容、出题规律、考查角度甚至长难句等诸多方面“吃透”这一系列书才是最佳选择。毕竟，您多陪“葫芦娃们”玩耍，你们的感情才会更好，小英雄们才会给您更多的帮助。书上的内容只有吃透了、消化了，才是“烤鸭”们自己的哦！不管它考题千变万化，“烤鸭”们都能应变自如。

4. 为什么每本书只有区区六七套题，是不是太坑了点？

小编个人认为题目“不在多、而在精”，把已有的几套题研究透彻了，那也是非常了不起的成就了。要知道许多人都卡在“囫囵吞枣”的境界，没有细嚼慢咽，品不出其中真味，体会不到六七套真题精微的奥妙之处，更发现不了其背后庞大而丰富的讯息。

5. 每篇文章、题目、答案都跟真实考试一模一样吗？为什么感觉有些文章看起来比官方真题中要更“肥”一些呢？难度与实际考试能一样吗？

《9 分达人系列》所收录的题目都是作者根据考试经验所编写的，是作者根据考试结束后考生的回忆还原而来。所以，每篇文章、题目和答案都跟作者所还原的那场考试中的真题是一模一样的。

不过，考虑到剑桥雅思考试委员会极有可能在下一次的考试中对文章或者题目进行细微的调整（考生应该能够领会其中的深意吧），所以保险起见，作者在还原每一篇的文章时也适当地保留或增加了一些信息。（为什么说保留呢？要知道，雅思考试中的许多文章都是改编自国外著名报刊或杂志上的文章。剑桥雅思考试委员会在编写考题的过程中很有可能视情况删减一些无关紧要的内容或者替换一些极为生僻的词汇等等。）所以，考生在实际使用这一系列书籍时会感觉有些文章偏长，但总体的难度其实与实际考试是差不多的。当然，这些增加的内容并不是毫无疑义的，它们都跟真题文章有着密不可分的联系，既能够帮助考生扩充知识面，还能够帮助考生训练做题速度。

至于题目和答案，如果考生人品爆发，很可能看到原封不动的内容。不过，鉴于剑桥雅思考试委员会可能会调整题目顺序，甚至细微地改动题目或题型，所以也有可能考生会遇到稍有区别的内容。如果“烤鸭”们的目的仅仅是通过这一系列书来押题的话，那么定要牢记每一道题目及其对应的答案，千万别弄错了哈。如果“烤鸭”们的目的是想通过学习这一系列书，稳步提升英语能力的话，待一步步“吃透”，会发现一切变化不过是“纸老虎”哦！

6. 有谁可以告诉我，为什么《9 分达人》（阅读系列第一本）最后一套题没！有！答！案！？

对于《9 分达人雅思阅读真题还原及解析》的读者而言，或许都存在同样的疑问。其实答案非常简单：最后一套题是作者随书附“赠”给读者的“福利”。这套附赠的题目是 2011 年雅思首场考试（即 2011 年 1 月 8 日）的阅读真题。不过，作者并未在书中公布该套真题的答案（当然也没有相应的题目详解和参考译文），而是把悬念留到了《9 分达人雅思阅读真题还原及解析 2》中去解答。大家应该对于每集电视剧最后的结点那种又爱又恨的感觉非常熟悉了吧，哇哈哈哈～

7. 为什么如此高大上的力作，纸张却像“盗版书”？

轻型纸答：人家好桑心哦！心都痛了！

为了保护广大读者的眼睛，为了保护我们可爱的地球，更为了各位“烤鸭”能够“轻”松应考，9 分达人阅读和听力系列都采用了轻型纸。这是一种更人性化的纸种，纸张比较厚，但是很轻，而且质感很好，做成书籍之后，拿在手里也不会感到重，所以非常方便携带。另外，这种纸不含荧光增白剂，采用原色调（轻型纸：人家不刺眼的哦！），具有天然特性，使用寿命也比一般的纸种长。在欧美等发达国家中，书店里 95% 以上的图书都是采用这种纸印刷，既环保，又可以保护大家在阅读的过程中视力不受伤害哟，而且超轻的重量，让不是女汉纸的萌妹纸也可以毫不费力把书捧在手心里了！鉴于 9 分达人口语和写作系列采用了双色排版，在轻型纸上呈现的视觉效果不太理想，所以这两个系列的书籍都使用了其他纸种。

最后，小编在此祝愿广大“烤鸭”、读者能够有所突破，修为猛进啦！

目 录

Test 1 …………………………………………………………………… 1

Test 2 …………………………………………………………………… 13

Test 3 …………………………………………………………………… 26

Test 4 …………………………………………………………………… 38

Test 5 …………………………………………………………………… 50

Test 6 …………………………………………………………………… 62

真题解析 ………………………………………………………………… 75

Answer Keys …………………………………………………………… 239

本书所收集文章及对应考试日期一览

Test 1

Review of Research on the Effects of Food Promotion to Children 2013年1月5日 2010年3月27日

The Bridge That Swayed 2013年3月23日 2009年3月5日

Internal Market: Selling the Brand Inside 2011年4月30日 2010年4月15日

Test 2

The Forgotten Forest 2013年1月12日

Storytelling, From Prehistoric Caves To Modern Cinemas 2013年1月12日 2010年7月17日 2010年6月26日

Living Dunes 2010年1月30日

Test 3

Classifying Societies 2013年3月9日

Tasmanian Tiger 2013年3月9日 2011年3月5日

Accidental Scientists 2013年3月9日 2010年4月24日

Test 4

Otters 2013年3月23日 2010年5月29日 2007年4月28日

Wealth in A Cold Climate 2014年1月25日 2006年7月22日

Musical Maladies 2013年1月12日

Test 5

Morse Code 2012年6月9日 2009年12月3日

From A Novice to An Expert 2010年10月23日 2009年2月28日 2007年9月8日

High Speed Photography 2007年3月31日

Test 6

Thomas Young The Last True Know-It-All 2012年7月21日 2010年11月20日

Antarctica – in from the cold? 2013年4月13日 2010年10月23日 2008年4月21日

Source of Knowledge 2013年2月23日

TEST 1

READING PASSAGE 1

*You should spend about 20 minutes on **Questions 1-13**, which are based on Reading Passage 1 on the following pages.*

Questions 1-7

Reading Passage 1 has seven paragraphs, **A-G**.

*Choose the most suitable heading for paragraphs **A-G** from the list of headings below.*

*Write the appropriate number, **i-x**, in boxes 1-7 on your answer sheet.*

List of Headings

- **i** General points of agreements and disagreements of researchers
- **ii** How much children really know about food
- **iii** Need to take action
- **iv** Advertising effects of the "Big Four"
- **v** Connection of advertising and children's weight problems
- **vi** Evidence that advertising affects what children buy to eat
- **vii** How parents influence children's eating habits
- **viii** Advertising's focus on unhealthy options
- **ix** Children often buy what they want
- **x** Underestimating the effects advertising has on children

1 Paragraph **A**
2 paragraph **B**
3 Paragraph **C**
4 Paragraph **D**
5 Paragraph **E**
6 Paragraph **F**
7 Paragraph **G**

REVIEW OF RESEARCH ON THE EFFECTS OF FOOD PROMOTION TO CHILDREN

This review was commissioned by the Food Standards Agency to examine the current research evidence on:

- *the extent and nature of food promotion to children*
- *the effect, if any, that this promotion has on their food knowledge, preferences and behaviour.*

A Children's food promotion is dominated by television advertising, and the great majority of this promotes the so-called 'Big Four' of pre-sugared breakfast cereals, soft-drinks, confectionary and savoury snacks. In the last ten years advertising for fast food outlets has rapidly increased. There is some evidence that the dominance of television has recently begun to wane. The importance of strong, global branding reinforces a need for multi-faceted communications combining television with merchandising, 'tie-ins' and point of sale activity. The advertised diet contrasts sharply with that recommended by public health advisors, and themes of fun and fantasy or taste, rather than health and nutrition, are used to promote it to children. Meanwhile, the recommended diet gets little promotional support.

B There is plenty of evidence that children notice and enjoy food promotion. However, establishing whether this actually influences them is a complex problem. The review tackled it by looking at studies that had examined possible effects on what children know about food, their food preferences, their actual food behaviour (both buying and eating), and their health outcomes (eg. obesity or cholesterol levels). The majority of studies examined food advertising, but a few examined other forms of food promotion. In terms of nutritional knowledge, food advertising seems to have little influence on children's general perceptions of what constitutes a healthy diet, but, in certain contexts, it does have an effect on more specific types of nutritional knowledge. For example, seeing soft drink and cereal adverts reduced primary aged children's ability to determine correctly whether or not certain products contained real fruit.

C The review also found evidence that food promotion influences children's food preferences and their purchase behaviour. A study of primary school children, for instance, found that exposure to advertising influenced which foods they claimed to like; and another showed that labelling and signage on a vending machine had an effect on what was bought by secondary school pupils. A number of studies have also shown that food advertising can influence what children eat. One, for example, showed that advertising influenced a primary class's choice of daily snack at playtime.

D The next step, of trying to establish whether or not a link exists between food promotion and diet or obesity, is extremely difficult as it requires research to be done in real world settings. A number of studies have attempted this by using amount of television viewing as a proxy for exposure to television advertising. They have established a clear link between television viewing and diet, obesity, and cholesterol levels. It is impossible to say, however, whether this effect is caused by the advertising, the sedentary nature of television viewing or snacking that might take place whilst viewing. One study resolved this problem by taking a detailed diary of children's viewing habits. This showed that the more food adverts they saw, the more snacks and calories they consumed.

E Thus the literature does suggest food promotion is influencing children's diet in a number of ways. This does not amount to proof; as noted above with this kind of research, incontrovertible proof simply isn't attainable. Nor do all studies point to this conclusion; several have not found an effect. In addition, very few studies have attempted to measure how strong these effects are relative to other factors influencing children's food choices. Nonetheless, many studies have found clear effects and they have used sophisticated methodologies that make it possible to determine that i) these effects are not just due to chance; ii) they are independent of other factors that may influence diet, such as parents' eating habits or attitudes; and iii) they occur at a brand and category level.

F Furthermore, two factors suggest that these findings actually downplay the effect that food promotion has on children. First, the literature focuses principally on television advertising; the cumulative effect of this combined with other forms of promotion and marketing is likely to be significantly greater. Second, the studies have looked at direct effects on individual children, and understate indirect influences. For example, promotion for fast food outlets may not only influence the child, but also encourage parents to take them for meals and reinforce the idea that this is a normal and desirable behaviour.

G This does not amount to proof of an effect, but in our view does provide sufficient evidence to conclude that an effect exists. The debate should now shift to what action is needed, and specifically to how the power of commercial marketing can be used to bring about improvements in young people's eating.

Questions 8-13

Do the following statements agree with the views of the writer in Reading Passage 1?

In boxes 8-13 on your answer sheet, write

YES	*if the statement agrees with the views of the writer*
NO	*if the statement contradicts with the views of the writer*
NOT GIVEN	*if it is impossible to say what the writer thinks about this*

8 There is little difference between the number of healthy food advertisements and the number of unhealthy food advertisements.

9 TV advertising has successfully taught children nutritional knowledge about vitamins and others.

10 It is hard to decide which aspect of TV viewing has caused weight problems of children.

11 The preference of food for children is affected by their age and gender.

12 Wealthy parents tend to buy more "sensible food" for their children.

13 There is a lack of investigation on food promotion methods other than TV advertising.

READING PASSAGE 2

*You should spend about 20 minutes on **Questions 14-26**, which are based on Reading Passage 2 below.*

THE BRIDGE THAT SWAYED

When the London Millennium footbridge was opened in June 2000, it swayed alarmingly. This generated huge public interest and the bridge became known as London's "wobbly bridge."

The Millennium Bridge is the first new bridge across the river Thames in London since Tower Bridge opened in 1894, and it is the first ever designed for pedestrians only. The bridge links the City of London near St Paul's Cathedral with the Tate Modern art gallery on Bankside.

The bridge opened initially on Saturday 10th June 2000. For the opening ceremony, a crowd of over 1,000 people had assembled on the south half of the bridge with a band in front. When they started to walk across with the band playing, there was immediately an unexpectedly pronounced lateral movement of the bridge deck. "It was a fine day and the bridge was on the route of a major charity walk," one of the pedestrians recounted what he saw that day. "At first, it was still. Then it began to sway sideways, just slightly. Then, almost from one moment to the next, when large groups of people were crossing, the wobble intensified. Everyone had to stop walking to retain balance and sometimes to hold onto the hand rails for support." Immediately it was decided to limit the number of people on the bridge, and the bridge was dubbed the 'wobbly' bridge by the media who declared it another high-profile British Millennium Project failure. In order to fully investigate and resolve the issue the decision was taken to close the bridge on 12th June 2000.

Arup, the leading member of the committee in charge of the construction of the bridge, decided to tackle the issue head on. They immediately undertook a fast-track research project to seek the cause and the cure. The embarrassed engineers found the videotape that day which showed the center span swaying about 3 inches sideways every second and the south span 2 inches every 1.25 seconds. Because there was a significant wind blowing on the opening days (force 3-4) and the bridge had been decorated with large flags, the engineers first thought that winds might be exerting excessive force on the many large flags and banners, but it was rapidly concluded that wind buffeting had not contributed significantly to vibration of the bridge. But after measurements were made in university laboratories of the effects of people walking on swaying platforms and after large-scale experiments with crowds of pedestrians were conducted on the bridge itself, a new understanding and a new theory were developed.

The unexpected motion was the result of a natural human reaction to small lateral movements. It is well known that a suspension bridge has tendency to sway when troops march over it in lockstep, which is why troops are required to break step when crossing such a bridge. "If we walk on a swaying surface we tend to compensate and stabilise ourselves by spreading our legs further apart—but this increases the lateral push". Pat Dallard, the engineer at Arup, says that you change the way you walk to match what the bridge is doing. It is an unconscious tendency for pedestrians to match their footsteps to the sway, thereby exacerbating it even more. "It's rather like walking on a rolling ship deck—you move one way and then the other to compensate for the roll." The way people walk doesn't have to match exactly the natural frequency of the bridge as in resonance—the interaction is more subtle. As the bridge moves, people adjust the way they walk in their own manner. The problem is that when there are enough people on the bridge the total sideways push can overcome the bridge's ability to absorb it. The movement becomes excessive and continues to increase until people begin to have difficulty in walking—they may even have to hold on to the rails.

Professor Fujino Yozo of Tokyo University, who studied the earth-resistant Toda Bridge in Japan, believes the horizontal forces caused by walking, running or jumping could also in turn cause excessive dynamic vibration in the lateral direction in the bridge. He explains that as the structure began moving, pedestrians adjusted their gait to the same lateral rhythm as the bridge; the adjusted footsteps magnified the motion—just like when four people all stand up in small boat at the same time. As more pedestrians locked into the same rhythm, the increasing oscillation led to the dramatic swaying captured on film until people stopped walking altogether, because they could not even keep upright.

In order to design a method of reducing the movements, an immediate research program was launched by the bridge's engineering designer Arup. It was decided that the force exerted by the pedestrians had to be quantified and related to the motion of the bridge. Although there are some descriptions of this phenomenon in existing literature, none of these actually quantifies the force. So there was no quantitative analytical way to design the bridge against this effect. The efforts to solve the problem quickly got supported by a number of universities and research organisations.

The tests at the University of Southampton involved a person walking on the spot on a small shake table. The tests at Imperial College involved persons walking along a specially built, 7.2m-long platform, which could be driven laterally at different frequencies and amplitudes. These tests have their own limitations. While the Imperial College test platform was too short that only seven or eight steps could be measured at one time, the "walking on the spot" test did not accurately replicate forward walking, although many footsteps could be observed using this method. Neither test could investigate any influence of other people in a crowd on the behavior of the individual tested.

The results of the laboratory tests provided information which enabled the initial design of a retrofit to be progressed. However, unless the usage of the bridge was to be greatly restricted, only two generic options to improve its performance were considered feasible. The first was to increase the stiffness of the bridge to move all its lateral natural frequencies out of the range that could be excited by the lateral footfall forces, and the second was to increase the damping of the bridge to reduce the resonant response.

Questions 14-17

*Choose **FOUR** letters, **A-I**.*

Write the correct letters in boxes 14-17 on your answer sheet.

Which **FOUR** of the following could be seen on the day when the bridge opened to the public?

A the bridge moved vertically
B the bridge swayed from side to side
C the bridge swayed violently throughout the opening ceremony
D it was hard to keep balance on the bridge
E pedestrians walked in synchronised steps
F pedestrians lengthened their footsteps
G a music band marched across the bridge
H the swaying rhythm varied to the portions of the bridge
I flags and banners kept still on the bridge

Questions 18-23

Complete the summary below.

Choose **NO MORE THAN TWO WORDS** *from the passage for each answer.*

Write your answers in boxes 18-23 on your answer sheet.

To understand why the Millennium Bridge swayed, engineers of Arup studied the videotape taken on the day of the opening ceremony. In the beginning they thought the forces of **18** _______ might have caused the movement because there were many flags and banners on the bridge that day. But quickly new understandings arose after series of tests were conducted on how people walk on **19** _______ floors. The tests showed people would place their legs **20** _______ to keep balance when the floor is shaking. Pat Dallard even believes pedestrians may unknowingly adjust their **21** _______ to match the sway of the bridge. Professor Fujino Yozo's study found that the vibration of a bridge could be caused by the **22** _______ of people walking, running and jumping on it because the lateral rhythm of the sway could make pedestrians adjust their walk and reach the same step until it is impossible to stand **23** _______.

Questions 24-26

Complete the table below.

Choose **NO MORE THAN THREE WORDS** *from the passage for each answer.*

Write your answers in boxes 24-26 on your answer sheet.

Test conducted by	Problems of the test
24 __________	Not enough data collection
25 __________	Not long enough
26 __________	Not like the real walking experience

READING PASSAGE 3

*You should spend about 20 minutes on **Questions 27-40**, which are based on Reading Passage 3 below.*

Internal Market: Selling the Brand Inside

When you think of marketing, you more than likely think of marketing to your customers: How can you persuade more people to buy what you sell? But another "market" is just as important: your employees, the very people who can make the brand come alive for your customers. Yet in our work helping executives develop and carry out branding campaigns, my colleagues and I have found that companies very often ignore this critical constituency.

Why is internal marketing so important? First, because it's the best way to help employees make a powerful emotional connection to the products and services you sell. Without that connection, employees are likely to undermine the expectations set by your advertising. In some cases, this is because they simply don't understand what you have promised the public, so they end up working at cross-purposes. In other cases, it may be they don't actually believe in the brand and feel disengaged or, worse, hostile toward the company. We've found that when people care about and believe in the brand, they're motivated to work harder and their loyalty to the company increases. Employees are united and inspired by a common sense of purpose and identity.

Unfortunately, in most companies, internal marketing is done poorly, if at all. While executives recognise the need to keep people informed about the company's strategy and direction, few understand the need to convince employees of the brand's power—they take it as a given.

Employees need to hear the same messages that you send out to the marketplace. At most companies, however, internal and external communications are often mismatched. This can be very confusing, and it threatens employees' perceptions of the company's integrity: They are told one thing by management but observe that a different message is being sent to the public. One health insurance company, for instance, advertised that the welfare of patients was the company's number one priority, while employees were told that their main goal was to increase the value of their stock options through cost reductions. And one major financial services institution told customers that it was making a major shift in focus from being a financial retailer to a financial adviser, but, a year later, research showed that the customer experience with the company had not changed. It turned out that company leaders had not made an effort to sell the change internally, so employees were still churning out transactions and hadn't changed their behavior to match their new adviser role.

Enabling employees to deliver on customer expectations is important, of course, but it's not the only reason a company needs to match internal and external messages. Another reason is to help push the company to achieve goals that might otherwise be out of reach. In 1997, when IBM launched its e-business campaign (which is widely credited for turning around the company's image), it chose to ignore research that suggested consumers were unprepared to embrace IBM as a leader in e-business. Although to the outside world this looked like an external marketing effort, IBM was also using the campaign to align employees around the idea of the Internet as the future of technology. The internal campaign changed the way employees thought about everything they did, from how they named products to how they organised staff to how they approached selling. The campaign was successful largely because it gave employees a sense of direction and purpose, which in turn restored their confidence in IBM's ability to predict the future and lead the technology industry. Today, research shows that people are four times more likely to associate the term "e-business" with IBM than with its nearest competitor.

Perhaps even more important, by taking employees into account, a company can avoid creating a message that doesn't resonate with staff or, worse, one that builds resentment. In 1996, United Airlines shelved its "Come Fly the Friendly Skies" slogan when presented with a survey that revealed the depth of customer resentment toward the airline industry. In an effort to own up to the industry's shortcomings, United launched a new campaign, "Rising," in which it sought to differentiate itself by acknowledging poor service and promising incremental improvements such as better meals. While this was a logical premise for the campaign given the tenor of the times, a campaign focusing on customers' distaste for flying was deeply discouraging to the staff. Employee resentment ultimately made it impossible for United to deliver the improvements it was promising, which in turn undermined the "Rising" pledge. Three years later, United decided employee opposition was undermining its success and pulled the campaign. It has since moved to a more inclusive brand message with the line "United," which both audiences can embrace. Here, a fundamental principle of advertising—find and address a customer concern—failed United because it did not consider the internal market.

When it comes to execution, the most common and effective way to link internal and external marketing campaigns is to create external advertising that targets both audiences. IBM used this tactic very effectively when it launched its e-business campaign. It took out an eight-page ad in the Wall Street Journal declaring its new vision, a message directed at both customers and internal stakeholders. This is an expensive way to capture attention, but if used sparingly, it is the most powerful form of communication; in fact, you need do it only once for everyone in the company to read it. There's a symbolic advantage as well. Such a tactic signals that the company is taking its pledge very seriously; it also signals transparency—the same message going out to both audiences.

Advertising isn't the only way to link internal and external marketing. At Nike, a number of senior executives now hold the additional title of "Corporate Storyteller." They deliberately avoid stories of financial successes and concentrate on parables of "just doing it," reflecting and reinforcing the company's ad campaigns. One tale, for example, recalls how legendary coach and Nike cofounder Bill Bowerman, in an effort to build a better shoe for his team, poured rubber into the family waffle iron, giving birth to the prototype of Nike's famous Waffle Sole. By talking about such inventive moves, the company hopes to keep the spirit of innovation that characterises its ad campaigns alive and well within the company.

But while their messages must be aligned, companies must also keep external promises a little ahead of internal realities. Such promises provide incentives for employees and give them something to live up to. In the 1980s, Ford turned "Quality Is Job 1" from an internal rallying cry into a consumer slogan in response to the threat from cheaper, more reliable Japanese cars. It did so before the claim was fully justified, but by placing it in the public arena, it gave employees an incentive to match the Japanese. If the promise is pushed too far ahead, however, it loses credibility. When a beleaguered British Rail launched a campaign announcing service improvements under the banner "We're Getting There," it did so prematurely. By drawing attention to the gap between the promise and the reality, it prompted destructive press coverage. This, in turn, demoralised staff, who had been legitimately proud of the service advances they had made.

Questions 27-32

Complete each sentence with the correct ending, ***A-E****, below.*

Write the correct letter, ***A-E****, in boxes 27-32 on your answer sheet.*

NB *You can use any letter more than once.*

27 A health company

28 A financial institution

29 A computer company

30 An airline

31 A sport shoe company

32 A railway company

A	alienated its employees by its apologetic branding campaign.
B	attracted negative publicity through its advertising campaign.
C	produced conflicting image between its employees and the general public.
D	successfully used an advertising campaign to inspire employees.
E	draws on the legends of the company spirit .

Questions 33-40

Do the following statements agree with the claims of the writer in Reading Passage 3?

In boxes 33-40 on your answer sheet, write

YES	*if the statement agrees with the claims of the writer*
NO	*if the statement contradicts with the claims of the writer*
NOT GIVEN	*if it is impossible to say what the writer thinks about this*

33 A strong conviction in the brand can contribute to higher job performance.

34 It is common for companies to overlook the necessity for internal communication.

35 Consumers were ready to view IBM as a leader in e-business before the advertising campaign.

36 United Airlines' failure in its branding campaign was due to the bad advice of an advertisement agency.

37 United Airlines eventually abolished its campaign to boost image as the result of a market research.

38 It is an expensive mistake for IBM to launch its new e-business campaign.

39 Nike employees claimed that they were inspired by their company tales.

40 A slight difference between internal and external promises can create a sense of purpose.

TEST 2

READING PASSAGE 1

*You should spend about 20 minutes on **Questions 1-13**, which are based on Reading Passage 1 below.*

The Forgotten Forest

Found only in the Deep South of America, longleaf pine woodlands have dwindled to about 3 percent of their former range, but new efforts are under way to restore them.

THE BEAUTY AND THE BIODIVERSITY of the longleaf pine forest are well-kept secrets, even in its native South. Yet it is among the richest ecosystems in North America, rivaling tallgrass prairies and the ancient forests of the Pacific Northwest in the number of species it shelters. And like those two other disappearing wildlife habitats, longleaf is also critically endangered.

In longleaf pine forests, trees grow widely scattered, creating an open, parklike environment, more like a savanna than a forest. The trees are not so dense as to block the sun. This openness creates a forest floor that is among the most diverse in the world, where plants such as many-flowered grass pinks, trumpet pitcher plants, Venus flytraps, lavender ladies and pineland bog-buttons grow. As many as 50 different species of wildflowers, shrubs, grasses and ferns have been cataloged in just a single square meter.

Once, nearly 92 million acres of longleaf forest flourished from Virginia to Texas, the only place in the world where it is found. By the turn of the 21st century, however, virtually all of it had been logged, paved or farmed into oblivion. Only about 3 percent of the original range still supports longleaf forest, and only about 10,000 acres of that is uncut old-growth—the rest is forest that has regrown after cutting. An estimated 100,000 of those acres are still vanishing every year. However, a quiet movement to reverse this trend is rippling across the region. Governments, private organisations (including NWF) and individual conservationists are looking for ways to protect and preserve the remaining longleaf and to plant new forests for future generations.

Figuring out how to bring back the piney woods also will allow biologists to help the plants and animals that depend on this habitat. Nearly two-thirds of the declining, threatened or endangered species in the southeastern United States are associated with longleaf. The outright destruction of longleaf is only part of their story, says Mark Danaher, the biologist for South Carolina's Francis Marion National Forest. He says the demise of these animals and plants also is tied to a lack of fire, which once swept through the southern forests on a regular basis. "Fire is absolutely critical for this ecosystem and for the species that depend on it," says Danaher.

Name just about any species that occurs in longleaf and you can find a connection to fire. Bachman's sparrow is a secretive bird with a beautiful song that echoes across the longleaf flatwoods. It tucks its nest on the ground beneath clumps of wiregrass and little bluestem in the open understory. But once fire has been absent for several years, and a tangle of shrubs starts to grow, the sparrows disappear. Gopher tortoises, the only native land tortoises east of the Mississippi, are also abundant in longleaf. A keystone species for these forests, its burrows provide homes and safety to more than 300 species of vertebrates and invertebrates ranging from eastern diamond-back rattlesnakes to gopher frogs. If fire is suppressed, however, the tortoises are choked out. "If we lose fire," says Bob Mitchell, an ecologist at the Jones Center, "we lose wildlife."

Without fire, we also lose longleaf. Fire knocks back the oaks and other hardwoods that can grow up to overwhelm longleaf forests. "They are fire forests," Mitchell says. "They evolved in the lightning capital of the eastern United States." And it wasn't only lightning strikes that set the forest aflame. "Native Americans also lit fires to keep the forest open," Mitchell says. "So did the early pioneers. They helped create the longleaf pine forests that we know today."

Fire also changes how nutrients flow throughout longleaf ecosystems, in ways we are just beginning to understand. For example, researchers have discovered that frequent fires provide extra calcium, which is critical for egg production, to endangered red-cockaded woodpeckers. Frances James, a retired avian ecologist from Florida State University, has studied these small black-and-white birds for more than two decades in Florida's sprawling Apalachicola National Forest. When she realised female woodpeckers laid larger clutches in the first breeding season after their territories were burned, she and her colleagues went searching for answers. "We learned calcium is stashed away in woody shrubs when the forest is not burned," James says. "But when there is a fire, a pulse of calcium moves down into the soil and up into the longleaf." Eventually, this calcium makes its way up the food chain to a tree-dwelling species of ant, which is the red-cockaded's favorite food. The result: more calcium for the birds, which leads to more eggs, more young and more woodpeckers.

Today, fire is used as a vital management tool for preserving both longleaf and its wildlife. Most of these fires are prescribed burns, deliberately set with a drip torch. Although the public often opposes any type of fire—and the smoke that goes with it—these frequent, low-intensity burns reduce the risk of catastrophic conflagrations. "Forests are going to burn," says Amadou Diop, NWF's southern forests restoration manager. "It's just a question of when. With prescribed burns, we can pick the time and the place."

Diop is spearheading a new NWF effort to restore longleaf. "It's a species we need to go back to," he says. Educating landowners about the advantages of growing longleaf is part of the program, he adds, which will soon be under way in nine southern states. "Right now, most longleaf is on public land," says Jerry McCollum, president of the Georgia Wildlife Federation. "Private land is where we need to work," he adds, pointing out that more than 90 percent of the acreage within the historic range of longleaf falls under this category.

Interest among private landowners is growing throughout the South, but restoring longleaf is not an easy task. The herbaceous layer—the understory of wiregrasses and other plants—also needs to be re-created. In areas where the land has not been chewed up by farming, but converted to loblolly or slash pine plantations, the seed bank of the longleaf forest usually remains viable beneath the soil. In time, this original vegetation can be coaxed back. Where agriculture has destroyed the seeds, however, wiregrass must be replanted. Right now, the expense is prohibitive, but researchers are searching for low-cost solutions.

Bringing back longleaf is not for the short-sighted, however. Few of us will be alive when the pines being planted today become mature forests in 70 to 80 years. But that is not stopping longleaf enthusiasts. "Today, it's getting hard to find longleaf seedlings to buy," one of the private landowners says. "Everyone wants them. Longleaf is in a resurgence."

Questions 1-5

Complete the notes below.

*Choose **NO MORE THAN TWO WORDS** from the passage for each answer.*

Write your answers in boxes 1-5 on your answer sheet.

Forest fire ensures that:

- Birds can locate their **1**_________ in the ground.
- The burrows of a species of **2**_________ provide homes to many other animals.
- Hardwoods such as **3**_________ don't take over.

Apart from fires lit by lightning:

- Fires are created by **4** _________ and settlers.
- Fires deliberately lit are called **5** _________.

Questions 6-9

Complete the flow-chart below.

Choose **ONE WORD ONLY** *from the passage for each answer.*

Write your answers in boxes 6-9 on your answer sheet.

How to increase the number of cockaded woodpeckers

Calcium stored in **6** ________

⇩

Shrubs are burned

⇩

Calcium released into **7** ________

⇩

Travel up to the leaves

⇩

8 ________ are eaten

⇩

Number of **9** ________ increases

⇩

More cockaded woodpeckers

Questions 10-13

Do the following statements agree with the information given in Reading Passage 1?

In boxes 10-13 on your answer sheet, write

TRUE	***if the statement agrees with the information***
FALSE	***if the statement contradicts the information***
NOT GIVEN	***if there is no information on this***

10 **The sparse distribution of longleaf pine trees leads to the most diversity of species.**

11 **It is easier to restore forests converted to farms than forests converted to plantations.**

12 **The cost to restore forest is increasing recently.**

13 **Few can live to see the replanted forest reach its maturity.**

READING PASSAGE 2

You should spend about 20 minutes on ***Questions 14-26****, which are based on Reading Passage 2 below.*

Storytelling, From Prehistoric Caves To Modern Cinemas

A It was told, we suppose, to people crouched around a fire: a tale of adventure, most likely—relating some close encounter with death; a remarkable hunt, an escape from mortal danger; a vision, or something else out of the ordinary. Whatever its thread, the weaving of this story was done with a prime purpose. The listeners must be kept listening. They must not fall asleep. So, as the story went on, its audience should be sustained by one question above all. What happens next?

B The first fireside stories in human history can never be known. They were kept in the heads of those who told them. This method of storage is not necessarily inefficient. From documented oral traditions in Australia, the Balkans and other parts of the world we know that specialised storytellers and poets can recite from memory literally thousands of lines, in verse or prose, verbatim—word for word. But while memory is rightly considered an art in itself, it is clear that a primary purpose of making symbols is to have a system of reminders or mnemonic cues—signs that assist us to recall certain information in the mind's eye.

C In some Polynesian communities a notched memory stick may help to guide a storyteller through successive stages of recitation. But in other parts of the world, the activity of storytelling historically resulted in the development or even the invention of writing systems. One theory about the arrival of literacy in ancient Greece, for example, argues that the epic tales about the Trojan War and the wanderings of Odysseus—traditionally attributed to Homer—were just so enchanting to hear that they had to be preserved. So the Greeks, c. 750-700BC, borrowed an alphabet from their neighbors in the eastern Mediterranean, the Phoenicians.

D The custom of recording stories on parchment and other materials can be traced in many manifestations around the world, from the priestly papyrus archives of ancient Egypt to the birch-bark scrolls on which the North American Ojibway Indians set down their creation-myth. It is a well-tried and universal practice: so much so that to this day storytime is probably most often associated with words on paper. The formal practice of narrating a story aloud would seem—so we assume—to have given way to newspapers, novels and comic strips. This, however, is not the case. Statistically it is doubtful that the majority of humans currently rely upon the written word to get access to stories. So what is the alternative source?

E Each year, over 7 billion people will go to watch the latest offering from Hollywood, Bollywood and beyond. The supreme storyteller of today is cinema. The movies, as distinct from still photography, seem to be an essentially modern phenomenon. This is an illusion, for there are, as we shall see, certain ways in which the medium of film is indebted to very old precedents of arranging 'sequences' of images. But any account of visual storytelling must begin with the recognition that all storytelling beats with a deeply atavistic pulse: that is, a 'good story' relies upon formal patterns of plot and characterisation that have been embedded in the practice of storytelling over many generations.

F Thousands of scripts arrive every week at the offices of the major film studios. But aspiring screenwriters really need look no further for essential advice than the fourth-century BC Greek Philosopher Aristotle. He left some incomplete lecture notes on the art of telling stories in various literary and dramatic modes, a slim volume known as *The Poetics*. Though he can never have envisaged the popcorn-fuelled actuality of a multiplex cinema, Aristotle is almost prescient about the key elements required to get the crowds flocking to such a cultural hub. He analyzed the process with cool rationalism. When a story enchants us, we lose the sense of where we are; we are drawn into the story so thoroughly that we forget it is a story being told. This is, in Aristotle's phrase, 'the suspension of disbelief'.

G We know the feeling. If ever we have stayed in our seats, stunned with grief, as the credits roll by, or for days after seeing that vivid evocation of horror have been nervous about taking a shower at home, then we have suspended disbelief. We have been caught, or captivated, in the storyteller's web. Did it all really happen? We really thought so—for a while. Aristotle must have witnessed often enough this suspension of disbelief. He taught at Athens, the city where theater developed as a primary form of civic ritual and recreation. Two theatrical types of storytelling, tragedy and comedy, caused Athenian audiences to lose themselves in sadness and laughter respectively. Tragedy, for Aristotle, was particularly potent in its capacity to enlist and then purge the emotions of those watching the story unfold on the stage, so he tried to identify those factors in the storyteller's art that brought about such engagament. He had, as an obvious sample for analysis, not only the fifth-century BC masterpieces of Classical Greek tragedy written by Aeschylus, Sophocles and Euripides. Beyond them stood Homer, whose stories even then had canonical status: *The Iliad* and *The Odyssey* were already considered literary landmarks—stories by which all other stories should be measured. So what was the secret of Homer's narrative art?

H It was not hard to find. Homer created credible heroes. His heroes belonged to the past, they were mighty and magnificent, yet they were not, in the end, fantasy figures. He made his heroes sulk, bicker, cheat and cry. They were, in short, characters—protagonists of a story that an audience would care about, would want to follow, would want to know what happens next. As Aristotle saw, the hero who shows a human side—some flaw or weakness to which mortals are prone—is intrinsically dramatic.

Questions 14-18

Reading Passage 2 has eight paragraphs, **A-H**.

Which paragraph contains the following information?

*Write the correct letter, **A-H**, in boxes 14-18 on your answer sheet.*

14 A misunderstanding of how people today get stories

15 The categorisation of stories

16 The fundamental aim of storytelling

17 A description of reciting stories without any assistance

18 How to make story characters attractive

Questions 19-22

Classify the following information as referring to

A adopted the writing system from another country

B used organic materials to record stories

C used tools to help to tell stories

*Write the correct letter, **A**, **B** or **C** in boxes 19-22 on your answer sheet.*

19 Egyptians

20 Ojibway

21 Polynesians

22 Greek

Questions 23-26

Complete the sentences below with **ONE WORD ONLY** *from the passage.*

Write your answers in boxes 23-26 on your answer sheet.

23 Aristotle wrote a book on the art of storytelling called ______.

24 Aristotle believed the most powerful type of story to move listeners is _____.

25 Aristotle viewed Homer's works as _______.

26 Aristotle believed attractive heroes should have some _______.

READING PASSAGE 3

You should spend about 20 minutes on ***Questions 27-40****, which are based on Reading Passage 3 on the following pages.*

Questions 27-33

Reading passage 3 has seven paragraphs, **A-G**.

Choose the correct heading for paragraphs ***A-G*** *from the list of headings below.*

Write the correct number, ***i-x****, in boxes 27-33 on your answer sheet.*

List of Headings

i	Shaping and reforming
ii	Causes of desertification
iii	Need combination of specific conditions
iv	Potential threat to industry and communication
v	An old superstition demystified
vi	Differences and similarities
vii	A continuous cycling process
viii	Habitat for rare species
ix	Replicating the process in laboratory
x	Commonest type of dune

27 Paragraph **A**

28 Paragraph **B**

29 Paragraph **C**

30 Paragraph **D**

31 Paragraph **E**

32 Paragraph **F**

33 Paragraph **G**

Living Dunes

When you think of a sand dune, you probably picture a barren pile of lifeless sand. But sand dunes are actually dynamic natural structures. They grow, shift and travel. They crawl with living things. Some sand dunes even sing.

A Although no more than a pile of wind-blown sand, dunes can roll over trees and buildings, march relentlessly across highways, devour vehicles on its path, and threaten crops and factories in Africa, the Middle East, and China. In some places, killer dunes even roll in and swallow up towns. Entire villages have disappeared under the sand. In a few instances the government built new villages for those displaced only to find that new villages themselves were buried several years later. Preventing sand dunes from overwhelming cities and agricultural areas has become a priority for the United Nations Environment Program.

B Some of the most significant experimental measurements on sand movement were performed by Ralph Bagnold, a British engineer who worked in Egypt prior to World War II. Bagnold investigated the physics of particles moving through the atmosphere and deposited by wind. He recognised two basic dune types, the crescentic dune, which he called "barchan," and the linear dune, which he called longitudinal or "sief" (Arabic for "sword"). The crescentic barchan dune is the most common type of sand dune. As its name suggests, this dune is shaped like a crescent moon with points at each end, and it is usually wider than it is long. Some types of barchan dunes move faster over desert surfaces than any other type of dune. The linear dune is straighter than the crescentic dune with ridges as its prominent feature. Unlike crescentic dunes, linear dunes are longer than they are wide—in fact, some are more than 100 miles (about 160 kilometers) long. Dunes can also be comprised of smaller dunes of different types, called complex dunes.

C Despite the complicated dynamics of dune formation, Bagnold noted that a sand dune generally needs the following three things to form: a large amount of loose sand in an area with little vegetation—usually on the coast or in a dried-up river, lake or sea bed; a wind or breeze to move the grains of sand; and an obstacle, which could be as small as a rock or as big as a tree, that causes the sand to lose momentum and settle. Where these three variables merge, a sand dune forms.

D As the wind picks up the sand, the sand travels, but generally only about an inch or two above the ground, until an obstacle causes it to stop. The heaviest grains settle against the obstacle, and a small ridge or bump forms. The lighter grains deposit themselves on the other side of the obstacle. Wind continues to move sand up to the top of the pile until the pile is so steep that it collapses under its own weight. The collapsing sand comes to rest when it reaches just the right steepness to keep the dune stable. The repeating cycle of sand inching up the windward side to the dune crest, then slipping down the dune's slip face allows the dune to inch forward, migrating in the direction the wind blows.

E Depending on the speed and direction of the wind and the weight of the local sand, dunes will develop into different shapes and sizes. Stronger winds tend to make taller dunes; gentler winds tend to spread them out. If the direction of the wind generally is the same over the years, dunes gradually shift in that direction. But a dune is "a curiously dynamic creature", wrote Farouk El-Baz in National Geographic. Once formed, a dune can grow, change shape, move with the wind and even breed new dunes. Some of these offspring may be carried on the back of the mother dune. Others are born and race downwind, outpacing their parents.

F Sand dunes even can be heard 'singing' in more than 30 locations worldwide, and in each place the sounds have their own characteristic frequency, or note. When the thirteenth century explorer Marco Polo encountered the weird and wonderful noises made by desert sand dunes, he attributed them to evil spirits. The sound is unearthly. The volume is also unnerving. Adding to the tone's otherworldliness is the inability of the human ear to localise the source of the noise. *Stéphane Douady* of the French national research agency CNRS and his colleagues have been delving deeper into dunes in Morocco, Chile, China and Oman, and believe they can now explain the exact mechanism behind this acoustic phenomenon.

G The group hauled sand back to the laboratory and set it up in channels with automated pushing plates. The sands still sang, proving that the dune itself was not needed to act as a resonating body for the sound, as some researchers had theorised. To make the booming sound, the grains have to be of a small range of sizes, all alike in shape: well-rounded. Douady's key discovery was that this synchronised frequency—which determines the tone of sound—is the result of the grain size. The larger the grain, the lower the key. He has successfully predicted the notes emitted by dunes in Morocco, Chile and the US simply by measuring the size of the grains they contain. Douady also discovered that the singing grains had some kind of varnish or a smooth coating of various minerals: silicon, iron and manganese, which probably formed on the sand when the dunes once lay beneath an ancient ocean. But in the muted grains this coat had been worn away, which explains why only some dunes can sing. He admits he is unsure exactly what role the coating plays in producing the noise. The mysterious dunes, it seems, aren't quite ready yet to give up all of their secrets.

Questions 34-36

Complete the sentences below.

Choose **ONE WORD ONLY** *from the passage for each answer.*

Write your answers in boxes 34-36 on your answer sheet.

34 _______ dune is said to have long ridges that can extend hundreds of miles.

35 According to Bagnold, an _______ is needed to stop the sand from moving before a dune can form.

36 Stéphane Douady believes the singing of dunes is not a spiritual phenomenon, but purely _______.

Questions 37-40

Complete the summary below.

Choose **ONE WORD ONLY** *from the passage for each answer.*

Write your answers in boxes 37-40 on your answer sheet.

There are many different types of dunes, two of which are most commonly found in deserts throughout the world, the linear dune and the **37** _______ dune, sometimes also known as the crescentic dune. It's been long known that in some places dunes can even sing and the answer lies in the sand itself. To produce singing sand in lab, all the sands must have similar **38** _______. And scientists have discovered that the size of the sand can affect the **39** _______ of the sound. But the function of the varnish composed by a mixture of **40** _______ still remains puzzling.

TEST 3

READING PASSAGE 1

*You should spend about 20 minutes on **Questions 1-13**, which are based on Reading Passage 1 below.*

CLASSIFYING SOCIETIES

Although humans have established many types of societies throughout history, sociologists and anthropologists tend to classify different societies according to the degree to which different groups within a society have unequal access to advantages such as resources, prestige or power, and usually refer to four basic types of societies. From least to most socially complex they are clans, tribes, chiefdoms and states.

Clan

These are small-scale societies of hunters and gatherers, generally of fewer than 100 people, who move seasonally to exploit wild (undomesticated) food resources. Most surviving hunter-gatherer groups are of this kind, such as the Hadza of Tanzania or the San of southern Africa. Clan members are generally kinsfolk, related by descent or marriage. Clans lack formal leaders, so there are no marked economic differences or disparities in status among their members.

Because clans are composed of mobile groups of hunter-gatherers, their sites consist mainly of seasonally occupied camps, and other smaller and more specialised sites. Among the latter are kill or butchery sites—locations where large mammals are killed and sometimes butchered—and work sites, where tools are made or other specific activities carried out. The base camp of such a group may give evidence of rather insubstantial dwellings or temporary shelters, along with the debris of residential occupation.

Tribe

These are generally larger than mobile hunter-gatherer groups, but rarely number more than a few thousand, and their diet or subsistence is based largely on cultivated plants and domesticated animals. Typically, they are settled farmers, but they may be nomadic with a very different, mobile economy based on the intensive exploitation of livestock. These are generally multi-community societies, with the individual communities integrated into the larger society through kinship ties. Although some tribes have officials and even a "capital" or seat of government, such officials lack the economic base necessary for effective use of power.

The typical settlement pattern for tribes is one of settled agricultural homesteads or villages. Characteristically, no one settlement dominates any of the others in the region. Instead, the archaeologist finds evidence for isolated, permanently occupied houses or for permanent villages. Such villages may be made up of a collection of free-standing houses, like those of the first farms of the Danube valley in Europe. Or they may be clusters of buildings grouped together, for example, the pueblos of the American Southwest, and the early farming village or small town of Çatalhöyük in modern Turkey.

Chiefdom

These operate on the principle of ranking—differences in social status between people. Different lineages (a lineage is a group claiming descent from a common ancestor) are graded on a scale of prestige, and the senior lineage, and hence the society as a whole, is governed by a chief. Prestige and rank are determined by how closely related one is to the chief, and there is no true stratification into classes. The role of the chief is crucial.

Often, there is local specialisation in craft products, and surpluses of these and of foodstuffs are periodically paid as obligation to the chief. He uses these to maintain his retainers, and may use them for redistribution to his subjects. The chiefdom generally has a center of power, often with temples, residences of the chief and his retainers, and craft specialists. Chiefdoms vary greatly in size, but the range is generally between about 5000 and 20,000 persons.

Early State

These preserve many of the features of chiefdoms, but the ruler (perhaps a king or sometimes a queen) has explicit authority to establish laws and also to enforce them by the use of a standing army. Society no longer depends totally upon kin relationships: it is now stratified into different classes. Agricultural workers and the poorer urban dwellers form the lowest classes, with the craft specialists above, and the priests and kinsfolk of the ruler higher still. The functions of the ruler are often separated from those of the priest: palace is distinguished from temple. The society is viewed as a territory owned by the ruling lineage and populated by tenants who have an obligation to pay taxes. The central capital houses a bureaucratic administration of officials; one of their principal purposes is to collect revenue (often in the form of taxes and tolls) and distribute it to government, army and craft specialists. Many early states developed complex redistribution systems to support these essential services.

This rather simple social typology, set out by Elman Service and elaborated by William Sanders and Joseph Marino, can be criticised, and it should not be used unthinkingly. Nevertheless, if we are seeking to talk about early societies, we must use words and hence concepts to do so. Service's categories provide a good framework to help organise our thoughts.

Questions 1-7

Do the following statements agree with the information given in Reading Passage 1?

In boxes 1-7 on your answer sheet, write

TRUE	*if the statement agrees with the information*
FALSE	*if the statement contradicts the information*
NOT GIVEN	*if there is no information on this*

1 There's little economic difference between members of a clan.

2 The farmers of a tribe grow a wide range of plants.

3 One settlement is more important than any other settlements in a tribe.

4 A member's status in a chiefdom is determined by how much land he owns.

5 There are people who craft goods in chiefdoms.

6 The king keeps the order of a state by using an army.

7 Bureaucratic officers receive higher salaries than other members.

Questions 8-13

Answer the questions below.

*Choose **NO MORE THAN TWO WORDS** from the passage for each answer.*

Write your answers in boxes 8-13 on your answer sheet.

8 What are made at the clan work sites?

9 What is the other way of life for tribes besides settled farming?

10 How are Çatalhöyük's housing units arranged?

11 What does a chief give to his subjects as rewards besides crafted goods?

12 What is the largest possible population of a chiefdom?

13 Which group of people is at the bottom of an early state but higher than the farmers?

READING PASSAGE 2

You should spend about 20 minutes on ***Questions 14-26****, which are based on Reading Passage 2 below.*

Tasmanian Tiger

Although it was called tiger, it looked like a dog with black stripes on its back and it was the largest known carnivorous marsupial of modern times. Yet, despite its fame for being one of the most fabled animals in the world, it is one of the least understood of Tasmania's native animals. The scientific name for the Tasmanian tiger is Thylacine and it is believed that they have become extinct in the 20th century.

Fossils of thylacines dating from about almost 12 million years ago have been dug up at various places in Victoria, South Australia and Western Australia. They were widespread in Australia 7,000 years ago, but have probably been extinct on the continent for 2,000 years. This is believed to be because of the introduction of dingoes around 8,000 years ago. Because of disease, thylacine numbers may have been declining in Tasmania at the time of European settlement 200 years ago, but the decline was certainly accelerated by the new arrivals. The last known Tasmanian Tiger died in Hobart Zoo in 1936 and the animal is officially classified as extinct. Technically, this means that it has not been officially sighted in the wild or captivity for 50 years. However, there are still unsubstantiated sightings.

Hans Naarding, whose study of animals had taken him around the world, was conducting a survey of a species of endangered migratory bird. What he saw that night is now regarded as the most credible sighting recorded of thylacine that many believe has been extinct for more than 70 years.

"I had to work at night," Naarding takes up the story. "I was in the habit of intermittently shining a spotlight around. The beam fell on an animal in front of the vehicle, less than 10m away. Instead of risking movement by grabbing for a camera, I decided to register very carefully what I was seeing. The animal was about the size of a small shepherd dog, a very healthy male in prime condition. What set it apart from a dog, though, was a slightly sloping hindquarter, with a fairly thick tail being a straight continuation of the backline of the animal. It had 12 distinct stripes on its back, continuing onto its butt. I knew perfectly well what I was seeing. As soon as I reached for the camera, it disappeared into the tea-tree undergrowth and scrub."

The director of Tasmania's National Parks at the time, Peter Morrow, decided in his wisdom to keep Naarding's sighting of the thylacine secret for two years. When the news finally broke, it was accompanied by pandemonium. "I was besieged by television crews, including four to five from Japan, and others from the United Kingdom, Germany, New Zealand and South America," said Naarding.

Government and private search parties combed the region, but no further sightings were made. The tiger, as always, had escaped to its lair, a place many insist exists only in our imagination. But since then, the thylacine has staged something of a comeback, becoming part of Australian mythology.

There have been more than 4,000 claimed sightings of the beast since it supposedly died out, and the average claims each year reported to authorities now number 150. Associate professor of zoology at the University of Tasmania, Randolph Rose, has said he dreams of seeing a thylacine. But Rose, who in his 35 years in Tasmanian academia has fielded countless reports of thylacine sightings, is now convinced that his dream will go unfulfilled.

"The consensus among conservationists is that, usually, any animal with a population base of less than 1,000 is headed for extinction within 60 years," says Rose. "Sixty years ago, there was only one thylacine that we know of, and that was in Hobart Zoo," he says.

Dr. David Pemberton, curator of zoology at the Tasmanian Museum and Art Gallery, whose PhD thesis was on the thylacine, says that despite scientific thinking that 500 animals are required to sustain a population, the Florida panther is down to a dozen or so animals and, while it does have some inbreeding problems, is still ticking along. "I'll take a punt and say that, if we manage to find a thylacine in the scrub, it means that there are 50-plus animals out there."

After all, animals can be notoriously elusive. The strange fish known as the coelacanth, with its "proto-legs", was thought to have died out along with the dinosaurs 700 million years ago until a specimen was dragged to the surface in a shark net off the south-east coast of South Africa in 1938.

Wildlife biologist Nick Mooney has the unenviable task of investigating all "sightings" of the tiger totalling 4,000 since the mid-1930s, and averaging about 150 a year. It was Mooney who was first consulted late last month about the authenticity of digital photographic images purportedly taken by a German tourist while on a recent bushwalk in the state. On face value, Mooney says, the account of the sighting, and the two photographs submitted as proof, amount to one of the most convincing cases for the species' survival he has seen.

And Mooney has seen it all—the mistakes, the hoaxes, the illusions and the plausible accounts of sightings. Hoaxers aside, most people who report sightings end up believing they have seen a thylacine, and are themselves believable to the point they could pass a lie-detector test, according to Mooney. Others, having tabled a creditable report, then become utterly obsessed like the Tasmanian who has registered 99 thylacine sightings to date. Mooney has seen individuals bankrupted by the obsession, and families destroyed. "It is a blind optimism that something is, rather than a cynicism that something isn't," Mooney says. "If something crosses the road, it's not a case of 'I wonder what that was?' Rather, it is a case of 'that's a thylacine!' It is a bit like a gold prospector's blind faith, 'it has got to be there'."

However, Mooney treats all reports on face value. "I never try to embarrass people, or make fools of them. But the fact that I don't pack the car immediately they ring can often be taken as ridicule. Obsessive characters get irate that someone in my position is not out there when they think the thylacine is there."

But Hans Naarding, whose sighting of a striped animal two decades ago was the highlight of "a life of animal spotting", remains bemused by the time and money people waste on tiger searches. He says resources would be better applied to saving the Tasmanian devil, and helping migratory bird populations that are declining as a result of shrinking wetlands across Australia.

Could the thylacine still be out there? "Sure," Naarding says. But he also says any discovery of surviving thylacines would be "rather pointless". "How do you save a species from extinction? What could you do with it? If there are thylacines out there, they are better off right where they are."

Questions 14-17

Complete the summary below.

Choose ***NO MORE THAN TWO WORDS*** *from the passage for each answer.*

Write your answers in boxes 14-17 on your answer sheet.

The Tasmanian tiger, also called thylacine, resembles the look of a dog and has **14** ________ on its fur coat. Many fossils have been found, showing that thylacines had existed as early as **15** ________ years ago. They lived throughout **16** ________ before disappearing from the mainland. And soon after the **17** ________ settlers arrived the size of thylacine population in Tasmania shrunk at a higher speed.

Questions 18-23

Look at the following statements (Questions 18-23) and the list of people below.

Match each statement with the correct person, ***A, B, C*** *or* ***D****.*

Write the correct letter, ***A, B, C*** *or* ***D****, in boxes 18-23 on your answer sheet.*

NB *You may use any letter more than once.*

18 His report of seeing a live thylacine in the wild attracted international interest.
19 Many eye-witnesses' reports are not trustworthy.
20 It doesn't require a certain number of animals to ensure the survival of a species.
21 There is no hope of finding a surviving Tasmanian tiger.
22 Do not disturb them if there are any Tasmanian tigers still living today.
23 The interpretation of evidence can be affected by people's beliefs.

List of People
A Hans Naarding
B Randolph Rose
C David Pemberton
D Nick Mooney

Questions 24-26

*Choose the correct letter, **A**, **B**, **C** or **D**.*

Write the correct letter in boxes 24-26 on your answer sheet.

24 Hans Naarding's sighting has resulted in

A government and organisations' cooperative efforts to protect thylacine.

B extensive interests to find a living thylacine.

C increase of the number of reports of thylacine worldwide.

D growth of popularity of thylacine in literature.

25 The example of coelacanth is to illustrate

A it lived in the same period with dinosaurs.

B how dinosaurs evolved legs.

C some animals are difficult to catch in the wild.

D extinction of certain species can be mistaken.

26 Mooney believes that all sighting reports should be

A given some credit as they claim even if they are untrue.

B acted upon immediately.

C viewed as equally untrustworthy.

D questioned and carefully investigated.

READING PASSAGE 3

You should spend about 20 minutes on ***Questions 27-40****, which are based on Reading Passage 3 on the following pages.*

Questions 27-32

Reading Passage 3 has seven paragraphs, **A-G**.

Choose the most suitable heading for paragraphs ***A-G*** *from the list of headings below.*

Write the appropriate number, ***i-x****, in boxes 27-32 on your answer sheet.*

List of Headings

i	Examples of some scientific discoveries
ii	Horace Walpole's fairy tale
iii	Resolving the contradiction
iv	What is the Scientific Method
v	The contradiction of views on scientific discovery
vi	Some misunderstandings of serendipity
vii	Opponents of authority
viii	Reality doesn't always match expectation
ix	How the word came into being
x	Illustration of serendipity in the business sector

27 Paragraph **A**

Example	*Answer*
Paragraph **B**	iii

28 Paragraph **C**

29 Paragraph **D**

30 Paragraph **E**

31 Paragraph **F**

32 Paragraph **G**

Accidental Scientists

A A paradox lies close to the heart of scientific discovery. If you know just what you are looking for, finding it can hardly count as a discovery, since it was fully anticipated. But if, on the other hand, you have no notion of what you are looking for, you cannot know when you have found it, and discovery, as such, is out of the question. In the philosophy of science, these extremes map onto the purist forms of deductivism and inductivism: In the former, the outcome is supposed to be logically contained in the premises you start with; in the latter, you are recommended to start with no expectations whatsoever and see what turns up.

B As in so many things, the ideal position is widely supposed to reside somewhere in between these two impossible-to-realise extremes. You want to have a good enough idea of what you are looking for to be surprised when you find something else of value, and you want to be ignorant enough of your end point that you can entertain alternative outcomes. Scientific discovery should, therefore, have an accidental aspect, but not too much of one. Serendipity is a word that expresses a position something like that. It's a fascinating word, and the late Robert King Merton—"the father of the sociology of science"—liked it well enough to compose its biography, assisted by the French cultural historian Elinor Barber.

C The word did not appear in the published literature until the early 19th century and did not become well enough known to use without explanation until sometime in the first third of the 20th century. Serendipity means a "happy accident" or "pleasant surprise", specifically, the accident of finding something good or useful without looking for it. The first noted use of "serendipity" in the English language was by Horace Walpole. He explained that it came from the fairy tale, called *The Three Princes of Serendip* (the ancient name for Ceylon, or present day Sri Lanka), whose heroes "were always making discoveries, by accidents and sagacity, of things which they were not in quest of".

D Antiquarians, following Walpole, found use for it, as they were always rummaging about for curiosities, and unexpected but pleasant surprises were not unknown to them. Some people just seemed to have a knack for that sort of thing, and serendipity was used to express that special capacity. The other community that came to dwell on serendipity to say something important about their practice was that of scientists, and here usages cut to the heart of the matter and were often vigorously contested. Many scientists, including the Harvard physiologist Walter Cannon and, later, the British immunologist Peter Medawar, liked to emphasise how much of scientific discovery was unplanned and even accidental. One of the examples is Hans Christian Ørsted's discovery of electromagnetism when he unintentionally brought a current-carrying wire parallel to a magnetic needle. Rhetoric about the sufficiency of rational method was so much hot air. Indeed, as Medawar insisted, "There is no such thing as The Scientific Method," no way at all of systematising the process of discovery. Really important discoveries had a way of showing up when they had a mind to do so and not when you were looking for them. Maybe some scientists, like some book collectors, had a happy knack; maybe serendipity described the situation rather than a personal skill or capacity.

E Some scientists using the word meant to stress those accidents belonging to the situation; some treated serendipity as a personal capacity; many others exploited the ambiguity of the notion. Yet what Cannon and Medawar took as a benign nose-thumbing at Dreams of Method, other scientists found incendiary. To say that science had a significant serendipitous aspect was taken by some as dangerous denigration. If scientific discovery were really accidental, then what was the special basis of expert authority? In this connection, the aphorism of choice came from no less an authority on scientific discovery than Louis Pasteur: "Chance favors the prepared mind." Accidents may happen, and things may turn up unplanned and unforeseen, as one is looking for something else, but the ability to notice such events, to see their potential bearing and meaning, to exploit their occurrence and make constructive use of them—these are the results of systematic mental preparation. What seems like an accident is just another form of expertise. On closer inspection, it is insisted, accident dissolves into sagacity.

F The context in which scientific serendipity was most contested and had its greatest resonance was that connected with the idea of planned science. The serendipitists were not all inhabitants of academic ivory towers. As Merton and Barber note, two of the great early-20th-century American pioneers of industrial research—Willis Whitney and Irving Langmuir, both of General Electric—made much play of serendipity, in the course of arguing against overly rigid research planning. Langmuir thought that misconceptions about the certainty and rationality of the research process did much harm and that a mature acceptance of uncertainty was far more likely to result in productive research policies. For his own part, Langmuir said that satisfactory outcomes "occurred as though we were just drifting with the wind. These things came about by accident." If there is no very determinate relationship between cause and effect in research, he said, "then planning does not get us very far." So, from within the bowels of corporate capitalism came powerful arguments, by way of serendipity, for scientific spontaneity and autonomy. The notion that industry was invariably committed to the regimentation of scientific research just doesn't wash.

G For Merton himself—who one supposes must have been the senior author—serendipity represented the keystone in the arch of his social scientific work. In 1936, as a very young man, Merton wrote a seminal essay on "The Unanticipated Consequences of Purposive Social Action." It is, he argued, the nature of social action that what one intends is rarely what one gets: Intending to provide resources for buttressing Christian religion, the natural philosophers of the Scientific Revolution laid the groundwork for secularism; people wanting to be alone with nature in Yosemite Valley wind up crowding one another. We just don't know enough—and we can never know enough—to ensure that the past is an adequate guide to the future: Uncertainty about outcomes, even of our best-laid plans, is endemic. All social action, including that undertaken with the best evidence and formulated according to the most rational criteria, is uncertain in its consequences.

Questions 33-37

*Choose the correct letter, **A**, **B**, **C** or **D**.*

Write the correct letter in boxes 33-37 on your answer sheet.

33 In paragraph A, the word "inductivism" means

A anticipate results in the beginning.

B work with prepared premises.

C accept chance discoveries.

D look for what you want.

34 Medawar says "there is no such thing as The Scientific Method" because

A discoveries are made by people with determined mind.

B discoveries tend to happen unplanned.

C the process of discovery is unpleasant.

D serendipity is not a skill.

35 Many scientists dislike the idea of serendipity because

A it is easily misunderstood and abused.

B it is too unpredictable.

C it is beyond their comprehension.

D it devalues their scientific expertise.

36 The writer mentions Irving Langmuir to illustrate

A planned science should be avoided.

B industrial development needs uncertainty.

C people tend to misunderstand the relationship between cause and effect.

D accepting uncertainty can help produce positive results.

37 The example of Yosemite is to show

A the conflict between reality and expectation.

B the importance of systematic planning.

C the intention of social action.

D the power of anticipation.

Questions 38-40

Answer the questions below.

*Choose **NO MORE THAN TWO WORDS** from the passage for each answer.*

Write your answers in boxes 38-40 on your answer sheet.

38 Who is the person that first used the word "serendipity"?

39 What kind of story does the word come from?

40 What is the present name of serendip?

TEST 4

READING PASSAGE 1

*You should spend about 20 minutes on **Questions 1-13**, which are based on Reading Passage 1 below.*

Otters

A Otters are semiaquatic (or in the case of the sea otter, aquatic) mammals. They are members of the Mustelid family which includes badgers, polecats, martens, weasels, stoats and minks, and have inhabited the earth for the last 30 million years and over the years have undergone subtle changes to the carnivore bodies to exploit the rich aquatic environment. Otters have long thin body and short legs—ideal for pushing dense undergrowth or hunting in tunnels. An adult male may be up to 4 feet long and 30 pounds. Females are smaller, around 16 pounds typically. The Eurasian otter's nose is about the smallest among the otter species and has a characteristic shape described as a shallow "W". An otter's tail (or rudder, or stern) is stout at the base and tapers towards the tip where it flattens. This forms part of the propulsion unit when swimming fast under water. Otter fur consists of two types of hair: stout guard hairs which form a waterproof outer covering, and under-fur which is dense and fine, equivalent to an otter's thermal underwear. The fur must be kept in good condition by grooming. Sea water reduces the waterproofing and insulating qualities of otter fur when salt water gets in the fur. This is why freshwater pools are important to otters living on the coast. After swimming, they wash the salts off in the pools and then squirm on the ground to rub dry against vegetation.

B Scent is used for hunting on land, for communication and for detecting danger. Otterine sense of smell is likely to be similar in sensitivity to dogs. Otters have small eyes and are probably short-sighted on land. But they do have the ability to modify the shape of the lens in the eye to make it more spherical, and hence overcome the refraction of water. In clear water and good light, otters can hunt fish by sight. The otter's eyes and nostrils are placed high on its head so that it can see and breathe even when the rest of the body is submerged. The long whiskers growing around the muzzle are used to detect the presence of fish. They detect regular vibrations caused by the beat of the fish's tail as it swims away. This allows otters to hunt even in very murky water. Underwater, the otter holds its legs against the body, except for steering, and the hind end of the body is flexed in a series of vertical undulations. River otters have webbing which extends for much of the length of each digit, though not to the very end. Giant otters and sea otters have even more prominent webs, while the Asian short-clawed otter has no webbing—they hunt for shrimps in ditches and paddy fields so they don't need the swimming speed. Otter ears are protected by valves which close them against water pressure.

C A number of constraints and preferences limit suitable habitats for otters. Water is a must and the rivers must be large enough to support a healthy population of fish. Being such shy and wary creatures, they will prefer territories where man's activities do not impinge greatly. Of course, there must also be no other otter already in residence—this has only become significant again recently as populations start to recover. A typical range for a male river otter might be 25km of river, a female's range less than half this. However, the productivity of the river affects this hugely and one study found male ranges between 12 and 80km. Coastal otters have a much more abundant food supply and ranges for males and females may be just a few kilometers of coastline. Because male ranges are usually larger, a male otter may find his range overlaps with two or three females. Otters will eat anything that they can get hold of—there are records of sparrows and snakes and slugs being gobbled. Apart from fish the most common prey are crayfish, crabs and water birds. Small mammals are occasionally taken, most commonly rabbits but sometimes even moles.

D Eurasian otters will breed any time where food is readily available. In places where condition is more severe, Sweden for example where the lakes are frozen for much of winter, cubs are born in Spring. This ensures that they are well grown before severe weather returns. In the Shetlands, cubs are born in summer when fish is more abundant. Though otters can breed every year, some do not. Again, this depends on food availability. Other factors such as food range and quality of the female may have an effect. Gestation for Eurasian otter is 63 days, with the exception of North American river otter whose embryos may undergo delayed implantation.

E Otters normally give birth in more secure dens to avoid disturbances. Nests are lined with bedding (reeds, waterside plants, grass) to keep the cubs warm while mummy is away feeding. Litter Size varies between 1 and 5 (2 or 3 being the most common). For some unknown reason, coastal otters tend to produce smaller litters. At five weeks they open their eyes—a tiny cub of 700g. At seven weeks they're weaned onto solid food. At ten weeks they leave the nest, blinking into daylight for the first time. After three months they finally meet the water and learn to swim. After eight months they are hunting, though the mother still provides a lot of food herself. Finally, after nine months she can chase them all away with a clear conscience, and relax—until the next fella shows up.

F The plight of the British otter was recognised in the early 60s, but it wasn't until the late 70s that the chief cause was discovered. Pesticides, such as dieldrin and aldrin, were first used in 1955 in agriculture and other industries—these chemicals are very persistent and had already been recognised as the cause of huge declines in the population of peregrine falcons, sparrowhawks and other predators. The pesticides entered the river systems and the food chain—micro-organisms, fish and finally otters, with every step increasing the concentration of the chemicals. From 1962 the chemicals were phased out, but while some species recovered quickly, otter numbers did not—and continued to fall into the 80s. This was probably due mainly to habitat destruction and road deaths. Acting on populations fragmented by the sudden decimation in the 50s and 60s, the loss of just a handful of otters in one area can make an entire population unviable and spell the end.

G Otter numbers are recovering all around Britain—populations are growing again in the few areas where they had remained and have expanded from those areas into the rest of the country. This is almost entirely due to law and conservation efforts, slowing down and reversing the destruction of suitable otter habitat and reintroductions from captive breeding programs. Releasing captive-bred otters is seen by many as a last resort. The argument runs that where there is no suitable habitat for them they will not survive after release and where there is suitable habitat, natural populations should be able to expand into the area. However, reintroducing animals into a fragmented and fragile population may add just enough impetus for it to stabilise and expand, rather than die out. This is what the Otter Trust accomplished in Norfolk, where the otter population may have been as low as twenty animals at the beginning of the 1980s. The Otter Trust has now finished its captive breeding program entirely. Great news because it means it is no longer needed.

Questions 1-9

Reading Passage 1 has seven paragraphs, **A-G**.

Which paragraph contains the following information?

*Write the correct letter, **A-G**, in boxes 1-9 on your answer sheet.*

***NB** You may use any letter more than once.*

1 A description of how otters regulate vision underwater

2 The fit-for-purpose characteristics of otter's body shape

3 A reference to an underdeveloped sense

4 An explanation of why agriculture failed in otter conservation efforts

5 A description of some of the otter's social characteristics

6 A description of how baby otters grow

7 The conflicted opinions on how to preserve

8 A reference to a legislative act

9 An explanation of how otters compensate for heat loss

Questions 10-13

Answer the questions below.

*Choose **NO MORE THAN TWO WORDS** from the passage for each answer.*

Write your answers in boxes 10-13 on your answer sheet.

10 What affects the outer fur of otters?

11 What skill is not necessary for Asian short-clawed otters?

12 Which type of otters has the shortest range?

13 Which type of animals do otters hunt occasionally?

READING PASSAGE 2

*You should spend about 20 minutes on **Questions 14-26**, which are based on Reading Passage 2 on the following pages.*

Questions 14-20

Reading Passage 2 has seven paragraphs, **A-G**.

*Choose the most suitable heading for paragraphs **A-G** from the list of headings below.*

*Write the appropriate number, **i-x**, in boxes 14-20 on your answer sheet.*

List of Headings

i	The positive correlation between climate and wealth
ii	Other factors besides climate that influence wealth
iii	Inspiration from reading a book
iv	Other researchers' results do not rule out exceptional cases
v	Different attributes between Eurasia and Africa
vi	Low temperature benefits people and crops
vii	The importance of institution in traditional views
viii	The spread of crops in Europe, Asia and other places
ix	The best way to use aid
x	Confusions and exceptions

14 Paragraph **A**

15 Paragraph **B**

16 Paragraph **C**

17 Paragraph **D**

18 Paragraph **E**

19 Paragraph **F**

20 Paragraph **G**

Wealth in A Cold Climate

Latitude is crucial to a nation's economic strength.

A Dr William Masters was reading a book about mosquitoes when inspiration struck. "There was this anecdote about the great yellow-fever epidemic that hit Philadelphia in 1793," Masters recalls. "This epidemic decimated the city until the first frost came." The inclement weather froze out the insects, allowing Philadelphia to recover.

B If weather could be the key to a city's fortunes, Masters thought, then why not to the historical fortunes of nations? And could frost lie at the heart of one of the most enduring economic mysteries of all—why are almost all the wealthy, industrialised nations to be found at latitudes above 40 degrees? After two years of research, he thinks that he has found a piece of the puzzle. Masters, an agricultural economist from Purdue University in Indiana, and Margaret McMillan at Tufts University, Boston, show that annual frosts are among the factors that distinguish rich nations from poor ones. Their study is published this month in the *Journal of Economic Growth*. The pair speculate that cold snaps have two main benefits—they freeze pests that would otherwise destroy crops, and also freeze organisms, such as mosquitoes, that carry disease. The result is agricultural abundance and a big workforce.

C The academics took two sets of information. The first was average income for countries, the second climate data from the University of East Anglia. They found a curious tally between the sets. Countries having five or more frosty days a month are uniformly rich, those with fewer than five are impoverished. The authors speculate that the five-day figure is important; it could be the minimum time needed to kill pests in the soil. Masters says: "For example, Finland is a small country that is growing quickly, but Bolivia is a small country that isn't growing at all. Perhaps climate has something to do with that." In fact, limited frosts bring huge benefits to farmers. The chills kill insects or render them inactive; cold weather slows the break-up of plant and animal material in the soil, allowing it to become richer; and frosts ensure a build-up of moisture in the ground for spring, reducing dependence on seasonal rains. There are exceptions to the "cold equals rich" argument. There are well-heeled tropical places such as Hong Kong and Singapore, a result of their superior trading positions. Likewise, not all European countries are moneyed—in the former communist colonies, economic potential was crushed by politics.

D Masters stresses that climate will never be the overriding factor—the wealth of nations is too complicated to be attributable to just one factor. Climate, he feels, somehow combines with other factors—such as the presence of institutions, including governments, and access to trading routes—to determine whether a country will do well. Traditionally, Masters says, economists thought that institutions had the biggest effect on the economy, because they brought order to a country in the form of, for example, laws and property rights. With order, so the thinking went, came affluence. "But there are some problems that even countries with institutions have not been able to get around," he says. "My feeling is that, as countries get richer, they get better institutions. And the accumulation of wealth and improvement in governing institutions are both helped by a favourable environment, including climate."

E This does not mean, he insists, that tropical countries are beyond economic help and destined to remain penniless. Instead, richer countries should change the way in which foreign aid is given. Instead of aid being geared towards improving governance, it should be spent on technology to improve agriculture and to combat disease. Masters cites one example: "There are regions in India that have been provided with irrigation—agricultural productivity has gone up and there has been an improvement in health." Supplying vaccines against tropical diseases and developing crop varieties that can grow in the tropics would break the poverty cycle.

F Other minds have applied themselves to the split between poor and rich nations, citing anthropological, climatic and zoological reasons for why temperate nations are the most affluent. In 350BC, Aristotle observed that "those who live in a cold climate...are full of spirit". Jared Diamond, from the University of California at Los Angeles, pointed out in his book *Guns, Germs and Steel* that Eurasia is broadly aligned east-west, while Africa and the Americas are aligned north-south. So, in Europe, crops can spread quickly across latitudes because climates are similar. One of the first domesticated crops, einkorn wheat, spread quickly from the Middle East into Europe; it took twice as long for corn to spread from Mexico to what is now the eastern United States. This easy movement along similar latitudes in Eurasia would also have meant a faster dissemination of other technologies such as the wheel and writing, Diamond speculates. The region also boasted domesticated livestock, which could provide meat, wool and motive power in the fields. Blessed with such natural advantages, Eurasia was bound to take off economically.

G John Gallup and Jeffrey Sachs, two US economists, have also pointed out striking correlations between the geographical location of countries and their wealth. They note that tropical countries between 23.45 degrees north and south of the equator are nearly all poor. In an article for the *Harvard International Review*, they concluded that "development surely seems to favour the temperate-zone economies, especially those in the northern hemisphere, and those that have managed to avoid both socialism and the ravages of war". But Masters cautions against geographical determinism, the idea that tropical countries are beyond hope: "Human health and agriculture can be made better through scientific and technological research," he says, "so we shouldn't be writing off these countries. Take Singapore: without air conditioning, it wouldn't be rich."

Questions 21-26

Complete the summary below.

Choose **NO MORE THAN TWO WORDS** *from the passage for each answer.*

Write your answers in boxes 21-26 on your answer sheet.

Dr William Masters read a book saying that a(an) **21** ________ which struck an American city hundreds of years ago was terminated by a cold frost. And academics found that there is a connection between climate and country's wealth as in the rich but small country of **22** ________. Yet besides excellent surroundings and climate, one country still needs to improve their **23** ________ to achieve long prosperity.

Thanks to resembling weather conditions across latitude in the continent of **24** ________, crops such as **25** ________ is bound to spread faster than from South America to the North. Other researchers also noted that even though geographical factors are important, tropical country such as **26** ________ still became rich due to scientific advancement.

READING PASSAGE 3

*You should spend about 20 minutes on **Questions 27-40**, which are based on Reading Passage 3 below.*

Musical Maladies

Norman M. Weinberger reviews the latest work of Oliver Sacks on music.

Music and the brain are both endlessly fascinating subjects, and as a neuroscientist specialising in auditory learning and memory, I find them especially intriguing. So I had high expectations of *Musicophilia*, the latest offering from neurologist and prolific author Oliver Sacks. And I confess to feeling a little guilty reporting that my reactions to the book are mixed.

Sacks himself is the best part of *Musicophilia*. He richly documents his own life in the book and reveals highly personal experiences. The photograph of him on the cover of the book—which shows him wearing headphones, eyes closed, clearly enchanted as he listens to Alfred Brendel perform Beethoven's *Pathétique* Sonata—makes a positive impression that is borne out by the contents of the book. Sacks's voice throughout is steady and erudite but never pontifical. He is neither self-conscious nor self-promoting.

The preface gives a good idea of what the book will deliver. In it Sacks explains that he wants to convey the insights gleaned from the "enormous and rapidly growing body of work on the neural underpinnings of musical perception and imagery, and the complex and often bizarre disorders to which these are prone." He also stresses the importance of "the simple art of observation" and "the richness of the human context." He wants to combine "observation and description with the latest in technology," he says, and to imaginatively enter into the experience of his patients and subjects. The reader can see that Sacks, who has been practicing neurology for 40 years, is torn between the "old-fashioned" path of observation and the new-fangled, high-tech approach: He knows that he needs to take heed of the latter, but his heart lies with the former.

The book consists mainly of detailed descriptions of cases, most of them involving patients whom Sacks has seen in his practice. Brief discussions of contemporary neuroscientific reports are sprinkled liberally throughout the text. Part I, "Haunted by Music," begins with the strange case of Tony Cicoria, a nonmusical, middle-aged surgeon who was consumed by a love of music after being hit by lightning. He suddenly began to crave listening to piano music, which he had never cared for in the past. He started to play the piano and then to compose music, which arose spontaneously in his mind in a "torrent" of notes. How could this happen? Was the cause psychological? (He had had a near-death experience when the lightning struck him.) Or was it the direct result of a change in the auditory regions of his cerebral cortex? Electroencephalography (EEG) showed his brain waves to be normal in the mid-1990s, just after his trauma and subsequent "conversion" to music. There are now more sensitive tests, but Cicoria has declined to undergo them; he does not want to delve into the causes of his musicality. What a shame!

Part II, "A Range of Musicality," covers a wider variety of topics, but unfortunately, some of the chapters offer little or nothing that is new. For example, chapter 13, which is five pages long, merely notes that the blind often have better hearing than the sighted. The most interesting chapters are those that present the strangest cases. Chapter 8 is about "amusia," an inability to hear sounds as music, and "dysharmonia," a highly specific impairment of the ability to hear harmony, with the ability to understand melody left intact. Such specific "dissociations" are found throughout the cases Sacks recounts.

To Sacks's credit, part III, "Memory, Movement and Music," brings us into the underappreciated realm of music therapy. Chapter 16 explains how "melodic intonation therapy" is being used to help expressive aphasic patients (those unable to express their thoughts verbally following a stroke or other cerebral incident) once again become capable of fluent speech. In chapter 20, Sacks demonstrates the near-miraculous power of music to animate Parkinson's patients and other people with severe movement disorders, even those who are frozen into odd postures. Scientists cannot yet explain how music achieves this effect.

To readers who are unfamiliar with neuroscience and music behavior, *Musicophilia* may be something of a revelation. But the book will not satisfy those seeking the causes and implications of the phenomena Sacks describes. For one thing, Sacks appears to be more at ease discussing patients than discussing experiments. And he tends to be rather uncritical in accepting scientific findings and theories.

It's true that the causes of music-brain oddities remain poorly understood. However, Sacks could have done more to draw out some of the implications of the careful observations that he and other neurologists have made and of the treatments that have been successful. For example, he might have noted that the many specific dissociations among components of music comprehension, such as loss of the ability to perceive harmony but not melody, indicate that there is no music center in the brain. Because many people who read the book are likely to believe in the brain localisation of all mental functions, this was a missed educational opportunity.

Another conclusion one could draw is that there seem to be no "cures" for neurological problems involving music. A drug can alleviate a symptom in one patient and aggravate it in another, or can have both positive and negative effects in the same patient. Treatments mentioned seem to be almost exclusively antiepileptic medications, which "damp down" the excitability of the brain in general; their effectiveness varies widely.

Finally, in many of the cases described here the patient with music-brain symptoms is reported to have "normal" EEG results. Although Sacks recognises the existence of new technologies, among them far more sensitive ways to analyze brain waves than the standard neurological EEG test, he does not call for their use. In fact, although he exhibits the greatest compassion for patients, he conveys no sense of urgency about the pursuit of new avenues in the diagnosis and treatment of music-brain disorders. This absence echoes the book's preface, in which Sacks expresses fear that "the simple art of observation may be lost" if we rely too much on new technologies. He does call for both approaches, though, and we can only hope that the neurological community will respond.

Questions 27-30

Choose the correct letter, ***A, B, C*** *or* ***D.***

Write the correct letter in boxes 27-30 on your answer sheet.

27 Why does the writer have a mixed feeling about the book?

A The guilty feeling made him so.

B The writer expected it to be better than it was.

C Sacks failed to include his personal stories in the book.

D This is the only book written by Sacks.

28 What is the best part of the book?

A the photo of Sacks listening to music

B the tone of voice of the book

C the autobiographical description in the book

D the description of Sacks's wealth

29 In the preface, what did Sacks try to achieve?

A make terms with the new technologies

B give detailed description of various musical disorders

C explain how people understand music

D explain why he needs to do away with simple observation

30 What is disappointing about Tony Cicoria's case?

A He refuses to have further tests.

B He can't determine the cause of his sudden musicality.

C He nearly died because of the lightening.

D His brain waves were too normal to show anything.

Questions 31-36

Do the following statements agree with the views of the writer in Reading Passage 3?

In boxes 31-36 on your answer sheet, write

YES	*if the statement agrees with the views of the writer*
NO	*if the statement contradicts with the views of the writer*
NOT GIVEN	*if it is impossible to say what the writer thinks about this*

31 It is difficult to give a well-reputable writer a less than favorable review.

32 Beethoven's *Pathétique* Sonata is a good treatment for musical disorders.

33 Sacks believes technological methods is not important compared with observation when studying his patients.

34 It is difficult to understand why music therapy is undervalued.

35 Sacks should have more skepticism about other theories and findings.

36 Sacks is impatient to use new testing methods.

Questions 37-40

Complete each sentence with the correct ending, ***A-F****, below.*

Write the correct letter, ***A-F****, in boxes 37-40 on your answer sheet.*

37 The dissociations between harmony and melody

38 The study of treating musical disorders

39 The EEG scans of Sacks's patients

40 Sacks believes testing based on new technologies

A	show no music-brain disorders.
B	indicates that medication can have varied results.
C	is key for the neurological community to unravel the mysteries.
D	should not be used in isolation.
E	indicate that not everyone can receive good education.
F	show that music is not localised in the brain.

TEST 5

READING PASSAGE 1

You should spend about 20 minutes on ***Questions 1-13****, which are based on Reading Passage 1 on the following pages.*

Questions 1-8

Reading passage 1 has eight paragraphs, **A-H**.

Choose the correct heading for paragraphs ***A-H*** *from the list of headings below.*

Write the correct number, ***i-xi,*** *in boxes 1-8 on your answer sheet.*

List of Headings

i	The advantage of Morse's invention
ii	A suitable job for women
iii	Morse's invention was developed
iv	Sea rescue after the invention of radiotelegraphy
v	The emergence of many job opportunities
vi	Standard and variations
vii	Application of Morse code in a new technology
viii	The discovery of electricity
ix	International expansion of Morse Code
x	The beginning of an end
xi	The move of using code to convey information

1 Paragraph **A**

2 Paragraph **B**

3 Paragraph **C**

4 Paragraph **D**

5 Paragraph **E**

6 Paragraph **F**

7 Paragraph **G**

8 Paragraph **H**

Morse Code

Morse code is being replaced by a new satellite-based system for sending distress calls at sea. Its dots and dashes have had a good run for their money.

A "Calling all. This is our last cry before our eternal silence." Surprisingly this message, which flashed over the airwaves in the dots and dashes of Morse code on January 31st 1997, was not a desperate transmission by a radio operator on a sinking ship. Rather, it was a message signalling the end of the use of Morse code for distress calls in French waters. Since 1992 countries around the world have been decommissioning their Morse equipment with similar (if less poetic) sign-offs, as the world's shipping switches over to a new satellite-based arrangement, the Global Maritime Distress and Safety System. The final deadline for the switch-over to GMDSS is February 1st, a date that is widely seen as the end of an era.

B The code has, however, had a good history. Appropriately for a technology commonly associated with radio operators on sinking ships, the idea of Morse code is said to have occurred to Samuel Morse while he was on board a ship crossing the Atlantic. At the time Morse was a painter and occasional inventor, but when another of the ship's passengers informed him of recent advances in electrical theory, Morse was suddenly taken with the idea of building an electric telegraph to send messages in codes. Other inventors had been trying to do just that for the best part of a century. Morse succeeded and is now remembered as "the father of the telegraph" partly thanks to his single-mindedness—it was 12 years, for example, before he secured money from Congress to build his first telegraph line—but also for technical reasons.

C Compared with rival electric telegraph designs, such as the needle telegraph developed by William Cooke and Charles Wheatstone in Britain, Morse's design was very simple: it required little more than a "key" (essentially, a spring-loaded switch) to send messages, a clicking "sounder" to receive them, and a wire to link the two. But although Morse's hardware was simple, there was a catch: in order to use his equipment, operators had to learn the special code of dots and dashes that still bears his name. Originally, Morse had not intended to use combinations of dots and dashes to represent individual letters. His first code, sketched in his notebook during that transatlantic voyage, used dots and dashes to represent the digits 0 to 9. Morse's idea was that messages would consist of strings of numbers corresponding to words and phrases in a special numbered dictionary. But Morse later abandoned this scheme and, with the help of an associate, Alfred Vail, devised the Morse alphabet, which could be used to spell out messages a letter at a time in dots and dashes.

D At first, the need to learn this complicated-looking code made Morse's telegraph seem impossibly tricky compared with other, more user-friendly designs. Cooke's and Wheatstone's telegraph, for example, used five needles to pick out letters on a diamond-shaped grid. But although this meant that anyone could use it, it also required five wires between telegraph stations. Morse's telegraph needed only one. And some people, it soon transpired, had a natural facility for Morse code.

E As electric telegraphy took off in the early 1850s, the Morse telegraph quickly became dominant. It was adopted as the European standard in 1851, allowing direct connections between the telegraph networks of different countries. (Britain chose not to participate, sticking with needle telegraphs for a few more years.) By this time Morse code had been revised to allow for accents and other foreign characters, resulting in a split between American and International Morse that continues to this day.

F On international submarine cables, left and right swings of a light-beam reflected from a tiny rotating mirror were used to represent dots and dashes. Meanwhile a distinct telegraphic subculture was emerging, with its own customs and vocabulary, and a hierarchy based on the speed at which operators could send and receive Morse code. First-class operators, who could send and receive at speeds of up to 45 words a minute, handled press traffic, securing the best-paid jobs in big cities. At the bottom of the pile were slow, inexperienced rural operators, many of whom worked the wires as part-timers. As their Morse code improved, however, rural operators found that their new-found skill was a passport to better pay in a city job. Telegraphers soon swelled the ranks of the emerging middle classes. Telegraphy was also deemed suitable work for women. By 1870, a third of the operators in the Western Union office in New York, the largest telegraph office in America, were female.

G In a dramatic ceremony in 1871, Morse himself said goodbye to the global community of telegraphers he had brought into being. After a lavish banquet and many adulatory speeches, Morse sat down behind an operator's table and, placing his finger on a key connected to every telegraph wire in America, tapped out his final farewell to a standing ovation. By the time of his death in 1872, the world was well and truly wired: more than 650,000 miles of telegraph line and 30,000 miles of submarine cable were throbbing with Morse code; and 20,000 towns and villages were connected to the global network. Just as the Internet is today often called an "information superhighway", the telegraph was described in its day as an "instantaneous highway of thought".

H But by the 1890s the Morse telegraph's heyday as a cutting-edge technology was coming to an end, with the invention of the telephone and the rise of automatic telegraphs, precursors of the teleprinter, neither of which required specialist skills to operate. Morse code, however, was about to be given a new lease of life thanks to another new technology: wireless. Following the invention of radiotelegraphy by Guglielmo Marconi in 1896, its potential for use at sea quickly became apparent. For the first time, ships could communicate with each other, and with the shore, whatever the weather and even when out of visual range. In 1897 Marconi successfully sent Morse code messages between a shore station and an Italian warship 19km (12 miles) away. By 1910, Morse radio equipment was commonplace on ships.

Questions 9-13

Do the following statements agree with the information given in Reading Passage 1?

In boxes 9-13 on your answer sheet, write

TRUE	***if the statement agrees with the information***
FALSE	***if the statement contradicts the information***
NOT GIVEN	***if there is no information on this***

9 Morse had already been famous as an inventor before his invention of Morse code.

10 Morse waited a long time before receiving support from the Congress.

11 Morse code is difficult to learn compared with other designs.

12 Companies and firms prefer to employ telegraphy operators from rural areas.

13 Morse died from overwork.

READING PASSAGE 2

*You should spend about 20 minutes on **Questions 14-26**, which are based on Reading Passage 2 below.*

From A Novice to An Expert

Expertise is commitment coupled with creativity. Specifically, it is the commitment of time, energy, and resources to a relatively narrow field of study and the creative energy necessary to generate new knowledge in that field. It takes a considerable amount of time and regular exposure to a large number of cases to become an expert.

An individual enters a field of study as a novice. The novice needs to learn the guiding principles and rules of a given task in order to perform that task. Concurrently, the novice needs to be exposed to specific cases, or instances, that test the boundaries of such principles. Generally, a novice will find a mentor to guide her through the process of acquiring new knowledge. A fairly simple example would be someone learning to play chess. The novice chess player seeks a mentor to teach her the object of the game, the number of spaces, the names of the pieces, the function of each piece, how each piece is moved, and the necessary conditions for winning or losing the game.

In time, and with much practice, the novice begins to recognise patterns of behavior within cases and, thus, becomes a journeyman. With more practice and exposure to increasingly complex cases, the journeyman finds patterns not only within cases but also between cases. More importantly, the journeyman learns that these patterns often repeat themselves over time. The journeyman still maintains regular contact with a mentor to solve specific problems and learn more complex strategies. Returning to the example of the chess player, the individual begins to learn patterns of opening moves, offensive and defensive game-playing strategies, and patterns of victory and defeat.

When a journeyman starts to make and test hypotheses about future behavior based on past experiences, she begins the next transition. Once she creatively generates knowledge, rather than simply matching superficial patterns, she becomes an expert. At this point, she is confident in her knowledge and no longer needs a mentor as a guide—she becomes responsible for her own knowledge. In the chess example, once a journeyman begins competing against experts, makes predictions based on patterns, and tests those predictions against actual behavior, she is generating new knowledge and a deeper understanding of the game. She is creating her own cases rather than relying on the cases of others.

The Power of Expertise

An expert perceives meaningful patterns in her domain better than non-experts. Where a novice perceives random or disconnected data points, an expert connects regular patterns within and between cases. This ability to identify patterns is not an innate perceptual skill; rather it reflects the organisation of knowledge after exposure to and experience with thousands of cases.

Experts have a deeper understanding of their domains than novices do, and utilise higher-order principles to solve problems. A novice, for example, might group objects together by color or size, whereas an expert would group the same objects according to their function or utility. Experts comprehend the meaning of data and weigh variables with different criteria within their domains better than novices. Experts recognise variables that have the largest influence on a particular problem and focus their attention on those variables.

Experts have better domain-specific short-term and long-term memory than novices do. Moreover, experts perform tasks in their domains faster than novices and commit fewer errors while problem solving. Interestingly, experts go about solving problems differently than novices. Experts spend more time thinking about a problem to fully understand it at the beginning of a task than do novices, who immediately seek to find a solution. Experts use their knowledge of previous cases as context for creating mental models to solve given problems.

Better at self-monitoring than novices, experts are more aware of instances where they have committed errors or failed to understand a problem. Experts check their solutions more often than novices and recognise when they are missing information necessary for solving a problem. Experts are aware of the limits of their domain knowledge and apply their domain's heuristics to solve problems that fall outside of their experience base.

The Paradox of Expertise

The strengths of expertise can also be weaknesses. Although one would expect experts to be good forecasters, they are not particularly good at making predictions about the future. Since the 1930s, researchers have been testing the ability of experts to make forecasts. The performance of experts has been tested against actuarial tables to determine if they are better at making predictions than simple statistical models. Seventy years later, with more than two hundred experiments in different domains, it is clear that the answer is no. If supplied with an equal amount of data about a particular case, an actuarial table is as good, or better, than an expert at making calls about the future. Even if an expert is given more specific case information than is available to the statistical model, the expert does not tend to outperform the actuarial table.

Theorists and researchers differ when trying to explain why experts are less accurate forecasters than statistical models. Some have argued that experts, like all humans, are inconsistent when using mental models to make predictions. That is, the model an expert uses for predicting X in one month is different from the model used for predicting X in a following month, although precisely the same case and same data set are used in both instances.

A number of researchers point to human biases to explain unreliable expert predictions. During the last 30 years, researchers have categorised, experimented, and theorised about the cognitive aspects of forecasting. Despite such efforts, the literature shows little consensus regarding the causes or manifestations of human bias.

Questions 14-18

Complete the flow-chart below.

Choose **NO MORE THAN THREE WORDS** *from the passage for each answer.*

Write your answers in boxes 14-18 on your answer sheet.

Novice: needs **14** ________ and ________ to perform a given task;
exposed to specific cases;
guided by a **15** ________ through learning

⇩

Journeyman: starts to identify **16** ________ within and between cases;
often exposed to **17** ________ cases;
contacts a mentor when facing difficult problems

⇩

Expert: creates predictions and new **18** ________;
performs task independently without the help of a mentor

Questions 19-23

Do the following statements agree with the information given in Reading Passage 2?

In boxes 19-23 on your answer sheet, write

TRUE *if the statement agrees with the information*
FALSE *if the statement contradicts the information*
NOT GIVEN *if there is no information on this*

19 Novices and experts use the same system to classify objects.

20 A novice's training is focused on memory skills.

21 Experts have higher efficiency than novices when solving problems in their own field.

22 When facing a problem, a novices always tries to solve it straight away.

23 Experts are better at recognising their own mistakes and limits.

Questions 24-26

Complete the summary below.

Choose **NO MORE THAN TWO WORDS** *from the passage for each answer.*

Write your answers in boxes 24-26 on your answer sheet.

Though experts are quite effective at solving problems in their own domains, their strengths can also be turned against them. Studies have shown that experts are less 24 ________ at making predictions than statistical models. Some researchers theorise it is because experts can also be inconsistent like all others. Yet some believe it is due to 25 ________, but there isn't a great deal of 26 ________ as to its cause and manifestation.

READING PASSAGE 3

*You should spend about 20 minutes on **Questions 27-40**, which are based on Reading Passage 3 below.*

HIGH SPEED PHOTOGRAPHY

A Photography gained the interest of many scientists and artists from its inception. Scientists have used photography to record and study movements, such as Eadweard Muybridge's study of human and animal locomotion in 1887. Artists are equally interested by these aspects but also try to explore avenues other than the photo-mechanical representation of reality, such as the pictorialist movement. Military, police, and security forces use photography for surveillance, recognition and data storage. Photography is used by amateurs to preserve memories, to capture special moments, to tell stories, to send messages, and as a source of entertainment. Various technological improvements and techniques have even allowed for visualising events that are too fast or too slow for the human eye.

B One of such techniques is called fast motion or professionally known as time-lapse. Time-lapse photography is the perfect technique for capturing events and movements in the natural world that occur over a timescale too slow for human perception to follow. The life cycle of a mushroom, for example, is incredibly subtle to the human eye. To present its growth in front of audiences, the principle applied is a simple one: a series of photographs are taken and used in sequence to make a moving-image film, but since each frame is taken with a lapse at a time interval between each shot, when played back at normal speed, a continuous action is produced and it appears to speed up. Put simply: we are shrinking time. Objects and events that would normally take several minutes, days or even months can be viewed to completion in seconds having been sped up by factors of tens to millions.

C Another commonly used technique is high-speed photography, the science of taking pictures of very fast phenomena. High-speed photography can be considered to be the opposite of time-lapse photography. One of the many applications is found in biology studies to study birds, bats and even spider silk. Imagine a hummingbird hovering almost completely still in the air, feeding on nectar. With every flap, its wings bend, flex and change shape. These subtle movements precisely control the lift its wings generate, making it an excellent hoverer. But a hummingbird flaps its wings up to 80 times every second. The only way to truly capture this motion is with cameras that will, in effect, slow down time. To do this, a greater length of film is taken at a high sampling frequency or frame rate, which is much faster than it will be projected on screen. When replayed at normal speed, time appears to be slowed down proportionately. That is why high-speed cameras have become such a mainstay of biology.

D In common usage, high-speed photography can also refer to the use of high-speed cameras that the photograph itself may be taken in a way as to appear to freeze the motion, especially to reduce motion blur. It requires a sensor with good sensitivity and either a very good shuttering system or a very fast strobe light. The recent National Geographic footage—captured last summer during an intensive three-day shoot at the Cincinnati Zoo—is unprecedented in its clarity and detail. "I've watched cheetahs run for 30 years," said Cathryn Hilker, founder of the zoo's Cat Ambassador Program. "But I saw things in that super slow-motion video that I've never seen before." The slow-motion video is entrancing. Every part of the sprinting cat's anatomy—supple limbs, rippling muscles, hyperflexible spine—works together in a symphony of speed, revealing the fluid grace of the world's fastest land animal.

E But things can't get any more complicated in the case of filming a frog catching its prey. Frogs can snatch up prey in a few thousandths of a second—striking out with elastic tongues. Biologists would love to see how a frog's tongue roll out, adhere to prey, and roll back into the frog's mouth. But this all happened too fast, 50 times faster than an eye blink. So naturally people thought of using high-speed camera to capture this fantastic movement in slow motion. Yet one problem still remains—viewers would be bored if they watch the frog swim in slow motion for too long. So how to skip this? The solution is a simple one—adjust the playback speed, which is also called by some the film speed adjustment. The film will originally be shot at a high frame (often 300 frames per second, because it can be converted to much lower frame rates without major issues), but at later editing stage this high frame rate will only be preserved for the prey catching part, while the swimming part will be converted to the normal speed at 24 frames per second. Voila, the scientists can now sit back and enjoy watching without having to go through the pain of waiting.

F Sometimes taking a good picture or shooting a good film is not all about technology, but patience, like in the case of bat. Bats are small, dark-colored; they fly fast and are active only at night. To capture bats on film, one must use some type of camera-tripping device. Photographers or film-makers often place camera near the bat cave, on the path of the flying bats. The camera must be hard-wired with a tripping device so that every time a bat breaks the tripping beam the camera fires and it will keep doing so through the night until the camera's battery runs out. Though highly-advanced tripping device can now allow for unmanned shooting, it still may take several nights to get a truly high quality film.

G Is it science? Is it art? Since the technique was first pioneered around two hundred years ago, photography has developed to a state where it is almost unrecognisable. Some people would even say the future of photography will be nothing like how we imagine it. No matter what future it may hold, photography will continue to develop as it has been repeatedly demonstrated in many aspects of our life that "a picture is worth a thousand words."

Questions 27-30

Look at the following ***organisms*** *(Questions 27-30) and the list of features below.*

Match each ***organism*** *with the correct feature,* ***A-D****.*

Write the correct letter, ***A-D****, in boxes 27-30 on your answer sheet.*

27 Mushroom

28 Hummingbird

29 Frog

30 Bat

A	too fast to be perceived
B	film at the place where the animal will pass
C	too slow to be visible to human eyes
D	adjust the filming speed to make it interesting

Questions 31-35

Complete the summary below.

*Choose **NO MORE THAN THREE WORDS** from the passage for each answer.*

Write your answers in boxes 31-35 on your answer sheet.

Fast motion (professionally known as time-lapse photography) and slow motion (or high-speed photography) are two commonest techniques of photography. To present before audiences something that occurs naturally slow, photographers take each picture at a **31** ______ before another picture. When these pictures are finally shown on screen in sequence at a normal motion picture rate, audiences see a **32** ______ that is faster than what it naturally is. This technique can make audiences feel as if **33** ______ is shrunk. On the other hand, to demonstrate how fast things move, the movement is exposed on a **34** ______ of film, and then projected on screen at normal playback speed. This makes viewers feel time is **35** ______.

Questions 36-40

Reading Passage 3 has seven paragraphs, **A-G**.

Which paragraph contains the following information?

*Write the correct letter, **A-G**, in boxes 36-40 on your answer sheet.*

36 a description of photography's application in various fields
37 a reference to why high-speed photography has a significant role in biology
38 a traditional wisdom that assures readers of the prospects of photography
39 a reference to how film is processed before final release
40 a description of filming shooting without human effort

TEST 6

READING PASSAGE 1

*You should spend about 20 minutes on **Questions 1-13**, which are based on Reading Passage 1 below.*

Thomas Young
The Last True Know-It-All

Thomas Young (1773-1829) contributed 63 articles to the *Encyclopedia Britannica,* including 46 biographical entries (mostly on scientists and classicists) and substantial essays on "Bridge," "Chromatics," "Egypt," "Languages" and "Tides". Was someone who could write authoritatively about so many subjects a polymath, a genius or a dilettante? In an ambitious new biography, Andrew Robinson argues that Young is a good contender for the epitaph "the last man who knew everything." Young has competition, however: The phrase, which Robinson takes for his title, also serves as the subtitle of two other recent biographies: Leonard Warren's 1998 life of paleontologist Joseph Leidy (1823-1891) and Paula Findlen's 2004 book on Athanasius Kircher (1602-1680), another polymath.

Young, of course, did more than write encyclopedia entries. He presented his first paper to the Royal Society of London at the age of 20 and was elected a Fellow a week after his 21st birthday. In the paper, Young explained the process of accommodation in the human eye—on how the eye focuses properly on objects at varying distances. Young hypothesised that this was achieved by changes in the shape of the lens. Young also theorised that light traveled in waves and he believed that, to account for the ability to see in color, there must be three receptors in the eye corresponding to the three "principal colors" to which the retina could respond: red, green, violet. All these hypotheses were subsequently proved to be correct.

Later in his life, when he was in his forties, Young was instrumental in cracking the code that unlocked the unknown script on the Rosetta Stone, a tablet that was "found" in Egypt by the Napoleonic army in 1799. The stone contains text in three alphabets: Greek, something unrecognisable and Egyptian hieroglyphs. The unrecognisable script is now known as demotic and, as Young deduced, is related directly to hieroglyphic. His initial work on this appeared in his Britannica entry on Egypt. In another entry, he coined the term Indo-European to describe the family of languages spoken throughout most of Europe and northern India. These are the landmark achievements of a man who was a child prodigy and who, unlike many remarkable children, did not disappear into oblivion as an adult.

Born in 1773 in Somerset in England, Young lived from an early age with his maternal grandfather, eventually leaving to attend boarding school. He had devoured books from the age of two, and through his own initiative he excelled at Latin, Greek, mathematics and natural philosophy. After leaving school, he was greatly encouraged by his mother's uncle, Richard Brocklesby, a physician and Fellow of the Royal Society. Following Brocklesby's lead, Young decided to pursue a career in medicine. He studied in London, following the medical circuit, and then moved on to more formal education in Edinburgh, Göttingen and Cambridge. After completing his medical training at the University of Cambridge in 1808, Young set up practice as a physician in London. He soon became a Fellow of the Royal College of Physicians and a few years later was appointed physician at St. George's Hospital.

Young's skill as a physician, however, did not equal his skill as a scholar of natural philosophy or linguistics. Earlier, in 1801, he had been appointed to a professorship of natural philosophy at the Royal Institution, where he delivered as many as 60 lectures in a year. These were published in two volumes in 1807. In 1804 Young had become secretary to the Royal Society, a post he would hold until his death. His opinions were sought on civic and national matters, such as the introduction of gas lighting to London and methods of ship construction. From 1819 he was superintendent of the Nautical Almanac and secretary to the Board of Longitude. From 1824 to 1829 he was physician to and inspector of calculations for the Palladian Insurance Company. Between 1816 and 1825 he contributed his many and various entries to the *Encyclopedia Britannica*, and throughout his career he authored numerous books, essays and papers.

Young is a perfect subject for a biography—perfect, but daunting. Few men contributed so much to so many technical fields. Robinson's aim is to introduce non-scientists to Young's work and life. He succeeds, providing clear expositions of the technical material (especially that on optics and Egyptian hieroglyphs). Some readers of this book will, like Robinson, find Young's accomplishments impressive; others will see him as some historians have—as a dilettante. Yet despite the rich material presented in this book, readers will not end up knowing Young personally. We catch glimpses of a playful Young, doodling Greek and Latin phrases in his notes on medical lectures and translating the verses that a young lady had written on the walls of a summerhouse into Greek elegiacs. Young was introduced into elite society, attended the theatre and learned to dance and play the flute. In addition, he was an accomplished horseman. However, his personal life looks pale next to his vibrant career and studies.

Young married Eliza Maxwell in 1804, and according to Robinson, "their marriage was a happy one and she appreciated his work." Almost all we know about her is that she sustained her husband through some rancorous disputes about optics and that she worried about money when his medical career was slow to take off. Very little evidence survives about the complexities of Young's relationships with his mother and father. Robinson does not credit them, or anyone else, with shaping Young's extraordinary mind. Despite the lack of details concerning Young's relationships, however, anyone interested in what it means to be a genius should read this book.

Questions 1-7

Do the following statements agree with the information given in Reading Passage 1?

In boxes 1-7 on your answer sheet, write

TRUE	*if the statement agrees with the information*
FALSE	*if the statement contradicts the information*
NOT GIVEN	*if there is no information on this*

1 'The last man who knew everything' has also been claimed to other people.

2 All Young's articles were published in *Encyclopedia Britannica.*

3 Like others, Young wasn't so brilliant when growing up.

4 Young's talent as a doctor surpassed his other skills.

5 Young's advice was sought by people responsible for local and national issues.

6 Young was interested in various social pastimes.

7 Young suffered from a disease in his later years.

Questions 8-13

Answer the questions below.

Choose ***NO MORE THAN THREE WORDS AND/OR A NUMBER*** *from the passage for each answer.*

8 How many life stories did Young write for the *Encyclopedia Britannica*?

9 What aspect of scientific research did Young focus on in his first academic paper?

10 What name did Young introduce to refer to a group of languages?

11 Who inspired Young to start his medical studies?

12 Where did Young get a teaching position?

13 What contribution did Young make to London?

READING PASSAGE 2

*You should spend about 20 minutes on **Questions 14-26**, which are based on Reading Passage 2 below.*

Antarctica – in from the cold?

A A little over a century ago, men of the ilk of Scott, Shackleton and Mawson battled against Antarctica's blizzards, cold and deprivation. In the name of Empire and in an age of heroic deeds they created an image of Antarctica that was to last well into the 20th century—an image of remoteness, hardship, bleakness and isolation that was the province of only the most courageous of men. The image was one of a place removed from everyday reality, of a place with no apparent value to anyone.

B As we enter the 21st century, our perception of Antarctica has changed. Although physically Antarctica is no closer and probably no warmer, and to spend time there still demands a dedication not seen in ordinary life, the continent and its surrounding ocean are increasingly seen to be an integral part of Planet Earth, and a key component in the Earth System. Is this because the world seems a little smaller these days, shrunk by TV and tourism, or is it because Antarctica really does occupy a central spot on Earth's mantle? Scientific research during the past half century has revealed—and continues to reveal—that Antarctica's great mass and low temperature exert a major influence on climate and ocean circulation, factors which influence the lives of millions of people all over the globe.

C Antarctica was not always cold. The slow break-up of the super-continent Gondwana with the northward movements of Africa, South America, India and Australia eventually created enough space around Antarctica for the development of an Antarctic Circumpolar Current (ACC), that flowed from west to east under the influence of the prevailing westerly winds. Antarctica cooled, its vegetation perished, glaciation began and the continent took on its present-day appearance. Today the ice that overlies the bedrock is up to 4km thick, and surface temperatures as low as -89.2deg C have been recorded. The icy blast that howls over the ice cap and out to sea—the so-called katabatic wind—can reach 300 km/hr, creating fearsome wind-chill effects.

D Out of this extreme environment come some powerful forces that reverberate around the world. The Earth's rotation, coupled to the generation of cells of low pressure off the Antarctic coast, would allow Astronauts a view of Antarctica that is as beautiful as it is awesome. Spinning away to the northeast, the cells grow and deepen, whipping up the Southern Ocean into the mountainous seas so respected by mariners. Recent work is showing that the temperature of the ocean may be a better predictor of rainfall in Australia than is the pressure difference between Darwin and Tahiti—the Southern Oscillation Index. By receiving more accurate predictions, graziers in northern Queensland are able to avoid overstocking in years when rainfall will be poor. Not only does this limit their losses but it prevents serious pasture degradation that may take decades to repair. CSIRO is developing this as a prototype forecasting system, but we can confidently predict that as we know more about the Antarctic and Southern Ocean we will be able to enhance and extend our predictive ability.

E The ocean's surface temperature results from the interplay between deep-water temperature, air temperature and ice. Each winter between 4 and 19 million square km of sea ice form, locking up huge quantities of heat close to the continent. Only now can we start to unravel the influence of sea ice on the weather that is experienced in southern Australia. But in another way the extent of sea ice extends its influence far beyond Antarctica. Antarctic krill—the small shrimp-like crustaceans that are the staple diet for baleen whales, penguins, some seals, flighted sea birds and many fish—breed well in years when sea ice is extensive and poorly when it is not. Many species of baleen whales and flighted sea birds migrate between the hemispheres and when the krill are less abundant they do not thrive.

F The circulatory system of the world's oceans is like a huge conveyor belt, moving water and dissolved minerals and nutrients from one hemisphere to the other, and from the ocean's abyssal depths to the surface. The ACC is the longest current in the world, and has the largest flow. Through it, the deep flows of the Atlantic, Indian and Pacific Oceans are joined to form part of a single global thermohaline circulation. During winter, the howling katabatics sometimes scour the ice off patches of the sea's surface leaving large ice-locked lagoons, or 'polynyas'. Recent research has shown that as fresh sea ice forms, it is continuously stripped away by the wind and may be blown up to 90km in a single day. Since only fresh water freezes into ice, the water that remains becomes increasingly salty and dense, sinking until it spills over the continental shelf. Cold water carries more oxygen than warm water, so when it rises, well into the northern hemisphere, it reoxygenates and revitalises the ocean. The state of the northern oceans, and their biological productivity, owe much to what happens in the Antarctic.

Questions 14-18

Reading Passage 2 has six paragraphs, **A-F**.

Which paragraph contains the following information?

*Write the correct letter, **A-F**, in boxes 14-18 on your answer sheet.*

14 The example of a research on building weather prediction for agriculture

15 An explanation of how Antarctic sea ice brings back oceans' vitality

16 The description of a food chain that influences animals' living pattern

17 The reference of an extreme temperature and a cold wind in Antarctica

18 The reference of how Antarctica was once thought to be a forgotten and insignificant continent

Questions 19-21

Match the natural phenomenon with the correct determined factor.

*Write the correct letter, **A-F**, in boxes 19-21 on your answer sheet.*

19 Globally, Antarctica's massive size and ________ would influence our climate.

20 ________ circulated under contributory force from wind blowing from the west.

21 The ocean temperature and index based on air pressure can help predict ________ in Australia.

A Antarctic Circumpolar Current (ACC)	**B** katabatic winds
C rainfall	**D** temperature
E glaciers	**F** pressure

Questions 22-26

*Choose the correct letter, **A, B, C** or **D**.*

Write the correct letter in boxes 22-26 on your answer sheet.

22 In paragraph B, the author intends to

A show Antarctica has been a central topic of global warming discussion in Mass media.

B illustrate how its huge sea ice brings food to millions of lives in the world.

C emphasise the significance of Antarctica to the global climate and ocean currents.

D illustrate the geographical location of Antarctica as the central spot on Earth.

23 Why should Australian farmers keep an eye on the Antarctic ocean temperature?

A It can help farmers reduce their economic loss.

B It allows for recovery of grassland lost to overgrazing.

C It can help to prevent animals from dying

D It enables astronauts to have a clear view of the Antarctic continent.

24 The decrease in the number of whales and seabirds is due to

A killer whales' activity around Antarctica.

B the correlation between sea birds' migration and the salinity level of the ocean.

C the lower productivity of food source resulting from less sea ice.

D the failure of seals to produce babies.

25 What is the final effect of the katabatic winds?

A Increasing the moving speed of ocean current

B Increasing the salt level near ocean surface

C Bringing fresh ice into the oceans

D Piling up the mountainous ice cap respected by mariners

26 What factor drives Antarctic water to move beyond the continental shelf?

A The increase of salt and density of the water

B The decrease of salt and density of the water

C The rising temperature due to global warming

D The melting of fresh ice into the ocean

READING PASSAGE 3

*You should spend about 20 minutes on **Questions 27-40**, which are based on Reading Passage 3 below.*

Source of Knowledge

A What counts as knowledge? What do we mean when we say that we know something? What is the status of different kinds of knowledge? In order to explore these questions we are going to focus on one particular area of knowledge—medicine.

B How do you know when you are ill? This may seem to be an absurd question. You know you are ill because you feel ill; your body tells you that you are ill. You may know that you feel pain or discomfort but knowing you are ill is a bit more complex. At times, people experience the symptoms of illness, but in fact they are simply tired or over-worked or they may just have a hangover. At other times, people may be suffering from a disease and fail to be aware of the illness until it has reached a late stage in its development. So how do we know we are ill, and what counts as knowledge?

C Think about this example. You feel unwell. You have a bad cough and always seem to be tired. Perhaps it could be stress at work, or maybe you should give up smoking. You feel worse. You visit the doctor who listens to your chest and heart, takes your temperature and blood pressure, and then finally prescribes antibiotics for your cough.

D Things do not improve but you struggle on thinking you should pull yourself together, perhaps things will ease off at work soon. A return visit to your doctor shocks you. This time the doctor, drawing on years of training and experience, diagnoses pneumonia. This means that you will need bed rest and a considerable time off work. The scenario is transformed. Although you still have the same symptoms, you no longer think that these are caused by pressure at work. You now have proof that you are ill. This is the result of the combination of your own subjective experience and the diagnosis of someone who has the status of a medical expert. You have a medically authenticated diagnosis and it appears that you are seriously ill; you know you are ill and have evidence upon which to base this knowledge.

E This scenario shows many different sources of knowledge. For example, you decide to consult the doctor in the first place because you feel unwell—this is personal knowledge about your own body. However, the doctor's expert diagnosis is based on experience and training, with sources of knowledge as diverse as other experts, laboratory reports, medical textbooks and years of experience.

F One source of knowledge is the experience of our own bodies; the personal knowledge we have of changes that might be significant, as well as the subjective experience of pain and physical distress. These experiences are mediated by other forms of knowledge such as the words we have available to describe our experience and the common sense of our families and friends as well as that drawn from popular culture. Over the past decade, for example, Western culture has seen a significant emphasis on stress-related illness in the media. Reference to being 'stressed out' has become a common response in daily exchanges in the workplace and has become part of popular common-sense knowledge. It is thus not surprising that we might seek such an explanation of physical symptoms of discomfort.

G We might also rely on the observations of others who know us. Comments from friends and family such as 'you do look ill' or 'that's a bad cough' might be another source of knowledge. Complementary health practices, such as holistic medicine, produce their own sets of knowledge upon which we might also draw in deciding the nature and degree of our ill health and about possible treatments.

H Perhaps the most influential and authoritative source of knowledge is the medical knowledge provided by the general practitioner. We expect the doctor to have access to expert knowledge. This is socially sanctioned. It would not be acceptable to notify our employer that we simply felt too unwell to turn up for work or that our faith healer, astrologer, therapist or even our priest thought it was not a good idea. We need an expert medical diagnosis in order to obtain the necessary certificate if we need to be off work for more than the statutory self-certification period. The knowledge of the medical sciences is privileged in this respect in contemporary Western culture. Medical practitioners are also seen as having the required expert knowledge that permits them legally to prescribe drugs and treatment to which patients would not otherwise have access. However there is a range of different knowledge upon which we draw when making decisions about our own state of health.

I However, there is more than existing knowledge in this little story; new knowledge is constructed within it. Given the doctor's medical training and background, she may hypothesise 'is this now pneumonia?' and then proceed to look for evidence about it. She will use observations and instruments to assess the evidence and—critically—interpret it in the light of her training and experience. This results in new knowledge and new experience both for you and for the doctor. This will then be added to the doctor's medical knowledge and may help in future diagnosis of pneumonia.

Questions 27-34

Reading Passage 3 has nine paragraphs, **A-I**.

Which paragraph contains the following information?

*Write the correct letter, **A-I**, in boxes 27-34 on your answer sheet.*

***NB** You may use any letter more than once.*

27 the contrast between the nature of personal judgment and the nature of doctor's diagnosis

28 a reference of culture about pressure

29 sick leave will not be permitted without professional diagnosis

30 how doctors' opinions are regarded in the society

31 the illness of patients can become part of new knowledge

32 a description of knowledge drawn from non-specialised sources other than personal knowledge

33 an example of collective judgment from personal experience and professional doctor

34 a reference that some people do not realise they are ill

Questions 35-40

Complete the notes below.

Choose **NO MORE THAN THREE WORDS** *from the passage for each answer.*

Write your answers in boxes 35-40 on your answer sheet.

Source of knowledge	Examples
Personal experience	Symptoms of a **35** ________ and tiredness Doctor's measurement by taking **36** ________ and temperature Common judgment from **37** ________ around you
Scientific evidence	Medical knowledge from the general **38** ________ e.g. doctor's medical **39** ________ Examine the medical hypothesis with the previous drill and **40** ________

真题解析

Reading Passage 1. REVIEW OF RESEARCH ON THE EFFECTS OF FOOD PROMOTION TO CHILDREN

词汇详解

underestimate *v.* 低估（很多带 under 的词汇都有“低，下面，不足”的意思。例如：underdeveloped 没有完全发育或发展的；underperform 表现不佳；understate 保守地讲或说；underplay 淡化……的重要性。）

review *n.&v.* 回顾；复习；复查（preview 是其反义词，意思是“预习，预览”。）

promotion *n.* 促进；提升；升职；（商品等的）促销（来自动词 promote，其中 mote 是词根，有“移动，运动”的意思，promote 就是“向前移动”，所以就是“促进，提升”的意思。相反的有 demote，也就是“使降级，使降职”的意思。）

commission *v.* 委任；授予；使服役 *n.* 委员会；委任，委托；佣金（来自动词 commit，其中词根 mit 代表“派出，派遣”，也就是英文 send 的意思，前缀 com 代表“共同，一起”，所以 commit 就有“托付，使承担义务”的意思。）

agency *n.* 代理；机构（美国中央情报局就是 CIA：Central Intelligence Agency。）

evidence *n.* 证据（它的形容词 evident 代表的意思是“明显的”，而人们常说的 self-evident 的意思就是“不言而喻的”。）

extent *n.* 程度（作文题中常说的“To what extent do you agree or disagree?”的意思就是“你在多大程度上同意或不同意？”）

preference *n.* 偏爱，偏好；偏爱的事物（来自动词 prefer，其中词根 fer 的意思是“拿着 carry”，前缀 pre 有“前面”的意思，于是 prefer 就表示拿起来放到所有其他事物的前面，也就变成“偏好，偏爱”的意思了。）

dominate *v.* 控制，支配；在……中占首要地位（来自拉丁语 dominus，也就是“master”的意思。所以，与其同源的词汇 domain 就是指一个人熟悉的领域，而且与拉丁语中表示“home”的意思的词汇 domus 非常相近。dominance 和 domination 都是 dominate 的名词，前者多指优势，支配地位；后者多指控制，统治。）

majority *n.* 大多数（来自形容词 major，其反义词则是来自形容词 minor 的 minority。所以少数民族就可以说成 ethnic minority。当然，汉族在中国就是 ethnic majority 了。）

cereal *n.* 谷物 *adj.* 谷物的（很多西方人早餐经常吃这个，其中有玉米片“cornflake”、燕麦“oat”，还有各种各样的葡萄干“raisin”等等，然后用牛奶一搅拌就可以吃了。）

confectionary *n.* 甜食；糖果店 *adj.* 甜食的（孩子们喜欢吃各种各样的 candies 和 sweets，但是吃多了会长蛀牙“tooth decay”。牙齿有个小洞洞“cavity”会很难受的，说不定还要带上牙套“teeth/dental brace”。）

savoury *adj.* 美味的，好吃的（可替代 delicious、yummy 和 tasty 等词，其同义词还有 palatable、ambrosial 等。动词是 savour，有“享受……的美味”的意思。）

outlet *n.* 出口，出路，排水口；批发商店；发泄（情感）的方法（奥特莱斯购物中心就是 Outlets 的音译；power outlet 指的就是电源插座。）

wane *v.* 衰落，变弱；（月）亏，缺 *n.* 衰退，衰败；月亏（月亮的阴晴圆缺用英文表达就是 wax and wane。当然，wax and wane 也指事物循环性的兴盛然后衰败，增长然后减弱等。wax 还有“蜡，蜡状物，给……上蜡”的意思。）

branding *n.* 打造品牌，品牌化（为品牌“brand”的动名词形式。与其相关的词汇还有许多，例如：trademark 商标；registered trademark 注册商标；logo 标志，标识。）

reinforce *v.* 加固，使更结实；加强；增援（force 有“力量”的意思，in 有“进入”的意思，前缀 re 表示“再一次，重复”。）

multi-faceted *adj.* 多面的，具有多个侧面的（名词 facet 有“平面，侧面，方面”的意思，前缀 multi 的意思是“很多，大量”。与 multi 相关的单词还有 multiple、multiply 等。）

merchandising *n.* 商品推销，销售规划（是单词 merchandise 的动名词形式，merchandise 作名词有“商品，货物”的意思，作动词有“销售，买卖”的意思。相关单词有：merchant 商人；merchantable 可买卖的，有销路的。）

tie-in *n.&adj.* 搭卖（的），捆绑销售（的）

recommend *v.* 推荐；建议（commend 有“推荐，表扬，托付”的意思，前缀 re 则表示“反复，重复”。）

theme *n.* 主题，题目；主旋律

fantasy *n.* 幻想，空幻；幻想作品（在书店里通常有科幻小说“sci-fi”区域和奇幻小说

"fantasy"区域。例如，著名的《指环王》*The Lord of the Rings* 以及《冰与火之歌》*A Song of Ice and Fire* 就是奇幻类作品。）

nutrition *n.* 营养（相关词汇有：nutrient 营养物，养料；nutritious 有营养的；malnutrition 营养不良；nutritionist 营养学家。）

establish *v.* 确定，证实；建立，创立（与其有关的 stable 表示"稳定的，稳固的"，所以从字面上看 establish 就表示"进入到稳定的状态"，于是就有"建立，创立"的意思。）

tackle *v.* 处理，对付

obesity *n.* 肥胖（是形容词 obese"肥胖的"的名词形式，obese 的近义词有 overweight、fat 等。）

cholesterol *n.* 胆固醇（其实胆固醇并不全是不好的，因为胆固醇有两种：high-density cholesterol 和 low-density cholesterol。其中后者才对身体有害，易导致心血管疾病"cardio-vascular diseases"。）

perception *n.* 感知能力；洞察力；理解，看法（来自动词 perceive，其中前缀 per 是"完全 thoroughly"的意思，ceive 是"拿到，拿着"的意思，所以 perceive 就是"完全拿到"，进一步就变成"理解，洞察"的意思。）

constitute *v.* 构成，组成（前缀 con 是"共同"的意思，词根 stitute 是"设置，放置"的意思，所以放到一起就变成了"构成，组成"的意思。该词的变形还有：constitution，可理解为全部法律的总纲放置在一起就变成了宪法；constituent 意为"成分，组成部分；选民"。）

context *n.* 上下文；背景，环境（该词是由表示"共同"的前缀 con 和表示"文本"的 text 组成。相关的词汇还有 pretext，意为"借口，托辞"。）

specific *adj.* 特定的，明确的，具体的 *n.* 特性，细节（电脑、汽车等的具体配置叫做 specs。）

advert *n.* 广告（是名词 advertisement 在英式口语中的说法，在美式口语中则更简短，只说 ad 就可以。）

exposure *n.* 暴露，揭发，曝光（来自动词 expose，expose 是由表示"出去"的前缀 ex 和表示"放置"的词根 pose 组成的。）

claim *v.* 声称，声明，断言；要求，索取；索赔 *n.* 声称，断言；索要之物；索款（相关词汇有：exclaim 呼喊，惊叹，大声说；proclaim 宣告，公布；disclaim 否认，拒绝承认；acclaim 欢呼，称赞，喝彩；reclaim 取回，收回。）

label *n.* 标签 *v.* 贴标签，把……称为

signage *n.* 标记；标识系统（来自动词 sign"签署，签名"。相关词汇还有：assign 指派，委派；consign 委托，托付，托运；resign 辞职，放弃。）

vending machine（自动）售货机（vend 就有"贩卖，出售"的意思，例如街边的小贩就叫做 street vendor。）

proxy *n.* 代理，代理人，代理权，（网络）代理服务器（翻墙利器，不可不知啊！听说过代理婚姻"proxy marriage"吗？新娘或新郎中有一方不能出席婚礼仪式，由别人来替代

参加的婚礼就叫做proxy marriage。)

resolve *v.* 使分解；解决；下决心，做决定

consume *v.* 消耗，消费（相关词汇有：consumption 消耗，consumer 消费者；consumerism 消费主义。）

amount to 共计，等同于，相当于（amount 作名词有“数量”的意思，例如 a large amount of 代表“大量的”，通常修饰不可数名词，而对应的 a large number of 通常修饰可数名词。）

incontrovertible *adj.* 无可辩驳的，不容置疑的（来自动词 controvert “争论，反驳，否定”。同义词还有 indisputable、inarguable、incontestable、irrefutable。）

attainable *adj.* 可获得的，可得到的（来自动词 attain “获得，达到”，同义词有 accomplishable、procurable、reachable、achievable。）

attempt *v.&n.* 试图，尝试（新闻中经常听到的谋杀未遂，英文就叫做 attempted murder。）

nonetheless *conj.* 虽然如此，但是，尽管

sophisticated *adj.* 复杂的，精致的；老练的，世故的（词根 soph 是“智慧”的意思，sophist 就是“诡辩家，博学者，智者”的意思。）

methodology *n.*（从事某一活动的）一套方法；方法学，方法论

independent *adj.* 独立的，不依靠别人的（美国的国庆节叫做独立日“Independence Day”，设定在每年的七月四日。）

downplay *v.* 贬低，轻视；不予重视；将……轻描淡写

principally *adv.* 主要地，首要地（principal 作名词时就有“负责人，主要的人，主角”的意思，还有“校长”的意思。）

cumulative *adj.* 积累的，渐增的（cumulate 作动词和形容词时均有“积累”的意思，还有动词 accumulate 也是“累积，积聚”的意思。）

understate *v.* 少说，保守地说

desirable *adj.* 令人满意的，值得拥有的，可取的

sufficient *adj.* 足够的，充足的（suffice 是其动词形式。）

shift *v.* 改变；转换，移动 *n.* 改变，转变

sensible *adj.* 明智的，合乎情理的（Jane Austen 的 *Sense and Sensibility* 就翻译为《理智与情感》。）

题目详解

Questions 1-7

思路

这种题型忌讳寻找主题句或中心句，因为每个人对段落中心思想的判断通常不同，而且

每个段落的首尾句也不一定是主题句或中心句，所以最好的解答方法应该是通过对每位考生都能读懂的标题进行反向思维，然后和段落内容进行比较，排除作答。

i. General points of agreements and disagreements of researchers

反向思维词：points of agreements and disagreements, researchers

反向思维：如果某段选此为标题，则该段落一般会出现具体的研究人员（一般为人名），并且讲到他们的观点的共同点和不同点。另外，也可能出现写作中最常见的句型之一：some people believe..., while others think...

ii. How much children really know about food

反向思维：这个标题的反向思维词并不明显，但是如果考生通读了全文，就知道整篇文章大概讲解食物促销对孩子的负面影响。所以，如果某段选此为标题，则该段落应该讲到孩子们对食物知识知之甚少，容易被食品促销误导。

iii. Need to take action

反向思维：这个标题的反向思维词也不明显，但是根据研究型文章的一般规律，“需要采取行动”一般会出现在研究型文章的后面，因为通常都是先讲研究发现的问题，然后再讲采取行动解决问题。

iv. Advertising effects of the “Big Four”

反向思维词：Big Four

反向思维：如果某段选此为标题，则该段落一定要提及“Big Four”。同时，该段落还要以“Big Four”的广告影响为主要内容，介绍这些广告是如何影响了孩子。

v. Connection of advertising and children's weight problems

反向思维词：weight problems

反向思维：如果某段选此为标题，则该段落应该提及孩子们的“weight problems”，而且该段落还可能会出现具体的体重数据。

vi. Evidence that advertising affects what children buy to eat

反向思维：这个标题的反向思维词不明显，但是如果某段选此为标题，则该段落要讲到广告对孩子的食品购买的影响，而且可能会出现具体的食品名称或品牌。

vii. How parents influence children's eating habits

反向思维词：parents, eating habits

反向思维：如果某段选此为标题，则该段落一定会提到“parents”。同时，该段落应该还会讲到具体的 eating habits，例如：过多地摄入甜食等等。

viii. Advertising's focus on unhealthy options

反向思维词：unhealthy options

反向思维：如果某段选此为标题，则该段落应该会提到一些具体的"unhealthy options"，例如：糖摄过多、油脂过量、食用过多膨化食品等等。

ix.　Children often buy what they want

反向思维：这个标题的反向思维词不明显，但是如果某段选此为标题，则该段落应该是讲广告的作用不大，对孩子没有什么影响。利用这个内容，很容易排除选项。

x.　Underestimating the effects advertising has on children

反向思维词：effects

反向思维：如果某段选此为标题，则该段落应该会提到一些具体的"effects"，但是重点会讲述人们低估了广告对孩子的影响，即原本以为影响小，而实际上影响大。

解答

1. ***Paragraph A***：作为开头段落，该段落前半部分先介绍了常见的面向儿童的广告内容，例如"Big Four"，而且介绍了食品促销的现状。后半部分则着重讲述广告充斥不良内容。据此，很明显地可以看出，与该段落对应的标题只有 iv. Advertising effects of the "Big Four" 和 viii. Advertising's focus on unhealthy options。如果该段落选 iv，按照之前的反向思维，应该要讲述"Big Four"的影响。而该段落显然根本未提及任何有关"Big Four"的广告影响，所以排除 iv，正确答案为 viii。
2. ***Paragraph B:*** 与该段落相关的标题有好几个：ii. How much children really know about food（对应 The review…possible effects on what children know about food…children's general perceptions of what constitutes a healthy diet…nutritional knowledge…）；v. Connection of advertising and children's weight problems（对应 …their health outcomes (eg. obesity or cholesterol levels)）；vi. Evidence that advertising affects what children buy to eat（对应 …their actual food behavior (both buying and eating)）。标题 ix. Children often buy what they want 与标题 x. Underestimating the effects advertising has on children 也有提及相关信息，但是很明显并非段落的主要内容，可以直接排除。标题 v 中的"weight problems"虽然对应原文中的"obesity"，但是该段落并没有以儿童肥胖为主要内容做文章，所以排除。标题 vi 中的"what children buy to eat"虽然对应原文"...their actual food behavior (both buying and eating)"，但是 B 段落也不是主要在讲儿童的购买行为，也可以排除。综上所述，该段落的标题应该为 ii。
3. ***Paragraph C:*** 段落中"…influences children's food preferences and their purchase behavior"对应标题 vi. Evidence that advertising affects what children buy to eat 和标题 x. Underestimating the effects advertising has on children。但是阅读段落后，很容易看出该段落讲到了广告的影响，但是根本未提及有关"underestimating"的事情，所以标

题 x 可以排除，正确答案为标题 vi。

4. ***Paragraph D:*** 段落中“...establish whether or not a link exists between food promotion and diet or obesity...”和后面反复提及的看电视、肥胖和儿童饮食之间的关系对应标题 v. Connection of advertising and children's weight problems，其他标题都未提及相关内容，所以正确答案为标题 v。

5. ***Paragraph E:*** 很明显地可以看出 E 段落中多处提及几个不同的研究及研究结果，甚至各研究结论还有所不同。其中之一说“This does not amount to proof”，另外的研究则说“many studies have found clear effects”，这完全对应了标题 i. General points of agreements and disagreements of researchers。尽管 E 段落没有提及具体的研究人员，但却提到了不同的观点。虽说标题 x. Underestimating the effects advertising has on children 也有一定的对应性，但是 E 段落完全没有提及与“underestimating”有关的信息，所以正确答案为标题 i。

6. ***Paragraph F:*** 段落首句“...these findings actually downplay the effect that food promotion has on children”对应标题 x. Underestimating the effects advertising has on children。段落最后提及的“...also encourage parents to take them for meals...”虽说对应标题 vii. How parents influence children's eating habits，但是全段并未具体讲述父母对孩子的饮食习惯的影响，反而只是在一个“For example”的举例当中略有提及，所以应当排除。综上所述，正确答案为标题 x。

7. ***Paragraph G:*** 很明显，在其他段落标题被选过之后，与此段落相对应的标题只有 iii. Need to take action（对应“The debate should now shift to what action is needed...”），所以正确答案为标题 iii。

Questions 8-13

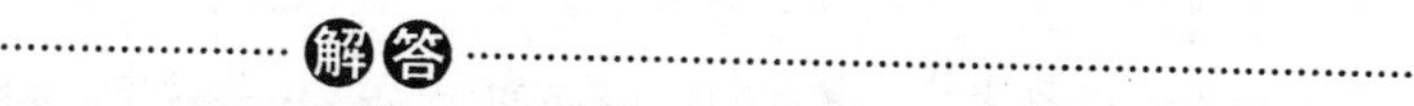

8. 利用顺序原则和细节信息“healthy food advertisements”与“unhealthy food advertisements”数量的比较，定位于原文段落 A 最后两句话“themes of fun and fantasy or taste（对应 unhealthy food advertisements）, rather than health and nutrition, are used to promote it to children. Meanwhile the recommended diet（对应 healthy food advertisements）gets little promotional support”，从上述内容可以很容易看出 unhealthy food 的广告多，而 healthy food 的广告少。题目与原文信息直接相反，所以正确答案为 No。

9. 利用顺序原则和细节信息“nutritional knowledge about vitamins and others”定位于原文段落 B 中间“In terms of nutritional knowledge, food advertising seems to have little influence on children's general perceptions of what constitutes a healthy diet”，由此可见电视广告并没有成功地教育孩子们关于营养的知识。题目与原文信息直接相反，所

以正确答案为No。

10. 利用顺序原则和细节信息“weight problems”定位于原文段落D中间“It is impossible to say, however, whether this effect is caused by the advertising, the sedentary nature of television viewing or snacking…”。题目与原文是同义表达，所以正确答案为Yes。

11. 利用顺序原则和细节信息“preference of food”以及“age and gender”在原文中无法找到与题目相对应的信息，所以答案为Not Given。

12. 利用顺序原则和细节信息“wealthy parents”以及“sensible food”定位于原文段落F最后一句话“…also encourage parents to take them for meals and reinforce the idea that this is a normal and desirable behavior”。这里虽然提及“parents”，但是并未讲到“wealthy parents”是否会为自己的孩子购买“sensible food”。题目在原文信息的基础上无法判断正误，所以正确答案为Not Given。

13. 利用顺序原则和细节信息“promotion methods”定位于原文段落F第二句话“the literature focuses principally on television advertising…”，对应题目所说的“lack of investigation on food promotion methods...”。题目与原文是同义表达，所以正确答案为Yes。

参考译文

关于食品促销对儿童影响的研究综述

本综述经由英国食品标准局委托开展，调查如下领域已获得的研究结果：

- *食品促销对儿童影响的程度和性质*
- *该促销对儿童的食品知识、喜好和饮食行为所产生的影响（如果存在的话）*

A 电视广告主导了面向儿童的食品促销，而且绝大多数是向儿童销售所谓的“大四类”：加糖的早餐麦片、软饮料、甜点和小吃。在过去十年当中，快餐店的广告迅速增多。有证据显示电视广告的主导地位已经开始下降。强有力的国际品牌形象的重要性加深了对结合电视与销售、“联合促销”和销售点活动这种多面交流的需求。广告所宣传的饮食与公众健康专家所推荐的饮食对比鲜明。有关健康和营养的主题反而被有趣、新奇或味道等内容所代替，被用来向儿童推销食品。与此同时，真正应该被提倡的饮食却只获得极少的推广支持。

B 有充分的证据显示，儿童会注意并且喜欢食品促销。但是要确定促销是否会对儿童造成影响却是一个复杂的问题。本综述通过检视食品促销可能对儿童自身的食品知识、食品偏好和实际饮食行为（包含购买和进食）以及导致的健康问题（例如肥胖和胆固醇水平）所带来的影响进行研究，以此解决上述问题。大多数的研究调查了食品广告，但是也有一部分研究调查了其他形式的食品促销。从营养知识方面来说，

食品广告似乎对儿童的健康饮食观念影响甚微，但是在特定情境下，它能对更加具体的营养方面的知识产生影响。例如，看到软饮料和麦片的广告会降低适龄儿童正确判断特定产品中是否含有真正水果的能力。

C 本综述也发现了食品促销影响儿童食物喜好和购买行为的证据。例如，一项针对小学生的研究发现，对广告的接触会影响学生所喜爱的食物；另外一项研究显示，自动贩卖机上的标签和标识对中学生的购买选择有影响。还有一些研究也显示，广告会影响儿童的饮食选择。比如，其中一项研究发现，广告会影响小学生每天课间玩耍时间的零食选择。

D 下一步，即尝试确定食品促销和饮食或肥胖之间是否存在联系的研究是非常难行的，因为这需要在现实环境中进行研究。有一些研究试图通过利用看电视的量替代接触广告的量来实现这一点。它们在看电视与饮食、肥胖和胆固醇水平之间建立了清晰的联系。不过却很难说这个影响是由广告造成的，还是由看电视时久坐不动或看电视时吃零食造成的。有项研究通过详细纪录儿童的电视观看习惯解决了这个问题。该研究显示，儿童观看的广告越多，所吃的零食和所消耗的卡路里就越多。

E 因此，研究文献确实指出食品促销正以多种方式影响儿童的饮食。这并不等同于确切的证据；正如上面所提及的，对于此类研究，确凿而毫无质疑的证据，简单来说，是不可能获得的。况且，也不是所有的研究都指向这个结论；有些研究就没有发现任何影响。除此以外，很少有研究去衡量，相对于那些其他影响儿童食物选择的因素，这些影响究竟有多大。尽管如此，许多研究发现了确切的影响，而且这些研究还使用了复杂的方法，使得确认以下内容成为可能：1）这些影响不是偶然发生的；2）它们独立于其他可能影响饮食的因素之外，例如父母的饮食习惯或态度；3）这些影响是发生在品牌和类别层面上。

F 此外，有两个因素显示，这些研究实际上低估了食品促销对儿童的影响。首先，研究文献主要集中于电视广告方面的研究；电视广告结合其他各种推销形式所累积的影响可能要大得多。其次，这些研究只考察了对个体儿童的直接影响，而低估了间接影响。例如，快餐店的促销可能不只影响儿童，还可能鼓励父母带他们在此就餐，进而强化一种观念，即这是正常且可取的行为。

G 这并不等同于证实了影响的存在，但是在我们看来，确实提供了充足的证据，使我们得出“影响是存在的”的结论。现在，关注的重点应该转移至我们该采取什么行动，尤其应该转移至如何利用广告营销的力量来促进年轻人改善饮食。

Reading Passage 2. The Bridge That Swayed

词汇详解

sway *v.&n.* 摇摆，摆动（该词在写作和口语中常用来表达一个人在事务上的立场或态度摇摆不定，也可以用来表达影响别人，例如：British commanders were also concerned that recent casualties could sway opinion. 英军长官也担心最近的死亡人数将会动摇民心。sway back and forth 就指的是像钟摆“pendulum”一样前后摆动。hold sway over 则表达的是“统治，控制”，例如：Today Taliban insurgents again hold sway over much of the Kandahar countryside. 现在，塔利班武装分子再次控制了大部分坎大哈郊区。）

millennium *n.* 一千年；千禧年（该词由词根 mille“千”和 ennium“年”组成，所以字面意思非常清晰。和 mille 相关的词根还有：dec 或 deca，表示“十”；cent 或 centi，代表“百”。于是就有了 decade 十年；century 百年；millennium 千年。如果再长一点还有 eon 亿万年。ennium 也可以组成很多词，例如：biennial 两年一次的；centennial 百年一次的。清华大学的百年校庆就叫做“centennial anniversary”。）

wobbly *adj.* 摇摆的，不稳定的（该词来自动词 wobble“晃动，摇摆不定”，人们还常用“wobble about”或“wobble around”来表达“左右晃动”。）

pedestrian *n.* 步行者，行人；没想象力的，平淡的（步行街就叫做“pedestrian street”。该词来自于词根 ped“脚”。与该词根相关的词汇还有：centipede 百足虫或蜈蚣；millipede 千足虫。pedicure 就是“足部治疗”，尤其是指提供脚趾和脚部指甲的护理。另外，值得一提的是表示“孩童”的词根也是 ped，例如：pediatrics 儿科；pedophilia 恋童癖；pedagogy 教育学。）

gallery *n.* 画廊，走廊（作为“走廊”的意思时，基本上就相当于 corridor。）

initially *adv.* 开始，最初（initial 作形容词时，意思是“最初的，开始的”。复数形式 initials 还可以用来指代人名的首字母，例如 John Hancock 的 initials 就是 JH，John Fitzgerald Kennedy 的 initials 就是 JFK。）

assemble *v.* 集合，收集；装配（assembly line 就是“生产线，装配线”。）

pronounced *adj.* 明显的，显著的；表达明确的（来自动词 pronounce“宣布，宣称”。虽然大家最熟悉的是其“发音”的意思，但是 pronounce 本身也有“公开宣布，宣称”的意思，因为词根 nounce 是“述说”的意思，前缀 pro 代表“向前”。例如，在婚礼上当新娘和新郎交换完戒指后，牧师就会说：“I now pronounce you husband and wife”，意思就是“我宣布你们为夫妻”。同义词有：marked、conspicuous、noticeable 等。与词根 nounce 相关的词汇还有：announce 宣布；renounce 否认，放弃；denounce 指责，控告等。）

lateral *adj.* 侧面的；横向的（unilateral 单边的；bilateral 双边的。在美式橄榄球中 lateral pass/throw 是“横向传球”。）

deck *n.* 甲板，舱板；层面；木质平台 *v.* 装饰；打扮（在船上如果听到船长说“clear the decks”，意思并非是让船员或乘客清扫甲板，而是“让大家离开甲板区域”，为下一步可能的行动做准备。当然现在在口语中也是一种形象的说法，是“get out of the way”或者“get out of the area”的意思，例如：Clear the decks! Here comes the teacher! 都闪开，老师来啦！on deck 是另外一个常见的说法，意思是“准备好，准备做什么事情”，例如：It was all hands on deck at the factory, labeling and bottling Shower Power to keep up with demand. 整个工厂全力开工，给“浴室动力”贴签、装瓶，来满足市场的需求。）

route *n.* 路，路线；航线 *v.* 按某路线发送（公交车中常用到这个词，例如 Route 101 就是 101 路车。另外自建 wifi 时，必不可少的路由器就叫做“router”。）

charity *n.* 慈善；施舍；慈善团体；仁爱，宽容（慈善的形式多种多样，其中最常见的应该就是捐赠“donation”。）

recount *v.* 详细叙述；重新计算（作为“叙述”时，就等同于 narrate，同义词还有 describe、recite、rehearse 等。）

sideways *adv.* 斜着，侧着 *adj.* 斜向一边的

wobble *v.* 晃动；摇摆不定 *n.* 摇动，晃动

intensify *v.* 增强，加剧（来自形容词 intense“强烈的，紧张的，热情的”。在单词后面加上后缀 fy 使其变成动词是英语中常见的一种构词法，意思是“to make or become”，例如：beautify 美化；nullify 使无效；verify 证实；purify 净化；clarify 使清晰等。）

retain *v.* 保持；记住（该词由表示“再一次”的前缀 re 和表示“持有”的词根 tain 组成，所以该词的字面意思就是“保持，保留”。）

rail *n.* 围栏，扶手；轨道；铁路（表示“扶手”的意思时，还可以用更加完整的词“handrail”。作为“轨道”的意思时，可以再加上前缀 de 变成 derail，意为“脱轨，出轨”。口语中还有“get/be back on the rails”的表达，字面意思就是“重新回到轨道上来”，是一种形象的表达。）

dub *v.* 起绰号；配音（口语中有个习语叫做“flub the dub”，意思就是“把事情搞砸了”。）

tackle *n.* 用具，装备；阻挡；阻截队员 *v.* 处理；与某人交涉；抢球；阻截（“tackle the issue of...”是一个常用的搭配，指的是“解决……的问题”。）

head on *adv.* 迎面地（head on 和其他单词组合在一起可以形成很多词组，例如：head on clash 迎头相撞；head on collision 正面碰撞；head on combat 正面战斗；head on confrontation 正面冲突等。）

undertake *v.* 承担，从事；答应，承诺（该词字面上的意思就是“从下面拿起”，很形象地就有了“承担”的意思，相当于“take upon oneself”。例如，中文成语“任劳任怨”就可以翻译成“to undertake a task despite criticism”或者“to bear the burden of office willingly”。值得一提的是该词的 ing 形式 undertaking 常被人们用来表示“努力从事的事情，事业”，相当于 enterprise。中文成语“骄兵必败”也常翻译为“a proud person often fails in his undertakings”。这里也送给广大考生一句 Napoleon Hill 曾经说过的话来共勉：“Every person who wins in any undertaking must be willing to cut all sources of retreat. Only by doing so can one be sure of maintaining that state of mind known as a burning desire to win.”）

exert *v.* 发挥；运用；努力（英语中“exert oneself to...”的表达，就等同于“try hard to...”或者“make an effort to...”，例如：Jerry exerted himself to please the new girl。而 exert influence 指的是“施加影响”。）

excessive *adj.* 过度的；过分的（来自动词 exceed，其中 ex 代表“出去”，词根 ceed 代表“走”，所以 exceed 的字面意思是“走出去”，后来再进一步引申，就变成了“超越，超出”的意思了。例如，超速就叫做“exceed the speed limit”。同义词有：surpass、overpass、outrun 等。）

banner *n.* 横幅；旗，旗帜（在口语中有一个习语叫做“under the banner of”，意思就是“在……的旗帜下，在……的名义下”。例如：She fought the election under the banner of equal rights. 她打着平等的旗号参加了竞选。该词代表“旗子”时，同义词有 flag、ensign、guidon 和 jack。尤其是 jack 也可以代表旗子，例如英国的国旗就叫做“the Union Jack”。）

buffet *v.* 反复敲打；连续猛击；打来打去 *n.*（火车）饮食柜台，（火车）餐车；自助餐（该词作“自助餐”时最为广大考生熟悉，作为动词表示“猛击或者敲打”时，同义词有 strike、batter、beat、flog、knock、pound 等。）

vibration *n.* 抖动；震动（在上课时为了防止手机铃声“ringtone”干扰课程的正常进行，往往要把手机调至振动或静音模式“set cellphone to vibrate or silent mode”，当然有些手机厂商把此功能叫做“set to meeting”，也就是“会议模式”。）

conduct *v.* 引导；带领；控制；传导；实施；执行 *n.* 行为，举止（作名词时重音在前，而作动词时重音在后。在学术文章中表达“进行实验，进行测试或者进行调查”时都常用到 conduct 一词，例如：conduct an experiment, a test, a survey 等。作为“引导”时，相当于动词 lead，同时还有很多和 lead 相似的词组，例如：conduct someone away (from...)、conduction someone into...、conduct someone out of... 等。此时名词 conductor 的意思就是乐队的“指挥”，或者公交车的“乘务员”。conductor 还有“导体”的意思，semiconductor 就是“半导体”。misconduct 代表“不当行为”。）

suspension *n.* 悬浮；暂停；悬挂；悬浮液（来自动词 suspend，其中 pend 是词根，代表“悬挂”，sus 是前缀，代表“下面”，所以该词的字面意思就是“在下面挂着，不上不下，中间悬着”。与词根 pend 相关的词汇还有：pendant 垂饰；depend 依靠；pendulum 钟摆；impend 迫近，即将发生；perpendicular 垂直等。词组 suspend someone from something 指的是“阻止某人参与或从事某事”。）

lock-step 锁步，步调一致

compensate *v.* 补偿，赔偿；报酬（根据消费者权益保护法“Consumer Protection Law”，尤其在“3.15”期间，如果购买的商品有瑕疵“defect”，可以直接向商家要求赔偿“compensation”，如果商家拒绝赔偿，可以向工商局“State Administration of Industry and Commerce，简称 SAIC”等有关机构投诉“complain”。）

exacerbate *v.* 使恶化；使加重（该词与 exasperate 接近，但是 exacerbate 更多表达的是“to make worse”，而 exasperate 更多的表示“to irritate, to anger”。同义词有 aggravate、worsen；反义词有：allay、alleviate、assuage、ease、mitigate、relieve 等。）

resonance *n.* 共鸣；反响；共振（该词的形容词形式是 resonant。该词词根 sona 或 soner 的意思就是“声音 sound”，所以该词字面的意思就是“发出回响 resound”。与该词根相关的词汇还有：sonic 音速的；consonant 一致的，符合的；dissonant 不和谐的，刺耳的；supersonic 超音速的。）

interaction *n.* 合作；互相影响，互动（前缀 inter 代表“两者之间，互相”，等同于 between；action 表示“行动”。）

subtle *adj.* 微妙的；敏感的；狡猾的；巧妙的（名词形式是 subtlety。中文成语“胸有城府”可以翻译成“subtle way of thinking”或者“hard to fathom”。同义词有：artful、crafty、delicate、scheming 等。）

absorb *v.* 吸收；吸引；吞并，合并；承担（词组“absorb oneself in...”指的是“沉迷于什么事物或做什么事情当中”。）

resistant *adj.* 有抵抗力的，抵抗的（来自动词 resist，其中词根 sist 代表“站立 stand”，字面意思就是“不站起来”，于是就延伸成“抵抗，反抗”的意思了。中文成语“难以抗拒，势不可挡”都可以用“impossible/hard to resist”来表达。英语中习语“line of least resistance”或者“path of least resistance”指的是“阻力最小的方向，最便当的方法，最省力的途径”，例如：People generally choose the line of least resistance. 人们一般采用最容易的办法。You can force them, but nature prefers configurations that follow the path of least resistance. 你可以强迫他们，但是大自然会选择那些阻力最小的构型。）

horizontal *adj.* 水平的；地平线的（该词是名词 horizon“地平线”的形容词形式，人们常说的“开阔视野”可以用英语“widen/broaden/expand one’s horizons”来表达。horizontal 的反义词是 vertical“垂直的”。）

dynamic *adj.* 动态的；动力的；精力充沛的 *n.* 动态；动力；动力学（同义词有：vigorous、energetic、robust、flush 等。作为“动力学”时，常用复数形式“dynamics”，而且可以和很多其他的前缀组合在一起，例如：aerodynamics 空气动力学；thermodynamics 热力学；hydrodynamics 流体力学等。）

gait *n.* 步态，步法（zombie gait 僵尸步；astronaut/spacewalk gait 太空步。）

magnify *v.* 放大；赞美；夸大（该词是形容词 magnificent“壮丽的，宏伟的”的变形。）

motion *n.* 运动；动作；提议 *v.* 打手势；示意（该词词根 mot 代表“运动”，例如：motive 动机；motivate 激励；locomotive 移动的；promote 促进。词组“put/set something in motion”的字面意思是“使什么东西开始移动”，等同于“开始”，例如：This does not mean that the changes set in motion in December will dissipate. 这并不意味着 12 月份作出的一系列变动将不复存在。set the wheels in motion 指的是"做什么事情，并由此引发一系列的行为 to do something that will cause a series of actions to start"。)

oscillation *n.* 振动；摆动；波动（来自动词 oscillate。词组"oscillate between..."就等同于"swing between..."，意思就是"在两者之间左右摆动，犹豫不决"。)

upright *adj.* 直立的；垂直的；正直的；诚实的（要让某人站直，可以跟他说："stand upright"。英语里有一句谚语叫做"An empty sack cannot stand upright"，意思就是说"a poor or hungry person cannot function properly 饿肚子或及其贫穷的人无法正常工作"。)

quantify *v.* 确定……的数量，量化

amplitude *n.* 振幅；广大，广阔（来自形容词 ample"足够的，充足的，丰富的"。)

retrofit *n.* 翻新，改进 *v.* 翻新，改型（其中前缀 retro 的意思是"向后，往回"，例如：retrospect 回顾，回想；retrogress 倒退，退化；retroaction 反作用。)

feasible *adj.* 可做的；可实行的；可能的（同义词有：achievable、attainable、possible、practicable、viable 等。)

stiffness *n.* 僵硬；生硬；顽固（来自形容词 stiff。英语中有很多关于 stiff 的词组或习语，例如：as stiff as a poker 刻板，生硬；keep a stiff upper lip 坚定不移，咬紧牙关，尤其是不流露出自己的悲伤或难过等。Even though he was only three years old, Jonathan kept a stiff upper lip the whole time he was in the hospital recovering from his surgery. 尽管乔纳森只有三岁，但是在医院手术恢复期间，他却能咬紧牙关坚强地挺过来。)

damping *n.* 阻尼，减幅（动词 damp 本身就有"抑制，减缓，减弱"的意思。例如，汽车上用来减轻路面颠簸的减震器，英语就叫做"damper"。)

题目详解

Questions 14-17

思路

一般情况下，这种多选多的选择题具有信息分散的特点，且通常具有归纳总结的特征，在雅思阅读中属于难题，所以应该放在做题顺序的最后，在其余细节题做完之后再来解答，此时更容易定位。做题过程中，只能分别针对每一个选项进行原文定位，根据原文信息进行判断。

不过这组题比较简单，因为题目信息相对集中，都是关于"on the day when the bridge opened to the public"所能观察到的现象，大多位于原文第二、三、四、五段。

解答

选项 A “the bridge moved vertically”中的“moved vertically”是选项的关键内容，意思是上下垂直移动或晃动。而根据原文多处信息，例如第二段第三句话中的“lateral movement”（侧向移动）和第六句话中的“sway sideways”（侧向摇摆），可以看出伦敦千年桥并没有上下摆动，而是朝两侧左右摇摆，所以该选项为错误选项，应该排除。

选项 B “the bridge swayed from side to side”，根据前面一题的分析，该选项正确。

选项 C “the bridge swayed violently throughout the opening ceremony”，该选项的关键信息是“swayed violently”（猛烈摇摆）和“throughout the opening ceremony”（贯穿开幕仪式的始终）。而原文第二段中间现场目击者的描述明显提及“At first, it was still. Then it began to sway sideways, just slightly”（一开始，桥梁并没有晃动，然后有轻微晃动），再然后“when large groups of people were crossing, the wobble intensified”（当人数变多时，晃动才加剧）。原文信息明显与该选项所说的“桥梁自始至终都在猛烈晃动”相反，所以该选项错误，应该排除。

选项 D “it was hard to keep balance on the bridge”，该选项内容在原文多处均有提及，例如原文第二段目击者的最后一句话“Everyone had to stop walking to retain balance and sometimes to hold onto the hand rails for support”。所以该选项正确。

选项 E “pedestrians walked in synchronised steps”，该选项的关键在于“synchronised steps”（同步步伐），原文第四、五段均有提及。第四段中间提及“It is an unconscious tendency for pedestrians to match their footsteps to the sway, thereby exacerbating it even more”，第五段最后提及“As more pedestrians locked into the same rhythm, the increasing oscillation led to the dramatic swaying captured on film…”，这里的“match their footsteps to the sway”和“locked into the same rhythm”对应选项中的“synchronised steps”。所以该选项正确。

选项 F “pedestrians lengthened their footsteps”，该选项的关键在于“lengthened their footsteps”（增大了他们的步伐）。而原文虽然在第四、五段提及关于行人步伐的理论，但是根本未提及行人是否“lengthened their footsteps”，所以该选项错误，应该排除。

选项 G “a music band marched across the bridge”，原文第二段开头虽然提及“band”，但是并未提及乐队是否也跟着过桥，只提到了人们伴随着乐队的演奏过桥（when they started to walk across with the band playing），所以该选项不正确，应该排除。

选项 H “the swaying rhythm varied to the portions of the bridge”，该选项的关键在于“portions of the bridge”（桥梁的不同部分）的摇摆节奏不同。该信息出现在原文第三段第三句话“…the center span swaying about 3 inches sideways every second and the south span 2 inches every 1.25 seconds"。这里明显能看出桥梁的中部与南部的摇摆节奏不同，与选项中的"varied to the portions of the bridge"对应，所以该选项正确。

选项I "flags and banners kept still on the bridge"，原文第三段中间明显提及"there was a significant wind blowing on the opening days…winds might be exerting excessive force on the many large flags and banners, but it was rapidly concluded that wind buffeting…"。原文这里提及虽然风力对桥上的旗帜和横幅有影响，但是并不足以使桥梁摆动。这也就是说桥上的"flags and banners"当天在风中是摆动的，而非静止的。所以该选项不正确，应该排除。

综上所述，**14-17**题的正确答案为B、D、E、H。

Questions 18-23

解答

18. 利用细节信息"flags and banners on the bridge"定位于原文第三段第四句话"Because there was a significant wind blowing on the opening days (force 3-4) and the bridge had been decorated with large flags, the engineers first thought that winds might be exerting excessive force on the many large flags and banners…"。原文这里提及工程师们最初认为是风对旗帜和横幅施加了过大的力 (exerting excessive force) 才导致桥梁晃动，对应题目中的"caused the movement"，所以正确答案为wind或winds。

19. 利用细节信息"new understandings"和"floors"以及顺序性原则定位于原文第三段最后一句话"after measurements were made in university laboratories of the effects of people walking on swaying platforms…a new understanding and a new theory were developed"。这里的"a new understanding and a new theory"对应题目中的"new understandings"，而且原文这里明显提及实验是关于"the effects of people walking on swaying platforms"，"platforms"对应题目中的"floors"，所以正确答案为swaying。

20. 利用细节信息"place their legs"和"keep balance when the floor is shaking"以及顺序性原则定位于原文第四段第三句话"If we walk on a swaying surface we tend to compensate and stabilise ourselves by spreading our legs further apart…"。这里的"stabilise ourselves"对应题目中的"keep balance"，"spreading our legs"对应题目中的"place their legs"，所以正确答案为further apart。

21. 利用细节信息"Pat Dallard"、"unknowingly adjust"和"to match the sway of the bridge"以及顺序性原则定位于原文第四段第五句话"It is an unconscious tendency for pedestrians to match their footsteps to the sway…"，这里的"unconscious"对应题目中的"unknowingly"，"match their footsteps to the sway"对应题目中的"adjust"和"to match the sway of the bridge"，所以正确答案为 footsteps。

22. 利用细节信息"Fujino Yozo"和"people walking, running and jumping"以及顺序性原则定位于原文第五段第一句话"...the horizontal forces caused by walking, running or jumping could also in turn cause excessive dynamic vibration in the lateral direction in the bridge"。很明显原文提及"walking, running or jumping"会导致"horizontal forces"，而这些"horizontal forces"又会反过来（in turn）导致桥梁的侧向振动（cause excessive dynamic vibration in the lateral direction in the bridge），所以正确答案为 horizontal forces。

23. 利用细节信息"impossible to stand"和顺序性原则定位于原文第五段最后一句话"...led to the dramatic swaying captured on film until people stopped walking altogether, because they could not even keep upright"。这里的"could not even keep upright"对应题目中的"impossible to stand"，所以正确答案为 upright。

Questions 24-26

24. 该题对应原文倒数第三段。原文中的"It was decided that the force exerted by the pedestrians had to be quantified...none of these actually quantifies the force. So there was no quantitative analytical way to design the bridge against this effect"对应题目所说的"Not enough data collection"，所以正确答案为 Arup。

25. 该题对应原文倒数第二段中间"While the Imperial College test platform was too short that only seven or eight steps could be measured at one time..."。这里的"test platform was too short"对应题目中的"Not long enough"，所以正确答案为 Imperial College。

26. 该题也对应原文倒数第二段中间"...the 'walking on the spot' test did not accurately replicate forward walking..."。这里的"did not accurately replicate forward walking"对应题目中的"Not like the real walking experience"，而"walking on the spot"就是该段落一开始所提及的 the University of Southampton 所做的实验，所以正确答案为 University of Southampton。

参考译文

摇摆桥

当伦敦千年桥在 2000 年 6 月开放时，它发生了剧烈的摇摆。这引起了公众的极大兴趣，该桥也因此被人们称作"摇摆桥"。

千年桥是继 1894 年开放的伦敦塔桥之后的第一座横跨伦敦泰晤士河的新建桥梁，而且也是第一座专门为行人设计的桥梁。该桥把伦敦市圣保罗大教堂附近区域和泰晤士河畔的泰特现代艺术展览馆连在了一起。

该桥最初于2000年6月10日星期六向公众开放。在开幕仪式上，一个一千多人的队伍聚集在桥梁的南侧，他们的前面还有一个乐队。当这一千多人伴随着乐队演奏开始过桥时，桥面立刻出现了人们完全未预料到的明显的侧向移动。“当时天气不错，这座桥也刚好在一个主要的慈善游行活动的线路上”，一个行人这样描述当时他所看到的一切，“起初，桥是静止的。然后它开始往两侧摇晃，但是很轻微。然后，几乎顷刻之间，当一大群人开始过桥时，摇摆加剧了。人们都不得不停下来以保持平衡，甚至有时候还要扶着扶手。”很快有关方面决定限制桥梁上过桥的人数，该桥也被一家媒体称作“摇摆桥”，并被该媒体宣称是另外一个高调的英国千年项目失败的案例。为了全面调查研究和解决摇摆的问题，有关方面做出了于2000年6月12日关闭该桥的决定。

该桥梁建设委员会的领导成员英国奥雅纳工程顾问公司（以下简称奥雅纳）决定直面问题。他们立刻开展了快速追踪研究项目来寻找原因和解决办法。这些尴尬的工程师们找到了当天的录像带。录像显示桥梁中间部分的侧向摆幅为每秒3英寸，而南边则为每1.25秒2英寸。由于开放当天风力较大（3到4级），而且桥梁上装点了很多大面积的旗帜，所以工程师们一开始以为可能是风对那许多大面积的旗帜和横幅施加了过大的风力。但是很快人们得出结论，认为风的冲击力不可能对桥的振动带来如此大的影响。在大学实验室里进行了人们在晃动平台上行走的测试和数据收集后，以及在进行了有大量行人参与的关于桥体本身的大规模实验之后，新的发现和新的理论诞生了。

桥梁意料之外的晃动是人们对细微的侧向移动的自然反应的结果。众所周知，吊桥容易在部队齐步过桥时发生摆动。正因如此，部队在过桥时会被要求碎步前进。“当我们走在一个摇摆的平面上时，我们倾向于分开双腿来弥补和保持身体稳定，但是这样做却会增加侧向的推力”。奥雅纳的工程师之一帕特·达拉德认为，人们会调整自己的走路方式以适应桥梁的运动。行人会让自己的步伐适应摇摆，这是一个无意识的倾向，这样反而会加剧桥梁的摆动。“这就像在摇摆的船甲板上行走一样——你需要朝一边踏一脚然后再朝另一边踏一脚来适应船的摆动”。人们走路的方式不需要像共振的情况一样与桥梁的振动频率精准吻合——两者之间的相互作用更加细微。当桥梁摆动时，行人会按照自己的方式调整自己的步伐。但问题是，当桥梁上的人数足够多时，叠加在一起所产生的侧向推力可能会超过桥梁所能承受的。于是，这个摆动就会加剧并且持续增强，直到人们开始感觉难以行走——他们甚至可能不得不抓紧扶手。

研究日本抗震桥梁Toda桥的东京大学教授藤野阳三认为，行走、跑步或跳动所产生的水平作用力反过来也会导致桥梁过度的侧向振动。他解释说，当建筑开始移动时，行人会根据桥梁的侧向振动节奏调整自己的步伐；而调整后的步伐又会加剧这种侧向振动——这就像四个人在一只小船里同时站起来一样。当越来越多的人调整到这个相同的节奏时，这种增强的振动就会导致我们在录像上所看到的剧烈的摆动，直到人们完全停止走动，因为他们甚至无法保持直立。

为了设计出一种能减轻摆动的方法，桥梁的工程设计方奥雅纳立刻开展了一个研究项目。专家认为行人所施加于桥梁的力必须要量化且需要与桥梁的摆动联系在一起。尽管在现有的研究文献中存在关于这个现象的相关描述，但是这些文献中没有任何一个文献对行人的力度进行了量化。因此，也就没有可量化的分析方法来设计桥梁使其消除摆动效应。解决该问题的努力很快就获得了许多大学和研究机构的支持。

南安普敦大学的实验是让一个人在一个小型振动台上原地踏步。帝国理工学院的测验则是让多人在一个特制的7.2米长的平台上行走，这个平台可以以不同的频率和摆幅朝侧面振动。这些实验都有其自身的局限性。一方面，帝国理工学院的实验平台太短，一次只能测量七到八步。另一方面，“原地踏步”的实验也不能精确地复制向前的行走，尽管这个方法可以观测到许多步伐。两者也都不能研究一群人中其他人对被测量者行为的影响。

这些实验室的研究结果提供了对桥梁进行改进的最初设计方案所需要的数据。但是，除非桥梁的使用受到极大的限制，否则只有两种通用改进桥梁的方案被认为可行。第一种方案就是增加桥梁的坚固性，把所有侧向自然振动频率都排除到行人侧向脚步力度所能影响的范围之外，第二种方案就是增加桥梁阻尼来降低共振反应。

Reading Passage 3. Internal Market: Selling the Brand Inside

词汇详解

internal *adj.* 内部的，内在的（其反义词为 external “外部的”，与内部和外部相关的词对还有 inside & outside、interior & exterior、intrinsic & extrinsic、inner & outer、inward & outward 等。）

brand *n.* 品牌，商标（其动名词形式为 branding，是“打造品牌，品牌化”的意思。与其相关的词汇还有：trademark 商标；registered trademark 注册商标；logo 标志，标识。）

executive *adj.* 执行的，经营管理的 *n.* 执行官，经理；行政部门（来自动词 execute “实施，执行”。该动词还有一个独特的含义，就是“处决，处死”的意思。CEO 首席执行官就是“chief executive officer”。）

campaign *n.* 运动；活动；战役 *v.* 参加或发起运动；参战，参加战役（如果该运动的波及面很广，甚至具有革命性的意义，则可以叫做 crusade。）

critical *adj.* 批评的；决定性的，关键的（来自动词 criticise “批评”，相关词汇有：critic

评论家，评论员；critique 评论文章，评论，发表评论。）

constituency *n.* 支持者，拥护者（来自动词 constitute "组成，构成，设立"；constituency 在政治上还有"选区，选区的选民"的意思。）

undermine *v.* 暗中破坏，逐渐削弱（under 有"下面"的意思，mine 有"挖矿"的意思，所以该词的字面意思就是"在下面挖矿"，越挖地基就越不稳定，于是就有"暗中破坏，逐渐削弱"的意思。相关词汇有 weaken、cripple、disable、debilitate 等。）

cross-purpose 相反的目的，不一致的目的，矛盾（类似这样构成的词还有很多，例如：著名的第一人称射击网游 CrossFire，在军事上是指交叉火力的意思；crossover 在车辆上指的是跨界车；cross-dressing 指的就是穿着异性的服装，男扮女装，女扮男装。）

disengage *v.* 放开，挣脱开；脱离（去掉否定前缀 dis 就变成了 engage，表示"参与，从事，与人交战"。）

hostile *adj.* 敌人的，敌对的；怀有敌意的 *n.* 敌对者，敌对物；敌方（名词形式为 hostility "敌意，对抗，反对"。相关词汇有：animosity 敌意，仇恨；enmity 敌意，敌对。）

motivate *v.* 激发，刺激，使有动机（名词 motive 有"动机"的意思，motivate 的同义词有 stimulate、impel、prick、goad。）

loyalty *n.* 忠诚，忠心（和 royalty "王族，王权"形似。）

unify *v.* 联合，统一，使一致（词根 uni 的意思就是"一"，由它引申出来的词还有 unity、unite、unanimous 等。unanimous 的意思为"全体一致的，一致同意的，无异议的"。）

inspire *v.* 鼓舞，激励；赋予灵感（词根 spir 是"呼吸"的意思。相关词汇有：respire 呼吸、respiratory 呼吸的；perspire 出汗；expire 断气，死亡，期满，出气。）

inform *v.* 通知，告知（information 就是通知的内容，也就是"信息"。informant 就是提供信息的人，也就是"报信人"。）

external *adj.* 外部的，外在的（为 internal 的反义词。）

mismatch *v.* 使不搭配，搭配不当

perception *n.* 感知能力；洞察力；理解，看法（来自动词 perceive，其中前缀 per 是"完全 thoroughly"的意思，ceive 是"拿到，拿着"的意思，所以 perceive 就是"完全拿到"，进一步就变成"理解，洞察"的意思。）

integrity *n.* 正直，诚实；完整（该词与 entire "全部的，整体的"同源，而且意思也接近。integrity 是一个重要的品质"virtue"，可以在口语中描述某个人物时使用，通常说成"... has/doesn't have integrity"。相关词汇有：integer 整数；integrate 使一体化，使整合。）

observe *v.* 观察；遵守

welfare *n.* 福利；幸福，繁荣

priority *n.* 优先的事物；优先权（是 prior "优先的，在……之前的"的名词。prior to 相当于 before。prioritise 意为"划分优先顺序，优先处理"。其实任何事物都应该统筹安排，为实现效果的最大化，我们要将最紧急的"most urgent"、最重要的"most important"事

情先做好，然后处理紧急但是不那么重要的事情，再然后处理不紧急但重要的事情，最后则处理既不紧急也不重要的事情。）

stock option 股票期权，优先认股权（是指在指定时期内定价定额购股权。）

reduction *n.* 减少，缩减（为 reduce 的名词形式。前缀 re 代表“往回，往后”，词根 duce 是引导“lead”的意思，所以 reduce 就是 to lead back，于是也就引申为“减少”。由词根 duce 变化出来的单词还有很多，例如：produce 生产，创造；induce 造成，引起；deduce 推论，推断，演绎；seduce 引诱，勾引；conduce 有益，有贡献，导致；transduce 从一种形态改变为另一形态，转换。）

institution *n.* 机构；建立

retailer *n.* 零售商（相关词汇有：retail 零售；wholesale 批发；wholesaler 批发商。）

churn out 快速生产；大量生产

transaction *n.* 交易，业务，事务

launch *v.* 发射；发动，开展活动计划等（火箭发射前的 10 秒倒计时叫做 10 seconds countdown。）

be credited for 被誉为，被认为……（词根 cred 的意思就是相信“believe”。）

embrace *v.* 拥抱；接受（前缀 em 有“进入”的意思，词根 brace 有“两胳膊”的意思，所以用两胳膊来环绕就是“拥抱，接受”的意思。）

align *v.* 使成一线；使结盟；排整齐（在使用 Microsoft Office Word 进行排版时，左对齐是 align to the left，右对齐就是 , align to the right。）

approach *v.* 接近，靠近；着手处理 *n.* 方法；途径；接近（要形容一个人平易近人，我们可以说他 approachable，相当于 easy-going。approach 在雅思阅读中表示“方法，手段”时，其同义词有 means、measure、way、method 等。）

restore *v.* 恢复；修复；归还（名词是 restoration。现在的电脑都比较先进，基本上都有一个系统恢复隐藏分区“a hidden partition for system restoration”，如果系统有任何问题或者遭受了严重的病毒侵袭“severe virus infection”，总是可以轻松地恢复到出厂设置“restore to factory setting”。）

associate *v.* 使联合；与……结交，交往（前缀 ad 表示“增强”的意思，拉丁语名词 socius 表示“同伴”的意思，而且前缀 ad 中的字母 d 会伴随词根的首字母发生变化。association 是名词，通常表示“联盟，协会”，例如美国国家篮球协会的英文全称就是 National Basketball Association，缩写为 NBA。此外，虽然为法语，但 Federation Internationale de Football Association 中的 Association 仍然表示“协会”的意思，中文全称为国际足球联合会，缩写为 FIFA。）

competitor *n.* 竞争者，竞争对手（同义词有 rival、challenger、contestant 等。）

take into account 考虑；重视（account 有“账目，账户”的意思。既然记到账户中，于是就有“考虑”的意思。）

resonate *v.* 引起共鸣；回响（前缀 re 表示“反复，再次”；拉丁语中 sonare 就含有“发声，响起”的意思。相关词汇有：sonar 声纳；sonant 发出声音的，有声音的；sonata 奏鸣曲。）
resentment *n.* 愤恨，怨恨（前缀 re 在这里表示“相反的，反向的”，词根 sent 则有“感觉 sense”的意思，所以“相反的感觉”就变成了“愤恨，不满”。表示“憎恶，讨厌，不满”的意思的单词除了动词 resent 之外，还有 loathe、detest、abhor 等。）
shelve *v.* 放在架子上；搁置起来（例如在国外念书期间，如果在图书馆中打工，shelving 就是其中一项重要工作，就是把大家还回来的书再按照类别重新放回到这些书本来的位置上。）
present *v.* 呈现；给予；展示；表达（很多同学在 PowerPoint 的帮助下做过的 presentation 就是这个单词的名词形式。）
survey *n.* 调查；测量；鉴定
reveal *v.* 显示，展现；揭露（前缀 re 表示“相反，反向”，词根 veal 其实就是 veil“面纱，遮盖物”，所以该词字面上的意思就是 uncover“揭开盖子”。西方国家大多数人相信上帝，他们常读的 *Holy Bible*《圣经》的最后一章就叫做“Revelation”，中文翻译过来就是“启示录”，因为使徒约翰“John the Apostle”在这一章里向人们展示了末世的事情，例如著名的 Armageddon、The Rapture、Judgment Day 等。形容词 revealing 也比较常用，尤其在口语中可以用来表达女孩子的衣服过于暴露。）
own up to 坦白，承认，供认（例句：Is there a way I can own up to my dark past and show that I have a bright future? 有没有办法让我既能坦白自己灰暗的过去，同时又能表明自己有着光明的未来？）
shortcoming *n.* 短处，缺点（同义词还有 weakness、demerit、weak point 和 frailty 等。）
differentiate *v.* 区分，区别（名词 differentiation 还有“微分”的意思，所以微分方程就叫做 differentiation equation。）
acknowledge *v.* 承认，供认；认可（某人的成就、地位、品质等）（该词是由 accord 中的 ac 加上 knowledge 构成的，字面意识就是“使知识一致，相符合”，进一步就变成了“承认”的意思。同义词还有 admit、avow、confess 等。）
incremental *adj.* 增加的，增量的（名词 increment 代表“增长量”。词根 cre 就代表“增长”的意思，例如 increase 就是由该词根构成的。相反，表示“减少”的词根是 diminish 中的 min。下面两个单词有助于记忆这两个词根：crescendo 和 diminuendo，它们分别代表声音上的逐渐增强和声音上的逐渐减弱。）
premise *n.* 前提，假设（同义词还有 presupposition、hypothesis、presumption、assumption、postulation 等。如果该词变成复数 premises 就有“契约所规定的土地及其上房屋”的意思。）
tenor *n.* 进展方向；要旨；男高音（例句：In fact, the tenor of the president’s speech to the pro-Israel lobby, and his remarks to the press before going into his meeting with Mr. Netanyahu,

were quite the opposite. 事实上，美国总统对亲以色列政治团体的讲话大意，以及他在与内塔尼亚胡会谈前面向媒体所做的评论大相径庭。）

distaste *n.* 厌恶，讨厌，不喜欢

discourage *v.* 使气馁，使沮丧；阻碍，劝阻

ultimately *adv.* 最后；基本上（形容词 ultimate 意为"最后的，根本的"。同源词汇有：ultima 最后一个音节；ultimatum 最后通牒；ultimacy 终极性，根本性。）

pledge *n.* 保证，誓言，诺言 *v.* 保证，发誓，许诺（如果一个人长期在美国生活并最终通过 naturalisation"归化"加入美国国籍，他就要在美国国旗前唱国歌并 pledge allegiance to the US constitution and laws"发誓效忠美国宪法和法律"。相关词汇有 promise、swear、vow、guarantee、oath。）

opposition *n.* 相反，反对；反对派，反对力量（来自动词 oppose"反对"。）

inclusive *adj.* 包括的，涵盖的（来自动词 include，其中词根 clud/clus 有关闭"close"的意思，于是 include 在字面上就是 enclose"包围起来"的意思。exclude 自然就是"赶出去再关上门"的意思，于是就进一步翻译为"排除在外，不包含"的意思；相关的词汇还有 recluse，意为隐居者，隐士。）

execution *n.* 执行，实施；处决（电脑中常见的可执行文件就是以扩展名 exe 结尾的，exe 是 executable 的缩写。动词原形是 execute，形容词 executive 还有"执行的，经营的"的意思。）

tactic *n.* 策略，手段；战术（最早成立于美国费城的特种警察部队 SWAT 的全称就是 Special Weapons and Tactics。）

declare *v.* 宣布；声明，声称；申报（词根 clare 就是 clear"清晰，明了"的意思，同时这里的前缀 de 并不代表"相反或移除"的意思，而是"去做"的意思，因为这里的 de 来自于古英语而不是拉丁语，所以该词字面意思就是"使清晰明了"。名词形式是 declaration，例如美国著名的《独立宣言》就是 *The Declaration of Independence*。）

vision *n.* 视力，视觉；影像，画面；幻影；想象力；视野（词根 vis 或 visio 是"看，看到"的意思。相关的词汇还有：visual 视觉的；visionary 有远见的，预言的，幻想的；visible 可以看到的；envision 想象，预见，展望。关于 vision，在《圣经旧约》箴言第 29 章第 18 节有这么一句话"Where there is no vision, the people perish"，缺少主的启示，人民就会放纵不羁。在 popular culture 当中人们还常用它表达"一个人没有理想，就会毁灭"这样的意思。）

stakeholder *n.* 股东（股票有多种讲法，最常见的就是 shares 和 stocks，相关的词汇还有：security 有价证券；bond 债券；stock option 股票期权。）

capture *v.* 捕获，捕捉（captive 被捕获的，被俘的，被监禁的；captivity 被俘，囚禁，束缚。）

sparing *adj.* 节约的；保守的（来自动词 spare"节省，节约；宽容，饶恕"。同义词有 frugal、thrifty、economical 等。反义词有 prodigal、profligate、spendthrift、squandering 等。）

symbolic *adj.* 符号的；象征性的，象征意义的（symbolism“象征，比喻”，是人们讲话和写作中常使用的一种表达法，例如莎士比亚在 *As You Like It* 中写道的“All the world's a stage, and all the men and women merely players; they have their exits and their entrances; And one man in his time plays many parts”，这里将世界比喻成舞台，把众人比喻成演员。）
signal *n.* 信号 *v.* 发出信号；表明，体现
transparency *n.* 透明，透明度（来自形容词 transparent。transparent 的同义词有 limpid、lucid、pellucid、see-through 等。）
corporate *adj.* 法人的，团体的；社团的；公司的（词根 corp 或 corpus 的含义是“身体”，所以该词字面上的意思就是“成为一个身体”，自然就引申为“团结”的意思和“公司”的意思。相关词汇还有 corporal“身体的”，所以体罚就是“corporal punishment”，当然也可以叫做“physical punishment”，相对应的词根 capita 表示“脑袋”，所以 capital punishment“惩罚脑袋的刑罚”也就是“死刑”了。）
deliberate *adj.* 故意的；蓄意的 *v.* 深思熟虑
parable *n.* 寓言（圣经中记载耶稣经常在 the Mount of Olives“橄榄山”上和 Jerusalem“耶路撒冷城”里用 parables 讲道，例如像著名的 *Parable of the Good Samaritan*。同义词有 allegory 和 fable，例如著名的 *Aesop's Fables*《伊索寓言》。）
reinforce *v.* 加固，使更结实；加强；充实；增援（force 是“力量”的意思，in“进入”，re“再一次”。）
recall *v.* 叫回，召回；使想起，回想（同义词有 remember、recollect、relive 等。）
legendary *adj.* 传说的，传奇的；极其著名的
waffle *n.* 华夫饼（一种西式烙饼）
prototype *n.* 原型，雏形，蓝本（前缀 proto 代表“原始的，最初的”，例如 protolanguage 指的就是 Derek Bickerton 语言起源理论中的“原始语言，早期人类语言”，protolanguage 和完整的 full language 的差异在于 protolanguage 中只有 lexical items，类似于汉语语法中的实词，而没有 full language 所具备的 grammatical items，接近于汉语语法中的虚词。）
innovation *n.* 改革，创新；新观念；新发明；新设施（其中词根 nova 就是 new“新的”的意思。例如 novice 这个单词就是“新手”的意思，加拿大的新斯科舍省就叫做 Nova Scotia，当然也可以音译为努瓦斯科舍省。同时还有 novel“小说”这个单词就来自于 nova 这个词根，因为每本小说都应该有新意，否则老调重弹就没什么意思了。）
incentive *n.* 激励；刺激；鼓励 *adj.* 刺激性的；鼓励性质的（同义词有 boost、encouragement、goad、impulse、incitement、motivation、stimulant、stimulus 等。）
rally *v.* 召集 *n.* 集合
slogan *n.* 口号，标语，广告语
justify *v.* 证明……有理；为……辩护；对……作出解释
credibility *n.* 可靠性，可信性；确实性（词根 cred 的意思就是“相信”，credit 就是大家

熟悉的“信用”，credible 就是“可信的”，incredible 就是“难以置信的”。对于一个考试来说，它就应该具备信度“credibility”和效度“validity”，信度就是说该考试能够可靠地、一致地“consistently”反映出该考试要测试的能力，不能第一次分数极高，第二次分数极低，第三次又是中间，否则就是缺乏 credibility 的表现；效度则是测量该考试能够准确反映考生能力的指标，也就是说该考试能反映出其计划测量的考生能力，例如我们绝对不能用数学考试来测量考生的英语水平，否则就是缺乏效度的体现。）

beleaguer *v.* 围攻；困扰（同义词是 besiege。）

premature *adj.* 过早的，提前的；早产的；草率的（和“早熟”不是一回事，早熟应该叫做“precocity”。）

prompt *adj.* 敏捷的；迅速的；立刻的；*v.* 提示，指点；促进；激起，唤起 *n.* 刺激物；提示（雅思写作给的题目，官方就把它叫做“prompt”，因为它提示了考生应该写些什么内容。）

demoralise *v.* 使士气低落，使意志消沉；使陷入混乱（morale 是“士气”，前缀 de 表示“离开，下降，相反”。）

legitimate *adj.* 合法的，合理的；正规的 *v.* 使……合法；给予……合法的地位（其中词根 leg 代表“法律”，相关词汇还有：legislation 立法；legal 合法的。）

alienate *v.* 使疏远，离间；使转移，放弃（人们在看过《异形》这部电影之后应该不会对 alien 这个单词感到陌生了，它还可以指外星人或外国人。）

apologetic *adj.* 道歉的，辩解的

conviction *n.* 确信，信念

abolish *v.* 废除，取消，撤销

boost *v.&n.* 提高，增进，增强

题目详解

Questions 27-32

解答

27. 该题对应文章第三段中间“One health insurance company, for instance…”。很明显可以看出这里所写的内容是一个例子，用以证明前一句的观点“They are told one thing by management but observe that a different message is being sent to the public”。所以正确答案为选项 C“produced conflicting image between its employees and the general public”。

28. 该题同样对应文章第三段中间“And one major financial services institution…”。很明显可以看出该题与前一道题所讲到的“health insurance company”一样都是为了说明观点“They are told one thing by management but observe that a different message is being sent to the public”的例子。所以正确答案同样为选项C“produced conflicting image between its employees and the general public”。

29. 该题对应文章第四段中间IBM的例子。原文在第四段中提及“IBM was also using the campaign to align employees around the idea of the Internet as the future of technology. The internal campaign changed the way employees thought about everything they did…it gave employees a sense of direction and purpose…”，这一切都在说明IBM的广告营销活动对员工产生了正面的、积极的作用，对应选项D“successfully used an advertising campaign to inspire employees”。所以正确答案为D。

30. 该题对应文章第五段United Airlines的例子。段落中“it sought to differentiate itself by acknowledging poor service and promising incremental improvements”对应选项A的“apologetic”，“a campaign focusing on customers' distaste for flying was deeply discouraging to the staff. Employee resentment ultimately made it impossible for United to deliver the improvements it was promising”对应选项A的“alienated its employees”。所以正确答案为选项A“alienated its employees by its apologetic branding campaign”。

31. 该题对应文章倒数第二段Nike的例子。段落中提及“Corporate Storyteller”讲述故事，以及“By talking about such inventive moves, the company hopes to keep the spirit of innovation that characterises its ad campaigns alive and well within the company”，对应选项E“draws on the legends of the company spirit”。所以正确答案为E。

32. 该题对应原文最后一段British Rail的例子。文章在段落最后明显提及“By drawing attention to the gap between the promise and the reality, it prompted destructive press coverage”，这里的“destructive press coverage”对应选项B的“negative publicity”。所以正确答案为选项B“attracted negative publicity through its advertising campaign”。

Questions 33-40

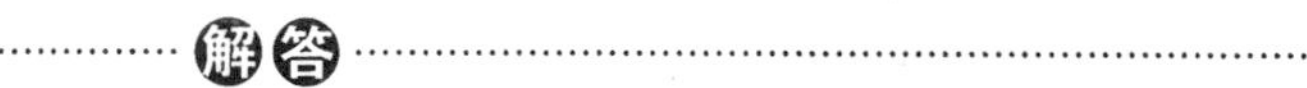

33. 利用细节信息“strong conviction in the brand”和顺序性原则定位于原文第一段倒数第二句话“when people care about and believe in the brand, they're motivated to work harder and their loyalty to the company increases”，这里的“believe in the brand”对应题目的“strong conviction in the brand”，“they're motivated to work harder”对应题目的“contribute to higher job performance”。题目与原文是同义表达，所以答案为Yes。

34. 利用顺序性原则定位于原文第二段第一句话“Unfortunately, in most companies, internal marketing is done poorly, if at all”，原文在这里提及大多数公司即使（if at all）做了“internal marketing”，也是做得很差（done poorly）。这里的“internal marketing”对应题目的“internal communication”，“done poorly, if at all”对应题目的“overlook”。

题目与原文是同义表达，所以正确答案为 Yes。

35. 利用细节信息“IBM”和“e-business”以及顺序性原则定位于原文第四段第三句话“In 1997, when IBM launched its e-business campaign…it chose to ignore research that suggested consumers were unprepared to embrace IBM as a leader in e-business”，原文这里明显提及在营销活动开始时消费者还没有准备好（unprepared）把 IBM 看作 e-business 的领袖，而题目却说消费者在活动开展之前就已经“ready to view IBM as a leader in e-business”，题目信息与原文信息明显相反，所以正确答案为 No。

36. 利用细节信息“United Airlines”和顺序性原则定位于原文第五段。原文在这里提及“United Airlines”开始了一个营销活动（launched a new campaign, “Rising”），但最后却失败了。失败的原因在该段落最后一句话有明确提及，即“a fundamental principle of advertising—find and address a customer concern—failed United because it did not consider the internal market”，也就是说失败的原因在于“United Airlines”没有能够充分地考虑“the internal market”，而非题目所说的“due to the bad advice of an advertisement agency”。题目信息与原文信息不相符，所以正确答案为 No。

37. 这道题的定位相对前一道题要简单。该题定位于原文第五段倒数第三句话“Three years later, United decided employee opposition was undermining its success and pulled the campaign”。原文这里提及联合航空公司撤销了这个营销活动（pulled the campaign），对应题目的“abolished its campaign”，但是否是为了“boost image”，原文并未提及。原文只提及联合航空公司认为“employee opposition”已经影响到了营销活动的成功，但是这个结论是否是由“market research”得出来的却不为人知。题目信息在原文信息的基础上无法判断，所以正确答案为 Not Given。

38. 利用细节信息“IBM”和顺序性原则定位于原文倒数第三段第二句话“IBM used this tactic very effectively when it launched its e-business campaign”，该段落后面也提及“This is an expensive way to capture attention, but if used sparingly, it is the most powerful form of communication”，很明显可以看出 IBM 做得较为成功，而题目却说这是一个“expensive mistake”。题目信息与原文信息直接相反，所以正确答案为 No。

39. 利用细节信息“Nike”和“company tales”定位于原文倒数第二段最后一句话“By talking about such inventive moves, the company hopes to keep the spirit of innovation that characterises its ad campaigns alive and well within the company”，原文在这里强调的是 Nike 的愿望（the company hopes…），而题目却说“employees claimed that they were inspired”。一个人或一个公司的愿望不一定最终实现，而题目却说实现了。原文其实并未提及 employees 是否被 inspired。题目信息在原文信息的基础上无法判断，所以正确答案为 Not Given。

40. 利用细节信息“A slight difference between internal and external promises”和顺序性原则定位于原文最后一段第一，第二句话“…companies must also keep external promises a little ahead of internal realities. Such promises provide incentives for employees and give them something to live up to…”，这里的“give them something to live up to”就对应题目的“a sense of purpose”。题目信息与原文信息是同义表达，所以正确答案为Yes。

参考译文

内部市场：品牌内部营销

当你想到市场营销时，你更有可能想到的是面向客户的市场销售：如何说服更多的人购买你的产品？但是另外一个“市场”也同等重要：你的雇员——能使品牌在你的客户面前真正焕发活力的那些人。然而在我们帮助企业领导者开发和推进品牌策略的工作中，我的同事和我发现这个至关重要的组成部分常常被企业所忽略。

为什么内部市场营销如此重要呢？首先，是因为这是最好的帮助雇员建立与自己所销售的产品或服务之间的强大感情联系的方法。没有这种联系，雇员极有可能破坏你的广告所期望达到的目标。在一些案例中，这种情况的发生是因为他们根本就不理解你向公众所作出的承诺，于是最终导致目标不一致。在另外一些案例中，这也许是因为他们并不相信这个品牌且同时有一种脱离感，甚至更糟糕的是，对公司充满敌意。我们发现当人们关心且相信品牌时，他们就会充满动力，从而更努力工作，同时他们对公司的忠诚度也会上升。雇员会因为共同的目的和身份而团结在一起。

不幸的是，在大多数公司中，即使实施了内部市场营销，那也是做得很糟糕。当企业领导者认识到使企业职员了解企业策略和发展方向的必要性时，却很少有人了解使雇员相信企业品牌力量的必要性——他们认为雇员理应是相信的。

企业员工需要听到与你向市场传达的相同的信息。然而在大多数企业中，内部和外部的交流经常是搭配不当的。这会使人感到非常困惑，同时还会影响员工对企业诚信的看法：企业管理层告诉他们一个信息，但是他们却发现一个不同的信息被传达给了公众。例如，一个医疗保险公司在广告中宣称病人的福祉是该企业的首要考虑，然而员工却被告知他们的首要目标是通过降低成本来增加他们的股票期权价值。还有另外一家重要的金融服务机构告诉顾客说他们正在做重大转型，从金融零售商转变成金融顾问。但是，一年过后，研究显示该机构的顾客体验并没有发生变化。原来，这家公司的领导并没有作出任何内部营销的努力，于是员工仍然在制造大量的交易，并没有改变他们的行为来对应他们新的顾问角色。

使员工能够满足客户的期望固然重要，但是这并不是一个企业需要使内部和外部信息一致的唯一原因。另外一个原因就是帮助企业实现非此而不能实现的目标。在1997年，当 IBM 开展电子商务营销时（这一营销活动被广泛地认为改变了其企业形象），它选择了忽略那项认为消费者还没有准备好接纳 IBM 作为电子商务领域的领导者的研究结论。尽管这在外界看来仿佛是在做外部市场营销的努力，但事实上 IBM 也在利用这个营销活动来统一雇员的观念，即认识互联网是科技的未来。这项内部营销活动改变了雇员对他们所做的一切事务的认识和思考方式，从产品命名到组织员工，再到销售方法。这项活动的成功很大程度上是因为它赋予了员工一种方向感和目标，而这一切又反过来恢复了员工对 IBM 预测未来和引领科技产业的能力的信任。今天，研究显示，人们更可能把“电子商务”和 IBM 联系在一起，而不是和它的直接竞争对手相联系。

也许更为重要的是，通过将员工考虑进来，企业能够避免创造一个无法引起共鸣的，或更糟糕的，一个会招致愤恨的企业口号。1996 年，联合航空公司就放弃了它的“飞翔在友好的天际”这一口号，当时正值一份关于乘客对航空业不满程度的调查报告出台。为了坦白航空业的缺点，联合航空公司开展了一项名为“上升”的新项目活动，通过承认差评服务和承诺更好的餐饮之类的改进来力图脱颖而出。尽管这个项目的时代主旨是合理的，但这个聚焦于乘客飞行不满度的项目深深地挫败了公司员工。员工们的愤慨最终使得公司无法履行它承诺的改进，这反过来又损害了“上升”项目的承诺。三年后，联合航空公司认识到员工的反对阻碍了项目的成功，于是终止了它。此后，“联合”成为了一个包容性更广泛的商标，它涵盖了所有的受众。从这里可以看出，广告的一个基本原则——找到并关注客户的需求——使得联合航空公司栽了跟头，因为它没有考虑内部市场。

当谈到如何执行时，连接内部与外部市场营销活动最普遍也最有效的方式是打造一个面向内外双方受众的公开广告。IBM 在开展电子商务活动时就非常有效地运用了这个策略。它在《华尔街日报》上刊登了一则八页的广告来宣扬自己的新愿景。这一信息不仅针对消费者，同时也面向公司内部股东。这种吸引注意力的方式很昂贵，但如果合理使用的话，它则是最有效的交流方式；事实上，你只需要做一次，就可以让公司的每一个人都读到它。而且这样做还有一个象征性优势。这样一种策略表明了这家公司非常重视自己的承诺；同时，它也展现了透明度——无论对内还是对外，都是同样的信息。

广告不是连接内外部营销的唯一方式。在耐克公司，有些高级经理人现在都加上了“企业说书人”的头衔。他们蓄意地回避了有关金融成就的故事和案例，而关注于“只是做事”的寓言上，以反映并强调公司的广告内容。例如，有一个故事让人们回想起耐克公司的创始人兼传奇教练比尔·鲍尔曼是如何为了给他的队伍打造更好的鞋子，而把橡胶倒入了自家的华夫锅，从而创造了著名的耐克华夫鞋底的原型。公司希望通过讲述这些富有创造力的举动，来保持它在广告中所体现的创新精神在公司内部的活力和盛行。

虽然他们的信息必须保持一致，但是企业也务必要使对外承诺稍微领先于内部现实，这样才能给员工带来激励，并给他们一个努力的目标。在 20 世纪 80 年代，福特公司将“质量是工作的第一要务”的内部战斗口号转为面向消费者的口号，来应对更便宜、更可靠的日本车所带来的威胁。虽然公司在这个口号被充分论证前就实施这一转变，但通过将口号张贴在公共场所，它激励了员工去战胜日本公司。然而，如果口号推出得过早，它也会丧失可信度。当陷入困境的英国铁路公司打着“我们正开往那里”的旗号，宣扬提高服务水平时，就为时过早了。它将人们的注意力拉到承诺与现实的差距上，这引起了毁灭性的媒体报道。反过来，这些报道使原本应该为他们所做的服务改善感到自豪的员工们意志消沉。

Reading Passage 1. The Forgotten Forest

词汇详解

pine *n.* 松树（其实对于大多数树木来说，人们并不需要了解太多的单词，除了一些著名的品种，例如像这里的松树“pine”，加拿大的标志之一枫树“maple”，身材妖娆的柳树“willow”，树懒考拉熊的最爱桉树“eucalyptus”，形似手掌的棕榈树“palm”，《乱世佳人》中十二橡树庄园的橡树“oak”。当然与树木相关的单词还有表达树木不同部分的树根“root”，树干“trunk”，树枝“branch”，树枝枝头的小树枝“twig”，树冠“canopy”；还有一些其他的词汇，例如小树苗“sapling”，针叶树“conifer”，落叶植物“defoliation plant”，蕨类植物“fern”等。）

dwindle *v.* 逐渐变小，缩小（同义词有：diminish、shrink、decrease、abate、lessen、lower 等；反义词有：escalate、increase、aggrandise、amplify、boost 等。）

range *n.* 范围（该词也可以作为动词使用，代表“涉及，包括”的意思，例如：If a piece of writing or speech ranges over a group of topics, it includes all those topics.）

restore *v.* 恢复，修复；归还（名词是 restoration。现在的电脑都很先进，基本上都有一个系统恢复隐藏分区“a hidden partition for system restoration”，如果系统有任何问题或者遭受了严重的病毒侵袭“severe virus infection”，我们总是可以轻松恢复到出厂设置“restore to factory setting”。）

biodiversity *n.* 生物多样性（前缀 bio 是“生物”的意思，例如：biology 生物学；biosphere 生物圈；biochemistry 生物化学；biodegradable 可生物降解的。）

ecosystem *n.* 生态系统（前缀 eco 是“生态，环境”的意思，例如：ecology 生态学；eco-friendly 生态友好的；ecocatastrophe 生态灾难；ecotourism 生态旅游；ecosphere 生态圈。）

rival *n.* 竞争对手 *v.* 与……竞争；比得上某人

prairie *n.*（尤指北美的）大草原，大牧场（其实就是一种 grassland，只不过 prairie 多指北美的草原，savanna 多指非洲的草原，相关的还有北极地区的苔原“tundra”。如果单纯只是指草地，例如房子或花园里的草坪，则叫“lawn”，如果是没有人看管而且还长有杂草的话就叫做“meadow”。放牧的草场则叫做“pasture”。）

species *n.* 物种，种类（英语词汇中比较少见的单复数一致的单词之一。类似的单复数一致的单词还有 sheep、fish、people、series、offspring、glasses、aircraft、advice 等。）

shelter *n.* 居所；避难所 *v.* 掩蔽；庇护；保护（该单词可以用在写作中论述房屋是功能性“functionality”——仅仅提供遮风挡雨的 shelter——重要，还是应该具备审美的艺术性“aesthetics”。）

habitat *n.*（动植物的）栖息地，居住地（相关单词有：habitant 居民；inhabit 居住。）

critically *adv.* 致命的，严重地；批判地（来自形容词 critical“批评的，决定性的，关键的”。相关词汇有：criticise 批评；critic 评论家；critique 评论文章，评论，发表评论。）

endanger *v.* 危及，使遭受危险（前缀 en 代表“进入”，所以 endanger 字面上就是“进入危险”的意思，类似的变形还有：enforce 实施；enact 规定，通过法案；encourage 鼓励。）

scatter *v.*（使）散开，（使）分散，驱散（同义词有 disperse、spread、strew、separate 等。）

savanna *n.*（非洲）大草原（通常没有树或者树很稀少。）

dense *adj.* 密集的，稠密的；浓密的，浓厚的（名词是 density“密度”。）

block *v.* 阻止；阻塞；遮挡；限制 *n.* 块；街区；<英>大楼，大厦；障碍物，阻碍（本来 block 就是“一个块状物”的意思，于是 building block 就有了“建筑砌块，基础材料”的意思，甚至还有儿童玩具中“积木”的意思。而且在写作中，当我们说某某物是什么什么的 building block 时就是指这个东西非常基础和重要，例如：Carbon molecules are the building blocks of all life on earth.）

trumpet *n.* 喇叭，小号（相关的乐器“musical instruments”还有：organ 风琴，也常指钢琴；pipe 管乐器；percussion 打击乐器；flute 笛子；drum set 架子鼓；cymbal 钹，镲；gong 锣；harp 竖琴。）

pitcher *n.* 一种水罐；（棒球）投手

Venus *n.* 维纳斯；金星（太阳系“solar system”中九大行星分别为：Mercury 水星、Venus 金星、Earth 地球、Mars 火星、Jupiter 木星、Saturn 土星、Uranus 天王星、Neptune 海王星、Pluto 冥王星。当然，后来 Pluto 被剥除了行星资格，因为天文学家发现它只是一个 kuiper belt 上的 kuiper object。）

lavender *n.* 薰衣草；淡紫色

shrub *n.* 灌木；灌木丛

fern *n.* 蕨类植物

catalogue *n.* 目录，一览表 *v.* 为……编目录；登记分类；记载，列入目录（美式拼写则简单很多，为 catalog。与 category“类别”长相相似；专门为生物进行分类研究的学科叫做 taxonomy“分类学”。）

acre *n.* 英亩（面积单位）

flourish *v.* 茂盛，繁荣；活跃，蓬勃（该词前面的 flour 是词根 flora 的变形，就是

flower“花”的意思，来自罗马神话中花之女神 Flora。相关的词汇有：florist 花农，花商；floriculture 养花业，花艺；florescence 开花，全盛期，花期。）

virtually *adv.* 实际上，实质上，事实上（形容词 virtual 在计算机领域还有“虚拟的”的意思，例如：virtual reality 虚拟现实；virtual flight 虚拟飞行驾驶。因为虚拟现实都是和计算机技术相关的，而计算技术又是广泛建立于半导体硅芯片的应用上的，所以计算机虚拟的或仿真的还可以被叫做“in silico”，而对应的在真实环境中，尤其是有机体内的则叫做“in vivo”，其中 vivo 在拉丁语中是“生命，活体”的意思，另外还有一种“in vitro”的说法，vitro 在拉丁语中是“玻璃”的意思，in vitro 指的就是在试管中，在生物体外，尤其是在一个可控环境中进行的实验、操作等，以上三种说法在生物学中最为常用。）

log *v.* 伐木，砍伐树木 *n.* 原木；日志，记录（如果看过谢耳朵也非常喜欢的 *Star Trek*《星际迷航》，也翻译作《星际旅行》的系列电视或动画的话，一定对片头的这句话非常熟悉：Captain's log 2145.67…）

pave *v.* 铺设；为……铺平道路；安排

oblivion *n.* 遗忘；湮没（任何事物或技能都是这样：use it or lose it。如果长期不使用，it will go into oblivion。Tom Cruise 2013 的好莱坞大片《遗落战境》的英文名就叫做 *Oblivion*。）

estimate *v.* 估计，估算；评价，评论（值得一提的是，该词的形容词 estimable 除了有“可估计的，能估量出来”的意思之外，还有“值得尊敬的”的意思。例如：He was an estimable, good natured man and a competent journalist. 他是一个值得尊重的、性情温和的而又称职的新闻记者。）

vanish *v.* 消失，突然不见；消亡，消逝（词根 van 与 vac 同义，都表示“空，没有”的意思，同根的还有：vanity 无价值，虚荣；vain 空虚的，徒劳的。同义词有 disappear、evaporate、dissolve 等。）

reverse *v.*（使）反转；（使）颠倒；掉换；（汽车）倒退，逆行（驾驶汽车是在国外生存的一项重要技能，汽车的档位分为 Manual Transition“手动挡”和 Auto Transition“自动挡”，其中自动挡的档位包括 P 代表的 park“驻车档”，R 代表的 reverse“倒车档”，还有 N 代表的 neutral“空挡”，以及 D 代表的 drive“驾驶档，行进档”。）

ripple *v.* 使泛起涟漪，在……上形成波痕 *n.* 涟漪，涟波，波纹（ripple effect 就是“涟漪效应”，当然也可以翻译成“连锁反应”。）

conservationist *n.* 自然资源保护者，生态环境保护者（来自动词 conserve，其中词根 serve 是“保存，保护”的意思。）

preserve *v.* 保护；保持，保存

associate *v.*（使）发生联系；（使）联合；结交；联想 *adj.*（用于等级或头衔前，表示稍有不同或略低）副的，准的（associate professor 指的是副教授，正教授是 full professor，不过在口语当中通常只说 professor，在美国的高校中，学生出于礼节，不管是正的还是

副的，都会称为 professor，原因你懂的。）

outright *adj.* 完全的；公开的 *adv.* 完全地，彻底地；坦率地；立即（与其形近的词汇还有 upright "直立的，垂直的，正直的，诚实的" 和 downright "完全的，十足的"。）

destruction *n.* 破坏，毁灭，消灭，灭亡（词根 struct 的意思是"build 建造"，再加上表示"相反，移除" 意思的前缀 de，于是就有了 "破坏，毁灭" 的意思了，直接反义词是 construct。）

demise *n.* 死亡，灭亡（前缀 de 表示"相反，取消或移除"，词根 mis 或 mit 代表"send 派出"，字面上是 "不再传递，不再派出" 的意思，于是就 "死翘翘" 了。同义词除了 death 还有 decease、expiry、expiration 等。）

sweep *v.* 打扫，清理；扫除；搜索；掠过（国家法定假日清明节就常被翻译成 Tomb Sweeping Day，因为这一天人们会以扫墓的形式来祭奠先人 "commemorate the dead"。）

sparrow *n.* 麻雀（雅思口语中曾经考过 bird 的话题，麻雀就是一种最常见的鸟，当然常见的鸟类还有：swallow 燕子；magpie 喜鹊；parrot 鹦鹉；lark 百灵，云雀；canary 金丝雀；nightingale 夜莺；owl 猫头鹰；woodpecker 啄木鸟；raven 乌鸦；eagle 鹰；hawk 隼；hummingbird 蜂鸟；flamingo 火烈鸟；peacock 孔雀；egret 白鹭。当然，还有在中国传统文化中非常流行的 "phoenix 凤凰"。）

secretive *adj.* 遮遮掩掩的，偷偷摸摸的；秘密的，不外露的（很容易可以看出来，该词是名词 secret "秘密" 的形容词形式。值得注意的是，和 secret 长相非常相似的一个单词 secrete 是 "分泌，隐匿，隐藏" 的意思，名词形式是 secretion。）

tuck *v.* 折叠；包起，裹起；挤进（在日常生活中人们常说的"把衬衫的下摆塞到裤子里去"，英文就叫做 "tuck the shirt into pants"。）

beneath *prep.&adv.* 在下面，在下方

clump *n.* 丛；笨重的脚步声

understory *n.* 林下叶层，林下植被

tangle *n.* 缠结的一团；混乱，纷乱 *v.*（使）缠结；乱作一团（词源上，该词可能是 entangle "使纠缠，使卷入，使混乱" 的简写形式，同义词还有：enmesh、ensnare、entrap 等。）

tortoise *n.* 乌龟（和 turtle 的差别在于，tortoise 通常指的是陆龟，而 turtle 则通常是指海龟，但是不管哪一种，在中国传统文化中都象征长寿 "longevity"。著名的 "龟兔赛跑" 的故事，英文就叫做 *The tortoise and the hare*。）

keystone *n.* 主旨，要旨，基础；拱心石

burrow *v.* 挖掘（洞穴），挖洞 *n.* 地洞（中国有句俗话叫做 "兔子不吃窝边草"，英文就可以翻译成 "The hare does not eat the grass around his burrow"，这种说法基本上也就等同于英文的 "Don't shit where you eat"，大家可以感受一下。）

vertebrate *n.&adj.* 脊椎动物（的）（生物学中分为界 "kingdom"、门 "phylum"、纲 "class"；目 "order"、科 "family"、属 "genus" 和种 "species"。其中界分为 animal kingdom "动物界"、plant kingdom "植物界" 和 microorganism kingdom "微生物界"。动物界又分

为 vertebrates “脊椎动物门”和 invertebrates “无脊椎动物门”。像人类就属于脊椎动物门里的 mammal “哺乳纲”，primate “灵长目”，hominid “人科”，homo “人属”，homo sapiens “智人种”。)

rattlesnake *n.* 响尾蛇(rattle 本来就是“发出格格嗒嗒的响声”的意思。作为人类的死对头，蛇的类别很多，单词自然也不少，例如：serpent 蛇，尤其是圣经里伊甸园中诱惑夏娃吃智慧树果实的蛇；python 蟒蛇；anaconda 亚马逊丛林里的巨蟒；cobra 眼镜蛇；viper 蝰蛇。有的蛇有毒，它的毒液“venom”是致命的“lethal”，而有的则是无害的。)

suppress *v.* 镇压，压制；止住，忍住；禁止（发表）；阻止，抑制（该词就是由表示“下面”的前缀 sub 和单词 press 组成的，sub 的字母 b 伴随词根 press 发生了变化。相近的词汇还有：oppress 压迫，压制；depress 使沮丧，使萧条，压低；repress 抑制，镇压，压抑。都和 press 有关。)

choke *v.* 阻塞；使窒息，哽噎（同义词有 suffocate、strangle 等。在一些银行抢劫的电影场景中，劫匪们为了防止自己的身份被认出来，一方面会 wear mask “戴面具”，另一方面也会在脖子上带一个 choker 来改变自己的声音。)

oak *n.* 橡树（《乱世佳人》*Gone with the Wind* 的女主人公 Scarlet O'Hara 就住在十二橡树庄园。)

overwhelm *v.* 淹没；压倒；覆盖；压垮（whelm 本身的意思是“反过来以遮盖”，于是 overwhelm 的字面意思就是“turn over, cover up”。类似于这样的构词还有：overhear 偷听，无意中听到；oversee 监督，监视，俯瞰；overcome 克服；overflow 溢出，过满而流出。)

set…aflame 放火使……燃烧

nutrient *n.* 养分，养料，营养物质（词根 nutri 来自动词 nourish，也就是“养育，培养”的意思，例如：nutrition 营养、nutritious 有营养的等。对于人体来说我们需要的 nutrients 有多种，例如能提供能量的 carbohydrate “碳水化合物”，组成身体各个部件的 protein “蛋白质”，以及在身体中起重要作用的各种 minerals “矿物质”。)

calcium *n.* 钙（人体必不可少的一种矿物质，组成人体骨骼的重要成分，如果缺钙“calcium deficiency”，则容易导致类似 osteoporosis “骨质疏松”这样的疾病。)

woodpecker *n.* 啄木鸟

avian *adj.* 鸟的，鸟类的（来自拉丁语 avis “鸟”，相关词汇还有：aviary 鸟笼，鸟舍；aviation 航空，飞行术；aviculture 养鸟。对应的，希腊语中表示“鸟”的单词是 pouli，于是也产生了这样的单词：poultry 家禽；poulterer 鸟贩，家禽贩。与该词相关的还有 avian flu “禽流感”，以及 2004 年 Leonardo DiCaprio 所主演的著名好莱坞大片 *Aviator*《飞行家》。)

sprawl *v.* 伸开四肢坐（躺）；蔓延；杂乱无序地拓展

clutch *v.* 抓紧，紧握；抓住，抓取 *n.* 一群，一窝（尤其是鸟蛋）（该词作动词时，同义词有 clench、grip、cling to、hold 等。除此以外，clutch 在汽车驾驶上还有一个独特的意思，就是“踩离合器”，或者作名词时直接指“离合器”。）

breed *v.* 产仔，繁殖（同义词有 reproduce、multiply、proliferate 和 propagate。在口语中，当我们讲“…is a rare breed”时，就是说某物很罕见，甚至很奇葩。）

territory *n.* 领土，版图；领地；领域，范围（美国先进的战区导弹防御系统 TMD 的全称就是“territory missile defense”。）

stash *v.* 隐藏，藏匿；贮藏（同义词有 cache、hoard、stockpile、store 等。）

pulse *n.* 脉搏，脉动

dwell *v.* 居住；细想或详述某事（词组 dwell on something 则表达对于事物“仔细思考，深思熟虑”。）

vital *adj.* 维持生命所必需的；至关重要的；生死攸关的（来自拉丁语 vita“生命”，与 vive 接近。生命当然重要了，所以 vital 就表示“至关重要”，vitality 则代表“生命力，活力”。）

prescribe *v.* 指定，规定；开具处方（词根 scribe 的意思是“书写”，而且 scribe 本身作为单词就是“抄写员，写字的文人”等，再加上前缀 pre“前面”，prescribe 的字面意思就是“提前写出各种各样的规章制度来规范和约束”。与该词根相关的词汇还有：scribble 潦草地写，乱写乱画；script 手记，文本，剧本；scripture 经文，经典；circumscribe 在周围画线，限制，限定；inscribe 雕，刻，题写；describe 描述，描绘；subscribe 签署，署名，认购，订阅；transcribe 誊写，转抄等。prescribe 作为开处方，prescription 作为处方也是与此相关的，因为医生只是提前把病人需要的药写下来，并没有直接把药给病人，病人必须去 pharmacy“药房”去取药，所以 prescribe 就有“开处方”的意思。）

deliberate *adj.* 故意的；蓄意的；深思熟虑的；慎重的 *v.* 权衡，考虑（该词来自 libra“天平，秤”，所以天秤座就叫做 Libra。再加上表示“去做，从事”的前缀 de，字面上该词就是“用天平去仔细衡量利弊，慎重考虑”的意思。deliberate 作动词时，其同义词有很多，例如：chew over、consider、contemplate、ponder、meditate、ruminate、weigh 等，作形容词则表示“仔细考虑过的”，进一步还可以表示“故意的”，接近 purposeful、intentional。）

drip *v.* 滴下，滴出 *n.* 滴答声（形同 drop，因为它就是 drop 的变形。意思接近的词汇有：dribble 滴下或作细流；trickle 滴，细细地流。）

oppose *v.* 反对，抗争；使相对，使对立；抵制（名词有 opposition“反对”和 opponent“对手”，形容词有 opposite“相反的”。同义词有 resist、withstand。）

catastrophic *adj.* 灾难的；惨重的，悲惨结局的（基本上等同于人们在口语中的常用表达“disaster of epic proportions”。名词形式是 catastrophe。同义词有 disastrous、calamitous 等。）

conflagration *n.* 大火，火灾

spearhead *v.* 当……的先锋；带头 *n.* 先锋，前锋；先头部队；矛头（英语和其他语言一样充满了各种各样的形象的说法，例如 head of state、seat of office、foot of the hill 等。）

herbaceous *adj.* 草本的（herb 就是“草药”，中药除了可以叫做“Chinese traditional medicine”外，还可以叫做“Chinese herbal medicine”。）

chew *v.&n.* 咀嚼（chewing gum 是大家熟悉的"口香糖"，词组 chew something over 表示对事物"仔细揣摩思考"。当描述食物平淡无味时，也可以说"…tastes like a chewing gum that's been chewed a million times"。）

convert *v.* 转变；皈依；兑换，换算（不同单位之间，例如 metric system"公制"与 imperial system"英制"之间的转换就叫做"convert"，转换表叫做"conversion table"。从一个宗教皈依到另一个宗教也叫做"convert"，而且该词还可以作为名词表达"皈依者"的意思。在车辆中 convertible 指的是"敞篷车"，因为它的软质车顶可以轻易收起。）

loblolly *n.* 火炬松

slash *n.* 斜线；刀痕，砍痕 *v.* 挥砍；大幅削减（标点符号中的斜线"/"就叫做"slash"，正斜线"/"和反斜线"\"可以分别叫做"forward slash"和"backward slash"。）

viable *adj.* 切实可行的；能自行生长发育的（来自于表示"生命"的词根 vie，viable 的字面意思是"可以活下来的"，那自然就可以代表"可行的"。）

vegetation *n.* 植被

coax *v.* 哄，用好话劝诱，哄骗（可以和 hoax"欺骗，骗局，恶作剧"一起记。）

prohibitive *adj.* 禁止的；禁止性的；抑制的；（价格等）过高的

seedling *n.* 秧苗，树苗（后缀 ling 和 let 都是"小化"词缀，所以 duckling 就是"小鸭子"，halfling 就是只有"正常人一半大小的小人"，也就是 hobbit 人。其他词汇有：youngling 年轻人；islet 小岛；droplet 一小滴水。）

resurgence *n.* 复活，复苏（来自动词 surge"猛地上升，波涛汹涌"，再加上前缀 re"再一次，反复"，于是就有了"重新焕发活力"的意思。同义词有 reanimation、rebirth、regeneration、revitalisation、renewal、rejuvenation 等。）

sparse *adj.* 稀疏的，薄的（其实从字面上来讲，该词来自于拉丁语的 spread out，所以自然就有"分散的，稀少的"的意思了。同义词有 meager、scarce、rare、scattered 等。）

题目详解

Questions 1-5

1. 利用细节信息"forest fire"、"birds"和"in the ground"定位于原文第五段前三句话"…you can find a connection to fire. Bachman's sparrow is a secretive bird…It tucks its nest on the ground beneath…"。原文信息"It tucks its nest on the ground…"对应题目中的"locate...in the ground"，所以正确答案为 nests。
2. 利用顺序原则和细节信息"burrows"定位于原文第五段中间"Gopher tortoises…A keystone species for these forests, its burrows provide home and safety to more than 300

species of vertebrates and invertebrates…”，这里很容易看出“Gopher tortoises”的“burrows”为300多个物种提供了家园。所以正确答案为tortoises。

3. 利用顺序原则和细节信息“hardwoods”定位于原文第六段第二句话“Fire knocks back the oaks and other hardwoods that can grow up to overwhelm longleaf forests”。这里的“overwhelm”对应题目中的“take over”，所以正确答案为oaks。
4. 利用顺序原则和细节信息“settlers”定位于原文第六段倒数第二、三句话“Native Americans also lit fires to keep the forest open…So did the early pioneers”。这里的“early pioneers”对应题目中的“settlers”，所以正确答案为Native Americans。
5. 利用顺序原则和细节信息“Fires deliberately lit”定位于原文第八段第二句话“Most of these fires are prescribed burns, deliberately set with a drip torch”，所以正确答案为prescribed burns。

Questions 6-9

解答

利用细节信息“cockaded woodpeckers”定位于原文第七段的后半部分：

6. 对应段落中“…calcium is stashed away in woody shrubs…”，原文中“stashed away”对应题目中的“stored”，所以正确答案为shrubs。
7. 对应段落中“when there is a fire, a pulse of calcium moves down into the soil and up into the longleaf”，原文中“moves down”对应题目中的“released”，同时原文的“up into the longleaf”对应流程图中下一步的“Travel up to the leaves”。所以正确答案为soil。
8. 对应段落中“…to a tree-dwelling species of ant, which is the red-cockaded's favorite food”，这里的“favorite food”对应题目中的“are eaten”，所以正确答案为Ants。
9. 对应段落最后一句话“…more calcium for the birds, which leads to more eggs, more young and more woodpeckers”。很明显，这里的“more young and more woodpeckers”对应流程图中下一步的“More cockaded woodpeckers”，所以正确答案为eggs。

Questions 10-13

解答

10. 利用细节信息“sparse distribution”和“diversity of species”定位于原文第二段前三句话“In longleaf pine forests, trees grow widely scattered, creating an open, park-like environment…This openness creates a forest floor that is among the most diverse in the world…”。原文中“grow widely scattered”对应题目中的“sparse distribution”，原文中“diverse”对应题目中的“diversity of species”。题目与原文表述的信息一致，所以正确答案为True。

11. 利用细节信息“farms”和“plantations”定位于原文倒数第二段后半部分“In areas where the land has not been chewed up by farming, but converted to loblolly or slash pine plantations, the seed bank…remains viable…In time, this original vegetation can be coaxed back. Where agriculture has destroyed the seeds, however, wiregrass must be replanted… the expense is prohibitive…”。很明显，这里提及如果转化成 plantations，最初的植被还能恢复（original vegetation can be coaxed back），但是如果转化成了农场（对应原文的“agriculture”），则很难恢复，而且花费出奇得高（the expense is prohibitive），而题目却说转化为农场后更容易复原。题目信息与原文信息相矛盾，所以正确答案为 False。
12. 利用顺序原则和细节信息“The cost to restore forest”定位于倒数第二段最后一句话“Right now, the expense is prohibitive, but researchers are searching for low-cost solutions”，但是这里只提及恢复森林价格昂贵，却未提及价格是否上升。题目信息在原文信息的基础上无法判断，所以正确答案为 Not Given。
13. 利用顺序原则和细节信息“replanted forest”和“maturity”定位于原文最后一段第二句话“Few of us will be alive when the pines being planted today become mature forests in 70 to 80 years”。很明显，题目信息与原文信息一致，所以正确答案为 True。

参考译文

被遗忘的森林

如今，只有在美国南方腹地才能找到长叶松森林，它的现有面积已经缩小到它的原面积的百分之三左右，但是人们正在努力使它们复原。

长叶松森林的美丽和生物多样性，甚至在其本土的南部，都是保存完好的秘密。然而，它却是北美最富有的生态系统之一，在物种数量方面，它完全可以媲美太平洋西北地区的高草草原和古森林。和那两个正在消亡的野生动物栖息地一样，长叶松森林也面临着严峻的威胁。

在长叶松森林中，树木都分散地生长在各处，从而形成一个开放的、公园般的环境，使它更像是热带大草原而不是森林。这些树木并没有稠密到遮住太阳。这种开放性造就了地球上最多样化的森林层，诸如多花的香石竹、喇叭状的猪笼草、捕蝇草、薰衣草和松林地带的马钱子等都生长在这里。仅在这一小块地方，就有多达 50 种不同品类的野花、灌木、草丛和蕨类植物。

从弗吉尼亚州到得克萨斯州，曾经有将近 9200 万英亩的长叶松森林繁荣生长，这是世界上探明的唯一一片生长区。但是到了 21 世纪，几乎全部的森林都被砍伐、铺平或开垦，并逐渐被遗忘了。只有大约 3% 的原面积仍然生长着长叶松，而这其中又仅剩约一万英亩的森林是没有被砍伐过的老龄林，其余的都是砍伐后的新生林。而且，估计每年仍有十万英亩的树林正在消失。不过好在，一场扭转这一趋势的运动正静悄悄地席卷这个地区。政府、民间组织（包括国家野生生物联盟（NWF））以及个体生态环境保护者正在寻找各种方式来保护现余的长叶松林，并为子孙后代种植新的森林。

搞清楚如何重建茂盛的松林也能够使生物学家们为这片栖息地的动植物提供帮助。在美国东南部，有将近三分之二的递减的、受威胁的或濒危的物种都依附于长叶松林。长叶松林的彻底破坏只是致使这些物种面临困境的部分原因，南卡罗来纳州弗朗西斯马里恩国家森林的生物学家马克·丹纳赫如此表示道。他认为这些动植物的死亡和缺少林火也有关系。南部森林曾经经常遭遇火烧。“林火对于这个生态系统以及依赖于它的物种来说，有着绝对重要的影响，”丹纳赫说道。

随便指名一个生长在长叶松林的物种，你都会发现它们和林火之间的联系。松林猛雀鹀是一种神秘的鸟，它优美的歌声常常回荡在长叶松林的低洼林木中。它把自己的巢筑在地面上，就在开放的下层植被狗尾草丛和须芒草丛下。但是，一旦有几年缺少林火，而灌木开始疯长，雀鸟就会消失。地鼠陆龟是生活在密西西比河流域的唯一的本土陆地龟，它在长叶松林中也有大量繁殖。地鼠陆龟在这些森林中扮演着极为重要的角色，有300多种脊椎和无脊椎动物（从东部菱形斑纹响尾蛇到穴蛙）以它挖掘的洞穴作为家园和庇护所。但当林火被抑制时，这种地鼠陆龟就会被封在洞中窒息而死。琼斯中心的生态学家鲍勃·米切尔说：“如果没有林火，我们就将失去这些野生生物。”

没有林火的话，我们还会失去长叶松林。林火能够抑制橡树和其他硬木的生长，否则它们会将长叶松林淹没。“它们是火之森林，”米切尔说道：“它们在美国东部的闪电之下不断进化。”此外，不只是闪电会引发森林之火。“美国本土居民也会点火来保持森林的开放，”米切尔说道：“早期殖民者也是这么做的，他们的这一做法帮助创造了我们今天所看到的长叶松林。”

林火还改变了长叶松林生态系统中的营养流动方式，对这些方式，我们才刚刚开始了解。举个例子，研究者发现频繁的林火能产生额外的钙，这对濒危的红冠啄木鸟的产蛋量起着决定性的作用。来自佛罗里达州立大学的一位退休的鸟类生态学家弗朗西斯·詹姆斯，已经在佛罗里达州广阔的阿巴拉契科拉国家森林里研究这种黑白相间的小型鸟类二十余年了。当她发现雌性红冠啄木鸟在领地被火烧后的首次繁殖期中会产下较多的一窝蛋时，她和她的同事就开始寻找答案。“我们发现，在森林没有被火烧时，钙质会被木本灌木吸收走，”詹姆斯说道：“但当森林被火烧了之后，就会有大量的钙质渗入到土壤中并被长叶松吸收。”最后，这些钙质又会沿着食物链往上，进入一种树栖蚂蚁的腹中，而这种蚂蚁则是红冠啄木鸟最喜爱的食物。结果就是：有更多的钙质提供给了这些啄木鸟，而这带来了更多的蛋、更多的幼雏以及更多的红冠啄木鸟。

现在，林火已经成为保护长叶松林及其野生生物的重要管理手段。绝大部分的林火都是按照规定，专门采用滴液点火器点燃的。尽管公众经常反对任何形式的放火以及由此产生的浓烟，但是这种低强度的燃烧能降低灾难性大火的风险。“森林总有一天会燃烧的，”国家野生生物联盟（NWF）南部森林的修复管理员阿马杜·迪奥普说道：“这只是时间问题。通过这些规定的燃烧，我们可以选择燃烧的时间和地点。”

迪奥普正在为国家野生生物联盟（NWF）重建长叶松林的项目扫清障碍。“这是一个需要复原的物种，”他说道。告诉土地所有者种植长叶松的好处是这个项目的一部分，他补充道，这项工作很快就能覆盖南部的九个州了。“现在，大部分的长叶松都生长在公共土地上，”佐治亚野生生物联盟主席杰里·麦科勒姆说道。他补充说：“私人土地才是我们的工作重心。”他还指出，超过90%的曾经生长过长叶松的土地都属于这个范畴。

整个南部地区的私人土地所有者的兴趣正不断攀升，但重建长叶松林并不是一件容易的差事。那些草本作物，即狗尾草等其他下层植被，同样需要重建。在那些没有被农垦破坏，但变成了火炬松或湿地松人工林的区域，土壤下的长叶松林的种子仍保持着生命力。最终，这些原生植物会回来的。但是，在种子已经被农耕破坏了的地区，狗尾草必须要重种。眼下，这项开销有些高，但研究者们正在寻找低成本的解决方式。

然而，重建长叶松林并不适用于目光短浅者。我们之中没有什么人能够活到七八十年后小松树长成大森林的那一天。但是这并不能阻挡长叶松的爱好者们。“现在，长叶松的幼苗已经越来越难买到了，”一个私人土地所有者说道：“每个人都想要买它们。长叶松正在复苏当中。”

Reading Passage 2. Storytelling, From Prehistoric Caves To Modern Cinemas

词汇详解

suppose *v.* 假定；猜想，推测；认为（人们在口语中说的“I suppose”基本上就等同于“I believe, I think”。该词是由表示“下面”的前缀 sub 和表示“put 放置”的词根 pose 组成，所以字面意思就是“to put under 放置在下面”，作为讲话的基础，那再进一步延伸就变成了“假定，猜测”的意思了。同义词有 calculate、conjecture、reckon、guess、estimate 等。）

crouch *v.* 屈膝，蹲伏；蜷伏（玩 FPS，first person shooter“第一人称射击游戏”的同学应该对该词不陌生，在键盘上按下 ctrl 键或 c 键就可以 crouch“蹲下”，降低射击时的 recoil“后坐力”，使得射击更准确，当然按下 z 键就可以 prone“匍匐”，进一步提高射击精准度以及降低被敌方发现的几率。当然，热爱电影的同学对于李安拍摄的《卧虎藏龙》应该也不陌生，其英文名就叫做 *Crouching Tiger, Hidden Dragon*。中文里的四字成语虎踞龙盘就可以翻译成 “where tigers crouch and dragons coil”。例句：The Longshan Valley is where tigers crouch and dragons coil; its terrain is just forbiddingly dangerous.）

encounter *v.&n.* 相遇，碰见；不期而遇（该词由前缀 en“进入”和词根 counter“对抗，相反”组成，所以 encounter 本身表达的是“对抗，冲突”的意思。）

remarkable *adj.* 异常的，引人注目的；卓越的；显著的；非凡的，非常（好）的（同义词有 bizarre、cranky、crazy、eccentric、erratic、funky、kinky、outlandish、queer、odd、strange 等。）

mortal *adj.* 致命的；终有一死的；极度的 *n.* 人类，凡人（人在知晓自己无法逃避死亡时往往会说“Mortal is human 人必有一死”这样的话。美国第 35 任总统 John F. Kennedy 在呼吁禁止核试验的演讲中曾经说过：“If we cannot end now our differences, at least we can make the world safe for diversity. For, in the final analysis, our most basic common link is that we all inhabit this small planet. We all breathe the same air. We all cherish our children's future. And we are all mortal.” 著名游戏《真人快打》的英文就叫做 *Mortal Kombat*。）

vision *n.* 视力，视觉；影像，画面；幻影；想像力；视野（词根 vis 或 visio 是“看，看到”的意思。相关的词汇还有：visual 视觉的；visionary 有远见的，预言的，幻想的；visible 可以看到的；envision 想象，预见，展望。关于 vision，在《圣经旧约》箴言第 29 章第 18 节有这么一句话“Where there is no vision, the people perish”，缺少主的启示，人民就会放纵不羁。在 popular culture 当中人们还常用它表达“一个人没有理想，就会毁灭”这样的意思。）

thread *n.* 线；线索；线状物；螺纹（在英语中有一种说法叫做“hang by a thread”，就是指“千钧一发，摇摇欲坠，岌岌可危”的意思。）

weave *v.* 编，织；迂回行进，穿行（著名的网页编辑软件 Abode Dreamweaver 就是要为网页创造者编制一个美好的梦。在英语中有一种说法叫做“weave in and out”，就用来表达车辆在繁忙的车流中“左右穿梭”。例如：The motorcycle wove in and out of traffic, leaving us far behind. 其实我觉得这个例子用在北京的 bicycle 上更贴切。首都，首堵嘛。）

prime *adj.* 最好的；首要的；最初的；基本的（每晚八点钟的电视黄金时间段就叫做“prime time”。数学里 prime number 代表的是“质数”或者也叫做“素数”。习语 in one's prime 代表的是“在一个人或事物的最佳状态下”。如果喜爱动画 *Transformers*《变形金刚》的话，对里面 autobots“汽车人大哥”Optimus Prime“擎天柱”必然会很熟悉，其实 Optimus Prime 本身的意思就是“最棒，一级棒”，因为 optimus 在拉丁语中就是“best”的意思，再加上 prime，那当然就是“best of the best”的意思啦，不过“擎天柱”的翻译还是不错的。）

sustain *v.* 维持；支撑，支持；遭受，忍受；供养（由前缀 sub“下面”和词根 tain“支持，hold”构成，所以该词字面意思就是“to hold/support from underneath 从下面支持”。sustainable 是形容词，中文里面常说的“可持续发展”，英文就叫做“sustainable development”。）

recite *v.* 背诵；叙述；列举（该词由前缀 re“再一次”和表示“引用”的单词 cite 组成，字面意思就是“再一次引用”，于是就变成了“背诵或者叙述”了。有些同学常把 recite 和 memorise 混为一谈，简单的翻译为“背”，这是不正确的。memorise 是把什么东西背下来，记在记忆力当中，而 recite 是把已经背下来的东西背诵出来。）

verse *n.* 诗，韵文；诗节，诗行；诗篇；（《圣经》中的）节

prose *n.* 散文

verbatim *adv.* 逐字地

mnemonic *adj.* 记忆的，有助于记忆的（该词来自于希腊记忆女神 Mnemosyne，她是掌管音乐的众缪斯“Muses”女神的母亲。mnemonic cue 就指的是“用来记忆的小特点或线索”，例如单词 anomaly“异常，反常”，它的 mnemonic cue 就是该词当中的 nomal，和 normal 长相相似，可以帮助记忆，尽管该词的 nomal 与 normal 没有任何关系。mnemonic device 指的是“记忆工具或方法”。）

cue *n.* 暗示，提示；线索（雅思口语考试的第二部分的口语卡片就叫做“cue card 线索 / 提示卡片”，为了帮助考生连续地讲够两分钟的内容，卡片上提供四个 cue questions“提示问题”。）

recall *v.* 叫回，召回；使想起，回想（同义词有 remember、recollect、remind、reminisce 等，不过这些词在使用上有些差异：remember 更多表示从记忆中不费力气地，轻松地想起来什么事物；recollect 则要费些力气，因为这些要回忆的事物可能已经 lost 或者印象不太深刻了；recall 则更多用来表达回忆事物，并且目的是为了发表什么讲话；remind 表示通过相似的事物、情景或某特征，例如触景生情，想起什么东西；reminisce 则常常用来表达一种怀旧的追忆。）

notch *n.*（V 字形的）槽口，刻痕 *v.* 在……上作刻痕，开槽口；作刻痕计算（在英文中有一种说法叫做“top notch”，最上面的刻痕当然就是“最高的，最好的，最棒的”，例如：top notch student 就指的是“成绩最好的学生”。）

successive *adj.* 连续的，相继的；继承的，接替的；逐次（该词是由 sub“下面”和词根 ceed“行走”及表示形容词词性的后缀 ive 组合而成，字面意思就是“在后面跟着走”，自然就是“后续的，继承的”了。相关词汇有：successor 继承者，继承人；proceed 进行，前往，继续做；exceed 超出等。）

literacy *n.* 识字；读写能力；精通文学（其中词根 lit 就代表“letter 字母”的意思。literate 字面上就是“认识字母”的，所以进一步引申为“有读写能力的，有文化修养的”。illiterate，如果连字母都不认识，那就一定是文盲了。literal 就代表“字面上的”，所以“字面上来讲”就可以翻译成“literally speaking…”，相关单词还有 transliterate，即把词或句

子等用另一个字母体系拼出，音译。）

epic *adj.* 史诗般的，叙事诗的；宏大的，壮丽的 *n.* 叙事诗；史诗（提到史诗，西方人最容易想起来的就是伟大的希腊诗人 Homer 荷马、在荷马史诗中最著名的 *Iliad* 伊利亚特和 *Odysseus* 奥德赛。）

attribute *v.* 认为……是，把……归于 *n.*（人或物的）属性，特质（该词的词根 tribute 是"给予"的意思，而且 tribute 本身就是一个单词，意思是"礼物，贡品或恭金"，所以 attribute 的意思就变成了"把……归于某人某事"了。tributary 就成了"给人上贡的人"，通常是一个附属国或被征服国的国君，而且也可以指河流的支流。contribute 当中的 con 代表"共同，一起"，大家一起给、一起提供就变成了"贡献"。）

enchanting *adj.* 使人喜悦的；令人陶醉的；迷人的（该词来自 chant "吟颂，咏唱"，尤其是在宗教场合，歌声往往是美丽动人的。en 代表"进入"，于是 enchant 就有了"迷人的，使人喜悦的"意思了。disenchantment 就变成了"不再着迷，不再喜欢"。）

parchment *n.* 羊皮纸；文凭；羊皮纸古文稿（该词来自动词 parch "使焦干，使干透"。想象一下羊皮被剥下来之后搭在架子上晒干，然后再被用来书写的过程，这一定非常复杂繁琐，更不用提那昂贵的价格 "not to mention its forbidding price"，可见造纸术 "the art of papermaking" 的伟大。）

trace *v.* 跟踪，追踪；追溯，探索 *n.* 痕迹，踪迹；微量，极少量（在雅思学习中一定要有一个系统的方法及可用的指标来追踪自己的学习进程 "trace one's learning progress"，否则学了，做了题了，却完全不知道自己的情况，好在哪里，差在哪里，哪里有问题，怎样可以解决等。not leave a trace behind 指的就是"不留下一丝痕迹"。在营养学中 trace minerals 指的就是"微量元素"。）

manifestation *n.* 表示，显示；示威（来自 manifest，作形容词时，意思是"明显的，明白的"，等同于 apparent、obvious、clear、clear-cut、evident、lucid、patent、unambiguous 等；作动词时，意思就是"显现，显示，使……清楚、清晰"。该词还有一个变形 manifesto，是"宣言"的意思，像著名的卡尔·马克思的《共产党宣言》就叫做 *The Communist Manifesto*。）

papyrus *n.* 纸莎草；纸莎草纸（这是古埃及人利用河边长的一种草制成的纸，亦可以用来表示记录在这种纸上的文献。）

archive *n.* 档案，文件；档案室（相关词汇有 file、document 和 dossier，因为它们都可以翻译成"文件"，且有时可以互换使用，所以人们往往区分不清楚。file 最初指的是可以把纸张整理在一起的工具，例如文件夹，于是就进一步引申为放在文件夹里的文件了，在电脑中可以指任何文件，例如图片，影像，或程序。而 document 则通常指打印或写在纸上的信息和传达这个信息的纸质介质，在电脑中则专指文本文档。archive 则指通过较长时间收集起来的文件，可能包含各个方面的内容；而 dossier 则专指关于某一个特定事物、人或事件的某个特定方面信息的文件 "detailed records on a particular person or subject"。）

bark *n.* 树皮，犬吠声 *v.* 犬吠，厉声说出（英语中的习语“bark up the wrong tree”，就是一种形象的说法，指的是“在批评或抱怨时，找错对象或认错目标了”。）

scroll *n.* 纸卷；书卷，画卷，卷轴 *v.* 卷起，滚动（鼠标左右键之间的滚轮就叫做“scroll wheel”，利用滚轮在屏幕上上下滚动也就叫做“scroll up, scroll down”。深受诸多玩家欢迎的《上古卷轴》游戏就叫做 *The Elder Scrolls*，也被玩家亲切地称呼为“老滚”。）

universal *adj.* 普遍的；全体的；全世界的（universal truth 就是“普遍真理”的意思，例如：Communism is a universal truth. 共产主义是一个普遍真理。）

narrate *v.* 叙述，讲述，作旁白（目前，中国电视史上最著名的旁白“narrator”应该就是赵忠祥了，他磁性的声音“magnetic voice”在《动物世界》及《人与自然》中精彩的解说“narration”是不少人童年难忘的回忆。）

assume *v.* 取得（权力）；承担，担任；假设，假定；认为

comic *adj.* 滑稽的，好笑的 *n.* 连环画，漫画（在日本漫画迅速兴起及广受欢迎的今天，很多书店的 Comics 书架都只会用来摆放欧美漫画，而日本漫画则会有一个单独的书架叫做 Manga，即“日文漫画”的意思。大受好评的一些作品，例如 *Dragon Ball*《七龙珠》，*Detective Conan* 或者有时候也翻译成 *Case Closed* 的《名侦探柯南》，*One Piece*《海贼王》，*Naruto*《火影忍者》，甚至少女漫画 *Sailor Moon*《美少女战士》都可以买到。）

access *n.* 通道，入径；机会，权利 *v.* 进入，访问；使用，获取（该词词根 cess 来自于另一个词根 cede 或 ceed，意思是“行走”。相关的词汇有：accede 加入，同意，任职；proceed 进行，前进；succeed 继承，继任，成功；recede 后退，减弱。）

supreme *adj.* 最高的；至高无上的；最重要的（supreme court 就是“最高法院”。Focus Interactive 出过一款 RTS“real time strategy 即时战略”游戏，叫做 *Supreme Commander*《最高指挥官》，也曾经风靡一时。在中文中有一种说法叫做“顾客至上”，英文翻译就要用到这个词，叫做“The customer reigns supreme”。）

distinct *adj.* 明显的，清楚的；有区别的（中文里常说的四季分明就用这个词“four distinct seasons”。distinctive 翻译为“有特色的，与众不同的，独特的”，在使用上和 distinct 要区分开来，例如我们只能说“four distinct seasons”，因为这四个季节的差异是清晰的，但是我们却可以说“What makes one of them distinctive?”，又如“What is distinctive about autumn in Canada is that tree leaves only change color and do not fall off to ground.”）

phenomenon *n.* 现象；奇迹（该词的复数是 phenomena。它的形容词 phenomenal 在口语和写作中经常被用来表达“非凡的，不寻常的，惊人的”意思，例如：Her performance tonight was absolutely phenomenal.）

precedent *n.* 前例，先例（来自动词 precede，其中词根 cede 为“走”的意思，所以 precede 自然就是“在前面行走”。precedent 的同义词有 previous、former、preceding、antecedent、anterior、prior 等。）

sequence *n.* 数列，序列，顺序；连续（该词与 sequel“续集，续篇”同源，都表示“在……

后面”的意思，而 prequel 是“前传”的意思。）

atavistic *adj.* 隔代遗传的，返祖性的（返祖现象就叫做“atavism”。）

pulse *n.* 脉搏；脉动（feel the pulse 就是“摸脉搏，切脉，号脉”的意思；take the pulse 就是“记脉搏，记心跳的快慢”；keep one's finger on the pulse of something 则指“把握事情的脉络和进展”。）

plot *n.*（戏剧、小说等的）故事情节 *v.* 设计情节；密谋，暗中策划（作动词表达暗中策划时，经常使用“plot against somebody/something”这样的搭配。在英式英语中还有“lose the plot”的习惯性表达，意思是“go crazy, become crazy”。）

embed *v.* 把……嵌入，使……插入；植入，栽种（该词还有另外一种拼写：imbed。）

script *n.* 手记，文本，剧本（该词来自于词根 scribe，意思是“书写”，而且 scribe 本身作为单词就是“抄写员，写字的文人”等。与该词根相关的词汇还有：scribble 潦草地写，乱写乱画；scripture 经文，经典；circumscribe 在周围画线，限制，限定；inscribe 雕，刻，题写；describe 描述，描绘；subscribe 签署，署名，认购，订阅；transcribe 誊写，转抄等。）

aspiring *adj.* 有志气的，有抱负的（来自动词 aspire 渴望，立志，追求。）

screenwriter *n.* 电影剧本作家；编剧家（电影剧本叫做“screenplay”。）

envisage *v.* 想象，设想，展望（该词是由表示“进入”的前缀 en 和 visage 组成，visage 是文学用语，是“脸，面容，外表，外观”的意思。其实这都和表示“看”的词根 vis 有关。）

actuality *n.*（常用复数）现状，现实，事实

multiplex *n.* 多厅影院，多银幕电影院（该词是由 multiple 和 complex 合成而来。multiple“多重的”，complex“综合大楼”，所以 multiplex 就用来指“有很多剧场或影院的大楼”。）

prescient *adj.* 有预知能力的，有先见之明的（该词的词根 scient 来自于拉丁语 scire，代表“知道”的意思，于是 prescient 就是“先知先觉”的意思。相关的词汇有：omniscient 全知的，什么都知道的；conscience 知觉，良心等。）

flock *n.* 鸟群；人群 *v.* 群集，成群结队（“物以类聚，人以群分”的英文表达就用到了这个词：“Birds of a feather flock together.”）

hub *n.* 轮毂；中心（汽车、自行车轮子中心装轴的部分就叫做“hub”，辐条叫做“spoke”，英语中词组“hub and spokes”就表示“轮轴放射状”的意思。在计算机中 hub 还可以代表“集线器”。在口语中人们也常用，例如：cultural hub 就指的是“文化枢纽”。）

analyze *v.* 分析（名词形式是 analysis。研究的最基本方法就是设计一定的指标然后进行数据收集“data collection”和数据分析“data analysis”。）

rationalism *n.* 理性主义，唯理论（来自形容词 rational“理性的”。相关词汇有：irrational 不理性的，盲目的；rationale 理念，原则，理论基础。）

suspension *n.* 悬浮，悬挂；暂停（来自动词 suspend，其中词根 pend 是“to hang 挂着”的意思，于是 suspend 就有“挂起来”的意思，再进一步延伸就有了“悬浮，暂停，延缓”的意思。

suspension 在汽车上指的是汽车的“悬挂系统”，悬挂调校好的话，就具有更好的舒适度“comfort”、操控“handling”或者运动性。）

stun *v.* 击晕，使昏厥；使目瞪口呆，使大吃一惊（“set phazer to stun”这句话对于《星际迷航》迷来说肯定不陌生，“设置相位枪为击昏模式”，曾经有多少少年希望自己能够加入联邦舰队“Federation Fleet”，拥有自己的星舰“Starship”和相位枪“Phased Energy Rectification Gun”，简称 Phazer。）

evocation *n.* 唤出，唤起，招魂（来自动词 evoke，其中词根 voke 就是“召唤，呼叫”的意思，所以 evoke 就有“召唤出来”的意思了。相关的词汇有：revoke 撤销，取消，废除；invoke 祈求；provoke 煽动。）

captivate *v.* 迷住，迷惑（该词在过去还有“capture 捕捉，捕获，抓捕”的意思。）

witness *n.* 目击者，见证人 *v.* 作证；见证（英语中常说的“bear witness to…”就是“为……做见证”的意思。值得一提的是，在美国法庭上，证人出席并给予证词之前，首先要把手按在圣经上宣誓“take an oath”。）

civic *adj.* 城市的；公民的，市民的

ritual *n.&adj.* 仪式（的）

recreation *n.* 消遣或娱乐（的方式）（该词和 entertainment 完全不同，recreation 主要是指各种各样的放松，多是自身的活动，而 entertainment 则侧重于各种表演，演出。）

respectively *adv.* 各自地，分别地

potent *adj.* 有效的；强有力的；有说服力的

capacity *n.* 容量；才能（英语中有一种说法叫做“Genius is an infinite capacity for taking pains”，指的是“天才从某种程度上来讲就是一种吃苦耐劳的无限能力”。）

enlist *v.* 征募；赢得……支持或帮助（该词经常被用在军事上，代表“征召士兵”的意思。）

purge *v.* 清除，（使）净化（该词来自 pure，所以就有了“净化”的意思。苏联历史上的大清洗就叫做“The Great Purge”。天主教教义中的 purgatory“炼狱”就认为罪人在炼狱中可以清除自己的罪恶，然后才有可能进入天堂。）

canonical *adj.* 依教规的；经典的（来自名词 canon“标准，准则，精品”。注意该词与 cannon“大炮，机关炮”发音一样，拼写只是一个字母之差，但是意思却相差很多。）

credible *adj.* 可信的（词根 cred 的意思就是“相信”，credit 就是大家熟悉的“信用”，credible 就是“可信的”，incredible 就是“难以置信的”。）

mighty *adj.* 有力的，强大的（might 是名词形式，代表“力量，能力和权威”。）

magnificent *adj.* 壮丽的；宏伟的；壮观的

sulk *v.* 生气，愠怒（主要指的是“生闷气”，甚至一言不发。常见的搭配是“sulk about”或者“sulk over”。）

bicker *v.* 争吵（并非真正的大吵大闹，而是因为鸡毛蒜皮的小事“petty nuisance”而进行的口角。）

protagonist *n.*（戏剧的）主角；（故事的）主人公；现实事件（尤指冲突和争端的）主要参与者

prone *adj.* 易于……的，有……倾向的；俯卧的

intrinsically *adv.* 从本质上（讲）（来自形容词 intrinsic “内在的”，反义词是 extrinsic。与内部和外部相关的词对还有 inside & outside、interior & exterior、internal & external、inner & outer、inward & outward 等。）

题目详解

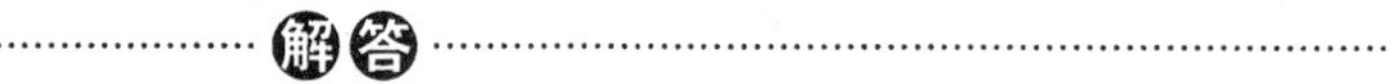

Questions 14-18

解答

14. 该信息出现在段落 D 中间靠后 “The formal practice of narrating a story aloud would seem—so we assume—to have given way to newspapers, novels and comic strips. This, however, is not the case...”。这里提及我们以为获取故事的途径已被 “newspapers, novels and comic strips” 所取代，而实际上并不是这样。这就是题目里所说的 “misunderstanding”。所以正确答案为 D。

15. 该信息出现在段落 G 中间 “Two theatrical types of storytelling, tragedy and comedy, caused Athenian audiences to lose themselves...”，这里的 “Two theatrical types of storytelling”，也就是亚里士多德所区分的 “tragedy and comedy” 对应题目所说的 “categorisation”。所以正确答案为 G。

16. 该信息出现在段落 A 中间 “...this story was done with a prime purpose. The listeners must be kept listening...”，很明显这里提及 “the fundamental aim of storytelling” 是 “The listeners must be kept listening”，所以正确答案为 A。

17. 该信息出现在段落 B “(stories) were kept in the heads of those who told them”，后面还提及 “...specialised storytellers and poets can recite from memory literally thousands of lines, in verse or prose...”，对应题目所说的 “reciting stories without any assistance”。所以正确答案为 B。

18. 该信息出现在段落 H 中间 “He made his heroes sulk, bicker, cheat and cry. They were, in short, characters—protagonists of a story that an audience would care about, would want to follow, would want to know what happens next”，这里 “audience would care about, would want to follow, would want to know what happens next” 对应题目信息 “attractive”。所以正确答案为 H。

Questions 19-22

19. 利用细节信息“Egyptians”很容易定位于原文段落D的第一句话“...the priestly papyrus archives of ancient Egypt...”。尽管考生不一定认识“papyrus”，但是很容易判断它不是从其他国家借鉴而来的“writing system”或一种帮助“tell stories”的“tools”，所以只能是“organic materials”。所以正确答案为B。

20. 利用细节信息“Ojibway”也定位于原文段落D的第一句话“...birch-bark scrolls on which the North American Ojibway Indians set down their creation-myth”，这里的“birch-bark”也对应选项B的“organic materials”，所以正确答案为B。

21. 利用细节信息“Polynesians”定位于原文段落C的第一句话“In some Polynesian communities a notched memory stick may help to guide a storyteller through successive stages of recitation”，很明显Polynesian会使用“notched memory stick”这种工具（tools）来帮助他们的storytelling，所以正确答案为C。

22. 利用细节信息“Greek”定位于原文段落C的最后“So the Greeks, c. 750-700BC, borrowed an alphabet from their neighbors in the eastern Mediterranean, the Phoenicians”，这里的“Phoenicians”对应选项A中的“another country”，所以正确答案为A。

Questions 23-26

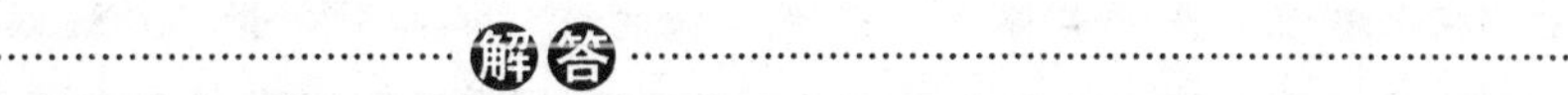

23. 利用细节信息“Aristotle”和“a book on the art of storytelling”定位于原文段落F第三句话“He (Aristotle) left some incomplete lecture notes on the art of telling stories in various literary and dramatic modes, a slim volume known as *The Poetics*”，很明显这里可以看出这本关于“the art of storytelling”的书叫做“*The Poetics*”，所以正确答案为*Poetics*。

24. 利用顺序原则和细节信息“most powerful type of story to move listeners”定位于原文段落G中间“Tragedy, for Aristotle, was particularly potent in its capacity to enlist and then purge the emotions of those watching the story unfold on the stage”，这里“particularly potent”对应题目中的“most powerful”；“enlist and then purge the emotions of those watching the story”对应题目中的“move listeners”，所以正确答案为tragedy。

25. 利用顺序原则和细节信息“Homer”定位于原文段落G倒数第二句话“... Homer, whose stories even then had canonical status: *The Iliad* and *The Odyssey* were already considered literary landmarks”。很明显可以总结出Aristotle把Homer的作品“*The Iliad* and *The Odyssey*”看成是“literary landmarks”。所以正确答案为landmarks。

26. 利用顺序原则和细节信息“attractive heroes”定位于原文段落H最后一句话“As

Aristotle saw, the hero who shows a human side—some flaw or weakness to which mortals are prone—is intrinsically dramatic"，这里"intrinsically dramatic"对应题目信息"attractive"，所以正确答案为 flaw 或 weakness。

参考译文

讲故事，从史前洞穴到现代影院

A 我们推测，人们曾围蹲在火堆旁听着这样的故事：一个关于冒险的，最有可能是和死亡密切相关的传说；一场不同寻常的捕猎，从致命危险中逃出生天；一个幻象或者其他不同寻常的场景。无论情节如何发展，所有故事在编造时都有一个基本目的，即必须让听众保持倾听下去的欲望。他们一定不能睡着。就这样，随着故事的发展，听众们都尤其应当被这样一个问题驱使着听下去：接下来会发生什么呢？

B 人类历史上最早的火边故事，我们已经无从得知了。它们存在于那些说书人的脑海中。这种靠记忆记录的方式并不一定就低效。据澳大利亚、巴尔干半岛以及世界上其他地区的口述传统记载，我们知道专职说书人或诗人能够逐字地背诵出上千行的诗篇或散文——一字不差。不过，尽管记忆本身被当作一门技艺，但我们明确地知道，创建符号的主要目的就是为了建立一个提示符或记忆线索系统，即能帮助我们唤醒脑海中特定信息的符号。

C 在一些波利尼亚群体中，刻有凹槽的记忆棒能引导说书人逐层背诵。但在世界其他地方，说书这一活动在历史上导致了书写体系的发展甚至是书写体系的发明与创造。例如，有一种观点认为，古希腊文学的产生是由于描述特洛伊战争和奥德修斯漂流记的史诗传说（一般认为是由荷马所作）太过动听，以至于人们不得不将故事记录下来。于是，希腊人在公元前 750-700 年间向他们的邻居，地中海东部的腓尼基人，借来了字母表。

D 从古埃及祭司的纸莎草纸档案到北美奥吉布韦印第安人记录他们创世神话的桦树皮卷，在世界各地的许多文化形式中，都能找到在羊皮纸或其他材料上记录故事的习惯。这是一种行之有效并且普遍适用的操作方法：甚至直到今天，大部分的故事或许都是以文字的形式呈现在纸上的。所以我们以为，叙述故事的正规方式似乎已经让位给报纸、小说和连环画了。然而，事情并非如此。据统计，通过书面文字获得故事的人在当代是否占大多数，仍然存疑。那么，另一个来源又是什么呢？

E 每年，超过 70 亿人口会去观看好莱坞、宝莱坞以及其他地方出品的最新电影。在当代，最大的说书人就是影院了。和静态照片明显不同，电影本质上看上去是一种现代技术现象。但这种观念是错误的，正如我们将看到的，电影媒介这一方式其实源

自于场景图片顺序展示的古老方式。任何一种视觉的故事叙述方式都必须从一开始就会认识到，所有的故事叙述都遵循着一个古老的原则：那就是，一个“好的故事”依赖于情节和角色刻画的形式模式，这已经深深地植入数代人的叙事实践中了。

F 每周都有数千份剧本出现在那些大型电影公司的办公桌上。那些希望有所作为的编剧并不需要另寻良方，他们只需将公元前 4 世纪希腊哲学家亚里士多德的思想视为最重要的信条即可。在用不同文学和戏剧模式来叙事的艺术上，亚里士多德留下了一些并不完整的讲义，这就是那本薄薄的《诗学》。尽管他从未设想过现在那充斥着爆米花的多厅影院，但亚里士多德却差不多预见性地指出了将人群吸引到这个文化中心所需的那些核心要素。他以冷静的理论主义分析了这一过程。当一个故事使我们入迷时，我们会忘记身处何地；我们会深深地陷入情节之中以至于忘记这只是一个虚构的故事。这就是亚里士多德的名言，“搁置质疑”。

G 我们熟悉这种感觉。如果当片尾闪过时，我们坐在自己的座位上，满怀悲痛；或者在看完逼真的惊恐场面后的好几天里，不敢在自己家里洗澡，那这时我们就已经“搁置质疑”了。我们已经被困在或者说沦陷在说书人的陷阱里了。那些故事真的发生过么？有那么一会儿，我们还真的认为确实发生过。亚里士多德一定见证了大量的这些“搁置质疑”。他曾在雅典讲学。在这座城市中，剧院发展成了市民举行日常仪式和进行娱乐的场所。故事叙述的两种戏剧类型，即悲剧和喜剧，使雅典观众分别陷入了悲痛和欢笑之中。对亚里士多德来说，悲剧能够尤为有效地唤起，然后净化那些观看故事在舞台上展开的观众的情感，于是他尝试找出那些说书人用以打动听众的要素。他不仅仅将公元前 5 世纪埃斯库罗斯、索福克勒斯和欧里庇得斯的希腊悲剧经典作为分析对象。在他们之上，荷马的作品尤其受到重视。荷马的故事作品甚至在当时就被视为经典：《伊利亚特》和《奥德赛》早已被认为是文学上的典范，所有的其他故事作品都应借此来衡量。那么荷马叙事艺术的秘诀是什么呢？

H 这并不难发现。荷马塑造了可信的英雄。他的英雄人物属于过去，他们强大、高尚，但是他们最终并非是虚无缥缈的幻想。在他的笔下，他的英雄们会发怒，会争吵，会欺骗，甚至会痛哭。简言之，他们是故事的主角，是观众们会关心，会追随，会期望得知剧情发展的故事的主人公。正如亚里士多德所看到的，一个具有人性化的一面，即拥有凡人缺陷或弱点的英雄本身就非常具有戏剧性。

Reading Passage 3. Living Dunes

词汇详解

reform *n.* 改革；改良；改造；改进 *v.* 改善；改革；重组（由表示“再一次”的前缀 re 与表示“形成”的 form 组合而成，字面意思就是“再次形成，形成新的形状”，于是就是“改革，改良”的意思了。中文中的“改过自新”就可以用这个词表达，翻译成“to reform and start afresh”。类似于表达“洗心革面”的习语还有“turn over a new leaf”，例句：Apparently he's turned over a new leaf and he's not drinking any more.）

desertification *n.* 沙漠化；沙化

communication *n.* 沟通；通讯，通信；交通（communication 除了表示普通的“交流”之外，还可以代表“道路交通系统”，例如“交通银行”就叫做“Bank of Communication”。）

superstition *n.* 迷信；迷信的思想、行为（中国人的迷信行为很多，例如：fortune-telling 算命；palm reading/palmistry 看手相；physiognomy 看面相等。）

demystify *v.* 使不再神秘

rare *adj.* 罕见的；稀有的；不寻常的；稀薄的；极好的

replicate *v.* 复制；重做；再造（replica 的意思就是“复制品”。同义词有：clone、copycat、duplicate、reduplicate、copy、reproduce 等。）

dune *n.* 沙丘

barren *adj.* 贫瘠的；不结果实的；不孕的；无价值的（该词与 infertile 都可以表示“不孕”，特指女性，因为男人不会怀孕，男人可以“不育”，叫做“sterile”。）

shift *v.* 改变；换挡；移动（开车时把车“挂到一挡”就是“shift into 1st gear”。）

crawl *v.* 爬行；缓慢地行进；巴结 *n.* 缓慢的爬行（词组“make someone's flesh crawl”的意思就是“使人起鸡皮疙瘩”，当然也可以说成“give someone goosebumps”。）

roll over 从（边上）滚下；（使）翻滚；（使）打滚

relentless *adj.* 无情的；残酷的；坚决的；不间断的（relent 的意思是“变温和”，加上否定后缀 less 就变成了“不变温和”，再进一步延伸就成了“无情的”的意思。）

devour *v.* 狼吞虎咽；吞食；吞没，毁灭

swallow *v.* 吞下，咽下；忍耐，忍受 *n.* 燕子；吞，咽（英文中说某事情是“hard to swallow”，意思就是指这件事情“难以置信”，例句：Her story was hard to swallow, and it finally was proven to be a lie. “swallow”作为“燕子”的意思时，有这样一句俗语叫做：“one swallow does not make a summer”，字面意思就是“不要看到一只燕子就以为夏天来了”，即“一燕不成夏”，言外之意就是“不能仅凭一点证据或线索就判断事物的是非”。）

displace *v.* 使（某人或某物）离开原位；替代，取代

prior to 在……之前

particle *n.* 微粒；颗粒；粒子（颗粒是由分子“molecule”构成，分子又由原子“atom”构成，原子由原子核“nucleus”和核外电子“electron”构成，原子核由质子“proton”和中子“neutron”构成，质子和中子又由夸克“quark”构成。总而言之，量子物理学“quantum physics”是无比玄妙。）

deposit *n.* 储蓄，存款；保证金；沉积物 *v.* 使沉积；寄存；放置

recognise *v.* 认出；识别；承认

crescentic *adj.* 新月形的

linear *adj.* 直线的，线形的；长度的（“线性代数”就叫做“linear algebra”。）

longitudinal *adj.* 经度的；纵向的；纵观的

ridge *n.* 背脊；山脊

prominent *adj.* 突出的；杰出的；显著地；重要的

comprise *v.* 包含，包括；组成，构成（“由……组成”的英文表达是“be comprised of…”。）

dynamics *n.* 动力学，力学

loose *adj.* 松动的；零散的；宽大的 *v.* 释放；射出（子弹或箭等）

vegetation *n.* 植物；植被，草木（当人们说到某地，例如沙漠缺乏植被时，用的就是 vegetation 这个词。在医学上，当某人因为某种原因变成植物人，这个植物人就叫做 vegetable。）

breeze *n.* 微风，和风；容易做的事，轻而易举的事 *v.* 飘然出现；信步走进；轻松完成

obstacle *n.* 障碍物；障碍物

momentum *n.* 动量；势头；动力；冲力

variable *adj.* 变化的；可变的；易变的 *n.* 可变因素；变量

merge *v.* 合并；融合；相融；融入；渐渐消失在另一物中

grain *n.* 谷物，粮食；颗粒；谷粒；（木材等的）纹理（词组“against the grain”的意思是“违反本性”，例句：What Mr. Lee has said really goes against the grain of our thinking. “a grain of truth”则指的是“一丁点真实的成分”，例句：If there were a grain of truth to your statement, I would trust you. 习语“take something with a grain of salt”意思就是“有所保留地相信某事”。）

steep *adj.* 陡峭的，陡的；过分昂贵的，过高的；急剧的 *v.* 浸泡；浸淫（在口语中，如果说某个东西是“a little steep”，意思就是说这个东西的“价格有点高”。）

collapse *v.* 坍塌；倒塌；崩溃

crest *n.* 山顶；浪峰；徽章；羽冠 *v.* 到达顶部（如果说某人是“on the crest of a wave”，意思是说此人“正处在顶峰时期”，好事接连不断。）

slip *v.* 滑倒；失足；溜走；滑落；下降 *n.* 滑；滑倒；小错误（“口误”就叫做“a slip of the tongue”。）

migrate *v.* 迁移；迁徙；移往；移居（从一个地方移居到另外一个地方就是“to migrate from one place to another place”。“migratory bird”就是“候鸟”。如果该词再加上表示“进入”的前缀“im/in”或表示“离开”的前缀“ex”的话就变成了 immigrate“移民进入”和 emigrate“移民离开”。）

breed *v.* 交配繁殖；饲养，培育；孕育；导致；使养成 *n.* 品种；种类，类型（英文中有很多关于 breed 的说法，例如：“familiarity breeds contempt”等同于中文的“亲不敬，熟生蔑”。说某人“生小孩生得多，生得快”，英文就可以说“breeds like rabbits”，因为兔子很能繁殖。如果说某人或某物是“rare breed”，就是说他或它“罕见，凤毛麟角”，例如：Warwick belongs to a rare breed of scientists who experiment on themselves.）

offspring *n.* 后代，子女，子孙；（动物的）幼崽

downwind *adv.* 顺风地

outpace *v.* 超过，赶过（out 在这里代表“超越”，例如：outwit 以智胜过；outnumber 数量上超过；outrun 跑得快；outsize 特大的；outlive 比……活得更长久等。）

weird *adj.* 怪异的；超自然的；奇怪的；不寻常的；古怪的（“weirdo”指的是“怪人”。）

attribute *v.* 认为……是，把……归于 *n.*（人或物的）属性，特质（该词的词根 tribute 是“给予”的意思，而且 tribute 本身就是一个单词，意思是“礼物，贡品或恭金”，所以 attribute 的意思就变成了“把……归于某人某事”了。tributary 就成了“给人上贡的人”，通常是一个附属国或被征服国的国君，而且也可以指河流的支流。contribute 当中的 con 代表“共同，一起”，大家一起给、一起提供就变成了“贡献”。）

volume *n.* 音量，响度；容量，体积；卷

unnerving *adj.* 使人紧张不安的；使人胆怯的

tone *n.* 声调，语调；色调；基调；音调，音质；语气（词组“set the tone”就是“确定基调”。）

otherworldliness *n.* 来世；冥间；理想世界

inability *n.* 无能；无力

localise *v.* 使局部化；使具有地方色彩

delve *v.* 探究；挖掘；钻研（该词本身的意思就是 dig“挖洞，挖掘”，等同于“excavate”，不过后来进一步地延伸，用来表达“examine a subject in detail and depth 钻研事物”，人们常用“delve into…”的组合。）

mechanism *n.* 机制；机械装置；（机械或装置的）结构，构造；技巧；程序

acoustic *adj.* 听觉的；声学的；原声的；声音的（“acoustic guitar”就是“原声吉他，木制吉他”，它靠的是振动箱的共振“resonance”来发声，另外一种是 electrical guitar“电吉他”，靠的是把电的信号转换成声音。）

haul *v.* 拖，拉

automated *adj.* 自动化的

resonate *v.* 共鸣；共振；回响（该词词根 sona 或 soner 的意思就是“声音”，所以该词的

字面意思就是“resound”，即“发出巨大的声音，回响”。）

theorise *v.* 创建理论；提出关于……的理论；使理论化

boom *v.* 发出隆隆声；迅速发展；繁荣 *n.* 隆隆声；繁荣；流行

synchronise *v.*（使）同步；（使）同时发生；（使）一致；校准

emit *v.* 发出；发射；排出；排泄

varnish *n.* 清漆，罩光漆 *v.* 给……涂上清漆

mineral *n.* 矿物；矿石；矿物质（人体健康必不可少的“微量元素”叫做“trace minerals”，常见的矿物质有：iron 铁；copper 铜；lead 铅；silver 银；gold 金；aluminum 铝；zinc 锌；nickel 镍；sodium 钠；magnesium 镁；potassium 钾；phosphorus 磷等。）

silicon *n.* 硅

manganese *n.* 锰

mute *adj.* 缄默的；哑的；不说话的 *n.* 哑巴；弱音器 *v.* 减弱……的声音；消除……的声音；使弱化；减弱，缓和

wear away 磨损；磨掉；消逝；衰退

题目详解

Questions 27-33

思路

这种题型忌讳寻找主题句或中心句，因为每个人对段落中心思想的判断通常不同，而且每个段落的首尾句也不一定是主题句或中心句，所以最好的解答方法应该是通过对每位考生都能读懂的标题进行反向思维，然后和段落内容进行比较，排除作答。

i. Shaping and reforming

反向思维词：reforming

反向思维：如果某段以此为标题，则该段落应该讲述沙丘成形的机制，而且也应该提及沙丘形状的变化，怎么从一个形状变成另外一个形状。

ii. Causes of desertification

反响思维词：causes

反向思维：如果某段以此为标题，则该段落必须提及沙漠化，而且重点讲解沙漠化的具体原因（而且不止一条原因，对应 causes），例如：植被的破坏、气候的变迁等等。

iii. Need combination of specific conditions

反向思维词：specific conditions

反向思维：如果某段以此为标题，则该段落应该讲到一些具体的条件，而且提及这些条

件都是必要条件，必须全部具备才能产生特定结果。

iv. *Potential threat to industry and communication*

反向思维词：threat, industry and communication（此处为交通，而非交流的意思）

反向思维：如果某段以此为标题，则该段落一定要提及工业和交通方面的内容以及沙丘对这两个领域的危害，例如：毁坏工厂和公路设施等等。

v. *An old superstition demystified*

反向思维词：an old superstition

反向思维：如果某段以此为标题，则该段落应该讲到一个具体的迷信，而且为了表达出“old”，还可能出现时间。

vi. *Differences and similarities*

反向思维：如果某段以此为标题，则该段落应该讲述不同沙丘间的相似之处和差异点。

vii. *A continuous cycling process*

反向思维词：continuous, cycling

反向思维：如果某段以此为标题，则该段落应该讲述一个具体的过程，然后重点描述这个过程是如何不停持续而且还自我循环。

viii. *Habitat for rare species*

反向思维词：rare species

反向思维：如果某段以此为标题，则该段落应该讲到一些具体的稀有物种，动物或植物，它们能够在沙丘上生活，而且还可能讲述它们是如何适应沙丘的严酷生存条件的。

ix. *Replicating the process in laboratory*

反向思维词：laboratory

反向思维：如果某段以此为标题，则该段落必须提到实验室、科学实验什么的，讲到在实验室中复制一个什么的过程，还可能出现具体的科学家名称或研究机构名称。

x. *Commonest type of dune*

反向思维词：commonest type

反向思维：如果某段以此为标题，则该段落应该讲述一种特定的沙丘，且对它有详细的描述，例如外观、分布以及如何分辨什么的。

解答

27. *Paragraph A:* 该段落非常简单，通读段落后很容易发现与该段落相关的标题只有一个 iv. Potential threat to industry and communication。段落开头就提及沙丘会破坏建筑，吞没车辆，威胁农作物和工厂。后面还讲到沙丘会吞噬村庄等等，所以正确答案为iv。

28. ***Paragraph B:*** 与该段落相关的标题有i. Shaping and reforming、vi. Differences and similarities和x. Commonest type of dune。虽然段落中讲到了新月形沙丘和线状沙丘的形状，但是并未讲述它们是如何形成的，或者它们的形状可以如何变化，所以标题i. Shaping and reforming应该排除。另外，段落中确实提及了新月形沙丘和线状沙丘的差异，例如：新月形沙丘是“it is usually wider than it is long”，线状沙丘是“longer than they are wide”，但这并非段落的主要内容，而且段落中并未提及两者的“similarities”，所以标题vi. Differences and similarities应该被排除。而标题x. Commonest type of dune就对应得很好，所以正确答案为x。

29. ***Paragraph C:*** 该段落也非常简单，与该段落对应的标题只有iii. Need combination of specific conditions，所以正确答案为iii。

30. ***Paragraph D:*** 与该段落相关的标题有i. Shaping and reforming和vii. A continuous cycling process。段落确实讲到沙丘的形成过程，但是却没有讲到“reforming”，相反的，整个段落说完沙丘的形成过程之后强调“The repeating cycle of sand...”，所以该段落只能选择vii。

31. ***Paragraph E:*** 段落D正确选择出答案之后，段落E的标题就好判断了。该段落开头提及风对沙丘形成的影响，然后又讲到沙丘的移动，沙丘形状的变化，甚至还提及诞生新沙丘，与此对应的标题只有i. Shaping and reforming，所以正确答案为i。

32. ***Paragraph F:*** 该段落讲到了沙丘唱歌的现象，而且开头还提及马可·波罗认为这种现象和鬼神有关，对应标题v. An old superstition demystified中的“An old superstition”，且其他标题信息都未提及，所以正确答案为v。

33. ***Paragraph G:*** 该段落也非常简单，段落明显提到Stéphane Douady的研究小组把沙子带回到实验室，然后在实验室里使这些沙子发出了声音，然后研究为什么这些沙子会发音的内容，与此对应的标题只有一个ix. Replicating the process in laboratory，所以正确答案为ix。

Questions 34-36

解答

34. 利用细节信息“long ridges”和“hundreds of miles”以及顺序性原则定位于原文段落B倒数第二句话“linear dunes are longer than they are wide—in fact, some are more than 100 miles (about 160 kilometers) long”，原文中的“longer than they are wide”对应题目的“long ridges”，“more than 100 miles”对应题目的“hundreds of miles”，所以正确答案为Linear。

35. 利用细节信息"Bagnold"和"stop the sand from moving"以及顺序性原则定位于原文段落C的倒数第二句话"and an obstacle, which could be as small as a rock or as big as a tree, that causes the sand to lose momentum and settle"，这里的"causes the sand to lose momentum and settle"对应题目的"stop the sand from moving"，所以正确答案为obstacle。

36. 利用细节信息"Stéphane Douady"和"not a spiritual phenomenon"定位于原文段落F的最后一句话"...believe they can now explain the exact mechanism behind this acoustic phenomenon"，所以正确答案为acoustic。

Questions 37-40

解答

37. 利用细节信息"linear dune"和"crescentic dune"定位于原文段落B第三句话"He recognised two basic dune types, the crescentic dune, which he called 'barchan', and the linear dune"，很明显原文提到crescentic dune也被叫做barchan，所以正确答案为barchan。

38. 利用细节信息"produce singing sand in lab"和"similar"定位于原文段落G第三句话"To make the booming sound, the grains have to be of a small range of sizes, all alike in shape: well-rounded"，原文这里的"all alike"就对应题目的"similar"，所以正确答案为shape。

39. 利用细节信息"size of the sand"和顺序性原则定位于原文段落G中间"Douady's key discovery was that this synchronised frequency—which determines the tone of sound—is the result of the grain size"，这里的"grain size"就对应题目的"size of the sand"，原文这里明显就说到沙砾的大小会影响"the tone of sound"，所以正确答案为tone。

40. 利用细节信息"varnish"定位于段落G倒数第四句话"...the singing grains had some kind of varnish or a smooth coating of various minerals..."，原文这里明显提到"varnish"是由不同的矿物质（minerals）所组成的，所以正确答案为minerals。

参考译文

充满生机的沙丘

当你想到一个沙丘时，你大脑中可能浮现出一堆贫瘠没有生命的沙子。但事实上沙丘却是活跃的天然形成物。它们能生长、变化和移动。它们也充斥着各种生命。有些沙丘甚至还能歌唱。

A 尽管不过是一堆被风吹到一起的沙子，沙丘却能淹没树木和建筑，无情地穿越公路，

吞噬道路上的车辆，并且威胁非洲、中东和中国的农作物及工厂。在某些地区，致命沙丘甚至淹没并吞噬城市。整个村庄消失在沙子下面。在一些案例中，政府为那些无家可归者建造新的村落，不过数年后又发现那些新的村落也被沙漠埋葬。阻止沙丘吞没城市和农业地区已经成为联合国环境保护项目的首要任务和目标。

B 一些关于沙漠运动最重要的实验和测量是由一位二战前在埃及工作的叫做拉尔夫·拜格诺的英国工程师进行的。拜格诺研究了沙砾在大气中运动和被风堆积的物理特性。他确认了两种最基本的沙丘类型，新月形沙丘，他也把它叫做 barchan 沙丘，以及线状沙丘，他也把它叫做纵向沙丘或 sief 沙丘（在阿拉伯语中 sief 是刀剑的意思）。新月形沙丘是最常见的沙丘类型。正如它的名字所示，这种沙丘形如弯月，两头尖尖，而且通常更宽。有些类型的新月形沙丘在沙漠表面可以比其他任何一种沙丘移动更快。线状沙丘则要比新月形沙丘更直,它的沙脊是它最大的特征。与新月形沙丘不同，线状沙丘更长——事实上，有些甚至超过 100 英里（大约 160 公里）长。沙丘还可以由很多不同的更小的沙丘组成，这也叫做复合型沙丘。

C 尽管沙丘的形成具有复杂的机制，但拜格诺注意到沙丘一般需要三个因素才能成型：在一块没有什么植被区域的一大堆松散的沙子——通常在海边或者干涸的河流、湖泊或海床上；能够移动这些沙砾的风；还需要一个小至石块大至树木的能够阻挡沙子，使其停止运动的障碍物。当这三个变量都满足时，一个沙丘就可以形成了。

D 当风把沙子吹起来时，沙子就开始移动，不过一般也只是离开地面一到两英寸，直到一个障碍物使其停下来。最重的沙砾就靠着障碍物沉积下来，于是一个小的沙脊或沙包就形成了。轻一点的沙子则落在障碍物的另一侧。风继续把沙子吹到这堆沙子的顶部，直到沙堆太陡峭，于是在自己的重力作用下塌了下来。塌下来的沙子就沉积下来，直到整个沙堆的坡度刚刚好可以使得这个沙丘稳定下来。沙子不停重复地由向风面一寸一寸攀上丘顶，又沿着沙丘滑面滑下来的过程使得整个沙丘可以往前沿着风吹的方向移动。

E 根据风速和风向以及当地沙砾的重量，沙丘也会变成很多不同的形状和大小。越强的风越容易产生较高的沙丘；越平缓的风越容易使沙丘更展开。如果数年来风向总保持一致，沙丘也就会朝那个方向前进。但是沙丘是“一个奇特且充满活力的产物”，法鲁克·埃尔·巴兹在《国家地理》杂志中如是写道。一旦沙丘形成，它就会生长、改变形状、随风迁徙，甚至还会诞生新的沙丘。其中一些沙丘“宝宝们”被“母亲”背负在背上。另一些则一出生就顺风而下，跑到“父母亲”的前面。

F 沙丘甚至会“歌唱”，人们在全球超过 30 个地方都可以听到它们的“歌声”，而且每个地方的“歌声”都有自己独特的频率或音调。13 世纪时，当探险家马可·波罗在接触到如此奇怪却又神奇的来自沙漠沙丘的声音时，他把这个现象归结于鬼神。这

声音不像是来自于这个世界。这音量也使人胆怯。人耳也很难辨别声音的源头，这更增加了其异次元特色。法国国家研究机构CNRS（法国国家科学研究中心）的史蒂芬·道阿地及其同事在深入研究了摩洛哥、智利、中国及阿曼的沙丘之后相信，他们现在已经可以解释这个声音现象背后的确切物理机制了。

G 该研究小组带了一些沙子回到实验室，把它们放到一些带有自动推板的槽里。这些沙子仍然发出了声音，这也就证明了沙丘本身并不像某些专家所认为的是产生声音的必要共振体。要产生这样的声音，沙砾的大小必须是在一个很小的范围之内，形状也必须相似：圆形。道阿地的核心发现就是这种同步的频率——能决定声音的音调——是由沙砾的大小决定的。沙砾越大，音调就越低。他通过仅仅测量沙砾的大小就成功地预测摩洛哥、智利和美国沙丘所发出的音调。道阿地还发现了这些能歌唱的沙砾有一种特定的由不同矿物质（硅、铁和锰）组成的光泽面或覆盖层，这可能是沙丘曾经在远古海洋下所形成的覆盖层。但是在那些失去声音的沙子上，这样的覆盖层已经被磨损掉了，这也解释了为什么有些沙丘可以歌唱，而有些不可以。但是他承认他不清楚这样的覆盖层在沙子产生声音的过程中起着什么作用。这些神秘的沙丘仿佛不愿意向人类揭示自己所有的奥秘啊。

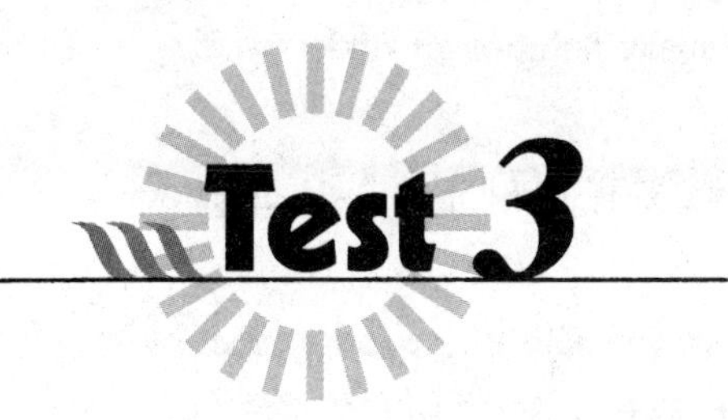

Reading Passage 1. Classifying Societies

词汇详解

classify *v.* 分类；把……列为密件（class 除了大家熟悉的“班级”的意思外，还有“等级，种类”的意思。例如，在生物学中，class 就指“纲”。所以 classify 就有“分门别类”的意思。在雅思阅读中还有一种分类题，题目中就有“Classify the following information as referring to”这样的要求。此外，如果文件比较机密，需要单独分类，那么就会归入机密级别“classified”。）

establish *v.* 建立，创建（该词是由前缀 e“进入”、词根 stable“稳定”以及后缀 ish 组成。）

sociology *n.* 社会学（词根 socio 代表“社会”，ology 代表“学科”。）

anthropology *n.* 人类学（词根 anthropo 代表“人类”，ology 代表“学科”。研究人类学的人经常说 anthropology 是覆盖面最广的学科“has the widest coverage”，因为只要是和人类相关的内容，没有人类学家不研究的。该学科也有诸多分支“branches”，例如：physical anthropology 主要研究人体；anatomy 也就是研究人体解剖；cultural anthropology 主要研究人类文化；social anthropology 主要研究人类社会等。）

unequal *adj.* 不平等的；不相称的

prestige *n.* 威望，声望

complex *adj.* 复杂的，合成的 *n.* 综合体（同义词有 complicated、intricate、involved 和 knotty，但是这些词汇各有侧重。complex 指复杂的不可避免“unavoidable result of a necessary combining”，但这并不意味失败“does not imply a fault or failure”，例如：a complex recipe。complicated 则强调问题理解、解决或解释上的困难“great difficulty in understanding, solving, or explaining”，例如：complicated legal procedures。intricate 则指不同部分之间互相交错到几乎无法分别掌握的地步“different parts are interlaces as to make it nearly impossible to follow or grasp them separately”，例如：an intricate web of deceit。involved 通常指极端的复杂且经常杂乱无章“extreme complication and often disorder”，例

如：a rambling, involved explanation。knotty 则指复杂和杂乱的情况使得问题解决或理解近乎不可能“suggests complication and entanglement that make solution or understanding improbable”，例如：knotty ethical questions。）

clan *n.* 宗族；氏族；大家族；宗派（在家族、氏族中通常有着祖先崇拜“ancestor worship”，那些早期祖先的物件也通常被神化“deify”。）

tribe *n.* 部落，部族（中文成语“一丘之貉”的英文就翻译成“jackals of the same tribe”。）

chiefdom *n.* 首领的地位，首领的权威；酋邦（该词来自 chief“酋长”。英文中有句俗是“too many chiefs and not enough Indians”，意思就是说“大家都争着做领导，而没有人愿意做小兵”。）

state *n.* 国家；州；状况，情况 *v.* 规定；陈述，声明（state 表示“国家”时，和 country 以及 nation 的侧重点完全不同。country 强调的是土地及土地上的一切，包括山川河流、丰富的物产以及生活在这里的人民，但不包括政府。例如：I love my country, but I hate the government。nation 则强调的是具有共同祖先、文化、语言的一群人。而 state 则主要指政治体制、政府，例如：police state、nation-state、city-state 等。police state 中文翻译过来就是“警察国家”，通俗地讲就是用警察或秘密警察来维持国家秩序和统治，通常制造白色恐怖，实施暴政，粗暴地干涉人们生活的社会，是一个贬义词。nation-state 指的是“单一民族国家”，有一个相对单一的民族自己统治自己。city-state 就是“由一个城市建立的国家”，自己管理自己，尤其是古希腊的城邦。当然，今天也有一些这样的国家，例如新加坡“Singapore”、迪拜“Dubai”等。在口语中，人们也简单地把美国称为“The States”。）

scale *n.* 规模；比例；级别；鱼鳞 *v.* 测量；刮……鳞片（在口语里关于 scale 的表达有很多，例如：scale up 和 scale down，分别指“使变大”和“使变小”。off the scale 则指“超出正常标准”，可以是好事，也可以是坏事。例如：China was just off the scale, hard to get your head round. 中国超出了我的想象，让人难以形容。Indeed, sovereign debt levels remain off the scale and unemployment continues to inch upward across the board. 实际上，主权债务水平依然高得离谱，失业率也在继续小幅攀升。）

seasonal *adj.* 季节的，季节性的；周期性的

exploit *v.* 开采，开发；利用；剥削（exploit 表示“利用”时相当于 utilise，是一个中性词，例如：exploit one's talents。但是作为“剥削”使用时则是一个彻头彻尾的贬义词。）

undomesticated *adj.* 未驯服的，未驯化的（来自形容词 domestic，而 domestic 又来自于拉丁语的 domus，是“房子”的意思，所以 domestic 的意思就是“家里的，家庭的”，进一步延伸为“内部的”。例如：domestic cat 家猫。domesticate 的意思就是“使成为家庭的一部分”，主要指“驯化动物或植物”。）

kinsfolk *n.* 亲属，亲戚，亲人（相当于 relative，同义词还有 blood、clan、kin、family、lineage 等。）

descent *n.* 下降；血统；斜坡（该词来自 descend，其中前缀 de 代表"减少，移除"，词根 scend 代表"攀爬 climb"，所以 descend 的字面意思很明显，就是"下降"。与该词根相关的词汇还有：ascend 上升；transcend 超越；condescend 屈尊等。）
disparity *n.* 不同；不等；不一致（来自形容词 disparate"完全不同的"。）
mobile *adj.* 移动的；流动的；易变的（手机就是 mobile phone，中国移动就叫做 China Mobile。作形容词表示"移动的"的意思时，相当于 movable、portable。该词还可以表示"易变的"，例如：mobile face"多变的脸"。）
consist *v.* 由……组成；存在于（该词作为"组成，构成"时，经常用在 consist of 这样的词组中，而且是主动语气，例如：The search engine mainly consists of three parts. 搜索引擎主要是由三个部分组成。consist 表示"存在于"时，等同于 lie in，例如：Liberty consists in the absence of obstructions. 自由在于没有阻碍。）
camp *n.* 营地；阵营；兵营 *v.* 宿营，露营（camping 就是"露营活动"了，campsite 是"露营地"，camp fire 就是营地的"篝火"。camp 作为"阵营"时有这样一个说法：have a foot in both camps，相当于中文的"脚踏两条船，两面讨好"。）
latter *adj.* 后者的；较后的（the latter 是"后者"，the former 就是"前者"。在英语中这样的指代很多，考生一定要弄清楚这些指代分别指的是什么。）
butchery *n.* 屠场；肉贩（来自名词 butcher"屠夫"。其实 butcher 也可以作动词使用，意思是"屠宰，屠杀"。英语中有一个习语叫做"as fit as a butcher's dog"，就是形容某人"极其健康"。）
mammal *n.* 哺乳动物（来自于拉丁语 mamma，意思是"乳房"。）
insubstantial *adj.* 无实体的，无实质的，非实在的（该词是由否定前缀 in 和 substantial 构成的。substantial 的意思是"大量的，牢固的，实质的"。人们常说的"巨大进步"，英文中就叫做"substantial improvement"。）
dwelling *n.* 住处，处所，寓所（来自动词 dwell"居住，住"。住在象牙塔里，人们就常说成"dwell in an ivory tower"。）
temporary *adj.* 临时的，暂时的（词根 tempor 来自于拉丁语 tempus，意思就是"时间"。）
debris *n.* 碎片，残骸
residential *adj.* 住宅的，适于作住宅的；与居住有关的
subsistence *n.* 存活，生存；生计（来自动词 subsist"维持生活，生存下去"，中文中"靠……生存下去"的英文表达就是"subsist on something"，例如：We can barely subsist on this amount of money. We need more! 我们仅靠着这一点点钱维持生计。我们需要更多！）
cultivate *v.* 耕作，种植；栽培（该词词根 cult 来自于拉丁语单词 cultus，意思是"培育"。考生熟悉的 culture 也来自于这个单词，culture 除了"文化"的意思外，还有"种植，培育"的意思，例如：aquaculture 水产养殖；aviculture 鸟类养殖；apiculture 蜜蜂养殖；horticulture 园艺；floriculture 养花等，在生物学上甚至还可以指微生物的"培养液，培养基"。）

nomadic *adj.* 游牧的；流浪的（nomad是名词，意思是“游牧的人”。所谓游牧就是没有固定居所，哪里能生存就往哪里去，或者漫无目的地游荡“roam aimlessly”。早期人类过的就是一种游牧生活，到处搜寻食物“forage”和狩猎“hunt”，后来人类学会了驯化植物和动物“domesticate plants and animals”，这时农业和畜牧业诞生了，人们便settle下来了。）
intensive *adj.* 加强的；密集的
livestock *n.* 家畜，牲畜
integrate *v.* 使一体化，使整合，合并（该词来自于拉丁语单词integer，就是“whole, entire的意思”。）
kinship *n.* 亲属关系（来自名词kin，意思就是“亲戚”。在英语中有这样的一些表达：kith and kin，意思是“朋友和亲人”，kith是较老的对朋友的称呼。one's next of kin指的是“某人最直系、最亲近的亲戚”，或者叫做“近亲”。）
pattern *n.* 模式；花样，图案；榜样，典范 *v.* 模仿；形成图案（pattern something after something指的是“仿照……的样子建造，仿制”。）
homestead *n.* 宅地；田产（指的是“房子和相连的土地”，通常是祖辈上留下来的。）
isolate *v.* 使隔离，使孤立
permanent *adj.* 永久的，永恒的，不变的 *n.* 烫发（同义词有：ceaseless、dateless、deathless、endless、eternal、immortal、everlasting、perpetual等。permanent作“烫发”时常用简写形式“perm”，例如：She got her hair permed at the salon.）
cluster *n.* 丛；簇；群 *v.* 丛生；群聚（英语中“cluster around...”和“cluster together”是常见的固定搭配，分别指“簇拥在……的周围”和“簇拥在一起”，相当于“bunch around...”和“bunch together”。）
pueblo *n.* 印第安人村庄
ranking *n.* 社会地位；顺序（国外学校或大学的排名就叫做“school/university ranking”。英国大学最权威的排名每年由*The Sunday Times*发布在http://www.thesundaytimes.co.uk/sto/University_Guide/。而美国大学最权威的排名由*US News & World Report*发布在http://www.usnews.com/rankings。）
lineage *n.* 血统，世系
ancestor *n.* 祖先，祖宗（来自动词antecede“先前，先行”，其中前缀ante代表“在……之前”，cede代表“行走”，所以该词字面意思就是“走在前面”；antecessor就是“前任者，前辈”。中文有一种说法叫做“光宗耀祖”，英文就可以翻译成“to bring honor to one's ancestors”。）
hence *adv.* 因此；从此
stratification *n.* 层化；分层（来自名词stratum“岩层，社会阶层”。值得一提的是stratum的复数形式是strata。stratify就是“使分层”，stratification就是stratify的名词形式。

该词近义词有 caste、order、class 等。）

specialisation *n.* 特别化；专门化

craft *n.* 技术，手艺，技艺；狡诈 *v.* 手工制作；精巧地制作

surplus *adj.* 过剩的；多余的；*n.* 剩余额；顺差；盈余（该词由 super 和 plus 组合而成，其意不言自明了。同义词有：overflow、overplus、plethora、redundancy、superfluity、excess、surfeit 等。）

foodstuff *n.* 食物，食品，粮食

periodical *n.* 期刊；杂志 *adj.* 周期的，定期的（period 本身的意思就是"周期"，所以 periodical 就有"周期的，定期的"意思。periodical 作为"期刊"的意思也很常用。期刊的类别有很多，有学术研究期刊"scholarly and research journals"，还有行业期刊"professional, trade and industry journals"，最后还有大众杂志"popular magazines"与报纸"newspapers"。如果考生关注雅思考试的文章来源，就会发现有相当一部分的 A 类阅读文章来自于 *New Scientist* 杂志，建议考生将其作为泛读材料使用。）

obligation *n.* 义务，责任（来自动词 oblige"强制，强迫"。英语中有很多关于 oblige 的表达，例如：oblige someone to do something 就是"要求某人做某事"。）

maintain *v.* 保持，维持；抚养，赡养（该词由 manu 和 tain 构成，其中 manu 代表"手"，tain 代表"持有"。汽车的维修和保养就叫做"maintenance"。）

retainer *n.* 家臣，侍从（来自动词 retain"持有，保留"。由词根 tain 组成的词汇还有：sustain 维持，支撑；attain 获得，获取；contain 包含；detain 拘留等。）

redistribution *n.* 重新分配

vary *v.* 变化；不同（该词在图表作文中用处颇大，词组"vary between…and …"就可以代表"两者之间的波动"，例如：The daytime temperatures vary between 80 and 90 degrees. 日间气温在 80 度与 90 度之间波动。）

feature *n.* 特征，特点；容貌，面貌；故事片 *v.* 以……为特色；由……主演（电影海报或介绍中经常会出现这个词，这里的 feature 就是"……做主演"。产品介绍和广告中也经常会出现"features…"，这里就是说该产品有什么特色。）

explicit *adj.* 明确的；详述的；不隐瞒的（该词来自动词 explicate"解释，说明"。它的反义词是 implicit"含蓄的"。implicit 来自动词 implicate"牵涉，涉及"。）

enforce *v.* 强迫人服从；实施，执行；加强（该词字面意思很清楚，en"进入"，force"力"，所以 enforce 就是"执行，实施"的意思了。那些执法队伍、公安、城管之类的都是"law enforcers"；说某人是执法工作人员，就可以说他"work in the law enforcement"。）

distinguish *v.* 区分，辨别；引人注目（在重要的场合中，尊敬的来宾的英文表达就是"distinguished guests"。作"区分"时，表达区别 A 与 B，人们常用词组"distinguish A from B"和"distinguish between A and B"。）

tenant *n.* 房客；佃户（英语中有一句俗语叫做“An empty house is better than a bad tenant.”字面意思就是“空房子比坏房客强”。）

bureaucratic *adj.* 官僚的，官僚主义的（来自名词 bureau“局，办事处”。该词最初指的是一种“写字台，办公桌”，可能早期在欧洲只有政府才有这样的桌子，所以后来就用来指政府的局或机关了。美国的 FBI 就是“Federal Bureau of Investigation 联邦调查局”，中国的公安局叫做“The Bureau of Public Security”。）

principal *adj.* 最重要的；主要的 *n.* 首长；校长；主要演员，主角（该词作为“主要的，首要的”时，同义词有很多，例如：arch、capital、cardinal、central、chief、dominant、key、leading、primal、primary、paramount 等。principal 作为“校长”时，通常指的是中小学的校长，大学校长一般叫做“president”。）

revenue *n.* 岁入，税收，收入

toll *n.* 通行费；长途电话费；钟声 *v.* 鸣钟（高速公路不收费就是“toll free”，收费公路就是“toll roads”，进出高速公路都有 toll gate“收费站”，toll booth 里会有人发卡和收费。toll-free telephone number 是“免费电话”。当 toll 作为“鸣钟”时，常搭配的说法是“death toll”，指的是“死亡人数”，例如：The estimated death toll could eventually reach 240. 当局估计遇难人数最终可能达 240 人。）

typology *n.* 类型学；象征主义，象征论（该词是由 type 和 ology 构成，所以字面意思就是“不同类型的学问”了。另外一个单词 topography“地形学”与其长相相似，但是也很好区分，因为它是由 top 加上表示“绘画、书写”的 graphy 组成，所以字面意思就是“绘制表面的样子”，再进一步延伸就是“地形学”了。）

elaborate *v.* 详细制定；详尽阐述 *adj.* 复杂的；精心制作的（该词是由表示“出去”的前缀 e 加上词根 labor 构成，所以该词字面意思就是“制作”。对某事物进行详尽解释通常用“elaborate on something”的表达。）

framework *n.* 构架，框架；结构

题目详解

Questions 1-7

解答

1. 利用细节信息“clan”和“economic difference”定位于原文 Clan 部分的第一个分段落的最后一句话“there are no marked economic differences or disparities in status among their members”。原文在这里清楚地提及氏族成员间不存在明显的经济差异或地位的不同。题目信息与原文信息一致，所以正确答案为 True。
2. 利用细节信息“farmers of a tribe”和所种植的“plants”定位于原文 Tribe 部分的第一

个分段落。虽然这里提及部落的食物主要来源于耕种的作物和驯化的牲畜（their diet or subsistence is based largely on cultivated plants and domesticated animals），但是并未提及农民种植的作物种类或者是否种植了各种不同的作物。题目信息在原文信息的基础上无法判断，所以正确答案为 Not Given。

3. 利用细节信息"settlement"和"tribe"以及顺序性原则定位于原文 Tribe 部分的第二个分段落的第二句话"Characteristically, no one settlement dominates any of the others in the region"。原文明显提及没有任何一种定居形式比其他定居形式更重要，而题目却说有一种定居形式比其他任何形式都重要。题目信息与原文信息明显相反，所以正确答案为 False。
4. 利用细节信息"chiefdom"和"status"定位于原文 Chiefdom 部分的第一个分段落的第三句话"Prestige and rank are determined by how closely related one is to the chief…"。这里原文明显提及地位（原文的"rank"对应题目的"status"）是由个人与酋长（chief）的亲近程度或关系所决定的，而题目却说是由成员所拥有的土地数量决定的（how much land he owns）。题目信息与原文信息不相符，所以正确答案为 False。
5. 利用细节信息"chiefdom"和"craft goods"以及顺序性原则定位于原文 Chiefdom 部分的第二个分段落的第一句话"Often, there is local specialisation in craft products…"。原文的"local specialisation"就是指专门生产"craft products"的职业或人员。题目信息与原文信息一致，所以正确答案为 True。
6. 利用细节信息"king"、"state"和"army"定位于原文 Early State 部分的第一个分段落的第一句话"the ruler (perhaps a king or sometimes a queen) has explicit authority to establish laws and also to enforce them by the use of a standing army"。这里的"establish laws"以及"enforce them"对应题目中的"keeps the order"，而且都是通过利用"army"来实现。题目信息与原文信息一致，所以正确答案为 True。
7. 利用细节信息"Bureaucratic officers"和"salaries"以及顺序性原则定位于原文 Early State 部分的第一个分段落，但是这里并没有提及"Bureaucratic officers"的收入情况，而只是提到"The central capital houses a bureaucratic administration of officials; one of their principal purposes is to collect revenue..."，也就是他们的职能。题目信息在原文信息的基础上无法判断，所以正确答案为 Not Given。

Questions 8-13

解答

8. 利用细节信息"clan"和"work sites"定位于原文 Clan 部分的第二个分段落的第二句话"…work sites, where tools are made or other specific activities carried out"。原文这里明显提到在"clan work sites"中制作的东西是 tools，所以正确答案是 tools。

9. 利用细节信息“tribes”和“settled farming”定位于原文 Tribe 部分的第一个分段落的第二句话“Typically, they are settled farmers, but they may be nomadic with a very different, mobile economy…”。原文这里提到部落中最典型的生活方式是固定的农耕，除此以外也可以是游牧的（nomadic）的生活，所以正确答案为 nomadic。

10. 利用细节信息“Çatalhöyük”和顺序性原则定位于原文 Tribe 部分的第二个分段落的最后一句话“Or they may be clusters of buildings grouped together, for example…the early farming village or small town of Çatalhöyük in modern Turkey”。原文这里明显提及 Çatalhöyük 的房子是“grouped together”，所以正确答案为 grouped/grouped together。

11. 利用细节信息“chief”和“crafted goods”定位于原文 Chiefdom 部分的第二个分段落的前两句话“Often, there is local specialisation in craft products, and surpluses of these and of foodstuffs are periodically paid as obligation to the chief. He uses these to maintain his retainers, and may use them for redistribution to his subjects”。原文这里明显提及多余的（surpluses）“craft products”和“foodstuffs”被定期地进贡给酋长，而酋长可能再把这些东西分发给自己的臣民（use them for redistribution to his subjects），所以正确答案为 foodstuffs。

12. 利用细节信息“population”和顺序性原则定位于原文 Chiefdom 部分的第二个分段落的最后一句话“Chiefdoms vary greatly in size, but the range is generally between about 5000 and 20,000 persons”。原文提及人口规模在 5000 到 20,000 之间，所以正确答案为 20,000。

13. 利用细节信息“early state”和“farmers”定位于原文 Early State 部分的第一个分段落的第三句话“Agricultural workers and the poorer urban dwellers form the lowest classes, with the craft specialists above…”。原文这里很明显地可以看出，农民和贫困的市民构成最低阶层，在他们上面的是“craft specialists”，所以正确答案为 craft specialists。

参考译文

社会分类

尽管人类在历史的不同时期建立了多种不同类型的社会，但社会学家和人类学家仍倾向于按照社会中不同群组可以接触到诸如资源、地位或权力的不同程度把不同的社会划分为四种基本类型。从最简单到最复杂依次为氏族、部落、酋邦和邦国。

氏族

氏族是由狩猎者和采集者组成的小规模社会，通常不超过百人，他们通过季节性的迁徙来开发和利用野生（未经驯化的）食物资源。大多数目前尚存的采猎者族群都是这种社会形式，例如坦桑尼亚的哈扎族或非洲南部的桑族。氏族的成员通常是通过血缘或婚姻联系在一起的亲属族人。这些氏族缺乏正式的领导，所以在氏族成员间也就没有明显的经济差异或地位的不同。

由于氏族是由迁徙的采猎者组成的，他们的活动场所就主要有季节性驻扎的营地和其他小一点但有特殊作用的地方。后者包括猎杀或屠杀大型哺乳动物的猎杀场或屠宰场以及制作工具或进行其他特定活动的工作场地。这样一个族群的（活动）大本营及其居住的遗迹也许能够证明他们没有真正意义上的居所或只有临时居所。

部落

部落一般要比采猎者的群体大，但是也不过几千人，他们的食物主要来自于种植的农作物和驯化的家畜。他们通常是典型的定居下来的农民，但是他们也可能过着一种非常不同的基于牲畜密集利用的移动经济式的游牧生活。部落通常是多群体社会，由不同的单一群体通过血缘关系融入到一个更大的社会中去。尽管有些部落存在官员，甚至“首都”或政府所在地，但这些官员缺乏有效地运用权力的经济基础。

部落最典型的定居方式是固定的农业庄园或村落。比较有特点的是，在特定的区域内，没有任何一个定居形式超过其他定居形式而占据主要地位。相反，考古学家发现，要么是单独的永久定居式庄园，要么是永久定居式村落。其中，这些村落可能是由一些独立的房子组成，例如欧洲多瑙河流域的最早期的农庄；或者它们可能是由集群的房子构成，例如美国西南部的印第安人村落和当今土耳其 Çatalhöyük 的早期农业村庄或小镇。

酋邦

这种社会形式依靠等级顺序（即人与人之间的不同社会地位）的原则运转。不同的家族（家族是一群声称有着共同祖先的人）按照声望来划分等级，并且地位高的家族和该社会整体都是由一个酋长所统治。声望和等级地位都是由个人与酋长的远近关系所决定，而且并不存在真正的阶级分化。酋长的角色至关重要。

通常，酋邦社会中有自己专门的工艺品的制造与生产链，剩余的工艺制品和食物会被定期地进贡给酋长。酋长则利用这些贡品来维持自己的家臣，而且也可能将它们重新分配给自己的臣民。酋邦通常有一个包含了庙宇、酋长及其家臣和工艺品工匠住宅的权力中心。酋邦的规模各不相同，但是通常在五千到两万人之间。

雏形邦国

这种社会形式保留了许多酋邦的特征，但是其统治者（可能是一个国王或者有时候是一个女王）拥有明确的权力来制定律法，并通过一支常规军队来实施它们。社会不再完全依靠血缘关系来维持：社会已经分化成不同的阶层。农民和更贫穷的市民构成了最低阶层，工艺品工匠高一个等级，祭司和统治者的家族则更高一等。统治者的职能和祭司的职能通常是区分开来的：宫殿与庙宇也有所不同。社会被看成是一个被统治者家族所拥有的领土，而在这片领土上，居住着有义务缴纳赋税的子民。中央首都拥有一个由官员组成的官僚行政机构；他们存在的主要目的之一就是收取收益（通常以赋税或捐税的形式出现），然后分配给政府、军队和工艺品工匠。许多早期的邦国构建了复杂的分配体系来维系这些必要的服务。

这个由埃尔曼·塞维斯提出，并由威廉·桑德斯和约瑟夫·马里诺详尽阐述的简单社会分类法有可以批判的地方，而且它不应该被轻率地使用。然而，如果我们企图研究早期社会，我们必须使用其相关的术语和概念。塞维斯的分类为我们提供了良好的能帮助我们组织思想的框架。

Reading Passage 2. Tasmanian Tiger

词汇详解

stripe *n.* 条纹，线条（美国国旗星条旗就叫做“the Stars and Stripes”，其中13条红白相间的条纹“red stripes alternating with white”代表最初独立的13个州，左上角的50颗星则代表目前美国的50个州。）

carnivorous *adj.* 食肉的（该词由carn“肉”和vorous“吃”构成。类似的词汇还有：herbivorous食草的；omnivorous杂食的。）

marsupial *n.* 有袋类动物 *adj.* 有袋的，袋状的（澳大利亚有各种各样的有袋类动物，著名的如：袋鼠kangaroo；考拉koala bear；树懒sloth；袋熊wombat；负鼠possum；小袋鼠wallaby；袋狸bandicoot等。）

fame *n.* 名声，名望（大多数考生所熟悉的famous就是fame的形容词形式。英语中有几个关于fame的说法，例如：house of ill fame指的是“妓院brothel”，这是委婉语“euphemism”，rise to fame指的是“变得出名，成名”，等同于become famous。）

fabled *adj.* 传说中的，虚构的（名词形式是fable，即“寓言”的意思，例如著名的《伊索寓言》*Aesop's Fables*。）

thylacine *n.* 袋狼（有袋类动物之一，现已绝迹。）

extinct *adj.* 灭绝的，绝种的；消逝的，破灭的（该词其实与动词extinguish“熄灭”同源，所以extinct就有了“灭绝的”意思。同义词有：bygone、dead、expired、nonextant、vanished；反义词有：alive、extant、existent、living。其实物种灭绝“species extinction”和新物种的出现“appearance/emergence of new species”是自然规律，正所谓物竞天择，适者生存。）

fossil *n.* 化石；老顽固，食古不化的人（fossil是研究生物进化理论的绝佳工具，但是进化论者却往往很难拿出强有力的证据证明人是猿猴进化而来的，因为中间缺少一个由猿进化至人的中间阶段的化石，这被称为the missing link，所以北京猿人头盖骨的发现具有重要意义，因为相当一部分生物学家和地质学家认为北京猿人就是the missing link，然而北京猿人头盖骨化石却在抗日战争期间不知去向，成为了一个谜。）

dig *v.* 挖掘；发掘；探究 *n.* 轻碰，轻戳，轻推；挖苦，讽刺（该词意思丰富，其中“挖，挖掘”是最常用的意思，例如：dig site就是“挖掘地”，dig a well就是“挖一个井”。值得一提的是，在口语里，dig经常代表“喜欢”的意思，如果一个人说他或她dig something，意思就是说他或她很喜欢这个事物。还有在吃饭的时候，主人说：“大家动筷子吧，大家开吃吧”，英语就是“let's dig in”，或者“dig in”。英语中还有很多关于dig的习语，例如：dig one's heels in中文对应的翻译就是“站稳脚跟”，其实就是说不动摇自己的观点或行动，还有dig one's own grave的中文翻译很明显，就是“自掘坟墓”。dig some dirt up on someone说的是“挖出某人不光彩的事情”，例如：The citizens' group dug up some dirt on the mayor and used it against her at election time.）

dingo *n.* 澳洲野犬（coyote和hyena同是野狗，看来老外对于狗真的是很有爱。）

captivity *n.* 被俘；囚禁（来自形容词captive“被俘的，被囚禁的”。当人们说“...is in captivity”就是说“……被关起来了”。同义词有：confinement、impoundment、imprisonment、incarceration等。）

unsubstantiated *adj.* 未经证实的，没有事实根据的

migratory *adj.* 迁移的，有迁居习惯的；流浪的（来自动词migrate“迁移，移居”。从一个地方移居到另外一个地方就是“to migrate from one place to another place”。“migratory bird”就是“候鸟”。如果该词再加上表示“进入”的前缀“im/in”或表示“离开”的前缀“ex”的话就变成了immigrate“移民进入”和emigrate“移民离开”。）

intermittent *adj.* 间歇的，断断续续的（来自动词intermit“使中断”。其中inter代表“两者之间”，mit是词根，代表“派出”。中间的东西出去了，不在了，于是就变成“中断”了。）

spotlight *n.* 聚光灯 *v.* 用聚光灯照；使注意，使突出或醒目（字面意思就是“照到一点上的光线”，这种光很亮，因为光线全部聚集在一起，舞台上常用这种灯光。英文中有种说法叫做put something in the spotlight，意思就是“聚焦，使人们关注该事物”。）

beam *n.* 梁；束；光线 *v.* 照射，射出光或热；笑容满面（著名美国科幻电视*Star Trek*《星际迷航》中的transporter“传送器”可以把企业号“Enterprise”的队员直接传送到一个地方，Captain Kirk经常说“Scotty, beam me down”。在《星际迷航》的宇宙中，transporter把人能量化后，再用光的形式传送来传送去，所以用的是beam。美国还有一个俚语性的表达“steam one's beam”，意思就是“使某人生气”。）

grab *v.* 抓住，夺得；取，拿；抢占，捞取；引人注意（到国外念书，学生可能会常常听到这样的表达“grab a bite”，其实意思就是“to get something to eat”，只不过大家这样讲更加有动作感，有气势罢了。类似的表达还有grab one's attention吸引某人的注意力；grab a chair弄个椅子坐下。英语中还有“up for grabs”，意思是“有什么东西或事物，你

可以去拿”，基本上等同于“for yours to take”，当然还有另外一个意思，既然谁想拿就能拿，那就是一片混乱“total chaos”，例如：This is a madhouse. The whole place is up for grabs.）

register *n.* 登记，注册；记录；登记簿；记录器 *v.* 登记，注册；记录；表达出，流露出

shepherd *n.* 牧羊人，羊倌 *v.* 带领，引导；护送（该词更多指普通的放羊人，基督教会里的“牧师”更多用“pastor”这个词。其实牧师是一个很好的职业，在美国的诸多职业学院中，神学院“divinity school”，又称“theological school”或“seminary”，独树一帜，因为牧师受人尊敬，而且收入也不差，所以神学院是绝对没有奖学金的，除了那些需要被派到边远地区传教的传教学“missiology”专业。而那些传教的人就是传教士“missionary”了。中国近代科学史和传教士有着密不可分的联系，从远的利玛窦 Matteo Ricci、汤若望 Johann Adam Schall von Bell，到近的司徒雷登 John Leighton Stuart 都为中国的科学进步乃至国家进步做出过巨大贡献。）

sloping *adj.* 倾斜的；有坡度的（关于 slope 的习语有不少，例如“…is on a slipper slope”就指的是“什么事情会导致问题或状况，或者是走下坡路”。slope down 是指“递减”，slope up 就是“递增”，而且还有一定的阻力。）

hindquarter *n.* 后腿及臀部（伴随着生活水平的提高，人们对于猪、牛、羊肉的讲究也越来越多，不同的部位适宜不同的烹饪方法和菜品。一般人们常分的部位有：leg 腿肉；loin 腰肉；blade shoulder 肩肉；arm shoulder 前肢肉；hock 蹄肉；head 头肉；side/belly 腹肉；rib 肋肉 / 骨。）

undergrowth *n.* 下层灌木丛

scrub *v.* 擦洗，刷洗；取消（原有安排）*n.* 灌木丛，矮树丛；擦洗（常见表达“scrub off”就是“用力擦掉污渍”。作为“灌木丛”时等同于“shrub”。）

accompany *v.* 陪伴，陪同；伴随；为……伴奏（该词由表达强化的前缀 ad 与表示“同伴”的 company 组合而成，所以该词的意思不言自明。accompany someone on a journey 就是指“在旅途中陪伴某人”，而 accompany someone on a musical instrument 就是“为某人提供伴奏”。）

pandemonium *n.* 喧闹，大混乱（该词由代表“全，总，泛”的前缀 pan 和代表“邪灵”的 demon 组成。该词是著名英国诗人 John Milton 在长篇诗作《失乐园》*Lost Paradise* 中创造出来的，描述堕落天使路西法“Lucifer”变身撒旦“Satan”后在地狱里创造的国度。）

besiege *v.* 包围，围困（该词由表示“使成为”的前缀 be 和名词 siege“围攻，围困”组成，所以字面意思也颇为清晰。类似的构词很多，例如：belittle 轻视，小看；befool 蒙蔽；beguile 欺骗；benumb 使麻木；befriend 成为朋友等。）

comb *n.* 梳子；鸡冠 *v.* 梳理；搜寻（该词最为大家熟悉的意思就是“梳头发 comb one’s hair”了。除此以外，该词意思很丰富，例如在本文中的意思是“彻底搜查”。当表示“搜索”时，常用的词组是“comb through…”，例如：I combed through my belongings, looking for the lost papers. 我搜遍了我所有的东西，寻找那丢失的文件。）

lair *n.* 巢穴，窝；（人的）藏身处（希特勒二战时期在波兰东北部森林深处的指挥总部就叫做 The Wolf's Lair。）

stage *n.* 时期，阶段；舞台；步骤 *v.* 上演，演出；筹办，举行；使出现（雅思口语考试的三个阶段就叫做"3 stages"，第一阶段"Stage 1: Introduction and Interview"就是"简单的介绍和对话"，第二阶段"Stage 2: Personal Long Talk"就是"个人长谈"，即考生要就一个口语卡片问题回答一到两分钟的内容，第三阶段"Stage 3: Two-way Discussion"就是"考生和考官之间深入的讨论"。stage 当然也可以指"表演的舞台"，当某人表演拙劣时，观众们就会"boo him/her off the stage"，boo 就是大家齐声发出的嘲讽或嘘声。如果有什么东西、事物或人"take the stage"或者"take center stage"，就是说"该人或事物变成大家关注的核心或焦点"。）

mythology *n.* 神话学；神话；虚幻的想法；错误的观点（"希腊神话"就是"Greek mythology"，其中最著名的神话著作应该就是古希腊诗人 Hesiod 的 *Theogony*《神谱》，重点介绍了诸神的诞生和氏谱，也穿插了诸多神灵间正义及爱情的故事。）

academia *n.* 学术界，学术环境

conservationist *n.* 自然资源保护者，环保主义者

curator *n.* 馆长，负责人

thesis *n.* 论文；毕业论文；论题；命题（thesis 一般指"硕士毕业论文"。一般性的论文，不管是本科还是硕士研究生的，都叫做"paper"。"本科毕业论文"称为"graduation paper"，"博士毕业论文"为"dissertation"。值得一提的是 thesis 的复数变形是 theses。）

panther *n.* 豹，黑豹，美洲狮（关于大型猫科动物"big cat"或者"feline animal"，豹子是一个很独特的类别，品种繁多，各个大洲及地区都有自己独特的品种，对应单词也变化多样，若不是专家，估计很难真正弄清楚。考生若感兴趣，可以研究以下各豹子的差异：leopard、panther、cheetah、cougar、jaguar、puma、mountain lion、bobcat、lynx。）

inbreed *v.* 近亲繁殖，生育（breed 作动词时的意思就是"培育，生育，繁殖"，这里 in 的意思就是"内部，里面"。）

punt *n.* 赌博；打赌

notorious *adj.* 臭名昭著的，声名狼藉的（中文成语"臭名远扬"就可以直接翻译成"notorious for one's misdeeds"，或者说成"be notorious far and wide"。）

elusive *adj.* 难以捉摸的；不易记住的；难以理解的；逃避的；难以达到的（来自动词 elude"逃避，使达不到"。elude 是由代表"出去"的 e 和代表"玩耍，戏剧"的词根 lude 构成。由 lude 构成的单词还有：allude 暗指，间接提到；delude 迷惑，蛊惑；prelude 序幕，前奏；ludicrous 可笑的，滑稽的等。）

coelacanth *n.* 腔棘鱼（人类常食用的鱼类很多，有淡水鱼"fresh water fish"和海鱼"sea/ocean fish"。淡水鱼中最大的品种就是目前对美国河湖生态造成巨大危害的 carp"鲤科"，其中有：鲤鱼 carp；鲢鱼 silver carp；草鱼 grass carp；青鱼 black carp。淡水鱼中还有一

个很大的品种，就是 catfish“鲶鱼”。其他的还有：鳟鱼 trout；鲈鱼 bass；桂鱼 mandarin fish；鲟鱼 sturgeon。鲟鱼全身上下所有的鱼骨“fish bones”都是可食用的“edible”，因为这些鱼骨全是软骨“soft bone/gristle”。海鱼的品种更多，最为大家所熟悉的有：鲑鱼/三文鱼 salmon；金枪鱼 tuna；沙丁鱼 sardine；鲱鱼 herring；鳗鱼 eel 等。）

proto-leg *n.* 原腿（proto 代表的意思是“原始的,最初的”。例如：protolanguage 原始语言；protohuman 原始人类；prototype 原型；protogalaxy 原始星系。）

specimen *n.* 样品，范例，（化验的）抽样

drag *v.* 拖，拉，拽，扯；缓慢而费力地移动；在地上拖着移动；缓慢前进 *n.* 拖累；累赘；绊脚石（在英语中关于 drag 的表达有很多，例如：“drag one's feet/heels”相当于中文的“拖着脚步”，意思主要是说做事情缓慢，原因在于根本就不想或不愿意去做。例句：We don't want to look as if we're dragging our heels over promoting women to senior positions. 此外，当我们说某人或者某事物是“a drag”，就是说他或它是“一个负担，一个拖油瓶”。）

unenviable *adj.* 艰难的，讨厌的，不值得羡慕的

investigate *v.* 调查；审查；研究（看到这个词很容易让人想到美国的 FBI，“Federal Bureau of Investigation”，即“联邦调查局”和 CSI，“Crime Scene Investigation”，即“犯罪现场调查”等。）

consult *v.* 商议，商量；咨询，请教；翻阅，参看（当该词用来表达“向某人咨询”时，常使用的结构是“consult someone about something”。单词 counsel 的意思接近，但是 consult 是“向专家咨询”，而 counsel 则是“专家提供建议”。）

authenticity *n.* 可靠性，确实性，真实性（软件的“正版”就可以说是“genuine”或者“authentic”，“盗版”叫做“pirate”。微软操作系统就会提供一个叫做“certificate of authenticity”的条码贴在操作系统盒子上或者预装系统电脑的机箱上。）

purportedly *adv.* 据称（该词前缀 pur 的意思是“往前，向外”，port 的意思是“carry”。purport 作名词时的意思是“大意，主旨”，作动词时的意思是“声称，自称，标榜”。）

on face value 从表面上看

submit *v.* 顺从，服从；提交，呈送；主张，认为（考生在网上填写“fill out”各种表格，最后提交的动作就叫做“submit”。）

amount to 共计，总计为，相当于

hoax *v.* 欺骗；戏弄 *n.* 骗局；恶作剧（网上经常有很多 hoax letters，例如：某非洲银行要你帮忙转账，且作为酬劳付给你多少钱这样的信件或者诅咒“curse”类信件，如果不转发 5 个人以上，厄运就会降临在你的头上等，这都是典型的 hoax letter。）

illusion *n.* 错觉；幻想；错误观念

plausible *adj.* 似乎有理的；花言巧语的（该词主要强调“表面上看起来可行，有说服力”，但是真正如何却不为人知。）

utterly *adv.* 完全地；彻底地；十足地（同义表达有 completely、thoroughly、through and through、absolutely 等。)

obsess *v.* 使着迷，使痴迷；牵挂，念念不忘（“为某物着迷”的英语表达是“be obsessed with”。）

bankrupt *adj.* 破产，倒闭；完全缺乏的 *v.* 使破产（该词词根 rupt 代表的意思是“破裂，断裂”。与该词根相关的词汇还有：rupture 破裂，裂开；abrupt 突然的，不连贯的；corrupt 腐败，败坏；disrupt 使分裂；erupt 爆发；interrupt 中断等。）

optimism *n.* 乐观；乐观主义（该词由词根 optimum“最佳的”和表示“观点，主义”的后缀 ism 组成，所以该词的字面意思就是“认为一切都会好起来的观点或看法”。反义词当然就是 pessimism“悲观主义”了。）

cynicism *n.* 冷嘲热讽；猜忌；愤世嫉俗；犬儒主义（该词词根为 cyn，意思是“狗”，所以翻译成“犬儒主义”非常贴切。所谓犬儒主义，就是像狗一样，看到什么事物都会叫两声，也就是看到任何事物都会批评一下，不相信人性，挑剔，尖酸刻薄等。）

prospector *n.* 勘探者，探矿者（该词前缀 pro 代表的意思是“向前”，词根 spect 的意思就是“看”。于是 prospect 的意思就是“前景或希望”。美国大学每年发给学生的招生简章就叫做“prospectus”。）

ridicule *n.&v.* 嘲笑，奚落，讥笑（和 ridicule 同样表示“嘲弄或奚落别人”的词汇还有 deride、mock 和 taunt，但是这几个单词各有侧重。ridicule 强调故意性和恶意嘲弄“deliberate and often malicious belittling”，例如：consistently ridiculed everything she said。deride 则重点强调轻视、瞧不起和通常苦毒的嘲讽“contemptuous and often bitter ridicule”，例如：derided their efforts to start their own business。mock 暗指通过模仿讽刺或假装尊重实际讽刺“scorn ironically expressed by mimicry or sham deference”，例如：youngsters began to mock the helpless wino。taunt 的讽刺则有侮辱和挑衅的意思“jeeringly provoking insult or challenge”，例如：hometown fans taunted the visiting team。）

irate *adj.* 盛怒的；暴怒的（来自名词 ire“愤怒，怒火”。irate 是指“正在发怒的”，而 irascible 则是指“容易发怒的”。）

highlight *n.*（图画或照片的）强光部份；最精彩的部分 *v.* 强调，突出；使醒目；用彩笔做标记

bemused *adj.* 困惑的；茫然的（同义词有 puzzled、bewildered、confounded 等。）

题目详解

Questions 14-17

解答

14. 利用细节信息“dog”和“fur coat”定位于原文第一段第一句话“Although it was

called tiger, it looked like a dog with black stripes on its back…"。这里的"looked like"对应题目信息"resembles"，所以正确答案是 black stripes。

15. 利用细节信息"fossils"定位于原文第二段第一句话"Fossils of thylacines dating from about almost 12 million years ago have been dug up at various places…"，意思是说发现的这些化石年代可以追溯到一千两百万年前，等同于说一千两百万年前就有袋狼了，所以正确答案为 12 million。

16. 利用细节信息"disappearing from the mainland"定位于原文第二段第二句话"They were widespread in Australia 7,000 years ago, but have probably been extinct on the continent for 2,000 years"。这里的"extinct on the continent"对应题目信息"disappearing from the mainland"，"widespread"对应题目信息"throughout"，所以正确答案为 Australia。

17. 利用细节信息"settlers"和"population in Tasmania shrunk at a higher speed"定位于原文第二段第四句话"Because of disease, thylacine numbers may have been declining in Tasmania at the time of European settlement 200 years ago, but the decline was certainly accelerated by the new arrivals"。这里的"settlement"对应题目中的"settlers"，"accelerated"对应题目中的"at a higher speed"，所以正确答案为 European。

Questions 18-23

18. 利用细节信息"attracted international interest"定位于原文第五段最后两句话"When the news finally broke… 'I was besieged by television crews, including four to five from Japan, and others from the United Kingdom, Germany, New Zealand and South America'"。这里的"news"指的就是 Naarding 看到袋狼的事情，对应题目中的"report of seeing a live thylacine"，原文里的来自各个国家的"television crews"对应题目中的"attracted international interest"，所以正确答案为 A。

19. 利用细节信息"reports are not trustworthy"定位于原文倒数第四段第一句话"And Mooney has seen it all—the mistakes, the hoaxes, the illusions and the plausible accounts of sightings"，该段落最后也提到了 Mooney 认为"reports are not trustworthy"的原因，所以正确答案为 D。

20. 利用细节信息"a certain number of animals"和"ensure the survival of a species"可以发现原文中有两处（第七段和第八段）提及了需要一定数量的个体才能保证物种存活的信息，但是题目中的"doesn't require a certain number"只有在原文第八段 David Pemberton 提到的"despite scientific thinking that 500 animals are required to sustain a population, the Florida panther is down to a dozen or so animals and, while it does have some inbreeding problems, is still ticking along”中有所体现，所以正确答案为C。

21. 利用细节信息“no hope of finding a surviving Tasmanian tiger”定位于原文第六段最后关于Randolph Rose的内容“Rose...is now convinced that his dream will go unfulfilled”，而Rose的“dream”就是前一句话中所提及的“he dreams of seeing a thylacine”。这里的信息对应题目信息“There is no hope of finding a surviving Tasmanian tiger”，所以正确答案为B。

22. 利用细节信息“Do not disturb them”定位于原文最后一段最后一句话“If there are thylacines out there, they are better off right where they are”。这里的“they are better off right where they are”对应题目信息“Do not disturb them”，所以正确答案为A。

23. 利用细节信息“interpretation of evidence”和“affected by people's beliefs”定位于原文倒数第四段最后几句话。这里Nick Mooney讲到“It is a blind optimism that something is, rather than a cynicism that something isn't...It is a bit like a gold prospector's blind faith...”，这都是在说人们倾向于相信自己想要相信的事物，容易受到自己信念的影响，对应题目信息，所以正确答案为D。

Questions 24-26

解答

24. 该题目仅凭“Hans Naarding's sighting”不好定位，需要结合题目选项信息排除、判断。选项A“government and organisations' cooperative efforts to protect thylacine”，利用这里的“government and organisations”可定位于原文第六段第一句话“Government and private search parties combed the region, but no further sightings were made”，这里明显提及的是政府和私人团体都去搜寻袋狼，而非一起保护袋狼，所以排除选项A。关于选项C“increase of the number of reports of thylacine worldwide”，虽然在第六段中间确实提及“the thylacine has staged something of a comeback”，后面也提及报告的数量很多，但是说的都是澳大利亚的报告，而非“reports of thylacine worldwide”，所以应该排除选项C。关于选项D“growth of popularity of thylacine in literature”，虽然在第六段中提及袋狼“becoming part of Australian mythology”，但是这并不是说袋狼在文学中的流行度上升，而是一种形象的说法，表达了发现或观察到袋狼的种种报告大多数只不过是传说，所以应该排除选项D。选项B“extensive interests to find a living thylacine”是对原文第六段整个段落的总结，既包含了政府和私人组织的努力搜寻，也包含了报告的增多等等，所以综上所述，正确答案为B。

25. 利用细节信息“coelacanth”很容易定位到原文倒数第六段。原文开头明显提及“animals can be notoriously elusive”，然后讲到人们最初认为这个物种已经灭绝，直到后来又在南非某海域捕获一只，这一切都是为了说明某些物种并不一定像大家所想的那样已经灭绝，对应选项 D “extinction of certain species can be mistaken”，所以正确答案为 D。

26. 利用细节信息 “Mooney” 和顺序性原则定位于原文倒数第三段。原文在这里说道 “Mooney treats all reports on face value”, “on face value” 的意思是 “就表面意思来说”，也就是指 Mooney 暂且相信每一个报告所说的东西，因为他 “never try to embarrass people, or make fools of them”，但是后面又隐晦地提及他也不会听到什么就立刻行动。选项 A “given some credit as they claim even if they are untrue” 与原文信息一致，所以正确答案为 A。

参考译文

塔斯马尼亚虎

尽管被叫做虎，但是却长得像狗，背上还有黑色的条纹，它就是现代已知最大的食肉有袋动物。然而，尽管它声名远扬，是最富有传奇色彩的动物之一，但它却是塔斯马尼亚最不被人们所了解的本土动物之一。塔斯马尼亚虎的学名是袋狼，人们认为它在 20 世纪就已经灭绝了。

可追溯到约近一千两百万年前的袋狼化石在维多利亚州、南澳和西澳等诸多地方都被挖掘出来。七千年前，它们曾广泛地分布于澳大利亚的各个角落，但是在澳大利亚大陆上，它们可能已经销声匿迹两千年了。人们认为这是由于八千年前野狗的到来所导致的。由于疾病，在两百年前欧洲人定居以前，塔斯马尼亚岛上的袋狼数量就可能已经在下降了，但是殖民者的到来肯定也加速了这种下降的趋势。已知的最后一只塔斯马尼亚虎于 1936 年死在霍巴特动物园。此后，这种动物就被官方认定为已灭绝。严格意义上而言，这意味着在过去 50 年中袋狼从未被官方所观察到或捕获。但是仍然有很多未经证实的目击报告。

因为研究动物的缘故，汉斯·纳尔丁去过全世界很多地方。当时，他正在研究一种濒临灭绝的候鸟。那天夜里，他见到了被许多人认为已经灭绝 70 余年的袋狼，这是到目前为止最可信的报道。

“我不得不在夜里工作，”纳尔丁接着讲述道。“我有一个时不时把大灯四处照照的习惯。当时光线落到了车前的一个动物身上，它距离我的车子不足 10 米。与其贸然行动去拿我的相机，我当时决定仔细记录分辨一下我所看到的。这个动物的大小与一只小牧羊犬的样子相当，是一只非常健硕的雄性。然而，使它区别于狗的是它有一个稍微倾斜的后臀以及一条非常粗壮的尾巴，这条尾巴是从它的脊柱部分直接延伸出来的。它的背上有 12 个清晰的条纹，一直延续到它的臀部。我非常清楚自己看到的是什么。就在我要拿起相机的时候，它就消失在茶树下层丛林和灌木丛中了。”

当时，塔斯马尼亚国家公园主管彼得·莫罗明智地决定把纳尔丁看到袋狼的事情保密两年。当消息最终泄露出去时，随之而来的是一片混乱。“我被各国电视台报道团队所包围，其中有四五个来自日本，其他的来自英国、德国、新西兰和南美，”纳尔丁如此说道。

政府和私人搜索团队彻底地搜查了整个区域，但是却没有任何进一步的发现。一如既往，塔斯马尼亚虎已经逃回它的巢穴，许多人坚持认为这样的秘密藏身处只存在于我们的想象中。但是从那时起，袋狼好像在某种程度上又回来了，成为澳大利亚“神话传说”的一部分。自从袋狼被认为灭绝以来，已经有过超过4000个声称发现袋狼的目击报告，而且如今每年平均有150个这样的官方报告案例。塔斯马尼亚大学动物学副教授伦道夫·罗斯说他做梦都想看到一只袋狼。但是，在塔斯马尼亚35年的学术生涯中实地考查了难以计数的关于发现袋狼的报告后，罗斯如今已经确信他的梦想将无法实现了。

“保育人士普遍认为，通常情况下，任何一个动物种群，如果其个体数量基数低于1000，那么这个动物种群在未来60年内就会走向消亡，”罗斯说道。“六十年前，我们所知道的袋狼只有一只，那就是在霍巴特动物园中的那一只，”他说。

大卫·彭伯顿博士是塔斯马尼亚博物馆和艺廊的动物学馆长，他的博士论文就是关于袋狼的。他说，尽管从科学上来讲，一个动物种群需要500个个体数量才能维持该动物种群的延续，但是佛罗里达黑豹的数量虽然只剩下十几只左右，而且还存在一定近亲繁殖的问题，却仍然没有灭绝。“我敢打赌，如果我们在灌木丛中找到一只袋狼，那就意味着那里至少还有50只袋狼。”

毕竟，动物是出了名的难以捉摸。就以腔棘鱼这一奇怪的鱼为例，它有着“原始的腿”，曾经被认为在七亿年前就已经和恐龙一起灭绝了，直到1938年有人在南非的东南海岸从防鲨网中拉出一条腔棘鱼。

野生生物学家尼克·穆尼的工作并不让人羡慕，他负责调查研究所有从20世纪30年代中期到现在为止的总共4000个，平均每年约150个的“目击”塔斯马尼亚虎的报告。上个月月末，关于几张数码照片的真实性，穆尼是第一个被请教的人。这几张照片据称是最近一名德国游客在州内丛林徒步旅行时拍摄到的。穆尼说，从表面上来看，这个目击报告以及那两张作为证明材料提交上来的照片，可以说是他看到的到目前为止最令人信服的证明这个物种还存活的案例之一。

当然，穆尼什么样的报告都见过——错误的、恶作剧的、幻想的和貌似可信的目击报告。据穆尼所说，除却恶作剧和骗局不谈，大多数目击报告者最后都相信自己看到的确实是袋狼，他们是如此坚信以至于他们甚至可以通过测谎仪的测试。其他提交过可信报告的人之后都会像那个迄今已提交99次报告的塔斯马尼亚人一样，陷入对塔斯马尼亚虎的痴迷之中。穆尼曾见过因此痴迷而破产和导致家庭破裂的案例。“那是对所观察事物的肯定的盲目乐观，而非否认所见之物的猜忌，”穆尼说道。“如果有什么东西从路中间穿过，问题往往不是‘那是什么？’而是‘那是一只袋狼！’这就有点像淘金者的盲目信仰，即‘这里一定有金子’。”

尽管如此，穆尼总是在表面上毫无疑义地对待每一个报告。“我从来不希望使人难堪，或者愚弄他们。但是，每当他们打电话给我时，而我却没有立即开车出发，这往往会被他们认为是在嘲弄他们。那些痴迷的人甚至会愤怒，因为在他们认为那儿一定有袋狼的时候，身处我这个位置的人竟然没有外出寻找。”

汉斯·纳尔丁在20年前看到带条纹的动物是“耗尽一生搜寻动物”最突出的事件，但是他却难以理解为何人们会浪费时间和金钱来寻找塔斯马尼亚虎。他说这些资源应该更好地用在拯救和保护塔斯马尼亚袋獾以及帮助那些因为澳大利亚湿地减少而导致群体数量下降的候鸟上面。

袋狼真的还存在吗？“当然”，纳尔丁如是说道。但是他还指出，发现任何尚且存活的袋狼是“没有任何意义的”。“你如何从灭绝的边缘拯救一个物种呢？你又能做什么呢？如果真的还有袋狼存活着，我们还是不要打扰它们为好。”

Reading Passage 3. Accidental Scientists

词汇详解

resolve *v.* 决定，决心；使分解，使解体；表决（该词的词根solve代表的意思是“松开，释放”，所以resolve就有“使分解，使解体”的意思。当然该词还可以代表“决心”，例如每年新春伊始，很多人就会定下新年打算“New Year’s resolution”。“某人决定做某事”就可以说“resolve to do something”，“通过坚定的决心”就说成“through firm resolve”。变成形容词resolute，意思就是“坚定的，果断的”；而变成irresolute，意思就是“优柔寡断的，犹疑不决的”。当然，在电脑里resolution还有“分辨率”的意思。）

contradiction *n.* 矛盾；否认；反驳（考生必须熟悉这个单词，因为雅思阅读中的“True/False/Not Given”题里的False就是用这个词来的动词形式“contradict”来定义的，“*if the statement contradicts the information*”就是False。该词由表示“相反”的前缀contra和表示“说话”的词根dict组成，所以该词本身的意思就是“反着说”。“自相矛盾”就可以说成“contradict one’s self”。）

serendipity *n.* 巧事；机缘凑巧

opponent *n.* 对手；竞争者；反对者（来自动词oppose，其中op是代表“反对”的前缀，是ob的变形，词根pose是“放置”的意思，所以oppose的字面意思是“反着放”，于是就变成了“反对”，而opponent也就变成“对手”了。同义词有：adversary、antagonist、foe、rival 等。）

sector *n.* 部门，领域，行业；地带，区域；扇形（该词来自于拉丁单词 secare，意思是“切”。所以 sect 就有“派系，学派，党派”的意思，section 就是“部分”，而 sector 就变成了“部门，领域”等意思了。）

paradox *n.* 悖论；似非而是的隽语；自相矛盾的人或事（该词由前缀 para“旁边，相关”，和词根 dox“想法，观点”组合而成。所以该词的意思首先是“和大众普遍接受的观点相反的内容”，然后才有“自相矛盾的观点或话语”。）

notion *n.* 观念；信念；理解（口语中有 have half a notion to do something 的表达，意思是“几乎决定要去做某事了”，尤其是一些不好的事情，例如：I have half a notion to go off and leave you here. 另外，not have the foggiest notion 的意思是“一点想法都没有”，类似于 not have the faintest idea。）

purist *n.* 纯粹主义者，正统主义者（同样由 pure 衍生而来的词汇还有：purism 纯粹主义；puritan 清教徒；purify 净化等。）

deductivism *n.* 演绎主义（来自动词 deduce“推理，演绎”，其中前缀 de 代表“相反”，词根 duce 代表“引导”，所以 deduce 就是“反着推导”的意思。名词形式是 deduction，形容词是 deductive，然后在单词后面加上 ism 就变成了“某某主义”了，这也是英语中常见的后缀。与词根 duce 相关的词汇还有：duct 管道；induce 劝诱；seduce 引诱；abduct 绑架；introduce 介绍；produce 创造等。）

inductivism *n.* 归纳法，归纳法优越论

premise *n.* 前提；假定（任何科学研究都是有前提或假设的，当然也可以叫做 assumption、presupposition 或 hypothesis。其中最基本的就是所研究的对象是可以被认知的，可以被研究的，就像宇宙学“cosmology”的最基本假设就是认为宇宙是可以被认知的“knowable”，否则一切研究都是白费力气的“futile”。）

suppose *v.* 假定；设想；认为，推断，料想（该词由代表“在下面”的前缀 sub 和表示“放置”的词根 pose 组成，所以该词的字面意思就是“to put under”的意思。很多考生单一地认为 suppose 是“猜想，假设，推测”的意思，其实 suppose 还可以表示“认为，具有……的看法”的意思，相当于“think”和“believe”。例如：I supposed I was early. 同义词有：calculate、conjecture、gauge、reckon 等。）

reside *v.* 住，居住于，定居于（该词由表示“回来”的前缀 re 和表示“坐下”的词根 side 组合而成，所以字面意思就是“sit back”，也就是留下来的意思。其名词形式 resident 是“居民”，residency 就是“定居，居住”的意思。例如，移民国外而申请的 PR 就是 permanent residency“永久居留权”。当 reside 表达“什么东西或性质在于/存在于什么”的时候，常用的表达是“reside in”，例如：Their arrogance, or anger or aloofness, are the things that reside in you as potentials, which is why you are so fiercely struggling against them. 他们的自大、愤怒或者冷漠是潜藏在你体内的，这就是为什么你如此强烈地抗争他们。）

alternative *adj.* 可替代的；可供选择的；另类的 *n.* 可供选择或替代的事物（该词由表示“变化”的 alter 变形为 alternate，然后再变化而来。alternate 常翻译为“交替变化的”，例如：“交流电”就叫做“alternating current”，简称为 AC；“直流电”就叫做“direct current”，简称为 DC。当我们说“某事物在两者之间变来变去”就可以用英文翻译为“alternate between ...and...”，但是词组“alternate with something/someone”指的是“替换”的意思，例如：I alternated with Fred as the lead in the school play.）

sagacity *n.* 精明；睿智，聪慧（该词和表示“英雄事迹”的 saga 没有任何关系。该词来自形容词 sagacious，而该词又来自于拉丁语 sagus，意思是“具有优秀的对事物捕捉和判断的能力”，所以 sagacity 和 sagacious 都有“精明，睿智”的意思了。同义词有：discernment、insight、perception、wisdom、sapience 等。）

quest *n.* 探索，追求，寻找 *v.* 探索；探求（当表示“寻找”时，常用的词组是“in quest of someone or something”，意思是“寻找某人或某物”，等同于“in search of someone or something”，例如：They went into town in quest of a reasonably priced restaurant. 他们进城寻找一个价格合理的饭店。当然 quest 也可以代表一个任务，不过通常是搜寻或调查任务“seek and investigate”，这时通常说“...is on a quest”。）

antiquarian *n.* 古文物研究者，收集古文物者 *adj.* 古文物研究的（该词由代表“之前”的前缀 ante 转化而成。ante 先变成 antique“古董，古玩”，然后再变成 antiquity“古老，古迹，古代”，再然后就变成 antiquarian，也就是收集或研究 antiquity 的人。）

rummage *v.* 翻找，搜寻；翻箱倒柜 *n.* 翻查，搜查（该词的主要意思就是彻底仔细地搜查，甚至搜查后把东西弄得乱七八糟。英语中有“rummage around somewhere for something”，意思就是“在某处四处乱翻或寻找某物”，还有“rummage through something”，即“在什么事物中翻找”等诸多说法。）

knack *n.* 诀窍，窍门；熟练技术，技巧（词组“have a knack of/for something”指的就是“擅长做某事”，相当于“be particularly good at something”。英语中还有一个词是 knick-knack，意思是“小的装饰品，饰物”，其中 knick 没有任何意思，纯粹是为了和 knack 构成谐音，在英语中这样的单词不少，例如：super-duper 很棒，极其出色；itsy-bitsy 非常之小；teeny-tiny 极小的；humpty-dumpty 矮胖的；okey-dokey 同意等。）

dwell *v.* 住，居住（“dwell in the past”指的是“沉溺于往事”，例如：Learn from the past, but don't dwell in the past. 从过去中学习，但不要停留于过去。）

vigorous *adj.* 有力的；精力充沛的；充满活力的（来自名词 vigor“活力，精力”。再加上表示“进入”的前缀 in 就变成了 invigorate，意思就是“使充满活力，使精力充沛”。）

contest *v.* 竞争；争取赢得；辩驳 *n.* 比赛；竞赛（该词由表示“共同，一起”的前缀 con 和表示“见证”的词根 test 构成，这里的 test 并非测试的 test，而是 testament 或 testimony 中表示“witness”的 test，所以该词的字面意思就是“召集所有人来观看”。同义词有：challenge、competition、combat、contention、dogfight、duel、face-off、tug-of-war 等。英

语中还有这样一种说法叫做“not going to win any beauty contest”，意思就是说“某某很丑，难看”。）

immunologist *n.* 免疫学者

electromagnetism *n.* 电磁；电磁学

unintentionally *adv.* 非故意地，非存心地（同义词有：nondeliberate、nonpurposive、unintended、involuntary、unwillingly 等。）

current *adj.* 现在的；最近的；流行的 *n.* 趋势；电流；水流；潮流（该词由表示“跑”的词根 curr 与形容词后缀 ent 构成。值得一提的是单词 car 也是来自于这个词根。同样由词该根衍生的词汇还有：concur 一致，同意；incur 遭遇，招致；occur 发生，出现；recur 复发，重现；cursory 匆忙的，草率的；cursive 潦草的，草书的；excursion 短途旅行；precursor 先驱等。英语中有这样一种说法叫做“swim against the tide”，意思就是“逆流而动，与大趋势背道而驰”。）

parallel *adj.* 平行的；类似的；并行的 *v.* 与……同时发生 *n.* 相似物；纬线

rhetoric *n.* 修辞；修辞学；华丽的文词

sufficiency *n.* 充足，充裕；足量；自满（来自动词 suffice“足够，使满足”。形容词形式是 sufficient，同义词有 enough 和 adequate。）

rational *adj.* 神智清楚的；理性的，理智的；合理的（rational 是 ration 的形容词，但是意思却相差较多。ration 指的是食品，药品等的定量配给，与代表“比例”的单词 ratio 同源。在物资稀缺的情况下实施按量配给也是非常理智、理性的。）

ambiguity *n.* 歧义；意义不明确；含糊的话；模棱两可（其中前缀 ambi 代表的意思是“二，双方面的”，也可以写成 amphi，例如单词：amphibian 两栖的，水陆两用的；amphicar 水陆两用车。同义词有：obscurity、ambivalence、equivocation、opacity、murkiness、inscrutability 等。）

benign *adj.* 温和的；仁慈的，善良的；良性的（该词在医学上指的是“良性的”，例如 benign tumor 良性肿瘤。）

nose-thumbing 轻蔑，瞧不起（该词其实指的是“用拇指擦鼻子的动作”，这在西方文化中是表示“轻蔑”的意思。英语中这样的表达很多，例如：竖起中指表示侮辱，英文叫做 give someone the finger；大拇指向上表示赞许，英文说 all thumbs up；食指中指交叉表示祝福或祈祷，英文叫做 keep the fingers crossed。）

incendiary *adj.* 引火的；纵火的；煽动性的 *n.* 燃烧弹（游戏中常用到的燃烧瓶 Molotov 就是 incendiary。）

denigration *n.* 诋毁；贬低；抹黑（该词的前缀 de 在这里并不表示否定，而是表示“使”，词根 niger 的意思是“黑色”，所以该词字面意思就是“抹黑，使变黑”，自然就有了“诋毁”的意思。）

aphorism *n.* 格言，警句（表示“格言、警句”的词汇还有：adage、saying、apothegm、 maxim、proverb 等，意思接近的还有 allegory、parable 和 fable。例如：圣经中记载耶稣经常在橄榄山“the mount of Olives”上和耶路撒冷城“Jerusalem”里用 parables 讲道，像著名的“Parable of the Good Samaritan 好撒马利亚人”，以及著名的 *Aesop's Fables*《伊索寓言》。）

dissolve *v.* 使溶解；使融化；使液化；消失；终止，解散（该词的词根 solve 代表的意思是“松开，释放”。固态物质溶入溶剂“solvent”，于是就形成了 solution“溶液”。在英语中，如果说某人“dissolve into tears/laughter”，就是说此人“突然大哭或大笑”。）

ivory *n.* 象牙；象牙制品；象牙色（“to live/dwell in an ivory tower”就是“住在象牙塔里”，除此以外，还有一个非常有趣的说法，就是“tickle the ivories”，意思就是“弹钢琴”，因为钢琴的按键曾经就是用象牙制成。）

rigid *adj.* 严格的；坚强的；不变的；坚硬的；不弯曲的；刚性的（rigid、rigorous 和 strict 都可以代表“严厉，严格”的意思。但是 rigid 主要强调绝不妥协，不容商量“uncompromising inflexibility”，例如：rigid rules of conduct。rigorous 则强调因要求高而导致困难等“imposition of hardship and difficulty”，例如：the rigorous training of recruits。strict 指不允许偏离标准、规则和要求“undeviating conformity to rules, standards, or requirements”，例如：strict enforcement of the law。）

misconception *n.* 误解；错误认识（该词前缀 mis 代表“偏，错误”，词根 cept 或 ceive 代表“收到”，所以 conception 表达的意思“设想，构想，想法”，而 misconception 就代表“错误的想法”了。由词根 ceive 或 cept 衍生出来的词汇很多，例如：receive 收到；deceive 欺骗；perceive 察觉；conceive 孕育等。）

drift *v.* 漂流；漂移；缓慢移动；堆积；使漂浮 *n.* 流动；趋势；偏航；气流；水流；吹聚物（著名电影《少年派的奇幻漂流》*The Life of Pi* 讲述的就是一个印度少年在海上和老虎一起漂流的故事。英语中有很多关于 drift 的表达，例如 drift apart 分开；drift away 离开，偏离；drift off to sleep 入睡；drift with the tide 随波漂流等。）

bowel *n.* 肠；内部（move one's bowels 就是“解大便”的委婉表达。）

capitalism *n.* 资本主义

spontaneity *n.* 自发性，自然发生（来自形容词 spontaneous“自发的，自然的，无意识的”。）

autonomy *n.* 自治；自治权；自主；自主权（该词由代表“自动，自己”的前缀 auto 和代表“法律”的词根 nomos 组成，所以字面意思很清晰。“自治区”就叫做“autonomous region”。）

invariably *adv.* 总是；不变的

regimentation *n.* 编组团队；组织化；系统化

...doesn't wash ……站不住脚，不能被接受

arch *n.* 拱；拱门；足弓；拱形物 *v.* 使成弓形；呈拱形覆盖

seminal *adj.* 精液的；影响深远的

purposive *adj.* 有目的的，故意的

buttress *n.* 扶壁；支撑物 *v.* 支持；给……以力量（英语词组 "buttress something up" 意思就是"提供支持"。）

lay groundwork 奠定基础

secularism *n.* 现世主义；世俗主义

ensure *v.* 确保；担保；保证

adequate *adj.* 足够的；合格的；合乎需要的（该词由前缀 ad 与词根 equa 组成，equa 就是"相等"的意思，所以该词的字面意思就是"使等同 to make equal"，再进一步延伸就变成"足够的"意思了。）

endemic *adj.* 地方性的；(某地或某集体中)特有的，流行的，难摆脱的(该词由代表"内部"或"进入"的前缀 en 和代表"人群"的词根 demos 组成，所以字面意思就是"在这一群人当中"。相似的单词还有 epidemic 和 pandemic，epi 的意思是"在……之上"，pan 的意思是"所有，全，总"，所以通俗来讲 endemic 是"地方上的"，epidemic 是"全国性的"，而 pandemic 就可以理解成"全球性的"。）

formulate *v.* 构想；规划；确切表达；认真阐述（来自名词 formula "公式"。）

题目详解

Questions 27-32

思路

这种题型忌讳寻找主题句或中心句，因为每个人对段落中心思想的判断通常不同，而且每个段落的首尾句也不一定是主题句或中心句，所以最好的解答方法应该是通过对每位考生都能读懂的标题进行反向思维，然后和段落内容进行比较，排除作答。

i. Examples of some scientific discoveries

反向思维词：Examples, scientific discoveries

反向思维：如果某段选这个标题，则该段落一定会提及一些具体的科学发现的例子，也就应该会出现该发现所对应的具体的科学家的名称和发现的时间等。

ii. Horace Walpole's fairy tale

反向思维词：Horace Walpole, fairy tale

反向思维：如果某段选这个标题，则该段落一定会出现 Horace Walpole 这个人名，同时也会提到"童话（fairy tale）"。该段落可能会讲解童话的内容，或者 Horace Walpole 对童话作出的贡献等。

iii. Resolving the contradiction

反向思维：如果某段选这个标题，则该段落一定会出现一个对立的内容。具体是什么的对立，考生在阅读文章之前可能无法判断。另外，该段落应该重点讲解如何解决这个对立。

iv. *What is the Scientific Method*

反向思维词：Scientific Method

反向思维：如果某段选这个标题，则该段落一定会出现“Scientific Method”，并且重点讲解它的内容和应用。

v. *The contradiction of views on scientific discovery*

反向思维词：contradictions of views

反向思维：如果某段选这个标题，则该段落一定会提及两个完全相反的观点，而且可能出现具体的提出观点的人名。

vi. *Some misunderstandings of serendipity*

反向思维词：misunderstandings, serendipity

反向思维：如果某段选这个标题，则该段落一定会讲到一些具体的对“serendipity”的误解。

vii. *Opponents of authority*

反向思维词：Opponents, authority

反向思维：如果某段选这个标题，则该段落应该提及具体的“authority”或者权威机构，而且还应该出现具体的反对者的列举或人名。

viii. *Reality doesn't always match expectation*

该段落不容易进行反向思维，但是通过阅读整篇文章应该很容易判断。

ix. *How the word came into being*

反向思维词：came into being（类似 birth 或 origin）

反向思维：如果某段选这个标题，则该段落一定会讲述一个词的来历，例如其词源，以及什么时间在什么地方第一次被使用等。

x. *Illustration of serendipity in the business sector*

反向思维词：business sector

反向思维：如果某段选这个标题，则该段落应该出现一个具体的商业领域的案例，比如说某公司成功地运用“serendipity”获得了商业上的巨大成功等。

解答

27. *Paragraph A:* 该段落主要介绍了科学发现的两种方式“deductivism”和“inductivism”，同时段落中有多处提及两者之间的对立（contradiction）关系，从开始的“paradox”、“...on the other hand”到后来的“these extremes”等。与该段落相关的标题只有 iii. Resolving the contradiction 和 v. The contradiction of views on scientific discovery。但 iii

并没有提及解决问题（Resolving）的相关内容，而且 iii 还是段落 B 的对应标题，理应排除，所以正确答案为 v。

28. ***Paragraph C:*** 该段落开头第一句话便提及“The word did not appear in the published literature until the early 19th century…”，这里明显是在讲“serendipity”一词的来源，与标题 ix. How the word came into being 相对应。虽然该段落后部分提及了“Horace Walpole”和“fairy tale”，但是并没有具体讲述该童话的情节内容或以该童话为核心，而是讲述 Horace Walpole 对“serendipity”的使用来源于一个童话，所以 ii 明显是一个干扰选项，应该排除。同时其他标题的信息也都未被提及。综上所述，正确答案为 ix。

29. ***Paragraph D:*** 该段落前半部分讲到古文物研究者（antiquarians）的工作具有“serendipity”的性质。然后作者又提到，科学家也认为“serendipity”很重要（The other community that came to dwell on serendipity to say something important about their practice was that of scientists）。在后半部分，作者又提及具体的科学家“Walter Cannon”和“Peter Medawar”来说明“how much of scientific discovery was unplanned and even accidental”，之后又讲到 Hans Christian Ørsted 的例子。与这些信息相关的标题为 i. Examples of some scientific discoveries。尽管段落中也提及标题 iv. What is the Scientific Method 中的“The Scientific Method”，但是该段落明显不是在解释说明 Scientific Method 是什么，所以该标题应该被排除。综上所述，正确答案为 i。

30. ***Paragraph E:*** 段落开头第一句话的“Some…; some…; many others…”讲述了人们对 serendipity 的不同误解，对应标题 vi. Some misunderstandings of serendipity。而其后出现的“…other scientists found incendiary…taken by some as dangerous denigration”和反问句“If scientific discovery were really accidental, then what was the special basis of expert authority?”也许会让有些考生认为该段落应该对应标题 vii. Opponents of authority，但是这里并未讲述反抗权威的人有哪些或者他们是如何反抗权威的，而是讲述众多科学家对“serendipity”的误用或滥用的憎恶，所以应当排除。综上所述，正确答案为 vi。

31. ***Paragraph F:*** 段落第三句话所提到的“two of the great early-20th-century American pioneers of industrial research—Willis Whitney and Irving Langmuir, both of General Electric—made much play of serendipity…”以及段落最后两句话“So, from within the bowels of corporate capitalism…The notion that industry was invariably committed to…”都对应标题 x. Illustration of serendipity in the business sector，其他标题的信息都未被提及，所以正确答案为 x。

32. ***Paragraph G:*** 该段落从第三句话“…what one intends is rarely what one gets”开始就可以很明显地看出其与标题 viii. Reality doesn’t always match expectation 的对应关系。段落中间和后面又讲到诸多“Unanticipated Consequences of Purposive Social Action”的例子，同时其他标题的信息也都未被提及。综上所述，正确答案为 viii。

Questions 33-37

解答

33. 原文中作者对“inductivism”的定义是“you are recommended to start with no expectations whatsoever and see what turns up”，也就是说开始时不加任何期待，接受出现的任何结果。选项A的“anticipate results in the beginning”明显与“start with no expectations”相反，所以排除。选项B的“work with prepared premises”所提及的“要有一个前提假设”明显是“deductivism”的研究方法，所以也排除。选项D的“look for what you want”也等同于寻找期待的结果，应该排除。选项C的“accept chance discoveries”就对应“inductivism”的“see what turns up”，所以正确答案为C。

34. 利用细节信息“Medawar”和他的那句话很容易定位到原文段落D。如果稍微往前多看一两句话的话，很容易看出作者在这里使用了诸多例子来说明科学中偶然的重要性（Many scientists, including the Harvard physiologist Walter Cannon and, later, the British immunologist Peter Medawar, liked to emphasise how much of scientific discovery was unplanned and even accidental），然后又提到了Hans Christian Ørsted的例子。正是在这些的基础上，作者写到“Indeed, as Medawar insisted, ‘There is no such thing as The Scientific Method,’ no way at all of systematising the process of discovery”。这里作者用到的“insisted”这个单词也说明了Medawar在这里要表达的意思和前面是一致的。选项A的“discoveries are made by people with determined mind（科学发现和决心的关系）”在原文这里明显没有提及，所以排除。选项B的“discoveries tend to happen unplanned”完全对应原文意思。选项C的“the process of discovery is unpleasant”所表达的“科学发现过程的不愉快”在原文中也没有被提及，应该排除。选项D的“serendipity is not a skill”是一个高难度的干扰选项，因为段落D开头提及“Some people just seemed to have a knack for that sort of thing, and serendipity was used to express that special capacity”，最后也有提到“serendipity described the situation rather than a personal skill or capacity”，但是根据前面的分析，Medawar讲这句话的目的与“serendipity”是否是一个“skill”完全不相关，所以必须排除。综上所述，正确答案为B。

35. 该题目细节词不明显，但是可以根据顺序性原则定位于原文段落E的第二、三句话“… other scientists found incendiary. To say that science had a significant serendipitous aspect was taken by some as dangerous denigration”，这里的“incendiary”和“denigration”都对应题目中的“dislike”。其中原因，作者在下一句话中做出了解释，即“If scientific discovery were really accidental, then what was the special basis of expert authority”，言外之意就是“这诋毁了很多科学家的权威”，对应选项D的“it devalues their scientific expertise”，所以正确答案为D。

36. 利用细节信息“Irving Langmuir”很容易定位到原文段落F的第三句话“As Merton

and Barber note, two of the great early-20th-century American pioneers of industrial research—Willis Whitney and Irving Langmuir, both of General Electric—made much play of serendipity, in the course of arguing against overly rigid research planning"，这里作者明显提及 Irving Langmuir "made much play of serendipity"，而且还反对 "rigid research planning"。其后 Langmuir 又提到 "a mature acceptance of uncertainty was far more likely to result in productive research policies"。其实，作者还是想用 Irving Langmuir 的例子来说明 serendipity 的重要性。选项 A 的 "planned science should be avoided" 容易被误选。原文虽然提及 "rigid research planning" 不好，而且 "misconceptions about the certainty and rationality of the research process did much harm"，但是并没有说 planning 应该被避免。况且 "then planning does not get us very far" 也是建立在 "If there is no very determinate relationship between cause and effect in research" 的条件之上。再者，作者在这里提及 Langmuir 是为了说明 "serendipity" 和 "mature acceptance of uncertainty" 的重要性，所以选项 A 可以排除。选项 B 的 "industrial development needs uncertainty" 虽然肯定了 "uncertainty"，与原文内容有所呼应，但是原文中并未讲到工业发展的任何内容，所以排除。选项 C 的 "people tend to misunderstand the relationship between cause and effect" 中的 "the relationship between cause and effect" 在原文中虽有提及，但是并未讲人们误解因果关系的内容，所以也应该排除。综上所述，正确答案为 D。

37. 利用细节信息 "Yosemite" 很容易定位到原文段落 G 的第三句话 "It is, he argued, the nature of social action that what one intends is rarely what one gets:…people wanting to be alone with nature in Yosemite Valley wind up crowding one another"，从这里不难看出，作者提到 Yosemite 的目的是为了说明冒号前面的内容 "what one intends is rarely what one gets"，也就是说现实往往和期望不一致，直接对应选项 A 的 "the conflict between reality and expectation"，所以正确答案为 A。

Questions 38-40

38. 该题目对应原文段落 C 的第三句话 "The first noted use of 'serendipity' in the English language was by Horace Walpole"，所以正确答案为 Horace Walpole。

39. 该题目对应原文段落 C 的最后一句话 "He explained that it came from the fairy tale…"，所以正确答案为 fairy tale。

40. 该题目对应原文段落 C 的最后一句话 "…*The Three Princes of Serendip* (the ancient name for Ceylon, or present day Sri Lanka)"，所以正确答案为 Sri Lanka。

参考译文

偶然的科学家

A 科学发现的核心存在着一个悖论：如果你已经知道你自己所要追寻的东西，那么找到它就很难算作一个发现，因为它早已被你预料到了；但是，另一方面，如果你完全不知道自己在找寻什么，那么当你找到它时，你也会浑然不知，如此一来，也就无所谓“发现”了。在科学哲学当中，这两个极端就反映在两个纯粹的形式上：演绎主义和归纳主义。在前者当中，结果应该合理地包含在开始的前提假设中；在后者当中，你被建议从一开始就不带任何期望，然后看看会发生什么事情。

B 正如在许多事情当中，最理想的情况被广泛地认为是存在于这两种不可能实现的极端情况中间的某个位置。你既希望有一个足够好的关于自己所找寻东西的设想，这样你才能在找到其他有价值的东西时感到惊喜，同时你也不想对最终结果有过多的预期，因为你也抱有着出现其他结果的期望。因此，科学发现应该有偶然的一面，但又不全然如此。“机缘巧合”一词就恰好能用来形容这种情况。它是一个令人着迷的词，已故的“科学社会学之父”罗伯特·金·默顿就非常喜欢它，并在法国文化史学家埃莉诺·巴伯的帮助下编写了关于它的来龙去脉。

C 该词直到19世纪早期才出现在正式出版物中，并且在20世纪前三分之一的某个时间之前还未被广泛使用，而且每次使用时还需要附带解释。“机缘巧合”指的是一个“愉快的机遇”或者“意外的惊喜”，尤其是指未经刻意寻找而意外发现的好的或有用的事物。第一个在英语中使用“机缘巧合”这个词的人是霍勒斯·沃波尔。他解释说，这个词来自于一个叫做《塞伦狄普三王子》的童话故事（塞伦狄普是锡兰或者今天的斯里兰卡的古称）。在这个故事中，主人公们总是意外或机敏地发现种种自己未曾期望的惊喜。

D 古文物研究者们跟随着沃波尔的脚步，也发现了这个词的用处，因为他们总是在到处翻查各种各样的新奇事物，所以意料之外的惊喜对他们来说并不陌生。有些人似乎就掌握了这样的诀窍，而“机缘巧合”就可以用来描述这种特殊的能力。另外一群强调“机缘巧合”在他们工作中的重要性的人就是科学家了。在他们那里使用“机缘巧合”的说法触及了问题的核心，因此常被人们争辩。许多科学家，包括哈佛生理学家沃尔特·坎农以及之后的英国免疫学家彼得·梅达沃都热衷于强调许多科学发现的产生是计划之外的，甚至是充满偶然的。诸多例子之一就是汉斯·克里斯蒂安·奥斯特不经意间把一根载流导线和一根磁针平行地放在一起而发现了电磁学。关于理性研究方法的花言巧语不过是夸夸其谈。事实上，正如梅达沃所坚持的，“真正的科学方法并不存在”，把科学发现的过程系统化是完全不可能的。真正重要的发现如果该出现了，那么不管怎样，它都一定会出现。而如果还不到时候，那么不

管你怎么努力寻找，都不可能找到。也许有些科学家，就好像一些藏书爱好者一样，有很好的诀窍；又或许“机缘巧合”实际上描述的是这种情形，而非一种个人的技巧或能力。

E 有些科学家使用这个词是为了强调这种情形中出现的偶然和意外；而另外一些则把“机缘巧合”看成是一种个人能力；还有许多人则利用了这个概念的模棱两可性。然而，坎农和梅达沃对“方法之梦”善意的轻蔑举动却使其他科学家感到不可接受。认为科学具有显著偶然性的说法被一些人认为是危险的诋毁。如果科学发现真的是偶然的，那专家权威的基础何在？就这一点上，一个在科学发现上有着毫不逊色权威的路易·巴斯德有一则关于选择的格言提到：“机会倾慕那些有准备的人”。当一个人在找寻别的事物时，偶然的发现确实可能发生，事情也可能会出现在计划或预料之外。但是注意到这些偶然，以及认识到它们潜在影响和意义，并对它们加以创造性地利用所需具备的能力都是系统性心理准备的结果。看似偶然的事情其实只不过是专业的另一种体现罢了。有科学家坚持认为，如果仔细观察，会发现“偶然”会渐渐转化为智慧。

F 在“计划性科学”概念的背景下，科学偶然性或“机缘巧合”的观点受到了最强烈的质疑，并获得了巨大的反响。“机缘巧合派”中并非所有人都高居学术象牙塔之上。正如默顿和巴伯所提及的，20世纪初的两位伟大的美国工业研究先驱，即通用电器的威利斯·惠特尼和欧文·朗缪尔，就在反对过度僵化的研究规划过程中充分利用了“机缘巧合”。朗缪尔认为对于研究过程肯定性和合理性的错误理解害处多多，而对非确定性的充分接纳更容易产生有效的研究政策。就他本人而言，朗缪尔认为令人满意的结果的“出现就好像我们只是随风飘荡一般，这些结果完全凭偶然产生”。如果在研究中没有非常确定的因果关系，他说：“那么计划也不可能带领我们走多远”。于是，在企业资本主义的内部就产生了强有力的例证，通过“机缘巧合”证实了科学的自发性和自主性。工业一定要致力于科学研究系统化的观念并非人人共识。

G 对默顿（一位人们认为是资深作者的人物）自身而言，“机缘巧合”代表了其社会科学理论的基本原理。在1936年，年轻的默顿写了一篇名为《目的性社会行为的意外结果》的开创性论文。他强调社会行为的本质决定了一个人所得到的通常并非他所期望的：科学革命中的自然哲学家本欲为基督教提供资源，最后却阴差阳错地奠定了现世主义的基石；人们本想在约塞米蒂峡谷享受与自然独处的时光，最后却发现大家都蜂拥至此。我们知道的就是不够，而且我们也永远不可能知道一切，因而无法确保过去能足以指引未来：结果的不确定性，甚至是对于我们最周密的计划，都是不可避免的。所有的社会行为，包括那些经过仔细揣测和精密制定的安排，在结果上也一定存在不确定性。

Test 4

Reading Passage 1. Otters

词汇详解

otter *n.* 水獭（有人常把 otter“水獭”和 beaver“河狸”搞混，其实两者是完全不同的动物，beaver 是 rodent“啮齿类动物”，而 otter 是 mustelid“鼬科动物”，两者相近的地方在于人类会为了它们的皮毛而残忍地猎杀它们。）

semiaquatic *adj.* 半水生的，半水栖的（前缀 semi 代表“半，一半”，词根 aqua 代表“水”。与 semi 相关的词汇有：semicircle 半圆；seminomadic 半游牧的；semifinal 半决赛；hemi-demisemiquaver 六十四分音符等。与 aqua 相关的单词有：aquatic 水生的；aquaculture 水产业；aquifer 地下含水层；aquarium 水族馆等。）

badger *n.* 獾 *v.* 纠缠；烦扰（当 badger 作动词表示“烦扰”的意思时，有这样一种说法叫做“badger someone to death”，字面意思再清楚不过了，就是“把某人烦死”。）

polecat *n.* 艾鼬，臭貂；臭鼬

marten *n.* 貂鼠，貂皮

weasel *n.* 鼬鼠，黄鼠狼 *v.* 逃避，推诿

stoat *n.* 白鼬

mink *n.* 水貂；貂皮；貂皮大衣

inhabit *v.* 居住在；栖居于（来自名词 habitat，意思是“栖息地，居住地”，所以 inhabit 很自然的就是“居住”的意思了。）

undergo *v.* 经历，遭受，承受（“经受风吹雨打”就可以说成“undergo hardship”。）

subtle *adj.* 微妙的；不明显的；机巧的；狡猾的；巧妙的；敏锐的（名词形式是 subtlety。中文成语“胸有城府”可以翻译成“subtle way of thinking”或者“hard to fathom”。同义词有：artful、crafty、delicate、scheming 等。）

carnivore *n.* 食肉动物，食虫植物（该词由 carn“肉”和 vore“吃”构成。类似的词汇还有：herbivore 食草动物；omnivore 杂食动物。）

tunnel *n.* 隧道；地道；洞穴通道 *v.* 开凿隧道；挖地道（英语中有一句俗语叫做“see the

light at the end of the tunnel"，类似于中文中的"车到山前必有路，柳暗花明又一村"。）

Eurasian *adj.* 欧亚的，欧亚人的 *n.* 欧亚混血儿

rudder *n.* 船舵；方向舵

stern *adj.* 严厉的；苛刻的；严峻的；难对付的 *n.* 船尾；末端（stern 作为"末端"的意思时，有这样一种说法叫做"from stem to stern"，意思就是"从一头到另一头，完全"的意思，例如：We overhauled the car from stem to stern. 我们把这辆车彻底翻修了一下。）

stout *adj.* 肥壮的；粗壮结实的；厚实牢固的；顽强的；坚毅的 *n.* 烈性黑啤酒（stout heart 就是"坚强勇敢的心"，stout-hearted 是形容词形式，意思就是"坚强而勇敢的"。）

taper *v.* 逐渐变窄 *n.* 细长蜡烛；木条；渐减（英文中常有"taper off"的说法，意思是"慢慢减弱或逐渐停止"，例如：Bob tried to taper off smoking again.）

waterproof *adj.* 不透水的，防水的 *v.* 使防水，使不透水 *n.* 防水衣物，雨衣（proof 就是"防……的"意思，例如：fireproof 防火的；bulletproof 防弹的；childproof 防小孩乱动乱摸的，对小孩安全的；mothproof 防蛀的等。）

equivalent *adj.* 相等的，相同的 *n.* 相等的东西（学习翻译时经常会听到某某说法或单词没有 direct equivalent/equivalence "直接等同物"，无法直接翻译过来，只能寻找 dynamic equivalent/equivalence，也就是只能意译或解释。）

thermal *adj.* 热的；热量的；保暖的；防寒的；温暖的 *n.* 上升的热气流（词根 therm 的意思就是"热"，于是 thermal 作为形容词就是"热的"的意思。由词根 therm 衍生出来的单词还有：thermostat 恒温器；thermometer 温度计；thermodynamics 热力学；thermosensitive 热敏的等。）

groom *v.* 擦洗，刷洗；梳理；培养；训练 *n.* 新郎；马夫，马倌（"groom someone for something"的意思就是"为某事、某场合精心准备或打扮"，例如：They are grooming the vice president for the top position.）

insulate *v.* 使隔音；使绝缘；使隔热；隔离（来自于拉丁语单词 insula "岛屿"。相关词汇还有：insular 海岛的；isolate 隔离；insulin 胰岛素等。词组 insulate someone/something against 的意思就是"保护某人或物免受……的影响或伤害"。）

squirm *v.* 动来动去，来回扭动，坐卧不宁；十分尴尬；羞愧难当

rub *v.* 擦；磨；搓；摩擦 *n.* 擦；抹；搓；揉（把某膏状物擦在某处就用 rub，比如把清凉油擦在太阳穴"temple"。英语中"rub salt in the wound"的意思就是"在伤口上抹盐"。英语中 rub 的词组很多，例如：rub against 往……上蹭 / 摩擦；rub at 在……上反复擦；rub away 擦去；rub down 用砂纸之类的东西把不平或粗糙的地方打磨掉并使其光滑；rub elbows with 接触，交往；rub one's nose in dirt 揭某人的底；rub off on someone/something 影响某人或某物；rub shoulders with 接触，交往，尤其是名人；rub someone the wrong way 使某人生气、发怒等。）

vegetation *n.* 植物；植被，草木（当人们说到某地，例如沙漠缺乏植被时，用的就是

vegetation这个词。在医学上，当某人因为某种原因变成植物人，这个植物人就叫做vegetable。）

scent *n.* 香味；气味；香水；嗅觉 *v.* 闻到；察觉，发觉；使具有香味（著名好莱坞电影《闻香识女人》英文就叫做*Scent of a Woman*。英语中还有一些关于scent的习语，例如："put/throw someone off the scent"的意思就是"使某人失去追寻的线索"，例句：The police were thrown off the scent for a while by false evidence given by two of the witnesses. 还有一个习语叫做"scent blood"，字面意思是"嗅到血腥的味道"，进一步延伸就是"发现别人的弱点并加以利用"，例句：The manager has already made some serious errors of judgement and it is clear that other employees scent blood.）

otterine *adj.* 水獭的（otter的形容词形式。）

modify *v.* 修饰；使改善；使改进；使缓和（该词与动词moderate同源。中学语法课上学到的形容词修饰名词，副词修饰动词中的"修饰"在英语中就叫做"modify"。）

lens *n.* 透镜，镜头；晶状体（"隐形眼镜"就叫做"contact lens"，如果是"美瞳"的就叫做"circle lens"。）

spherical *adj.* 球形的，球状的

refraction *n.* 折射；折光（该词由前缀re与表示"破坏"的词根fract组合而成。与词根fract相关的词汇还有：fracture骨折，破碎；fraction小部分；infraction违反；diffract衍射等。）

nostril *n.* 鼻孔（nasal"鼻子的，鼻腔的"以及nose"鼻子"都是由拉丁词nasus变换而来。中文俗语"一个鼻孔出气"就可以翻译成"breathe through the same nostril"。）

submerge *v.* 潜入水中，淹没；湮没，掩盖

whisker *n.* 细须；连鬓胡子（小猫咪两边的胡须就叫做whisker。英语中有一些关于whisker的表达法，例如："by a whisker/by a whisker's breadth"指的是"一丁点，仅仅"，等同于英语单词"barely"，例句：Last time she raced against the Brazilian she won by a whisker. 英语中"within a whisker of something"指的是"非常接近"，例句：An asteroid came within a whisker of crashing into the earth.）

muzzle *n.* 枪口，炮口；（防止动物咬人的）口套；（狗、马等动物的）鼻口 *v.*（给狗等）戴口套；使缄默，钳制（言论）

vibration *n.* 颤动；震动；（感情的）共鸣

murky *adj.* 阴暗的；昏暗的；朦胧的；含糊的；暧昧可疑的；浑浊的（同义词有dim、dusky、gloomy、darkish、foggy、misty等。）

steer *v.* 驾驶；操纵，控制；引导（汽车的"方向盘"就叫做"steering wheel"，"左右打方向"就叫做"steer left/steer right"。英文中"steer clear of something/someone"指的是"刻意避开某人或物"。"a bum steer"则指的是"错误或无用的信息"，例句：The bus driver gave us a bum steer and we ended up miles from where we wanted to go.）

hind *adj.*（常指动物腿）后面的 *n.* 雌鹿（军事爱好者应该对这个单词很熟悉，著名的米格 24 武装直升机就被军迷们称为“Hind 雌鹿”。当然该词在英语中最常用的意思是“后部，后面的”，副词 behind 就来自于此。）

flex *v.* 弯曲，活动 *n.* 花线；皮线（词组“flex something out of shape”的意思是说“使某物弯曲变形”，甚至在美式英语中，如果说某人是“flexed out of shape”，则是指此人“非常生气”，例句：The boss was completely flexed out of shape. 词组“flex one's muscles”的字面意思指的是“挽起胳膊把肌肉露出来以显示力量”，形象点则指“展示力量”，例句：The attorney general is flexing his legal muscles to enforce gun control laws.）

vertical *adj.* 垂直的，竖立的 *n.* 垂直线

undulation *n.* 波动；波荡（该词词根 unda 的意思就是“波浪”,所以 undulate 就是“起伏，波动”，undulation 是它的名词形式。）

webbing *n.* 脚蹼；带子；结实的带状织物

digit *n.* 数字，数位；手指；拇指；脚趾（本文中 digit 指的是“足趾”，但是 digit 最常用到的意思是“数字，数位”，例如：12 is a two-digit number；256 is a three-digit number。digital 就是“数字的，数码的”，各种各样的“数码设备”就是“digital device”。）

prominent *adj.* 突出的；显著的；著名的（名词形式是 prominence，英语中还有“come into prominence”的说法，意思就是“变得知名”。）

claw *n.* 爪，脚爪；（水生有壳动物的）钳；爪形器具 *v.*（用爪子或手指甲）抓，撕，挠

shrimp *n.* 虾，小虾；矮小的人 *v.* 捕或捉小虾（有关虾的单词很多，从小到大基本上有 shrimp、prawn、lobster。还有一些虾叫法独特，例如大家常说的皮皮虾，其实学术语叫做螯虾，英文叫做“crayfish”。）

ditch *n.* 沟；渠 *v.* 摆脱，抛弃；挖沟；修沟；迫降（“把某人甩掉”或者“把男女朋友甩掉”也可以用“ditch”或者“dump”。因为 ditch 还有“迫降”的意思，所以英语中还有 last-ditch effort 的表达，意思就是“a final effort 最终的努力”，例如：It was a last-ditch effort. I didn't expect it to work.）

paddy *n.* 水稻；水田；发火；发怒（“稻田”也叫做“paddy field”。但是英语中“paddy wagon”的意思就比较独特，指的是用来运送犯人到监狱的“囚车”，因为 paddy 在俚语中有警察的意思。）

valve *n.* 阀；阀门；活门；气门；（心脏或血管的）瓣膜；活塞

constraint *n.* 限制；约束；限定（该词由表示“共同”的前缀 con 与表示“拉紧,使紧张”的词根 strain 组成，所以字面意思不言自明。同义词有：continence、discipline、refrainment、repression、restraint、self-control 等。）

wary *adj.* 谨慎的，小心翼翼的，警惕的（该词与 aware 都来自词根 ware，意思是“小心，谨慎”。同义词有：alert、cautious、chary、circumspect、gingerly、guarded、careful 等。）

impinge *v.* 对……有明显作用（或影响）；妨碍，侵犯（常用到的组合是 impinge on/upon someone or something。）

overlap *n.* 重叠部分；重叠量；重叠时间，交接时间 *v.* 重叠；交叠（前缀 over 代表的是“在……之上”，lap 在这里是“折叠”的意思，所以 overlap 的字面意思很清晰，就是“在上面叠加”。由 over 构成的词汇很多，例如：overcoat 外套大衣；overcome 克服，战胜；overlook 忽略，俯瞰；oversee 监督；overview 纵览，概述；overhear 偷听等。）

sparrow *n.* 麻雀（虽然雅思阅读中从来不考查有关鸟的单词，但偶尔还是会涉及关于鸟的题目，所以了解一些最常见的鸟类词汇还是必要的。除了 sparrow“麻雀”之外，小时候常常唱到的“小燕子”叫做“swallow”，当然 swallow 作动词时还有“吞，咽”的意思。另外，还有代表和平的鸽子“dove”，“pigeon”虽然也是鸽子但是不是野生的，而且颜色也通常是灰色；美丽的金丝雀“canary”；优美动听的云雀“skylark”；捕虫能手啄木鸟“woodpecker”，昼伏夜出的猫头鹰“owl”；空中猛禽老鹰“eagle”、condor“秃鹰”、hawk“隼”；美丽的孔雀“peacock”；直上青天的白鹭“egret”；祝寿的仙鹤“crane”；粉红的火烈鸟“flamingo”；不会飞的鸵鸟“ostrich”；笨笨的企鹅“penguin”等。当然所有鸟类中大家最为熟悉的莫过于鸡“chicken”、鸭“duck”、鹅“goose”啦。）

slug *n.* 鼻涕虫；子弹；假硬币 *v.* 用力打，猛击（slug 表示“猛击”时，常有“slug it out”的词组，意思是“两人竞争第一或最高职位”，或者表示“两人激烈辩论或争吵”，例句：Will the rest of the country find these teams interesting enough to watch them slug it out on TV for seven games?）

gobble *v.* 狼吞虎咽；贪婪地吃；咯咯叫（基本上就等同于“eat like a horse”，与其相反的就是小口小口地吃“nibble”或者“eat like a bird”。）

prey *n.* 被捕食的动物；猎物；受害者；受骗者 *v.* 捕食；坑骗；欺凌（“成为……的猎物”英文常用“fall prey to somebody/something”来表达，当然也可以用来表达“受到不良影响”，例如：Patients may fall prey to dishonest salespeople who say they can cure their pain.）

crayfish *n.* 淡水螯虾；小龙虾（泛指“龙虾、龙虾肉”一般用 lobster；crayfish 特指“淡水龙虾”；prawn 指“对虾、明虾、大虾”；langouste 是法语中的龙虾，常出现在法式菜单中；shrimp 则一般指“小虾”；mantis shrimp 则是“皮皮虾”。）

mole *n.* 鼹鼠；色素痣；内奸（英文中有一种说法叫做“make a mountain out of molehill”，意思就是“小题大做”。）

breed *v.* 交配繁殖；饲养，培育；孕育；导致；使养成 *n.* 品种；种类，类型（英文中有很多关于 breed 的说法，例如：“familiarity breeds contempt”等同于中文的“亲不敬，熟生蔑”。说某人“生小孩生得多，生得快”，英文就可以说“breeds like rabbits”，因为兔子很能繁殖。如果说某人或某物是“rare breed”，就是说他或它“罕见，凤毛麟角”，例如：Warwick belongs to a rare breed of scientists who experiment on themselves.）

cub *n.* 幼兽，崽；幼童军；毛头小伙子；新手

gestation *n.* 怀孕；怀孕期；（思想、计划等的）构思，酝酿，孕育（孕期保健非常重要，

如果没有照顾好孕妇就可能出现流产“miscarriage”或早产“premature birth”等现象。）

embryo *n.* 胚，胚胎；胚芽；萌芽时期

implantation *n.* 培植；灌输；植入

den *n.* 兽穴；兽窝；窝点；书斋；书房（英语中有很多关于 den 的习语，“the lion’s den”指的就是“险境，令人为难的境地，尴尬境地”，例句：It’s your turn for the lion’s den. Gordon wants to see you in his office now. 还有另外一个说法，“beard the lion in his den”有点类似于“太岁头上动土”或“虎口拔牙”的意思，或者说地直白一点就是“在别人的领域上挑战对方”，例句：I must beard the lion in his den and go and ask the boss for a day off next week.）

disturbance *n.* 打扰；干扰；骚乱；动乱；障碍；失调（该词由表示“偏离，分开”的前缀 dis 和表示“搅动”的词根 turb 组成，而后缀 ance 则表示“状况，状态”。与词根 turb 相关的词汇还有：turbulence 骚乱；turbid 浑浊的；turbine 涡轮；turmoil 混乱；perturb 扰乱等。）

nest *n.* 鸟窝，鸟巢；巢穴；安乐窝；藏匿处 *v.* 筑巢；嵌套（关于 nest 的习语和习惯性表达非常多，“nest together”就是中文的俗话“窝在一起”，指的是“紧凑地呆在一起”；“stir up a hornet’s nest”就是“捅了马蜂窝”；“foul one’s own nest”则指的是“伤害自己的利益，使自己处于不利地位”，例句：The boss really dislikes Mary. She certainly fouled her own nest when she spread those rumors about him. 英语中还有一句格言叫做“birds in their little nests agree”，意思是说“同一家人或住在一起的人应该努力和平相处”。）

bedding *n.* 寝具（类似于这样的单词变形还有：lighting 光线，灯光系统；plumbing 管道系统；wiring 线路等。）

reed *n.* 芦苇（还可以指管乐器，如笛子等的“簧片”，这可能是由于早期的簧片就是用芦苇制成的。）

litter *n.* 杂物，垃圾；一窝幼崽 *v.* 使杂乱；乱扔（标语牌“no littering”就是“请勿乱扔杂物”了。）

wean *v.* 使断奶

blink *v.* 眨眼睛；闪烁 *n.* 眨眼睛（习语“blink at something”可以是字面意思“看着某物眨眼睛”，也可以形象地指“对某事睁一只眼，闭一只眼”，当然更常见的说法实际上是“turn a blind eye to…”。习语“on the blink”指的是“出故障，不管用”，例句：Every computer in the office is on the blink again. 词组“in the blink of an eye”则指的“一眨眼的功夫”，形容很快。）

chase *v.* 追捕；追求；追寻（常与 after 连用）；镂刻 *n.* 追捕；追赶（英语中说某人“always chase rainbows”指的是此人“好高骛远，喜追求刺激华丽但不切实际的东西”，例如：He can’t seem to settle down and enjoy life. He’s always chasing rainbows. chase 还有一些常见组合，例如：chase away 赶走，撵走；chase around 撵得到处跑；chase down 追踪。除

此以外，还有很多常用习语，例如：wild-goose chase 徒劳之举，白费力气的追求；chase one's own tail 费力做事，却收效甚微；"Go chase yourself!" 则是说"走开，别烦我！"。）

conscience *n.* 良心；良知；愧疚（该词的词根来自于拉丁语 scire，代表"知道"的意思，前缀 con 代表"全部"，所以字面意思是"知道自己的所有过错"，内心自责，当然就是"良心发现"了。英语中有许多关于 conscience 的习语和俗语："a guilty conscience needs no accuser" 基本上就等同于中文的"做贼心虚"的意思，例句：Even though no one noticed him eating most of the cookies, Peter felt so bad about it that he told us what he had done. A guilty conscience needs no accuser. 中文成语"问心无愧"，英文则翻译成"have a clear conscience"；"…in all/good conscience" 则是说"凭良心，公平地"，例句：In good conscience, I could not recommend that you buy this car.）

plight *n.* 苦难；困境；苦境

pesticide *n.* 杀虫剂，农药（pest 是"害虫"，词根 cide 是"杀死"。由词根 cide 衍生出来的词汇还有：suicide 自杀；insecticide 杀虫剂；homicide 杀人；genocide 种族屠杀；patricide 弑父；matricide 弑母等。）

dieldrin *n.* 狄氏剂；地特灵（一种杀虫剂）

aldrin *n.* 艾氏剂；阿特灵（一种杀虫剂）

persistent *adj.* 持续的；连绵的；坚持不懈的（"我坚持，我成功"就是"I will persist until I succeed"。）

peregrine *n.* 游隼

falcon *n.* 猎鹰

predator *n.* 掠夺者；捕食性动物；剥削者（知道电影 AVP 吗？全称是 *Alien Vs. Predator*，中文翻译为《异形大战铁血战士》。美国著名无人机"掠食者"的英文也叫做 Predator。）

phase out 逐步淘汰，逐渐停止（反义词是"phase in"，意为"逐步采用、逐步实施"。在物理学中，"in phase"是指"同位相，协调地"；"out phase"则是"位相不一致、不合拍"的意思。）

fragment *n.* 碎片；片段 *v.*（使）碎裂，破裂，分裂（该词词根 frag 代表"打碎，打破"，由 frag 衍生出来的词汇还有：fragile 脆弱的，易碎的；fraction 小部分，碎片，分数；fracture 破碎，骨折；fractal 分形等。电脑磁盘使用时间长了就会出现一些数据碎片，"整理碎片"就叫做"defragment"。）

decimation *n.* 多数人的杀害；大量毁灭（来自动词 decimate，其中词根 dec 意思是"十"，该词本身是指罗马军队惩罚反叛者或叛逃者的方式：每十个人分成一组，然后杀死每个组里的第十个人。）

unviable *adj.* 不能独立生存的

last resort 终极手段；最后一招；最后依靠；最后的解决办法

impetus *n.* 动力；促进；动量；惯性

regulate *v.* 调节；控制；管理

legislative *adj.* 立法的；制定法律的（其中 legis 代表"法律"，相关词汇还有：legislation 立法，法律；legal 合法的；legitimate 合法的；legislature 立法机关等。）

compensate *v.* 补偿；赔偿

题目详解

Questions 1-9

思路

这种题型适合通过题目信息进行反向思维，然后和段落内容进行比较，得出答案。

解答

1. 根据反向思维信息"regulate vision underwater"推测，原文对应段落中应该出现关于水獭视觉方面的信息，例如在水下怎样才可以看得清楚，看东西有什么特征，怎样利用视觉的不同特性捕食等，甚至还有可能出现水下多少米的能见度等内容。该题目的对应信息出现在原文段落 B 的第三、四句话"Otters have small eyes…they do have the ability to modify the shape of the lens in the eye to make it more spherical, and hence overcome the refraction of water"，这里讲到水獭可以通过调整眼睛晶状体的形状来克服水中折射作用的影响。原文中的"modify the shape of the lens in the eye to make it more spherical"对应题目中的"regulate vision"，所以正确答案为 B。
2. 根据反向思维信息"body shape"和"fit-for-purpose characteristics"推测，原文对应段落中应该出现描述水獭具体身形的内容，例如水獭的身形是肥胖或瘦小或流线型等，脑袋以及四肢有什么特征等，然后提及这些身形特点又能实现哪些独特的目的等。该题目的对应信息出现在原文段落 A 中间，从"Otters have long thin body"开始，一直到"This forms part of the propulsion unit..."。原文在这里描述了水獭的身形、四肢、体长、鼻子和尾巴，而这一切特征都是为了"exploit the rich aquatic environment"。综上所述，正确答案为 A。
3. 根据反向思维信息"underdeveloped sense"推测，原文对应段落中应该出现水獭的一个具体的感官，例如触觉、嗅觉或听觉等，并有可能说它发育不好或者退化了等内容。该题目的对应信息位于段落 B 的第三句话"Otters have small eyes and are probably short-sighted on land"。原文前面提及水獭的嗅觉像狗一样灵敏，第三句话则说水獭极有可能近视。这里的"short-sighted"对应题目中的"underdeveloped sense"，所以正确答案为 B。
4. 根据反向思维信息"why agriculture failed "和"in otter conservation efforts"推测，

原文对应段落中应该提及农业方面的一系列词汇，例如农作物、农机、农药等，以及这些东西对水獭数量的影响等。该题目的对应信息位于段落F中间“Pesticides, such as dieldrin and aldrin, were first used in 1955 in agriculture…otter numbers did not—and continued to fall into the 80s”，原文这里提及农业方面对水獭数量的影响主要在于化学杀虫剂“dieldrin”和“aldrin”的使用，所以正确答案为F。

5. 根据反向思维信息“social characteristics”推测，原文对应段落中应该提及水獭种群中不同个体之间如何互相交往，是否有等级之分，是否有领地意识甚至劳动分工等社会特征方面的内容。该题目的对应信息位于段落C的第三、四句话“Being such shy and wary creatures, they will prefer territories…there must also be no other otter already in residence”，原文这里讲述到水獭的害羞（shy）和小心（wary）并且具有领地意识（no other otter already in residence），这些都对应题目中的“social characteristics”，所以正确答案为C。
6. 根据反向思维信息“how baby otters grow”推测，原文对应段落中应该提及小水獭的不同生长阶段，如几天、几个星期、几个月等。该题目的对应信息位于段落E中间“At five weeks they open their eyes…At seven weeks…”，很明显可以看出原文这里是在讲小水獭的成长过程，所以正确答案为E。
7. 根据反向思维信息“conflicted opinions”推测，原文对应段落中应该提及两个相反的观点，甚至还可能出现具体的提出观点的人名。该题目的对应信息位于段落G中间的人们对于“captive breeding programs”的看法：一方面“where there is no suitable habitat for them they will not survive after release”，另一方面“where there is suitable habitat, natural populations should be able to expand into the area”，所以正确答案为G。
8. 根据反向思维信息“a legislative act”推断，原文对应段落中应该提及一个具体的法律上的行为，例如立法禁止破坏栖息地，或者废除不利于水獭保护的法律等。该题目的对应信息位于段落G的第二句话“This is almost entirely due to law and conservation efforts…”，这里的“law”对应题目中的“legislative act”，所以正确答案为G。
9. 根据反向思维信息“heat loss”和“compensate for”推测，原文对应段落中应该提及具体的体温方面的信息、具体的温度，或者有关防止热量流失的弥补方法等。该题目的对应信息位于段落A最后对于水獭皮毛作用的描述，尤其是倒数第五句话“…underfur which is dense and fine, equivalent to an otter's thermal underwear”讲到水獭的绒毛就像保暖内衣一样可以保暖御寒，所以正确答案为A。

Questions 10-13

解答

10. 利用细节信息“outer fur”和顺序性原则定位于原文段落A倒数第三句话“Sea water

reduces the waterproofing and insulating qualities of otter fur when salt water gets in the fur”。原文这里明显提及海水（中的盐分）会降低水獭皮毛的防水性能和隔离作用，所以正确答案为 sea water 或 salt water 或 salt。

11. 利用细节信息“Asian short-clawed otters”和顺序性原则定位于原文段落 B 倒数第二句话“…the Asian short-clawed otter has no webbing—they hunt for shrimps in ditches and paddy fields so they don't need the swimming speed”，原文这里提及亚洲短爪水獭没有蹼膜是因为它们不需要游泳速度，所以正确答案为 swimming speed。

12. 利用细节信息“shortest range”和顺序性原则定位于原文段落 C 中间“Coastal otters have a much more abundant food supply and ranges for males and females may be just a few kilometers of coastline”，而且前一句中也提及河獭的活动范围一般在“12 and 80km”之间，而“coastal otters”只有几公里而已，由此可以推测出它们的活动范围最小，所以正确答案为 coastal otters。

13. 利用细节信息“animals”、“otters hunt occasionally”和顺序性原则定位于原文段落 C 最后一句话“Small mammals are occasionally taken, most commonly rabbits but sometimes even moles”，而且因为题目问的是“Which type of animals”（哪种类别的动物），而不是某个具体的动物，所以正确答案为 small mammals。

参考译文

水獭

A 水獭是半水栖的哺乳动物（或者对海獭来说是完全水栖的）。它们是鼬科动物中的一员，其他的鼬科动物还包括獾、臭猫、貂鼠、黄鼠狼、白鼬和水貂。它们在地球上已经繁衍生息了三千万年，在这漫漫岁月里，它们那食肉性身体已悄然发生细微的变化来更好地适应和利用丰富的水域环境。水獭身躯细长，四肢短小，非常适合在茂密的灌木丛中穿梭或在地洞中捕猎。一只成年雄性水獭可以长到 4 英尺长，30 磅重，雌性水獭则小很多，通常只有 16 磅左右。欧亚水獭的鼻子大概是所有水獭物种中最小的，而且呈一个独特的浅“W”形。水獭尾巴（或者称为尾舵或尾部）的基部粗壮，且往尾端逐渐变细变平。这形成了水獭在水下快速前行的部分推进系统。水獭的毛分为两种：粗壮的针毛形成外面的防水层，而下面浓密纤细的绒毛则等同于水獭的保暖内衣。水獭的皮毛必须通过梳理来保持最佳状态。一旦含盐的海水渗入水獭的皮毛中，其皮毛的防水性能和隔离作用就会降低。这也就是为什么淡水池对生活在海边的水獭如此重要的原因。游泳过后，它们会在水池里把盐分洗掉，然后在地上不停地扭动身体，把水在植被上蹭干。

B 水獭能利用气味在陆地上进行捕猎、交流以及发现危险。水獭的嗅觉感官极有可能和狗一样灵敏。水獭的眼睛很小，而且在陆地上极有可能近视，但是它们却有调整

眼睛中晶状体的形状的能力，使其变得更圆，并借此来克服水中折射作用的影响。在清晰的水域和光线充足的情况下，水獭可以通过视力来捕鱼。水獭的眼睛和鼻孔都在头部的高处，这样它们就可以在身体甚至完全浸泡在水中的情况下观察和呼吸。它们生长在口鼻处的长长的胡须可以感知到周围鱼的存在。这些胡须能探测到鱼儿游泳时尾部拍打水所产生的振动。这使得水獭在浑浊的水中也可以捕获猎物。在水下，除了需要控制方向的时候，水獭都把腿紧紧地贴靠在身体两侧，它们的后尾部则像垂直的波浪一样上下摆动。河獭还有蹼膜，一直延伸到每个指头的大部分，近乎指尖。巨型水獭和海獭甚至具有更大的蹼膜，而亚洲短爪水獭却没有蹼膜，它们在水渠和稻田里捕捉小虾，所以并不需要追求游泳的速度。水獭的耳朵还有阀门，可以保护它们免受水压的伤害。

C 许多制约因素和水獭的喜好限制了适合水獭生存的栖息地。水当然是必须的，河流也必须足够大，能保证养活一定数量的健康鱼群。水獭是既害羞又谨慎的动物，所以它们更喜欢人类活动影响不大的地方。当然，那里还不能已经生活有其他水獭——这也只有在最近水獭数量开始回升时才显得重要。雄性河獭的活动范围通常可以达到25公里，而雌性河獭的活动范围连这个数值的一半都不到。但是，河流能否提供充足的食物也会对水獭的活动范围产生巨大的影响，一项研究发现，雄性水獭的活动范围在12到80公里之间。沿海水獭因为有充裕的食物供给，所以雄性水獭和雌性水獭的活动范围可能都只有海岸线附近的几公里。正因为雄性水獭的活动范围更大，所以一只雄性水獭可能会发现自己的活动区域与两到三个雌性水獭的活动区域重叠了。水獭会食用任何能捕捉到的食物——有记录显示麻雀、蛇和蛞蝓都可以成为水獭的食物。除了鱼之外，水獭最常捕捉的猎物有螯虾、螃蟹和水鸟。小型哺乳动物偶尔也会成为水獭的腹中美餐，最常见的是兔子，有时候甚至是鼹鼠。

D 欧亚水獭会在食物充足的任何时机繁殖后代。在条件恶劣的地方，例如在冬天大多数时间湖水结冰的瑞典，幼崽会在春天出生。这样可以确保在恶劣气候再次到来之前，它们已经发育完全。在设得兰群岛，幼崽会出生在鱼群丰盛的夏天。尽管水獭每年都可以产生新的后代，但是有些却选择不这么做。这也取决于食物充足与否。其他因素，例如食物的范围和雌性水獭的体质也会有影响。欧亚水獭的妊娠期为63天，其中北美河獭的情况例外，它们的胚胎着床时间会更长。

E 水獭通常会在更安全隐秘的巢穴中生产，以确保不受打扰。它们的巢穴会铺满苇草、水岸植物和其他杂草来保证当水獭妈妈外出觅食时，幼崽能保持温暖。幼崽的数量通常在一到五只之间（两只或三只最为常见）。由于某些不为人知的原因，海獭的幼崽数量要少一些。在第五周的时候，小水獭们会睁开眼睛——每只重量不过700克。七周的时候，它们断奶并且开始进食固体食物。十周的时候，它们离开巢穴，第一次看到阳光。三个月过后，它们终于接触到水并且开始学习游泳。八个月大的时候，

它们开始狩猎，尽管水獭妈妈仍然提供大量食物。最终，九个月之后，水獭妈妈安心地把小水獭们赶出家门，自己则松口气——直到下一只雄性水獭的出现。

F 英国水獭的境况早在60年代早期就被人们发现了，但是直到70年代人们才发现导致水獭数量下降的主要原因。类似于地特灵和阿特灵这样的杀虫剂在1955年首次被应用于农业和其他工业领域——这些化学品非常持久，并已经被认定为是导致游隼、雀鹰和其他捕食鸟类数量急剧下降的原因。这些杀虫剂进入到河系以及食物链中——从微生物、鱼类最终进入水獭的身体，这些化学品也就一步步地逐渐积聚。从1962年开始，这些化学杀虫剂被逐步淘汰，尽管有些物种的数量快速恢复过来，但是水獭的数量却没有——反而持续下降，一直到80年代。这很有可能主要是因为栖息地的破坏和它们常常死于车轮之下。由于50年代和60年代水獭的突然大量死亡导致的群体分散，一个区域中仅仅几只水獭的丧生就可以导致整个种群无以为继且最终灭绝。

G 目前，全英国的水獭数量都在回升——在仅有的几个水獭存活下来的区域，它们的种群数量再次增长并且扩散到全国其他地方。这几乎完全是由于法律的作用和保护工作的努力，减缓甚至扭转了适合水獭生活的栖息地的破坏，同时从人工圈养繁殖计划中重新引入水獭。把圈养的水獭放归自然被许多人认为是最后手段。他们争论说在没有合适栖息地的地方，放归自然后它们也无法存活，而在有合适栖息地的地方，它们的数量会自然地扩张并覆盖该区域。不过，把圈养的水獭放归到四分五裂的、脆弱的水獭种群中也有可能推动整个种群数量的稳定和增长，而不再灭绝。这就是水獭基金项目在诺福克所完成的工作。在20世纪80年代初，诺福克的水獭数量曾经一度低至20只左右。如今，水獭基金项目已经完全结束了人工圈养繁殖计划。这是一个好消息，因为这意味着圈养繁殖已经没有必要了。

Reading Passage 2. Wealth in A Cold Climate

词汇详解

correlation *n.* 相互关系；相关性（该词是由前缀com“共同”与relation组合而成。correlation所表达的相互关系主要是不同现象、不同事物、不同统计或数学变量间的联系。动词形式是correlate，表达两者之间有相互关系时，常用介词with，比如correlate something with something和correlate with something。）

inspiration *n.* 灵感；鼓舞人心的人或事；启发灵感的人或事物；妙计（词根spire是“呼吸”的意思，传说上帝用泥土造了亚当，然后在亚当的鼻孔里吹了一口气，于是亚当就变成了活人。相关词汇有：respire 呼吸；respiratory 呼吸的；perspire 出汗；expire 死亡，过期；aspire 渴望，立志追求。）

rule out 用直线划掉；宣布……不可能，排除……的可能性

exceptional *adj.* 优秀的；杰出的；例外的；特别的（来自动词 except“把……除外”，其中前缀 ex 代表“出去”，词根 cept 代表“拿”。名词是 exception，而且可以组成很多词组或习语，例如：make an exception“破例”，还有一句俗话叫做“the exception proves the rule”，意思是“正因存在例外，才证明有普遍规律”。）

attribute *v.* 认为……是，把……归于 *n.*（人或物的）属性，特质（该词的词根 tribute 是“给予”的意思，而且 tribute 本身就是一个单词，意思是“礼物，贡品或恭金”，所以 attribute 的意思就变成了“把……归于某人某事”了。tributary 就成了“给人上贡的人”，通常是一个附属国或被征服国的国君，而且也可以指河流的支流。contribute 当中的 con 代表“共同，一起”，大家一起给、一起提供就变成了“贡献”。）

Eurasia *n.* 欧亚大陆（变成形容词就是 Eurasian，可以指“欧亚大陆的”，也可以是“欧亚混血儿”。）

institution *n.*（大学、银行等规模大的）机构；惯例，制度；建立；社会福利机构

latitude *n.* 纬度；纬度地区（“经度”就是“longitude”，还有一个单词叫做“altitude”，意思是“高度”。经度和纬度在一起就可以表达地理上的坐标“coordinate”。）

crucial *adj.* 关键性的；决定性的（词根 cruc 本身的意思是“cross 十字交叉口，十字架”。同样由 cruc 衍生出来的单词还有：crusade 十字军东征；excruciate 施酷刑，折磨；crucify 钉在十字架上；cruciform 十字形的等。）

mosquito *n.* 蚊子（口语中还常把蚊子叫成 mozzie，因为在单词后面加上 y 或者 ie 这样的词缀会变得可爱，例如：doggy 狗狗；piggy 猪猪；birdie 鸟鸟；ducky 鸭鸭，所以 mozzie 就是蚊蚊啦。）

anecdote *n.* 趣闻，轶事（长相与 antidote“解药”相近，注意区分。）

epidemic *n.* 流行病；（迅速的）泛滥，蔓延 *adj.* 流行性的（该词由代表“在上面”的前缀 epi 和代表“人群”的词根 demos 组成，所以字面意思就是“在一大群人之上”。相似的单词还有 endemic 和 pandemic，en 的意思是“在……之内”，pan 的意思是“所有，全，总”，所以通俗来讲 endemic 是“地方上的”，epidemic 是“全国性的”，而 pandemic 就可以理解成“全球性的”。）

recall *v.* 叫回，召回；使想起，回想 *n.* 记性；召回令（该词在口语里常用来表示“想起”，可以用来替换 remember，也可以用 recollect 和 reminisce 来表达相同的意思。英语中有句俗语叫做“word spoken is past recalling”，意思就是说“一旦什么话说出口，对别人或事物造成不良影响或伤害，就无法挽回”，相当于中文的“覆水难收”，例句：Hilary apologised for having called Mark's suit cheap, but Mark was still offended. A word once spoken is past recalling.）

decimate *v.* 大批杀害（其中词根 dec 意思是“十”，该词本身是指罗马军队惩罚反叛者或叛逃者的方式，每十个人分成一组，然后杀死每个组里的第十个人。）

frost *v.* 使结霜；（在蛋糕上）撒糖霜 *n.* 霜冻；严寒天气（英文中“严寒”也叫做“Jack Frost”，这是对恶劣天气的拟人化称呼，来自于盎格鲁撒克逊传说。英文中还常有“stay frosty”的说法，意思就是“保持警醒”，相当于“stay alert”，因为高温使人慵懒，低温使人清醒。）

inclement *adj.* 恶劣的（指天气寒冷或潮湿的等，前缀 in 代表否定，clement 的意思是气候“温和的”或指人“宽大仁慈的”，所以该词的意思不言自明。）

enduring *adj.* 持久的；耐久的

annual *adj.* 每年的；一年一次的；年度的；一年的 *n.* 年刊；一年生植物（该词词根 annus 的意思是“年”，所以 annual 就是“每年一次的”，biannual 就是“一年两次的”。相对应的是 ennium 也是“年”，但是 biennial 是“两年一次的”，centennial 是“百年一次的”，例如，清华大学的百年校庆就叫做“centennial anniversary”。）

distinguish *v.* 区分，辨别；引人注目（在重要的场合中，尊敬的来宾的英文表达就是“distinguished guests”。作“区分”时，表达区别 A 与 B，人们常用词组“distinguish A from B”和“distinguish between A and B”。）

speculate *v.* 推断，猜测，推测；投机（该词词根 spec 的意思就是“看”，由它衍生出来的词汇还有：spectacle 眼镜；spectate 观看；circumspect 谨慎小心的；respect 尊敬；prospect 前景；suspect 怀疑等。“对某事物进行猜测”可以使用“speculate about/on something”的表达，如果 speculate 表示“在……项目或事情上投机”就可以用“speculate in/on something”的表达，例句：Jeff made a fortune speculating in cotton.）

snap *v.* 断裂；拍照；（使啪的）打开，关上；厉声说；咬 *n.* 一阵（通常指寒冷的）天气；拍照（的快门声）；开或关（的声音）；（物体）断裂（该词的意思相当丰富，一定要结合语境来判断。例如：snap fingers 打响指；the twig snapped 小树枝啪的一下折断了；snap a shot 拍照片，相当于 take a shot。与 snap 相关的习语很多，“snap to it”或者“snap it up”的意思就是“快点 hurry up”。“snap out of something”的意思就是“从不好的经历或情绪中恢复过来”，例句：She's filled with grief, and just can't seem to snap out of it.）

otherwise *adv.* 否则；不然；另外；除此之外

tally *n.* 记录；积分表；账 *v.* 计算；使……符合；吻合（词组“tally something up”的意思就是“add something up”，而“tally with something”则指的是“与……相符合”。）

uniformly *adv.* 一致地；相同地（uni 代表“一”，form 是“形式”，所以字面意思很清晰。）

impoverish *v.* 使贫穷；使贫瘠（前缀 im 是“进入”，词根 pover 是“贫穷”，例如：poverty。）

chill *v.* 使很冷；使冰冷；使恐惧 *n.* 寒冷；受寒 *adj.* 寒冷的（人们口语中常说的“chill out”就相当于“cool out”，意思是“calm down”，即“镇定下来”。当 chill 表示“冷”

时，有很多词组，例如：chill to the bone 和 chill to the marrow，其中 bone 是“骨头”，marrow 是“骨髓”，所以意思就是“冻到骨头里”了。“send chills down/up one's spine”的意思就是“使人脊背一凉 / 一阵冷汗”。)

render *v.* 使成为；使变得；翻译；使处于某状态；回报；递交；熔化（词组“render something down”的字面意思是“把……熔化”，用来形象地表达“把事物精化，简化”，相当于“boil down”。“render something in/into something”的意思是“把……转变成……”。)

ensure *v.* 确保；担保；保证

moisture *n.* 水分；湿气；潮气(形容词是 moist“潮湿的”，动词有“moisten”和“moisturise”，差异在于 moisten 是“使……变得湿润”，而 moisturise 则是“增加湿度”。英语中还有一个习语叫做“moist around the edges”，意思就是“伶仃大醉”，例句：Charlie is more than moist around the edges. He is soused.)

well-heeled *adj.* 富有的（同义词有：affluent、deep-pocketed、opulent、silk-stocking、wealthy、well-off、well-to-do、moneyed 等。)

superior *adj.*（在级别、地位上）更高的；（在品质上）更好的；有优越感的 *n.* 上级；上司

crush *v.* 压坏；压伤；挤压变形；压碎；破坏 *n.* 迷恋；拥挤的人群

overriding *adj.* 最重要的；首要的；凌驾一切的

attributable *adj.* 可归因于；可能由于

route *n.* 路，路线；航线 *v.* 按某路线发送（公交车常用到这个词，例如 Route 101 就是 101 路车。另外自建 wifi 时，必不可少的路由器就叫做“router”。)

affluence *n.* 富足；富裕（该词来自形容词 affluent，由表示“加强”的前缀 ad 和表示“流动”的词根 flu 组成，字面意思就是“不停流动的”，进一步就延伸为“富裕的”。)

destine *v.* 注定；指定；命定；预定（“命中注定发生或要做什么事情”英文可以使用“destined for something”这样的表达。)

penniless *adj.* 一文不名的；贫穷的（字面意思就是“一个便士都没有”。penny 在雅思听力中也常出现，但是非常值得考生注意的是，penny 的复数不是 pennies，而是 pence。)

irrigation *n.* 灌溉；水利

vaccine *n.* 疫苗（“注射疫苗”就叫做“vaccinate”或者“inoculate”。)

split *v.* 分裂；分开 *n.* 分歧；裂缝；劈叉（“a split second”指的是“一瞬间 an instant”。口语里“I've got to split”的意思是“我要先闪了”。大家一起去餐馆吃饭的话，“AA 制”就可以说“let's split the bill”。“split up”就是两个人“分开，分手”。)

cite *v.* 引用，引述；举例；表扬

anthropological *adj.* 人类学的

germ *n.* 微生物；细菌

align *v.* 使成一线；使结盟；排整齐（在使用 Microsoft Office Word 进行排版时，“左对齐”就是“align to the left”，“右对齐”就是“align to the right”。)

domesticate *v.* 驯养
dissemination *n.* 散播，宣传
boast *v.* 自夸；自吹自擂 *n.* 引以为傲的事物；自夸的话
livestock *n.* 家畜，牲畜
be bound to 一定要……；必定；势必；注定
equator *n.* 赤道
ravages *n.* 破坏；损害；毁坏（动词形式是 ravage。）
write off 把（车辆等）毁坏，报废；注销；认定……失败
terminate *v.* 使停止，结束，终结

题目详解

Questions 14-20

思路

这种题型忌讳寻找主题句或中心句，因为每个人对段落中心思想的判断通常不同，而且每个段落的首尾句也不一定是主题句或中心句，所以最好的解答方法应该是通过对每位考生都能读懂的标题进行反向思维，然后和段落内容进行比较，排除作答。

i. *The positive correlation between climate and wealth*

反向思维词：positive correlation

反向思维：如果某段以此为标题，则该段落应该主要讲述气候和财富之间的正面联系，也就是说优良的气候带来财富，恶劣的气候带来贫困。当然，段落中也可能出现具体的气候的描述，例如湿润和干燥的气候、寒冷和温暖的气候、内陆和沿海的气候等等（应该以寒冷气候为主，因为文章标题就有 cold climate），以及具体国家或地区的财富的描述（很可能是目前世界上发达的欧美国家）。

ii. *Other factors besides climate that influence wealth*

反向思维词：other factors

反向思维：如果某段以此为标题，则该段落一定会讲述到气候不再是唯一的决定性因素，而是存在很多影响财富的其他因素，例如政治、科技、文化、历史等因素。政治的不稳定、战争的频发和科技的落后都会导致国家或地区经济发展的缓慢或落后。

iii. *Inspiration from reading a book*

反向思维词：a book

反向思维：如果某段以此为标题，则该段落一定会提及一本具体的书，还可能出现该书的书名、作者及主要内容等等，然后讲述从该书获得的灵感。

iv. Other researchers' results do not rule out exceptional cases

反向思维词：other researchers, exceptional cases

反向思维：如果某段以此为标题，则该段落应该提及其他具体的研究，也就是说，可能出现具体的研究人员（人名）、研究内容，当然一定会讲到研究结果。同时该段落应该还会提及一些具体的例外的案例。

v. Different attributes between Eurasia and Africa

反向思维词：Eurasia and Africa, attributes

反向思维：如果某段以此为标题，则该段落一定要出现 Eurasia 和 Africa，而且主要讲述 Eurasia 和 Africa 之间一些特性的差异，并采用对比的方法描写。

vi. Low temperature benefits people and crops

反向思维词：low temperature, crops

反向思维：如果某段以此为标题，则该段落可能出现具体的低温度数，例如零下 5 度，零下 10 度等等，而且主要讲述低温对人和农作物的好处，例如瑞雪兆丰年之类的内容。

vii. The importance of institution in traditional views

反向思维词：institution, traditional views

反向思维：如果某段以此为标题，则该段落应该提及 institution 或者法律、政府等具体的 institution，而且也应该出现一些具体的传统观点。

viii. The spread of crops in Europe, Asia and other places

反向思维词：crops, Europe, Asia, other places

反向思维：如果某段以此为标题，则该段落应该出现 Europe、Asia 和其他地区，同时提及一些具体的农作物，例如水稻、小麦等农作物传播的案例。

ix. The best way to use aid

反向思维词：aid

反向思维：如果某段以此为标题，则该段落应该提及援助方面的内容，而且主要讲述最好的援助方法是什么，而且也可能出现传统援助方法的优劣。

x. Confusions and exceptions

反向思维词：exceptions

反向思维：其实很难想到与该标题对应段落的具体内容，因为该标题过于抽象，但是如果某段以此为标题，则该段落应该出现一些具体的例外的案例。

解答

14. *Paragraph A:* 该段落的标题非常容易选择。很明显，与该段落相关的标题只有 iii.

Inspiration from reading a book，所以正确答案为 iii。

15. ***Paragraph B:*** 浏览完该段落可以发现与该段落相关的标题有 i. The positive correlation between climate and wealth 和 vi. Low temperature benefits people and crops。虽然该段落确实提及寒冷和国家财富有一定联系，但是并没有详细地进行描述，例如描述寒冷导致财富，炎热导致贫困，也没有具体的案例，同时并没有进行具体的两者之间关联的剖析，只是提出问题或者说是猜想。相反的，段落中却明确地提出了寒冷有一定的好处，即可以杀死害虫，消灭热带疾病等，所以综上所述正确答案为 vi。

16. ***Paragraph C:*** 浏览完该段落可以发现与该段落相关的标题有 i. The positive correlation between climate and wealth、ii. Other factors besides climate that influence wealth、iv. Other researchers' results do not rule out exceptional cases 和 x. Confusions and exceptions。虽然该段落提及了一些其他因素，例如得天独厚的地理位置和政治等因素，但是并非以此为主要内容讲述它们对国家财富的影响，所以应该排除 ii。该段落也提及新加坡与香港的例外情况，对应 exceptional cases，但是这也不是段落的主要内容，也不是其他 researchers 的研究内容，更没有提及 Confusions 方面的内容，所以也应该排除 iv 和 x。综上所述，正确的答案为 i。

17. ***Paragraph D:*** 浏览完该段落发现与该段落相关的标题有 ii. Other factors besides climate that influence wealth 和 vii. The importance of institution in traditional views。虽然该段落提及 institution，但是只讲到 institution 是众多 other factors 其中之一，另外还提及了贸易路线等。综上所述，正确答案为 ii。

18. ***Paragraph E:*** 浏览完该段落很明显可以发现与该段落相关的标题只有一个，就是标题 ix. The best way to use aid，所以正确答案为 ix。

19. ***Paragraph F:*** 浏览完该段落发现与该段落相关的标题有 v. Different attributes between Eurasia and Africa 以及 viii. The spread of crops in Europe, Asia and other places。该段落中虽然确实提及谷物的传播，但这只是其中的一个细节，是为了说明 "Eurasia is broadly aligned east-west, while Africa and the Americas are aligned north-south" 带来的好处，而且不仅如此，还带来了 "faster dissemination of other technologies such as the wheel and writing"，所以应该排除 viii。综上所述，正确答案为 v。

20. ***Paragraph G:*** 浏览完该段落信息，同时排除之前已经选过的标题后不难发现，此时与该段落对应的标题只有 iv. Other researcher's results do not rule out exceptional cases 和 x. Confusions and exceptions。该段落明显提及到 Other researchers（John Gallup 和 Jeffrey Sachs）的研究，同时也提及新加坡的例子来说明地理决定论（geographical determinism）不可取，与标题 iv 对应非常好，而且该段落也没有提及任何与标题 x 中 Confusions 相关的信息，所以标题 x 应该排除。综上所述，正确答案为 iv。

Questions 21-26

21. 利用细节信息“a book”和“American city”以及顺序性原则定位于原文段落A前两句话“Dr William Masters was reading a book...the great yellow-fever epidemic that hit Philadelphia in 1793”。原文中的“Philadelphia”就对应题目中的“American City”，所以该题正确答案为yellow-fever epidemic。
22. 利用细节信息“rich but small country”定位于原文段落C中间“For example, Finland is a small country that is growing quickly...”，原文这里的“For example”就对应题目中的“as”，“growing quickly”就对应题目中的“rich”，所以该题正确答案为Finland。
23. 利用细节信息“besides excellent surroundings and climate”以及“long prosperity”定位于原文段落D第二句话“Climate, he feels, somehow combines with other factors—such as the presence of institutions, including governments, and access to trading routes—to determine whether a country will do well”，原文这里“Climate...combines with other factors...such as...access to trading routes”对应题目中的“besides excellent surroundings and climate”，“do well”对应题目中的“long prosperity”。很明显可以看出，除了地理位置和气候因素外，institutions包括governments也很重要，也需要改进，所以该题正确答案为institutions或governments。
24. 利用细节信息“resembling weather conditions across latitude”以及“continent”定位于原文段落F中间“in Europe, crops can spread quickly across latitudes because climates are similar”，原文这里“climates are similar”对应题目中的“resembling weather conditions”，所以该题正确答案为Europe。
25. 利用细节信息“crops”和“spread faster than from South America to the North”以及顺序性原则定位于原文段落F中间“One of the first domesticated crops, einkorn wheat, spread quickly from the Middle East into Europe; it took twice as long for corn to spread from Mexico to what is now the eastern United States”，原文这里“it took twice as long for corn to spread from Mexico to what is now the eastern United States”对应题目中的“faster than from South America to the North”，所以该题正确答案为einkorn wheat。
26. 利用细节信息“tropical country”和“scientific advancement”以及顺序性原则定位于原文段落G最后一句话“Human health and agriculture can be made better through scientific and technological research...Take Singapore: without air conditioning, it wouldn't be rich”，原文这里“scientific and technological research”就对应题目中的“scientific advancement”，所以该题正确答案为Singapore。

参考译文

气候与财富

纬度对一个国家的经济实力至关重要。

A 威廉·马斯特斯博士在读一本关于蚊子的书籍时突然获得了一个灵感。"曾经有一个故事记录了美国费城1793年发生的黄热病大流行的事情，"马斯特斯回忆道。"这场流行病重创了这个城市，直到初霜的来临。"恶劣的天气冻死了蚊子，使得费城得以恢复生机。

B 马斯特斯认为，如果天气可以是一个城市财富的关键，那为什么不能是国家财富积累的关键呢？霜降会是最持久的经济发展奥秘之一的核心吗？为什么几乎所有富有的、经济发达的国家都出现在40度以上的纬度呢？经过两年的研究，他认为自己找到了解决谜题的关键。来自印第安纳州普渡大学的农业经济学家马斯特斯和波士顿塔夫茨大学的玛格丽特·麦克米兰认为每年的霜冻是区别穷国和富国的因素之一。他们的研究成果被发表在本月的《经济增长杂志》上。这对专家还推测冷空气的到来有两个主要好处——能够冻死破坏农作物的害虫，还能够冻死传播疾病的生物，例如蚊子。这样的结果就是高产的农业和充裕的劳动力。

C 这两位学者收集了两组信息。第一组是国家的平均收入，第二组是来自于东安格利亚大学的气候数据。他们发现了这两组数据中有一个有趣的吻合。那些每月有5个或以上霜冻日子的国家全都非常富有，而那些少于5个霜冻日的国家则非常贫困。于是他们怀疑这个5天非常关键；这也许是杀死土壤中的害虫所需要的最少的时间。马斯特斯还说："例如，芬兰是一个发展很快的小国，但是同样作为小国的玻利维亚却没有任何的发展。也许气候和这个现象有一定关系。"事实上，有限的霜冻对农民有巨大的好处。低温能杀死害虫或使它们丧失行动能力；寒冷的天气还能减缓土壤中植物和动物材料的分解，使得土壤更加肥沃；同时霜冻还能保证开春前土壤中湿度的增加，降低对季节性雨水的依赖。当然"寒冷等同于财富"的论述也是有例外的。例如富有的热带地区香港和新加坡，它们就是占据了优越的贸易地理位置的结果。同样的，并不是所有的欧洲国家都是有钱的——在那些前共产主义国家中，经济潜力完全被政治所破坏。

D 马斯特斯还强调气候永远不可能是压倒一切的因素——国家财富的成因极其复杂，不能简单地归结于一个因素。他认为，气候和其他因素——例如包括政府在内的社会制度的存在和是否接近贸易路线——以某种方式结合在一起共同决定了一个国家能否很好地发展。马斯特斯说，传统上经济学家认为社会制度对经济的影响最大，因为它能够以法律和财产权利等形式为国家带来秩序。有了秩序，财富也随之而来，他们如是认为。"但是仍然会有一些问题甚至是具备很好的社会制度的国家也难以克

服的，”他说道。“我感觉，随着国家财富的增长，它们也会逐渐催生出更好的社会制度。而且财富的积累和社会制度的进步都得益于良好的环境，例如气候。”

E 他坚持认为，这并不意味着热带国家在经济上就完全没有希望，并注定贫穷。富国应该改变援助穷国的方式。与其帮助改善穷国的政府制度，不如把更多的援助资金用在改善农业和抵抗疾病的技术上。马斯特斯引用了一个例子，说道：“印度一些地区获得了灌溉上的援助——农业生产因此大大提高，同时居民健康也得到改善。”提供抵御热带疾病的疫苗和开发多样的适合生长于热带的农作物能够打破贫困。

F 其他一些专家则专注于富国和穷国之间的差异，引用人类学、气候和动物学的因素来解释为什么温带气候的国家最为富足。早在公元前350年，亚里士多德就观察到“那些居住在寒冷气候的人们……充满了活力”。加州大学洛杉矶分校的贾雷德·戴蒙德在他的《枪支、细菌和钢铁》中指出，欧亚大陆大致上是从东到西对应的，而非洲和美洲大陆则是南北连成一线的。所以，在欧洲，农作物可以沿着纬度快速传播，因为气候是相似的。最早被人类种植的农作物之一，单粒小麦，就快速地从中东地区传播到了欧洲；而玉米却花了两倍的时间从墨西哥传播到今天的美国东部。这种便捷的沿着相似纬度在欧亚大陆间的传播也意味着其他技术，例如轮子和文字能更快捷地传播，戴蒙德如是推测。这个区域也骄傲地享有着驯化的家畜，它们能为人们提供肉食、毛线以及田地里的劳力。享受着如此的自然优势，欧亚大陆注定了在经济上会腾飞的。

G 两位美国经济学家，约翰·盖洛普和杰弗里·萨克斯也曾指出国家的地理位置和财富之间的惊人联系。他们注意到赤道南北23.45度之间的热带国家几乎全部都是贫穷的。在《哈佛国际评论》的一篇文章中，他们得出的结论是“发展看起来确实更倾顾温带区域的经济体，尤其是北半球以及那些避开了社会主义和战争蹂躏的国家”。但是马斯特斯也警告说要反对那种认为热带国家完全没有希望的地理决定论：“人类健康和农业可以通过科学和技术研究得到提升，”他讲道，“所以我们不应该忽视这些国家。就拿新加坡来说吧，没有空调，这个国家是不可能富有的。”

Reading Passage 3. Musical Maladies

词汇详解

malady *n.* 弊病；疾病（mal在英文当中是一个表示“坏”的前缀，例如：malevolent 恶毒的；malnutrition 营养不良；maladministration 弊政；malfunction 故障，失灵等。）

fascinate *v.* 使着迷，使人迷（同义词有 allure、bewitch、captivate、enchant、charm 等。）

subject *n.* 主题，话题；科目；研究对象

neuroscientist *n.* 神经科学家（该词的前缀 neuro 代表“神经”的意思，例如：neural 神经的，神经系统的；neurosis 神经机能病，神经衰弱症；neuron 神经元；neurology 神经病学。）

auditory *adj.* 听觉的（词根 audi 或 audio 代表“声音或听觉”，来自于拉丁语。相关的词汇有：audible 可以听到的；audiobook 有声读物；auditorium 礼堂，会堂；audience 听众。）

intriguing *adj.* 有趣的；迷人的（基本上和 fascinating 的意思一致，但是 intrigue 作动词时却有“搞阴谋诡计”的意思，例如：intrigue with someone against someone 表示“和某人一起阴谋策划来反对某人”。）

musicophilia *n.* 音乐欣欢症（该词其实在字典上并不存在，而是该文章作者为了描述一种现象而创造出来的单词。musico 就代表“音乐”，philia 由表示“喜爱”的 phile 和表示“疾病或病理现象”的 ia 组成，这两个部分组合在一起就变成了“音乐欣欢症”，代表那些对音乐喜欢的不得了甚至接近病态的现象。）

neurologist *n.* 神经病学家

prolific *adj.* 多产的；众多的；富饶的；丰硕的（和 proliferate“猛增”同源。）

confess *v.* 承认，坦白，供认（在罗马天主教中还有“忏悔，悔过”的意思。电视里经常可以见到这样的镜头：一个天主教信徒进入到一个大教堂中，在教堂的一侧有一个木制小黑屋“confession box”，叫做“告解室”，虔诚的信徒就会说“Father, I've sinned. 神父啊，我犯罪了”，然后神父就会说“上帝已经原谅了你的罪过，我的孩子，不要再犯罪了”等等。）

reaction *n.* 反应；反动（前缀 re 代表“相反”的意思。knee-jerk reaction 就是著名的“膝跳反射”。口语里常说的 gut reaction 就是“直觉反应”，还有类似的 gut feeling 就是“直觉”。）

enchant *v.* 使心醉；使迷惑（chant 在英语中是“吟颂，咏唱”的意思，尤其是指宗教中的，例如天主教的 Gregorian Chant、佛教的 Buddhist Chant 和伊斯兰教的 Muslim Chant。前缀 en 代表“进入”，于是 enchant 就是“进入到吟颂、咏唱当中去”，于是也就有了“使陶醉，使入迷”的意思。）

be borne out by 被……证实（来自词组 bear out，意思是“证实，证明”。）

erudite *adj.* 博学的，有学问的（其中 rudi 是词根，是“rude”的意思，前缀 e 相当于 ex，代表“出去”，于是字面意思就是“离开了粗俗，进而变成博学”的意思了。同义词有：educated、knowledgeable、learned、lettered、scholarly、well-read；反义词有：benighted、ignorant、uneducated、unlettered、unlearned、unscholarly。）

pontifical *adj.* 教皇的；固执武断的（该词来源于名词 pontiff“罗马教皇，主教”，变成形容词则指“具备教皇权威的”，进一步还可以指“傲慢，武断”。）

preface *n.* 序言，引语；开端，前奏

insight *n.* 洞察力；眼光；领悟

glean *v.* 搜集；拾（当人们说“glean something from something”时，通常表达的是“收集别人剩下的东西”，例如拾落穗，但是如果说 glean something from somebody 时，则通

常是指“通过搜集人们的只言片语弄清楚某事情的缘由或真相”。)

enormous *adj.* 巨大的，庞大的（该词是由表示“出去”的前缀e和表示“标准”的词根norm组成，所以enormous的字面意思就是“离开了标准，不同寻常”，后来就常指数量、大小、程度等的巨大。同义词有：colossal、elephantine、gargantuan、gigantic、grand、immense、jumbo、leviathan、mammoth、massive、monstrous、tremendous、titanic等。)

underpinning *n.* 基础材料；基础（pin作名词时是“针，别针，大头针”的意思，作动词则是“压住，用钉子钉住”的意思。了解了pin的意思就不难理解为什么underpin具有“支持，加固，加强”的意思，于是underpinning也就有“基础”的意思。)

bizarre *adj.* 离奇的；奇怪的（近义词有：absurd、fantastic、fanciful等。另外有一个词与该词发音相近，要注意区分：bazaar“巴扎”，来自于波斯语，原指的是中东地区的“杂货市场”，现在还可以指“百货商店”。)

context *n.* 上下文；背景，环境（该词是由表示“共同”的前缀con和表示“文本”的词根text组成，相关的词汇还有表示“借口，托辞”的pretext。)

tear *v.* 撕裂，撕（雅思考试时监考官会明确地告诉考生，不可以“tear off or remove any test material from the question booklet”，否则就算是违规，会被立即终止考试。词组“be torn between”表达的是在两个事物之间“难以抉择，左右为难”。)

newfangled *adj.* 新奇的，新制的（同义词有：modernistic、ultramodern、state-of-the-art、up-to-date；反义词有：antiquated、archaic、oldfangled、old-fashioned。)

take heed of 留心，注意（Take heed of what he says, if you want to succeed. 假如你想成功，就得留意他说的话。该词组的意思基本等同于beware，同时heed本身就可以作动词使用，意思是“注意，留心，留意”。例句：But few at the conference in London last week heeded his warning. 但在上周于伦敦召开的大会上，几乎没有人留意他的警告。)

contemporary *adj.* 当代的，现代的；同时代的，同属一个时期的（该词由前缀con“共同”以及词根tempor组成，该词根来自于拉丁语tempus，意思就是“时间”，于是该词字面意思就是“来自于共同时间”。与该词根相关的词汇有：temporal 时间的，世俗的；temporary 临时的，暂时的；extemporise 即兴创作，即席演奏等。尤其是temporary的这个词，在电脑中经常会遇到一些电脑运行过程中产生的临时文件，这些文件名的后缀就是temporary的缩写tmp，文件夹Temp也就是“临时文件夹”了。)

sprinkle *v.* 洒，撒（同义词有scatter、spray、strew等。把什么东西洒在什么上面通常用“sprinkle something on/onto something”的组合。sprinkler就是草坪上常见的“喷水器”，而且建筑物中天花板上防止火灾蔓延的洒水系统就叫做“sprinkler system”。)

haunt *v.* 常出没或闹鬼；时常萦绕心头（中文中我们说一个地方或房子闹鬼就可以用这个词汇，例如：a place/house is haunted。中文的鬼在英语中应该翻译为ghost，但是各种精怪要翻译为spirit，千万不能翻译成god。英语中“come back to haunt someone/return to haunt someone”指的是“受什么东西反复困扰，挥之不去”，尤其是不好的回忆或者错误的决定导致的负面影响。中文中的“故地重游”也可以翻译成 revisit old haunts。)

consume *v.* 消耗，消费(consumption 消耗；consumer 消费者；consumerism 消费主义)

crave *v.* 渴望；恳求(同义表达有：covet、desire、ache for、hunger for、itch for、long for、lust for、thirst for、yearn for 等。)

compose *v.* 组成,构成；创作；使镇定,使安定(该词由前缀 com“共同”,词根 pose“放置”组合而成，字面意思就是“放置在一起”。作为“组成，构成”时基本上等同于 compound, constitute，作为“创造，创作”时等同于 produce。composer 就是“作曲家”，composition 代表“作文”。作为“使镇定，使安定”时，基本上就等同于“pull yourself together”，人们常说“compose yourself”。composure 就是“沉着，冷静”。)

spontaneous *adj.* 自发的；自然的(与该词接近的词汇有 impulsive、instinctive、automatic、mechanical 等，但是意思或所强调的内容却有差异。spontaneous 强调一种自然性，没有任何刺激的、自发的、内在的“lack of prompting, a naturalness”，例如：a spontaneous burst of applause。impulsive 则强调在情感或形式的压力之下做出的举动“acting under stress of emotion or spirit of the moment”，例如：impulsive acts of violence。instinctive 强调未经过判断或自我意识“action involving neither judgment nor will”，例如：Blinking is an instinctive reaction。automatic 指的是没有思维或情感的参与，而且通常意味着可预测的反应“action engaging neither the mind nor the emotions, and often with predictable response”，例如：His denial was automatic。mechanical 则指没有生机，甚至敷衍了事“lifeless, often perfunctory”，例如：a mechanical teaching method。)

torrent *n.* 急流；爆发，迸发(torrential rain“暴雨”，不是一般的雨，而是 heavy downpour“倾盆大雨”。当然 torrent 不一定非得是“雨或水”，也可以是形象的表达，例如某人讲话滔滔不绝，就可以说此人“talk like unceasing torrent”。)

cerebral *adj.* 大脑的；理智的(来自名词 cerebrum“大脑”。)

cortex *n.* 大脑皮层(雅思中虽然会出现一些大脑方面的专业词汇，例如：hypothalamus“下丘脑”、orbital prefrontal lobe“眶前额叶”等，但是并不会真正考查这些单词的意思。)

electroencephalography *n.* 脑电图，脑电图学(该词由 electro“电的”、encephal“脑的”以及 graph“图像”构成。与 electro 相关的词汇很多，例如：electricity 电流；electrode 电极；electrocute 电击；electron 电子等。与 encephal 相关的词汇有：encephalitis 脑炎；encephalopathy 脑病。与 graph 相关的词汇有：geography 地理；electrocardiograph 心电图仪；graphology 笔迹学；ideograph 象形文字；topography 地形学。)

trauma *n.* 创伤；损伤；痛苦(动词 traumatise 就是“使受伤害，使受精神创伤”的意思。通常受过巨大创伤的人，那些痛苦的经历“bad memories”经常会 return to haunt them。)

subsequent *adj.* 后来的，随后的(该词由 sub“下面”与词根 sequi“跟随”构成，所以字面意思非常清晰。与该词根相关的词汇还有：sequel 后记，后传；consequence 后果，结果；sequence 顺序，次序；obsequious 奉承的，谄媚的；sequacious 盲从的。）

conversion *n.* 转变；兑换（来自动词 convert，其中 con 代表“共同”，vert 代表“转动”，所以 convert 就是“转变，转换”的意思。）

decline *v.&n.* 下降；衰退；辞谢（下降的意思最为广大考生熟知，其实 decline 还可以用来表达“拒绝，谢绝”。例如，当考生收到多所院校的 offer 时，自己不得不接受其中之一，而 decline the others。当表示“拒绝”时，相近的词汇还有 refuse、reject、repudiate 和 spurn，但是意思各有侧重。decline 强调礼貌的谢绝，尤其是谢绝邀请或礼物“courteous refusal especially of offers or invitations”。refuse 更多指对要求或请求的拒绝，且态度坚定，不留情面“denial of something asked for”，例如：refused to lend them the money。reject 则指专横、傲慢地拒绝，抛弃“peremptory refusal by sending away or discarding”，例如：The editor rejected the manuscript as unpublishable。repudiate 则不同，它更多强调因为虚假、未授权或没有价值而抛弃“casting off or disowning as untrue, unauthorised or unworthy of acceptance”，例如：teenagers who repudiate the values of their parents。spurn 强调蔑视，瞧不起“contempt or disdain in rejection or repudiation”，例如：a spurned lover。）

undergo *v.* 经历；遭受，承受（经受风吹雨打就可以说成“undergo hardship”。）

delve *v.* 探究；挖掘；钻研（该词本身的意思就是 dig“挖洞，挖掘”，等同于“excavate”，不过后来进一步地延伸，用来表达“examine a subject in detail and depth 钻研事物”，人们常用“delve into…”的组合。）

amusia *n.* 乐感丧失症（这个词是作者自己创造的，与之前的 musicophilia 一样是字典中不存在的。前缀 a 表示“否定”，musi 代表“音乐”，后缀 ia 说明是“一种病”，再根据文中对于 amusia 的解释“an inability to hear sounds as music”，该词就是“乐感丧失症”。）

dysharmonia *n.* 和音错乱（与 amusia 一样是作者自己创造的词汇，dys 代表“否定”，harmoni 代表“和音”，ia 代表“疾病”，而且原文又解释说 dysharmonia 是“a highly specific impairment of the ability to hear harmony, with the ability to understand melody left intact”，也就是说能够听出旋律，但是却无法听出其中的和音。）

impairment *n.* 损害，损伤(来自动词 impair。虽然有人认为该词字面意思是“不再是一对”，自然就是“损害，损伤”了，但实际上该词的构成并非如此，im 代表“进入”，pair 是来自拉丁语的 peiorare，意思是“使变糟糕”，ment 构成名词，所以 impair 本身的意思是“to damage or make worse”。听觉受损或视觉受损就用到 impair，分别是“hearing impaired”和“visually impaired”，其实分别是 deaf 和 blind 的委婉表达“euphemism”。）

intact *adj.* 完整的（该词由否定前缀 in 和代表“碰触，触摸”的词根 tact 组成，所以该词字面意思是“untouched”，也就是“完整的”。）

dissociation *n.* 分离；解体（association 的反义词。例句：Almost the first lesson they learn is how to dissociate emotion from reason. 如何将理智和情感分开几乎可以说是他们所学的第一课。）

to one's credit 值得赞扬，可取之处（其实该词组不好直接翻译，但是字面意思就是"认可某人的行为或言论"，因为 cred 这个词根的意思就是"相信"。）

underappreciate *v.* 未正确评价或充分赏识（under 再加上另外一个单词来表达"没有充足地怎么样或者低于"是英语中常见的组合，例如：underachiever 落后的人或学生；underage 未成年；underact 不充分地表演，不卖力地演；undercharge 少收钱。与 under- 这种构词相对应的就是 over-，例如：overachiever 成绩超过预料的人或学生；overact 过火地表演；overcharge 要价过高，收费过多；overage 超龄等。）

realm *n.* 领域，范围；王国

therapy *n.* 治疗，疗法（是医学中除了医药、手术之外的另外一种重要的治疗方法，通常用来治疗身体、精神或行为上的错乱"disorder"，而且常作为辅助型手段。）

intonation *n.* 语调，声调

aphasic *adj.* 失语症的（该词来自名词 aphasia"失语症"。由表示否定的前缀 a，表示"说话"的词根 phasis 以及表示"疾病"的词缀 ia 组成。相关的词汇还有：dysphasia 语言障碍症。）

stroke *n.* 划水动作；中风；（打、击等的）一下；一笔，笔画 *v.* 轻抚，抚动（stroke 的含义非常丰富，在游泳里，不同的泳姿就用 stroke 来表达，例如：breast stroke 蛙泳；back stroke 仰泳；butterfly stroke 蝶泳；free stroke 自由泳。）

demonstrate *v.* 证明，证实，论证；显示，展示；演示；游行示威

animate *v.* 使有生气，赋予……以生命 *adj.* 有生命的，有生气的

posture *n.* 姿势；看法，态度，立场 *v.* 故作姿态；装样子（坐姿、站姿都用到了这个词，分别翻译为"sitting posture"和"standing posture"。词组 posture as someone/something 指的是"装作某人/物的姿态"，或者"在姿势上模仿某人/物"，例如：Carla entered the ballroom, posturing as a grand duchess of somewhere. 卡拉走进舞厅，摆出一副仿佛来自什么地方的大公夫人的样子。）

revelation *n.* 启示；揭发，披露；被揭露的真相（来自动词 reveal。其中前缀 re 表示"相反，反向"，词根 veal 其实就是 veil"面纱，遮盖物"，所以该词字面上的意思就是 uncover"揭开盖子"。）

implication *n.* 含意，含义；言外之意

oddity *n.* 怪异，反常，古怪；怪人，怪事（形容词是 odd。数学里 odd number 是"奇数"，even number 是"偶数"，prime number 是"质数或素数"。）

localisation *n.* 地方化，局部化

alleviate *v.* 减轻，缓和（该词由表示"强化"的前缀 ad 与表示"轻"的词根 levis 组成，当然 ad 伴随词根 levis 的首字母变形成 al。由词根 levis 组成的词汇还有：elevate 提起，升起；levitate 使浮于空中；levity 轻浮。该词的同义词有很多：relieve、lighten、assuage、mitigate 和 allay，但这些词的意思略有差异。relieve 指的是缓和以使得能够承受"lifting of enough of a burden to make it tolerable"，例如：Take an aspirin to relieve the pain。alleviate 则强调短暂性和部分减轻、缓和 “temporary and partial lessening of pain or distress”，例如：The lotion alleviated the itching。lighten 强调减少负担 “reduce a burdensome or depressing weight”，例如：Good news would lighten our weight。assuage 强调软化或者甚至使痛苦的东西感到舒适 “softening or sweetening what is harsh or disagreeable”，例如：Ocean breezes assuaged the intense heat。mitigate 指减轻或降低痛苦的事物所带来的影响 “moderating or countering the effect of something violent or painful”，例如：the need to mitigate barbaric laws。allay 指有效地降低恐惧或人的警觉 “effective calming or soothing of fears or alarms”，例如：allayed their fears。）

symptom *n.* 症状，征兆

aggravate *v.* 加重，使恶化；激怒（该词由表示“加强”的前缀 ad 和表示“沉重”的词根 grav 组成，而且 ad 伴随词根首字母变形为 ag。同样由 grav 组成的单词还有：grave 严肃的，庄重的；gravity 重力，引力；gravitate 下沉，下降。）

antiepileptic *adj.&n.* 抗（癫）痫的（药物），镇（癫）痫的（药剂）

medication *n.* 药物；药物治疗；药物处理（当我们说谁谁是 “on medication”，意思就是说他正在进行药物治疗。）

damp *adj.* 潮湿的 *v.* 使潮湿；抑制 *n.* 湿气

compassion *n.* 怜悯，同情，恻隐之心（该词由前缀 com “共同” 与词根 pass “感情” 组合在一起，其意不言自明。同义词有：commiseration、sympathy。）

pursuit *n.* 追求；追赶（来自动词 pursue。Will Smith 的著名电影《当幸福来敲门》英文片名就叫做 *The Pursuit of Happiness*。）

avenue *n.* 林荫路；大街；途径，手段（avenue 的缩写是 ave，street 的缩写是 st，road 的缩写是 rd。）

diagnosis *n.* 诊断；判断

题目详解

Questions 27-30

解答

27. 根据细节信息 “mixed feeling about the book” 和顺序原则定位于原文第一段最后一句话 “...my reactions to the book are mixed”，但是这里并没有提及原因。原因实际上出现在前一句话 “So I had high expectations of *Musicophilia*...”，也就是说作者对这本书期望很高，但是却不得不说（feeling a little guilty reporting...）自己的感受是 “mixed”，言外之意就是讲这本书未达到自己的期望。对应这个信息的选项是 B。原文中虽然出现了 “guilty” 这个词，但是并不是说作者做了什么不好的事而让他感到 “guilty”，

而是表达了作者不得不对这本书作出负面评价的无奈，况且这个“guilty” feeling 也是他的“mixed” reactions 的一部分，而不是原因，所以选项 A 不正确，应该被排除。原文明显在第二段开头提及了“He richly documents his own life in the book and reveals highly personal experiences”，而选项 C 却说“Sacks failed to include his personal stories in the book”，这与原文内容相反，所以排除。第一段倒数第二句话提及 Oliver Sacks 是一个“prolific author”，即多产的作家，这与选项 D“This is the only book written by Sacks”信息相反，所以选项 D 也应该被排除。综上所述，正确答案为选项 B。

28. 利用细节信息“best part of the book”和顺序原则定位于原文第二段第一句话“Sacks himself is the best part of *Musicophilia*”，第二句话接着讲述“He richly documents his own life in the book and reveals highly personal experiences”，也就是说作者认为该书最好的部分在于 Sacks 对自己的经历的描述，对应选项 C“the autobiographical description in the book”。选项 A“the photo of Sacks listening to music”，虽然原文也有提及，但这只是此书最好的部分的一个表现，或者按照作者的原话“a positive impression that is borne out by the contents of the book”，即一个由书籍内容所支持的留给读者的正面印象，而非最好的部分，所以应该排除。虽然原文第二段最后也提及本书写作的语气“steady and erudite but never pontifical…neither self-conscious nor self-promoting”，表示肯定，但是这也并非此书最好的部分，所以排除。选项 D“the description of Sacks's wealth”完全和原文不相关，原文的“richly documents…”指的根本不是财富，所以也被排除。综上所述，正确答案为选项 C。

29. 利用细节信息“preface”和顺序原则很容易定位于原文第三段，但是因为题目问到“what did Sacks try to achieve”属于归纳总结的内容，所以无法定位到具体的任何一个句子，需要阅读全段，然后再利用排除法对选项一一进行判断。选项 A“make terms with the new technologies”，意为和新技术妥协或达到一个平衡点。原文第三段最后提及的“Sacks…is torn between the 'old-fashioned' path of observation and the newfangled, high-tech approach: He knows that he needs to take heed of the latter, but his heart lies with the former”就对应这个信息，他知道新技术很重要，是必须考虑的，但是又真的喜欢简单的传统的观察研究，所以需要在两者之间找一个平衡。虽然不能一眼就看出这个选项是正确答案，但是可以先待选。选项 B“give detailed description of various musical disorders”，即详细地描述了多种乐感失调症，原文段落虽然提及“…the complex and often bizarre disorders to which these are prone”，但是这里明确说到，作者是想传达从这些研究和文献中获取的灵感，而并非对这些病症进行描述，所以排除。选项 C“explain how people understand music”，与选项 B 的问题类似，原文虽然提及“musical perception and imagery”，但是并非是要解释人们如何认知或欣赏音乐的，所以也排除。选项 D“explain why he needs to do away with simple observation”，解释为什么他要废除使用“simple observation”，这个信息明显与原文相反，正如前面提到，原文明确表示 Sacks 非常喜欢使用简单的传统的观察研究，所以该选项必须排除。综上所述，正确答案为选项 A。

30. 利用细节信息“Tony Cicoria”、“disappointing”和顺序原则定位于原文第四段最后两句话“There are now more sensitive tests, but Cicoria has declined to undergo them; he does not want to delve into the causes of his musicality. What a shame!”也就是说，作者感到非常遗憾或失望是因为有很多更敏感的测试可以进行，但是却被 Cicoria 拒绝了（declined to undergo them），这个信息明显对应选项 A“He refuses to have further tests”。选项 B“He can't determine the cause of his sudden musicality”似乎和该段落倒数第二句话中“he does not want to delve into the causes of his musicality（他不愿意深究自己突如其来的乐感的缘由）”有联系，实则完全不相关，所以排除。选项 C“He nearly died because of the lightening” 和 选 项 D“His brain waves were too normal to show anything”虽然在原文中都有提及，但是都不是作者感到失望的原因，所以也应该排除。综上所述，正确答案为选项 A。

Questions 31-36

31. 该题目的细节词不明显，但是可以利用顺序原则和第 32 题的定位提示定位到原文第一段最后一句话“And I confess to feeling a little guilty reporting that my reactions to the book are mixed”。这里作者明显提及自己在对 Oliver Sacks 的作品作出负面评价时“feeling guilty”，对应题目信息“difficult to give…a less than favorable review”。题目信息与原文信息一致，所以正确答案为 Yes。

32. 利用细节信息“Beethoven's Pathétique Sonata”很容易定位到原文第二段中间“...shows him wearing headphones, eyes closed, clearly enchanted as he listens to Alfred Brendel perform Beethoven's Pathétique Sonata”，但是原文并没有提及这个音乐是否能治愈“musical disorders”，只是提及书的封面上有 Sacks 的一张听音乐时陶醉的照片。题目信息在原文信息的基础上无法判断，所以正确答案为 Not Given。

33. 利用细节信息“observation”和“technological methods”的比较以及顺序原则定位于原文第三段最后“Sacks…is torn between the 'old-fashioned' path of observation and the newfangled, high-tech approach: He knows that he needs to take heed of the latter, but his heart lies with the former”。原文明显讲到 Sacks 对于“observation”和“technological methods”左右为难（torn between），他明显喜欢“observation”，但是又认为“technological methods”一样重要（he needs to take heed of the latter），而题目却说“technological methods”在“observation”面前不重要。题目信息与原文信息直接相反，所以正确答案为 No。

34. 利用细节信息“music therapy”和顺序原则定位于原文第六段开头“To Sacks's credit, part III, 'Memory, Movement and Music', brings us into the underappreciated realm of music therapy”。这里虽然提及“music therapy”不被人们重视（对应题目信息“undervalued”），但是并未讲到“why music therapy is undervalued”，更未提及理解这个原因容易与否。题目信息在原文信息的基础上无法判断，所以正确答案为 Not Given。

35. 利用细节信息“other theories and findings”和顺序原则定位于原文倒数第四段最后一句话“And he tends to be rather uncritical in accepting scientific findings and theories”，再加上前面作者对 Sacks 的负面评价不难看出，作者认为 Sacks 毫无保留地接受其他研究发现或理论是不应该的，对应题目所说的“Sacks should have more skepticism”。题目信息与原文信息一致，所以正确答案为 Yes。

36. 利用细节信息“new testing methods”和顺序原则定位于原文最后一段第二句话“Although Sacks recognises the existence of new technologies…he does not call for their use”。原文明显说到 Sacks 没有使用“new technologies”（对应题目信息“new testing methods”），而题目却说 Sacks 迫不及待地（impatient）要使用新的测试方法。题目信息与原文信息直接相反，所以正确答案为 No。

Questions 37-40

解答

37. 利用细节信息“harmony and melody”定位于原文倒数第三段倒数第二句话“…loss of the ability to perceive harmony but not melody, indicate that there is no music center in the brain”，对应选项 F“show that music is not localised in the brain”。尽管选项 E“indicate that not everyone can receive good education”中的 education 在原文倒数第三段最后一句话也被提及，但是完全不是“The dissociations between harmony and melody”所表明的内容，应该被排除。所以正确答案为选项 F。

38. 利用细节信息“treating musical disorders”和顺序原则定位于原文倒数第二段的全部内容。原文明显提及没有真正的“cures”，而且治疗效果也不同（their effectiveness varies widely），与选项 B“indicates that medication can have varied results”对应，所以正确答案为选项 B。

39. 利用细节信息“EEG”和顺序原则定位于原文最后一段第一句话“in many of the cases described here the patient with music-brain symptoms is reported to have 'normal' EEG results”，对应选项 A“show no music-brain disorders”，所以正确答案为选项 A。

40. 利用细节信息“new technologies”和顺序原则定位于原文最后一段的最后两句话“Sacks expresses fear that 'the simple art of observation may be lost' if we rely too much on new technologies. He does call for both approaches…”这里作者明显提及Sacks认为observation和new technologies都要使用（He does call for both approaches），对应选项D“should not be used in isolation”，所以正确答案为选项D。

参考译文

音乐“病”

诺曼·M·温伯格对奥利弗·萨克斯关于音乐的最新作品的评论。

音乐和大脑都是使人无尽着迷的课题，尤其是作为一个声音习得和记忆方面的神经学专家，我发现它们更是令人着迷。因此，我对于神经病学家兼高产作家奥利弗·萨克斯的最新著作《恋音乐》有着较高的期待。但我不得不愧疚地承认我对这本书的感受是复杂的。

萨克斯本人是《恋音乐》这本书中最棒的部分。在这本书中，他丰富地纪录了自己的生活并揭示了极具个人色彩的经历。在书的封面上放着他的照片——戴着耳机，双眼闭合，聆听着阿尔弗雷德·布伦德尔演奏贝多芬的《悲怆奏鸣曲》时那种陶醉的神情——给人留下了正面的印象。当然，书的内容也证实了这一点。整本著作里，萨克斯的语气沉稳而博学，但又决不自以为是。他既不害羞，也不自我标榜。

前言部分很好地介绍了书的主要内容。其中，萨克斯解释说他想传达从“大量及快速增长的关于音乐认知和音乐意象的神经学以及其易导致的复杂且经常奇特的失调案例”中获得的灵感。他也强调了“观察这门简单艺术”和“人文环境的丰富性”的重要性。他说他想“把观察和描述与最新的技术结合在一起”，同时充满想象力地去领会自己的病人和研究对象的经验。读者可以看到，萨克斯，一个具有40年经验的神经学家，在“过时的”观察研究和最新的高科技研究方法之间左右徘徊：他知道后者的必要性，但是他的心却在前者。

这本书主要包含了对案例的详细描述，其中大多数涉及萨克斯在自己的学术生涯中见到的病人。对当代神经学报道的简要讨论遍布全书。第一部分“音乐幽灵”以一个奇怪的病例开头：托尼·西科里拉，一个不懂音乐的中年外科医生在一次被闪电击中之后疯狂地爱上了音乐。他突然开始渴望聆听钢琴乐，而在此前却对钢琴乐全然不感兴趣。他开始弹奏钢琴，然后开始谱曲，这些曲子就像是一波又一波的乐符自发地在他的大脑中形成。这是怎么回事呢？是心理学因素导致的吗（当闪电击中他时，他经历了一场濒死体验）？还是他大脑皮层中的听觉区域改变的直接结果呢？在20世纪90年代中期，也就是在那场创伤和“皈依”音乐之后不久，脑电波图还显示着他的脑电波都是正常的。现在还有更敏感的测试可以做，但是西科里拉拒绝参与；他不想深入研究这突如其来的乐感的缘由。这真是令人遗憾！

第二部分"不同的乐感"所涉及的话题更广，但是不幸的是，有些章节几乎甚至没有给人带来任何新意。例如，长达五页的第十三章仅仅提到了失明者的听力比正常视力的人要好。最有趣的章节要数那些讲述不同寻常病例的章节。第八章是关于"失音症"和"合音错乱症"，分别指无法欣赏音乐的症状和不能听到合音但是却能欣赏音乐旋律的特定障碍。这些特定的"不协调"在萨克斯所描述的病例中都能找到。

值得赞赏的是，萨克斯在第三部分"记忆、运动和音乐"中带领我们进入了未得到充分赏识的音乐治疗领域。第十六章解释了"旋律声调治疗法"是如何被用来帮助表达性失语症患者（指那些在中风或大脑损伤后不能口头表达自己的想法的人）再次流利地说话。在第二十章中，萨克斯展示了音乐近乎奇迹般的力量。这种力量使得帕金森氏症患者和其他具有严重运动协调障碍的人，甚至那些肢体已经僵化形成奇怪姿势的人，再次充满活力地运动起来。科学家现在还不能解释音乐是如何达到这个效果的。

对于不熟悉神经科学和音乐行为的读者来说，《恋音乐》可能是一本具有启发性的读物。但是这本书却并不能满足那些寻找萨克斯所描述的这些现象的原因和含义的人。原因之一就在于萨克斯仿佛更愿意讨论病人，而不是讨论试验。并且，他倾向于毫无保留地接受科学发现和理论。

固然，人们对于与音乐相关的大脑奇异现象了解极少。但是，萨克斯其实本可以发掘出更多关于他和其他神经学专家所做出的观察以及那些成功治疗案例所带来的启迪。例如，他本应该指出在音乐欣赏的诸多组成部分中，许多特定的不协调（比如，丧失辨别合音而非旋律的能力）就意味着大脑中不存在音乐中枢。正因为很多读过此书的人都极其可能认为所有的思想行为都有对应的大脑中枢，所以这本书错过了一个很好的纠正观念的机会。

人们能够得出的另外一个结论是，我们似乎并没有一个能治愈有关音乐的神经学疾病的"灵药"。一种药物也许能减轻一个病人的症状，但却能使另一个病人的病情恶化，或者能在同一个病人的身上体现出好坏两种截然不同的效果。书中提及的治疗方法几乎毫无例外地都采用了抗癫痫的药物，这些药物一般来说不过是"浇灭"了大脑的兴奋度；这些治疗方法的有效性也各不相同。

最后，在书中所描述的许多案例中，患有与音乐相关的大脑病症的病人都显示出"正常的"脑电波测试结果。尽管萨克斯知晓存在更先进的技术，而且其中还具有和标准神经学脑电波测试相比更灵敏的分析脑电波的方法，但他却并没有使用。事实上，尽管他显示出了对病人的极大同情，但是他并没有传达出追寻新的诊断和治疗与音乐相关的大脑疾病的方法的紧迫性。这一点正好对应了前言中萨克斯所表达出的担忧，即如果我们过分依赖新技术，"观察研究这一简单艺术就会消失"。虽然他也确实呼吁两种方法并行，但是我们只能寄期望于神经学界能作出回应。

Test 5

Reading Passage 1. Morse Code

词汇详解

radiotelegraphy *n.* 无线电报（该词由 radio 与 telegraphy 组合而成。radio 是“无线电”，telegraphy 是“电报”。其中前缀 tele 代表的意思是“远”，例如：telephone 听到远处的声音，电话；telecom 和远处的人交流，电信；television 看到远处的事物，电视；telescope 往远处看，望远镜；teleport 拿到远处，瞬间移动等。）

emergence *n.* 出现；显现

variation *n.* 变化，变动；变异

expansion *n.* 扩大；扩展；膨胀

distress *n.* 悲痛；危难；困境；贫困 *v.* 使痛苦，使贫困（distress、suffering、misery 和 agony 在英语中都可以表示“忧伤，痛苦”，但是 distress 强调外在的而且通常是短暂的肉体或精神上的压力“external and usually temporary cause of great physical or mental strain and stress”，例如：the hurricane put everyone in great distress。而 suffering 则强调有意识地忍受痛苦或忧伤“conscious endurance of pain or distress”，例如：the suffering of famine victims。misery 侧重于由疾病、贫穷或损失所带来的不幸“the unhappiness attending especially sickness, poverty or loss”，例如：the homeless live with misery every day。agony 则暗示痛苦过于强烈而难以忍受“pain too intense to be borne”，例如：in agony over the death of their child。“distress call”指的是飞机、船舶等的“求救信号”。）

have a good run 运行良好；干得不错；持续时间久

eternal *adj.* 永恒的，永久的；似乎不停的；不朽的（同义词有：ageless、dateless、enduring、everlasting、immortal、imperishable、lasting、perennial、perpetual、timeless 等。值得一提的是，英语中有一种说法“pass on into”或者“enter eternal life”，意思就是说某个人“死了”，这里的“eternal life”是一种委婉表达法“euphemism”。）

flash *v.* 使闪光，使闪亮；闪现；出示；迅速传播，传送 *n.* 闪光；闪光灯；动画；一瞥 *adj.* 突发的；豪华的，阔气的；爱显摆的（“手电筒”就叫做“flashlight”，当然英国人会把它

叫做“torch”。英语中有很多关于 flash 的词组或习语，例如：“quick as a flash”的意思就是“很快，马上”，相当于“swift as lightning”；“flash something around”是指“到处炫耀”；“flash a smile”或者“flash a smile at someone”指的是“露出微笑”，而且通常是快而短暂的；“flash across one's mind”就是说想法在人的头脑中“一闪而过”；“in a flash”就是“一闪之间”，也是非常快。老外学习语言或者记忆一些知识点时，通常会用到“flashcard 教学用的抽示卡”，就是把单词或知识点记在卡片上，有空就从兜里掏出来看一看。）

desperate *adj.* 绝望的；拼命地；极度渴望的；危急的；孤注一掷的（英文当中有句俗话叫做“desperate diseases must have desperate remedies”，相当于中文的“重症还得猛药治”，意思就是说“对困难或危险的处境可以采取极端的措施”，或者还可以说成“desperate times often call for desperate measures”。变形成“desperado”，意思就是“亡命之徒”。“despair”就是“绝望”。）

transmission *n.* 播送；传送；传动装置

radio *n.* 无线电通讯；收音机；无线电广播节目；无线电收发设备 *v.* 用无线电发送信号

sink *v.* 下沉，沉没；下降，降低 *n.* 洗涤槽；洗碗池

decommission *v.* 使退役

sign-off *n.* 广播完毕的信号

switch *n.* 开关；突变；转辙器 *v.* 转变，改变；转换

maritime *adj.* 海的；海事的；海上的；沿海的

appropriate *adj.* 适当的；恰当的；合适的 *v.* 占用；挪用；拨（款）

single-mindedness *n.* 一心一意；专心

rival *n.* 对手；竞争者 *v.* 与……竞争；比得上

spring *n.* 春季；泉水；弹簧；弹性；跳跃 *v.* 跳跃；反弹（本文中主要是“弹簧”的意思。）

there is a catch 其中有诈，有圈套

bear *n.* 熊 *v.* 忍受；承担；支撑；具有，拥有（名字或头衔）；带有（某种标记或外观特征）；生育（与 bear 相关的词组有很多，例如：bear off 离开；bear out 证明，证实；bear testimony to 为……作证；bear the brunt of 首当其冲；bear with 忍受；bear witness to 作证；grin and bear it 任劳任怨，逆来顺受等。）

sketch *n.* 草图；素描；梗概 *v.* 草拟；作速写；作素描；画草图（“a thumbnail sketch”指的是“简单的描绘”；“sketch something in”指的是“把……描绘进去”；“sketch something out”也是“描绘”的意思。）

scheme *v.* 策划，图谋 *n.* 计划；方案（英文中有种说法叫做“in the scheme of things”，意思是说“某事物在整个事态或一连串的事件当中”。）

devise *v.* 想出，设计；发明

tricky *adj.* 狡猾的；复杂的，棘手的

grid *n.* 金属格栅；方格图案；坐标方格；电力网（power grid 就是“输电网”，大型央企“国

家电网”就是“State Grid Corporation of China”。）

transpire *v.* 蒸发，散发；被发现，为人所知

facility *n.* 设备，设施；装置；场所；天赋，才能

dominant *adj.* 占优势的，强大的；专横的（来自动词dominate“控制”，dominate又来自拉丁语的dominus，也就是“master”的意思，所以与其同源的词汇domain就是指一个人熟悉、擅长的“领域”了。dominance和domination都是它的名词，前者多指“优势，支配地位或优越性”，而后者多指“控制，统治”。）

revise *v.* 修订；改变；修正

rotate *v.* 旋转或转动；使轮流（来自于拉丁语rota“轮子”。同样由rota变形过来的单词有：rotund圆胖的；rotor转子。）

hierarchy *n.* 等级制度；层级

deem *v.* 认为，视为

lavish *adj.* 慷慨的；大方的；丰富的；大量的（同义词有：profuse、exorbitant、extravagant、immoderate、excessive、plethoric等。）

banquet *n.* 宴会，盛宴 *v.* 宴请；参加宴会

adulatory *adj.* 奉承的（动词形式是adulate。另外有两个长相相似的单词，分别是adulterate“掺假”和adultery“通奸”，看来adults都不干好事啊。）

tap *v.* 轻拍，轻叩，轻敲；用（手指或脚）打节拍；利用，发掘；窃听 *n.* 龙头，阀门；轻轻敲击；踢踏舞；电话窃听（“tap someone's telephone”就是“在某人的电话上安装窃听装置”。）

standing ovation 长时间起立鼓掌；起立致敬

throb *n.* 跳动；震动；颤动 *v.* 抽痛；有规律地颤动，震响；跳动

instantaneous *adj.* 瞬间的；即时的

heyday *n.* 全盛期

precursor *n.* 前驱；先锋；先兆；初期形式（该词由表示“在……之前”的前缀pre和表示“跑”的词根curr组成，所以字面意思就是“先驱”。同义词有：foregoer、harbinger、herald、forerunner等。）

lease *n.* 租约，租契 *v.* 租用，租借（“lease something to someone”就是“把某物租给某人”；“give something a new lease of life”的意思是说“给予新的生机或活力”。）

题目详解

Questions 1-8

思路

这种题型忌讳寻找主题句或中心句，因为每个人对段落中心思想的判断通常不同，而且

每个段落的首尾句也不一定是主题句或中心句，所以最好的解答方法应该是通过对每位考生都能读懂的标题进行反向思维，然后和段落内容进行比较，排除作答。

i. *The advantage of Morse's invention*

反向思维词：advantage

反向思维：如果某段落选此为标题，则该段落应该重点讲述莫尔斯电码的优点，例如高效、方便迅捷、成本低廉、回报丰厚等。

ii. *A suitable job for women*

反向思维词：women

反向思维：如果某段落选此为标题，则该段落应该具体讲述女性。以女性为中心，讲述和电报相关的工作如何对女性有好处，甚至还可能出现和男性的对比等。

iii. *Morse's invention was developed*

反向思维：如果某段落选此为标题，则该段落应该位于文章的开头前几段，因为整篇文章都是在讲莫尔斯电码的，所以它的诞生一般先写，然后是之后的发展等。

iv. *Sea rescue after the invention of radiotelegraphy*

反向思维词：Sea rescue, radiotelegraphy

反向思维：如果某段落选此为标题，则该段落应该会出现专业词汇"radiotelegraphy"，但是出现该词的段落并不意味着一定要选，而是可以待选，直至排除或确认为正确答案；而且该段落应该主要讲述海事救援方面的内容，甚至有可能出现具体的案例。

v. *The emergence of many job opportunities*

反向思维：如果某段落选此为标题，则该段落应该主要讲述工作方面的内容，以及出现许多就业机会等，虽然具体提及什么详细的内容不容易确定，但是总可以最后排除解答。

vi. *Standard and variations*

反向思维：该标题不容易进行反向思维，但是如果某段落选此为标题，则该段落应该提及一个什么东西的具体标准，然后讲述这个标准可能在不同国家、不同地区有许多不同的"variations"。

vii. *Application of Morse code in a new technology*

反向思维词：a new technology

反向思维：如果某段落选此为标题，则该段落应该会讲述一个具体的新技术，以及莫尔斯电码在其中的应用等。

viii. *The discovery of electricity*

反向思维：如果某段落选此为标题，则该段落应该重点讲述电的发现，甚至会出现具体的科学家和科学实验，以及电被发现的时间等。

ix. International expansion of Morse Code

反向思维词：International

反向思维：如果某段落选此为标题，则该段落可能会出现具体的世界各国的名称或具体的地名以体现莫尔斯电码的在国际范围内的扩张，或者也可能以数据的形式体现。

x. The beginning of an end

反向思维词：beginning

反向思维：该标题也不容易进行反向思维，但是如果是讲述某一个事物或事件的"beginning"，一般会出现具体的时间。

xi. The move of using code to convey information

反向思维：如果某段落选此为标题，则该段落应该提到以前不是用"code"来传递信息，后来因为某种原因开始使用"code"来"convey information"。

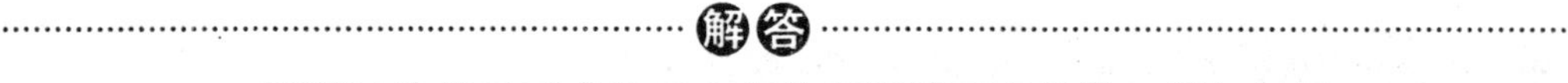

1. ***Paragraph A:*** 浏览该段落后不难发现大多数标题都可以排除，例如标题 v. The emergence of many job opportunities，因为该段落根本未提及任何与工作相关的信息。唯有标题 iv. Sea rescue after the invention of radiotelegraphy 中的"sea rescue"、标题 x. The beginning of an end 中的"beginning"和标题 xi. The move of using code to convey information 中的"using code to convey information"和该段落有点联系。但是标题 iv 中的"radiotelegraphy"在该段落中完全没有提到，所以应该排除；该段落也并非着重讲述标题 xi 所代表的人们是怎么开始使用电码来传递信息的，反而提及莫尔斯代码终止使用了，也应该排除。只有标题 x 与段落相关，而且该段落中也确实提及自 1992 年开始许多国家已经逐渐用 GMDSS 来替代莫尔斯电码，即对应标题中的"beginning"，也对应标题的"end"。所以综上所述，正确答案为标题 x。
2. ***Paragraph B:*** 与该段落相关的标题分别有 iii. Morse's invention was developed、viii. The discovery of electricity 和 xi. The move of using code to convey information。该段落虽然提及关于莫尔斯产生了发明电报的想法，但是并未提及他的发明是如何"develop"出来的，所以标题 iii. Morse's invention was developed 对应得并不贴切，可以排除。标题 viii. The discovery of electricity 中的"electricity"虽然在该段落中有所提及，但是并不是在具体讲电被发现的过程，而只是提及最新的电力理论上的进步使莫尔斯产生了发明电报的想法，所以也应该排除。标题 xi. The move of using code to convey information 的内容虽然在该段落中的对应并不是非常直接，但是莫尔斯"taken with the idea of building an electric telegraph to send messages in codes"的新想法以及"Morse

succeeded"确实对应了"The move of using code to convey information"。所以综上所述，正确答案为标题 xi。

3. ***Paragraph C:*** 与该段落相关的标题有标题 i. The advantage of Morse's invention 和标题 iii. Morse's invention was developed。虽然段落开头就提及"Compared with rival electric telegraph designs…Morse's design was very simple: it required little more than a 'key'"，对应标题 i 中的"advantage"，但是作者很快又讲到"there was a catch"，再然后又详细描述了莫尔斯的最初设计以及他在助手的帮助下对自己的设计进行了改善。由此可见，标题 i 不太合适，如果改成"The advantage and disadvantage of Morse's invention"或许还值得考虑。况且，在段落 D 的辅助下，考生不难判断段落 C 应该选标题 iii. Morse's invention was developed。所以综上所述，正确答案为标题 iii。
4. ***Paragraph D:*** 通过阅读该段落，考生应该很容易发现与该段落相关的标题只有标题 i. The advantage of Morse's invention，所以正确答案为标题 i。
5. ***Paragraph E:*** 虽然该段落开头提及"As electric telegraphy took off in the early 1850s"，与标题 viii. The discovery of electricity 中的"electricity"有相关性，但是该段落并未提及任何关于发现电力的内容，应该排除。剩下的唯一和该段落有联系的只有标题 vi. Standard and variations，对应段落中提到的"European standard"和"a split between American and International Morse"，所以正确答案为标题 vi。
6. ***Paragraph F:*** 与该段落相关的标题有 ii. A suitable job for women 和 v. The emergence of many job opportunities。段落最后虽然提及"Telegraphy was also deemed suitable work for women"，以及"a third of the operators...were female"，但是这明显只是该段落的一个细节信息，并非该段落的主要内容，应该排除。而标题 v. The emergence of many job opportunities 的信息在该段落中得到了很好的对应，比如电报次文化的兴起为农村人口提供了进城工作的机会，甚至还为女性提供了工作机会。所以综上所述，正确答案为标题 v。
7. ***Paragraph G:*** 这道题目相对简单，在读完该段落后，很容易发现与该段落相关的标题只有 ix. International expansion of Morse Code，所以正确答案为标题 ix。
8. ***Paragraph H:*** 与该段落相关的标题有 iv. Sea rescue after the invention of radiotelegraphy 和 vii. Application of Morse Code in a new technology。很明显该段落虽然提及"radiotelegraphy"，但是并没有详细讲述其发明之后对"Sea rescue"有什么样的影响等，所以标题 iv 应该排除。而标题 vii 就对应得很好。段落中间提及的"Morse code, however, was about to be given a new lease of life thanks to another new technology"，以及最后提及的"Morse radio equipment was commonplace on ships"都对应"Application of Morse Code in a new technology"（莫尔斯电码在新技术中的应用）。所以综上所述，正确答案为标题 vii。

Questions 9-13

解答

9. 利用顺序性原则和细节信息“before his invention of Morse code”定位于原文段落 B 的第三句话“At the time Morse was a painter and occasional inventor”，原文这里明显提及莫尔斯只是一个“occasional inventor”，而题目却说莫尔斯在发明莫尔斯电码之前就已经“famous as an inventor”。题目信息与原文信息直接相反，所以答案为 False。
10. 利用细节信息“support from the Congress”和顺序性原则定位于原文段落 B 的最后一句话“it was 12 years, for example, before he secured money from Congress to build his first telegraph line”，原文提及莫尔斯等候了 12 年，与题目信息“waited a long time”相对应。题目信息与原文信息一致，所以答案为 True。
11. 利用细节信息“difficult to learn”和“compared with other designs”定位于原文段落 D 的第一句话“the need to learn this complicated-looking code made Morse’s telegraph seem impossibly tricky compared with other, more user-friendly designs”，原文这里的“impossibly tricky”对应题目中的“difficult to learn”，“compared with other, more user-friendly designs”对应题目中的“compared with other designs”。题目信息与原文信息是同义表达，所以答案为 True。
12. 利用细节信息“operators from rural areas”定位于原文段落 F 后半部分的信息。原文这里虽然提到了“rural operators”的内容，但只是说他们位于报务员等级的底层（At the bottom of the pile were slow, inexperienced rural operators），以及电报操作的工作使得他们可以进城务工并获得更高收入（rural operators found that their new-found skill was a passport to better pay in a city job），原文并未提及公司是否更愿意雇佣来自乡下的报务员。题目信息在原文信息的基础上无法判断，所以答案为 Not Given。
13. 利用细节信息“Morse died”和顺序性原则定位于原文段落 G 的第三句话“By the time of his death in 1872...”，原文这里虽然提及莫尔斯辞世于 1872 年，但是并未提及是什么原因。题目信息在原文信息的基础上无法判断，所以答案为 Not Given。

参考译文

莫尔斯电码

莫尔斯电码正被一个新的基于卫星的系统所取代，.用来在海上发送求救信号。它的电码已经被人们使用许久。

A “呼叫！呼叫！这是我们陷入永久沉默之前的最后一次呼叫。”然而让人们吃惊的是，这条在 1997 年 1 月 31 日流传于广播电台的用莫尔斯电码发送的信息并非是一

个来自正在下沉的船上无线电报务员的绝望求助。事实上，这是一条标志在法国水域结束使用莫尔斯电码来发送求救信号的信息。自 1992 年开始，随着世界船运转向使用一个新的基于卫星的全球海上遇险和安全系统（GMDSS），世界各国纷纷采用相似（可能会欠缺诗意）的信号来标志自己的莫尔斯电码设备的退役。切换到 GMDSS 的最终期限是 2 月 1 日，这一天被广泛认为是一个时代的终结。

B 但是莫尔斯电码却有着优良的历史。作为往往和沉船无线电报务员相关的一项技术，莫尔斯电码的想法据说最初是塞缪尔·莫尔斯在一艘横渡大西洋的轮船上突然想到的。那个时候，莫尔斯只是一个画家，偶尔也做做发明，但是当同船的一位乘客和他分享关于电力理论最新进展的时候，莫尔斯突然有了一个建设电报机并用电码传播信息的想法。其实在过去一个世纪的大部分时间里，已经有许多其他发明家尝试做相同的事情。莫尔斯成功了，而且被人们称作“电报之父”，其中部分原因就在于他的执著与坚持——例如，他用了 12 年的时间才从美国国会获得款项来建设自己的第一条电报线路——但也有技术方面的原因。

C 和其他竞争对手的电报设计（例如英国威廉·库克和查尔斯·惠特斯通的针式电报机）相比，莫尔斯的设计非常简单：它只需要一个“按键”（实际上是一个弹簧承载式开关）来发送信息，一个会发出咔嗒声的“发声器”来接收信息，以及一根连接两者的电线。尽管莫尔斯的硬件设计很简单，但是却有一个问题：为了使用该设备，报务员必须要学会那套以莫尔斯的名字命名的点与线的电码。起初，莫尔斯并没有打算使用点或线的组合来代表不同的字母。根据他在横渡大西洋的旅途过程中在本子上记录下来的笔记来看，他的第一套电码使用了点和线来代表 0 至 9 十个数字。莫尔斯的想法是这样的，他认为信息可以由一连串的数字组成，而这些数字又分别对应一个特殊数字编码字典中的单词和词组。但是莫尔斯之后放弃了这个想法，并在其助手阿尔弗莱德·维尔的帮助下设计出了用点和线组成一个个字母拼成信息的莫尔斯电码字母表。

D 起初，学习这个看起来非常复杂的电码表的需求使得莫尔斯电报和其他用户易学的设计比起来过于复杂困难。例如，库克和惠特斯通的电报就是使用五个针脚从菱形网格中挑出字母。尽管这意味着任何人都可以轻松使用，但是它却需要在电报站之间连接五根电线。而莫尔斯的电报只需要一根。很快人们也发现，有些人具有使用莫尔斯电码的天赋。

E 随着电报在 19 世纪 50 年代的兴起，莫尔斯电报迅速占据了主导地位。在 1851 年它被采纳为欧洲标准，使得不同国家的电报网络可以直接连接在一起。（然而英国却坚持使用针式电报一段时间，没有加入这个标准）。到这时为止，莫尔斯电码自身也进行了一些修改，加入了注音符和其他国家的文字，这也导致了一直持续到今天的美国莫尔斯电码和国际莫尔斯电码的分裂。

F 在国际海底电缆中，人们用一个小型可旋转的镜子所反射的左旋和右旋光线来分别表示点和线。与此同时，一个确切的具有自己的习俗和词汇的电报次文化，以及一个基于报务员收发电报电码速度的等级制度也应运而生。第一流的报务员一分钟可以收发45个单词，他们从事报业新闻的传播，牢牢掌握了大城市里收入最好的工作。在这个等级的底层是那些收发缓慢、来自乡下的报务员，其中大多数都是兼职。但是，随着他们使用莫尔斯电码的熟练程度的提升，这些乡下的报务员发现，他们新掌握的技能是一个能使他们在城市中获得更高收入的通行证。报务员很快就充斥了整个新兴中产阶层。收发电报也被认为是一项适合女性的工作。截至1870年，美国最大的位于纽约的西联电报公司中，有三分之一的报务员是女性。

G 在1871年的道别仪式上，莫尔斯本人向全球报务员宣布了再见。在盛大的宴席和诸多奉承的演说之后，莫尔斯坐在了一个电报桌前，手指放在连接了美国各电报线的按键上，伴随着人们长久的起立和掌声，敲出了自己最后的道别。当莫尔斯在1872年辞世之时，全球已经真正很好地通过电报联系在一起：在超过六十五万英里的电报线和三万英里的海底电缆里，莫尔斯电码在不停地传输信息；两万个城镇和乡村业已连入环球电报网络。正如今天互联网常被称作“信息高速公路”，当时的电报也被称作“思想的瞬时通道”。

H 但是到了19世纪80年代，随着完全不需要专业技能便可操作的电话和自动电报（电传打字机的雏形）的发明，莫尔斯电报作为尖端科技的鼎盛时期已然即将终止。然而，莫尔斯电码却因另一项新技术而即将获得新生：无线电。在1896年古列尔莫·马可尼发明无线电报之后，莫尔斯电码在海上应用的潜力显现了出来。有史以来第一次，船舶与船舶之间以及船舶与岸上之间可以无视天气状况和是否在可视范围内互相通讯。1897年，马可尼成功地在沿岸电报站和一艘意大利战船之间（相距19公里/12英里）发送了一条莫尔斯电码讯息。截至1910年，莫尔斯无线电通信设备已经成为船舶上的标配。

Reading Passage 2. From A Novice to An Expert

词汇详解

novice *n.* 初学者，新手（其中词根nova就是“new新”的意思，于是novice这个单词就是“新手”的意思。加拿大的新斯科舍省就叫做Nova Scotia，当然也可以音译为努瓦斯科舍省。同时还有novel“小说”这个单词就来自于nova这个词根，因为每本小说都应该有新意，否则老调重弹就没什么意思了。“新手”还有其他的表达法：newbie、rookie、 recruit、beginner、tenderfoot、freshman、neophyte、apprentice、abecedarian 等。）

expertise *n.* 专门知识或技能

commitment *n.* 承诺；投入；奉献；花费（来自动词 commit。其中词根 mit 代表“派出，派遣”，也就是英文 send 的意思，前缀 com 代表“共同，一起”，所以 commit 就有“使承担义务”的意思。）

be coupled with 和……联合，结合

concurrently *adv.* 同时发生地（该词来自动词 concur“同时发生，一致，同意”，其中 con 代表“一起”，词根 curr 代表“跑”。同样由词根 curr 衍生出来的词汇还有：incur 遭遇，招致；occur 发生，出现；recur 复发，重现；cursory 匆忙的，草率的；cursive 潦草的，草书的；excursion 短途旅行；precursor 先驱等。）

boundary *n.* 分界线；界限；范围

mentor *n.* 导师，指导者

acquire *v.* 获得，取得；学到（AIDS“艾滋病”的全称就是 Acquired Immune Deficiency Syndrome。acquire 的名词形式是 acquisition。）

chess *n.* 棋，国际象棋（象棋是一种策略型平板游戏“strategy board game”，在西方其他常见的平板游戏还有：checkers 西洋跳棋；monopoly 强手棋；scrabble 拼字游戏；reversi 黑白棋；backgammon 西洋双陆棋等。）

pattern *n.* 模式，方式；花样，图案；榜样，典范；模型；样品 *v.* 模仿某物；形成图案（“pattern something after something”指的是“仿照……的样子建造，仿制”。）

journeyman *n.* 学徒期满的职工；熟练工

maintain *v.* 保持，维持；保养，维护；抚养，赡养（其中 manus 代表“手”，tain 代表“持有”。）

offensive *adj.* 无礼的，冒犯的；令人不快或讨厌的；进攻的，攻势的 *n.* 进攻，攻势（该词是动词 offend 的变形，由代表“反对”的前缀 ob 和代表“击打”的词根 fend 构成。名词形式是 offense。当为了说明事实，但又不是有意冒犯时，人们常说“no offense”或者“mean no offense”的表达，例如：I'm really sorry. I meant no offense. It was simply a slip of the tongue. 此时，如果听者没有往心里去就会说“no offense taken”，当然“take offense”就指的是“往心里去，而且觉得受到侮辱”的意思了。）

defensive *adj.* 防御用的；防守的；戒备的，自卫的 *n.* 守势（来自动词 defend。英语里有个说法叫做“The best defense is a good offense”，意思就是“最好的防守就是进攻”。习语“spring to one's defense”是形象地表达“立刻为自己或某人辩解”，强调快，例如：We sprang to Mary's defense when she was accused of doing wrong.）

hypothesis *n.* 假设，假说（该词由表示“在……下面”的前缀 hypo 和表示“放置”的词根 thesis 组合而成，所以该词的字面意思就是“放在下面的东西”，也就是“underlying assumption”了。与 hypo 相关的词汇有：hypotension 低血压；hypodermic 皮下的；hypothermia 低温症；hypochondria 忧郁症；hypocrisy 虚伪；hypoxia 缺氧症等。与 thesis 相关

的词汇有：thesis 论文；antithesis 对立；synthesis 合成；parenthesis 括号，插入语等。）
transition *n.* 过渡；转变；变迁（还可以用来指“过境”。来自动词 transit。很多城市的快速公交系统 BRT 的全称就是“Bus Rapid Transit”。）
superficial *adj.* 表面的；肤浅的；缺乏深度的（该词由表示“在……上”的 super 和 face 组成，所以字面意思再清晰不过了。“美貌就是表面的，肤浅的”，英文常说“beauty is only skin deep”。）
perceive *v.* 意识到；察觉，发觉；理解
domain *n.* 范围，领域；领土
random *adj.* 任意的；随机的；胡乱的（词组“at random”表达的意思是“随便地，随意地”。）
innate *adj.* 天生的；先天的；固有的（该词由表示“进入或内部”的前缀 in 和表示“出生”的词根 nat 组成。由 nat 组成的单词还有：natal 出生的；prenatal 出生前的；nation 国民，民族；neonate 新生儿等。）
perceptual *adj.* 知觉的，有知觉的
utilise *v.* 利用，使用
comprehend *v.* 理解，领会；包含（该词前缀 com 代表“共同”，词根 prehend 代表“抓住”，所以字面意思就是“全部抓住”，于是就有“理解，领会，包含”的意思。同样由词根 prehend 衍生出来的词汇还有：apprehend 逮捕；reprehend 斥责；misapprehend 误解等。其形容词 comprehensive 常表示“综合的”意思，例如：comprehensive guide 综合指南。）
criterion *n.*（评判的）标准，尺度（该词的复数形式为 criteria，雅思写作与口语考试的“评分标准”就叫做“marking criteria”。）
monitor *n.* 显示器；监测仪；监控人员；班长 *v.* 监视；检测；监督；监听
heuristics *n.* 启发法；探索法
actuarial *adj.* 保险精算的
outperform *v.* 做得比……更好，胜过
theorist *n.* 理论家
inconsistent *adj.* 不一致的；不协调的；前后矛盾的
bias *n.* 偏见，成见；偏心；偏爱 *v.* 使倾向一方；使有偏见（“on the bias”的意思就是“成对角地”。）
cognitive *adj.* 认知的；认识的（该词词根 gno 代表的意思就是“知道 know”，相关的词汇还有：agnostic 不可知论的；gnosis 真知；prognosis 预测；recognise 认出等。）
consensus *n.* 意见一致；共同看法（该词来自动词 consent “同意”，而 consent 又是由表示“共同，一起”的前缀 con 和表示“感觉”的词根 sent 构成，所以不难理解该词为“同意”的意思。人们在口语中常说的“达成一致意见”，英文就叫做“reach a consensus”。）
manifestation *n.* 表示，显示；示威（来自 manifest，作形容词时，意思是“明显的，明白的”，等同于 apparent、obvious、clear、clear-cut、evident、lucid、patent、unambiguous 等；作

动词时，意思就是"显现，显示，使……清楚、清晰"。该词还有一个变形 manifesto，是"宣言"的意思，像著名的卡尔·马克思的《共产党宣言》就叫做 *The Communist Manifesto*。）

题目详解

Questions 14-18

解答

14. 利用顺序性原则和细节信息"perform a given task"定位于原文第一段第二句话"The novice needs to learn the guiding principles and rules of a given task in order to perform that task"。原文这里明显提及新手需要学习"guiding principles and rules"（指导性原则和规则）来完成任务，所以正确答案为 guiding principles 和 rules。

15. 利用顺序性原则和细节信息"guided…through learning"定位于原文第一段第四句话"a novice will find a mentor to guide her through the process of acquiring new knowledge"，这里的"the process of acquiring new knowledge"对应题目中的"learning"，所以正确答案为 mentor。

16. 利用顺序性原则和细节信息"within and between cases"定位于原文第二段第一、二句话"the novice begins to recognise patterns of behavior within cases and, thus, becomes a journeyman…the journeyman finds patterns not only within cases but also between cases"。原文中的"recognise"和"find"都对应题目中的"identify"，所以正确答案为 patterns of behavior 或 patterns。

17. 利用顺序性原则定位于原文第二段第二句话"With more practice and exposure to increasingly complex cases…"，原文明显提及"journeyman"面临的案例更多是"complex cases"，所以正确答案为 complex。

18. 利用顺序性原则和细节信息"creates predictions"定位于原文第三段第一、二句话"When a journeyman starts to make and test hypotheses about future behavior…Once she creatively generates knowledge"和倒数第二句话"makes predictions based on patterns, and tests those predictions against actual behavior, she is generating new knowledge…"，原文中的"make hypotheses"和"makes predictions"都对应题目的"creates predictions"，而且原文中还讲到专家能在经验的基础上创造新知识（new knowledge），所以正确答案为 knowledge。

Questions 19-23

解答

19. 利用细节信息"classifying objects"定位于原文第五段第二句话"A novice, for example, might group objects together by color or size, whereas an expert would group the same objects according to their function or utility”。原文中的“group objects”对应题目中的“classifying objects”，而且原文明显提及新手通常按照颜色或大小把物品编排在一起，而专家是按照物品的功用分类，两者的分类方法明显不一样。题目信息与原文信息直接相反，所以答案为 False。

20. 利用细节信息“memory skills”和顺序性原则定位于原文第六段第一句话“Experts have better domain-specific short-term and long-term memory than novices do”。原文这里虽然提及了“memory”方面的信息，但只是说专家在自己领域方面的长短期记忆力都比新手强，并未提及新手的训练是否“focused on memory skills”。题目信息在原文信息的基础上无法判断，所以答案为 Not Given。

21. 利用细节信息“higher efficiency”和顺序性原则定位于原文第六段第二句话“Moreover, experts perform tasks in their domains faster than novices and commit fewer errors while problem solving”。原文中明显提及专家完成任务更快、错误更少，这里的“faster”和“commit fewer errors”对应题目的“higher efficiency”。题目信息与原文信息表达一致，所以答案为 True。

22. 利用顺序性原则定位于原文第六段倒数第二句话“Experts spend more time thinking about a problem to fully understand it at the beginning of a task than do novices, who immediately seek to find a solution”。原文中明显提及新手是立即设法寻找解决方案，原文中的“immediately seek to find a solution”对应题目中的“tries to solve it straight away”。题目信息与原文信息表达一致，所以答案为 True。

23. 利用细节信息“mistakes and limits”定位于原文第七段第一句话和最后一句话“experts are more aware of instances where they have committed errors…Experts are aware of the limits of their domain knowledge…”。原文中明显提到专家更擅长发现自己的错误和了解自己领域知识的局限。题目信息与原文信息表达一致，所以答案为 True。

Questions 24-26

解答

24. 利用细节信息“making predictions”和“statistical models”定位于原文倒数第二段第一句话“Theorists and researchers differ when trying to explain why experts are less accurate forecasters than statistical models”。而且综合倒数第三段所讲述的内容，很明显可以看出专家在预测未来方面比统计模型要“less accurate”，所以正确答案为 accurate。

25. 利用细节信息“inconsistent”、“Yet some believe”和顺序性原则定位于原文最后一段第一句话“A number of researchers point to human biases to explain unreliable expert predictions”。原文明显提及有些研究者认为是人的偏见导致了问题的产生，所以正

确答案为human bias。

26. 利用细节信息"cause and manifestation"和顺序性原则定位于原文最后一段最后一句话"the literature shows little consensus regarding the causes or manifestations of human bias"。原文明显提及对于偏见产生的原因（causes）和表现（manifestations），现有研究文献中没有一致见解（shows little consensus），原文中的"little"对应题目中的"there isn't a great deal of"，所以正确答案为consensus。

参考译文

从新手到专家

专长是努力加上创造力。它尤其指的是在一个相对狭小的研究领域中所投入的时间、精力和资源，以及在该领域中产生新知识所必需的创造性能量。一个人需要付出大量的时间和接触大量的案例才能成为专家。

每个人在刚进入某个领域时都是新手。新手需要学习一个具体任务的指导性原则和规则才能执行这个任务。与此同时，新手还需要接触具体的案例或事例来检验这些原则以及它们的适用范围。通常情况下，新手会寻找一个指导者来指引她获取新知识的过程。举一个非常简单的例子，这就像是一个人在学习象棋。象棋新手会寻找导师来教导她比赛的目标、棋盘的大小、不同棋子的名称、每个棋子的功用、棋子的移动规则以及赢得比赛或输掉比赛的必要条件。

假以时日，在大量的练习之后，新手开始认出不同案例中的行为模式，于是变成一个熟练工。在更多的练习和接触到更为复杂的案例之后，熟练工不仅能够找到案例之中的规律和联系，甚至还能发现案例之间的规律与联系。更重要的是，熟练工了解到这些规律随着时间的推移经常会重复地出现。熟练工仍旧会和导师保持定期联系来解决特定的难题和学习更加复杂的策略。回到象棋选手的例子，该选手开始学习开局要领、进攻和防守的比赛策略，以及胜利和失败的种种情况。

当一个熟练工开始基于过去的经验对未来的行为做出假设并测试假设时，她就开始进入新的阶段了。一旦当她能够创造性地产生知识，而非简单地把表面的规律联系在一起，她就变成了一个专家。此时，她对自己的知识充满了自信，也不再需要导师的指导——她能对自己的知识负责了。再次回到象棋的例子，一旦一个熟练工开始和专家级选手比赛，开始基于规律做出预测或判断，并且根据对手的真实表现检验自己的判断，她就在创造新的知识并加深对比赛的理解。这时，她在创造属于她自己的案例，而非依赖于别人的案例。

专长的优势所在

专家在自己的研究领域内比非专家人士更能发现有意义的规律。在新手看来是随机的或没有任何联系的数据点的地方，专家却能够把案例内以及案例间的常见规律联系在一起。这种发现规律的能力并非天生的察觉能力，而是反映了一个人在接触并体验了成千上万个案例之后对知识的组织能力。

专家对自己的研究领域的理解也远远大于新手，而且能够运用更高层次的原则来解决问题。例如，新手可能会按照颜色或者大小将事物分组，而专家则会根据它们的功能和用途来分类。专家在自己的研究领域中对数据意义的理解和对衡量变量的不同标准的利用要比新手好很多。专家能够认出对特定问题具有最大影响的变量，进而把自己的重心放在这些变量上。

和新手相比，专家具有更好的与领域相关的短期和长期记忆力。此外，专家在自己的领域中比新手完成任务更快，解决问题时犯的错误更少。有趣的是，专家解决问题的方式也和新手不一样。专家在任务之初会花更多的时间来思考以便完全理解整个问题，而新手却会立刻设法寻找问题的解决方案。专家会借助以往案例中的知识来创建思维模式以便解决问题。

和新手相比，专家也更善于自我审视，更能意识到自己所犯错误或没能理解问题所在的种种情景。专家也更经常地检查自己的解决方案，并且能在自己错过解决问题的必要信息时意识到这种情况。专家对自己专业领域知识的局限性也有较强的认识，并且能运用自己领域中的原理或原则来解决经验之外的问题。

专长的矛盾之处

专长的优势也可能成为劣势。尽管我们可能会期望专家能对未来做出精准的预测，但是他们却并不太擅长这一点。自20世纪30年代以来，研究人员一直在测试专家预测的能力。精算数据统计表被用来衡量专家的表现，以判定他们是否比简单的统计模型更善于预测。七十年后，在两百多个涉及各个领域的实验的支持下，答案显然是：否。在提供了等量的特定案例信息的情况下，精算数据统计表在预测未来的表现上和专家的表现一样好，或者更好。即便在一个专家获取了比统计模型更具体的案例信息的情况下，专家也未必能比精算数据统计表的表现更出色。

理论学家和研究者对于为什么专家在预测未来方面没有统计模型精准的情况有不同的看法。有些人辩称，和所有人一样，专家在使用思维模式进行预测时也会前后不一致。也就是说，一个专家在某月预测X时所使用的思维模式和他在下一个月预测X时所使用的思维模式会不一样，尽管这两次使用了完全相同的案例和数据。

也有许多研究者指出专家预测不可靠的现象是由人类偏见导致的。在过去三十年间，研究者在预测认知方面做了大量的分类、实验及理论工作。尽管如此，现有的研究文献对人类偏见产生的原因及表现仍没有达成一致。

Reading Passage 3. High Speed Photography

词汇详解

inception *n.* 开始，开端

locomotion *n.* 运动；移动；运动力；移动力（该词词根 mot 代表“运动”，例如：motive 动机；motivate 激励；locomotive 移动的；promote 促进，推动等。）

avenue *n.* 林荫道；大街；途径；手段（在雅思阅读和听力考试当中，任何标准的缩写都是可以接受的，所以如果考生不会拼写 avenue，可以只写它的缩写形式“ave.”。其他常见的表示地址的缩写形式还有：rd. 对应 road；st. 对应 street；blvd. 对应 boulevard；blk. 对应 block；bldg. 对应 building；fl. 对应 floor；rm. 对应 room 等。）

mechanical *adj.* 机械的；机械制造的；呆板的

representation *n.* 表现；陈述；代表

pictorialist *n.* 运用绘画风格的人（尤指非营利性的艺术摄影师）

surveillance *n.* 监视，监督

amateur *n.* 业余爱好者（该词来自于法语的 amour“恋情”，所以 amateur 就是“热爱……事物的人”。）

preserve *v.* 保护；维护；保存；保持；腌制 *n.* 果酱；腌菜；独有或专有的活动

visualise *v.* 设想；想象；使可见；视觉化

lapse *n.* 失误，疏忽；过失，过错；时间间隔（词组“lapse from grace”指的是“失势，失宠”，例句：The child was told that if he ever smoked even one cigarette, he would lapse from grace for certain.）

timescale 时间，时段

perception *n.* 感知能力；洞察力；理解，看法（来自动词 perceive，其中前缀 per 是“完全 thoroughly”的意思，ceive 是“拿到，拿着”的意思，所以 perceive 就是“完全拿到”，进一步就变成“理解，洞察”的意思。）

incredibly *adv.* 难以置信地；非常地（来自形容词 incredible“难以置信的”，其中词根 cred 的意思是“相信”。）

subtle *adj.* 微妙的；不明显的；机巧的；狡猾的；巧妙的；敏锐的（名词形式是 subtlety。中文成语“胸有城府”可以翻译成“subtle way of thinking”或者“hard to fathom”。同义词有：artful、crafty、delicate、scheming 等。）

sequence *n.* 顺序，次序；一连串相关事件或行动；片段，连续镜头

frame *n.* 框架，边框；构架；骨架；眼镜框；镜头，画面 *v.* 框住；给……装框；陷害，诬告；制定，拟定；表达（词组“frame something in something”的意思就是“把某物放在……的框架内”，例句：Let us frame the photograph in a wood frame rather than a metal one. 如果

再进一步延伸，还可以表示“以某种特定的方式来表达思想”，例句：He framed his comments in very simple language. 当 frame 作为“陷害”的意思时，人们常用“…is framed”这样的表达，基本等同于“be set up”。）

interval *n.* 间隔时间；幕间休息（中文中的“有规律性的间隔”，英文就翻译为“at regular intervals”。）

shrink *v.* 收缩，缩小；变小；退缩，畏缩（英语中有一个非常形象的表达“shrinking violet”，意思就是“羞怯的人”。）

phenomenon *n.* 现象；奇事；非凡的人或事物（该词的复数形式是 phenomena。它的形容词 phenomenal 在口语和写作中经常被用来表达“非凡的，不寻常的，惊人的”的意思，例如：Her performance tonight was absolutely phenomenal.）

hover *v.* 盘旋；彷徨；踌躇（“气垫船”就叫做“hovercraft”。）

nectar *n.* 花蜜；果汁；（古希腊神话中的）众神饮的酒；琼浆玉液

flap *n.* 襟翼；拍动，拍打；慌乱 *v.* 扑动（翅膀）；振翅；摆动

flex *v.* 弯曲，活动 *n.* 花线；皮线（词组“flex something out of shape”的意思是说“使某物弯曲变形”，甚至在美式英语中，如果说某人是“flexed out of shape”，则是指此人“非常生气”，例句：The boss was completely flexed out of shape. 词组“flex one's muscles”的字面意思指的是“挽起胳膊把肌肉露出来以显示力量”，形象点则指“展示力量”，例句：The attorney general is flexing his legal muscles to enforce gun control laws.）

precisely *adv.* 精确地，确切的，准确的；恰好，正是；确实如此

sample *n.* 样品；标本 *v.* 取样；试用；品尝（口语中常说的“品尝各种美食佳肴”就用到这个单词“sample different food/cuisines/delicacies”。）

project *v.* 放映；投射；预计，推断；计划，预订；传播 *n.* 项目；工程；计划；课题

proportionately *adv.* 成比例地，相称地

mainstay *n.* 支柱；中流砥柱；主要的依靠

motion blur 动态模糊（指的是电影或动画中快速移动的物体造成的明显的模糊、拖动痕迹。在电脑游戏的图像设置“graphics setting”中通常有 motion blur 这个选项，设置这个选项为开启可以增加游戏画面的真实感或电影效果“cinematic effect”。）

sensor *n.* 传感器；感应器

shutter *n.* 遮板；百叶窗；快门

strobe *n.* 闸门；闪光灯

footage *n.* 影片，影片片段，镜头

unprecedented *adj.* 前所未有的；无前例的；空前的（该词是 precedent 的否定变形。而 precedent 又来自于 precede，其中词根 cede 为“走”的意思，所以 precede 自然就是“在前面行走，先行”的意思，unprecedented 就变成了“史无前例的”了。precedent 的同义词有 previous、former、preceding、antecedent、anterior、forgoing、prior 等。）

entrancing *adj.* 使人神魂颠倒的；使人入神的（en 代表“进入”，trance 是“出神”。）

sprint *v.&n.* 冲刺，全速短跑（“百米冲刺”就叫做“100 meters sprint”。）

supple *adj.* 柔软的；灵活的；易弯曲的

limb *n.* 肢，腿，臂，翼；树的主枝（习语“out on a limb”的字面意思指的是“站在树枝上”，常用来表达“处于危险境地，缺乏他人支持”。词组“tear somebody limb from limb”就是“把某人的胳膊腿全卸下来”，常用来指代“猛烈的攻击”。）

ripple *v.* 使泛起涟漪，在……上形成波痕 *n.* 涟漪，涟波，波纹（ripple effect 就是“涟漪效应”，当然也可以翻译成“连锁反应”。）

spine *n.* 脊柱；脊椎

symphony *n.* 交响乐，交响曲（前缀 sym 是“共同，相同”，词根 phone 代表“声音”。同样由 phone 衍生出来的单词还有：phonetics 语音学；cacophony 刺耳的声音；microphone 话筒；telephone 电话等。）

fluid *n.* 液体，流体 *adj.* 流体的，流动的；不固定的；动作灵活而优美的

prey *n.* 被捕食的动物；捕获物；受损害者 *v.* 捕食（“成为……的猎物”英文常用“fall prey to somebody/something”来表达，当然也可以用来表达“受到不良影响”，例如：Patients may fall prey to dishonest salespeople who say they can cure their pain.）

snatch *v.* 迅速抓住；抢夺（词组“snatch someone/something away from…”的意思是“从…夺回 / 夺得某人或事物”，“snatch someone out of the jaws of death”或者“snatch someone from the jaws of death”都指的是“从死亡线把某人救过来”，相近的“snatch victory from the jaws of defeat”就指的是“在最后一刻获得胜利”。）

elastic *adj.* 有弹力的；可伸缩的；灵活的 *n.* 松紧带（迪斯尼动画片《超人总动员》中超能先生 Mr. Incredible 的老婆就是 Elastgirl，中文翻译为“弹力女超人”，因为她的身体无比柔软，而且还非常 elastic，可以随意伸缩。）

adhere *v.* 黏附；附着；坚持（该词由表示“加强”的前缀 ad 和表示“黏附”的词根 here 组合而成。英文中表达“坚持什么事”常用“adhere to something”的组合。同样由词根 here 衍生出来的词汇还有：cohere 凝聚，连贯；inhere 固有，生来即存在；hereditary 遗传的等。）

blink *v.* 眨眼睛；闪烁 *n.* 眨眼睛（习语“blink at something”可以是字面意思“看着某物眨眼睛”，也可以形象地指“对某事睁一只眼，闭一只眼”，当然更常见的说法实际上是“turn a blind eye to…”。习语“on the blink”指的是“出故障，不管用”，例句：Every computer in the office is on the blink again. 词组“in the blink of an eye”则指的“一眨眼的功夫”，形容很快。）

skip *v.* 跳过，略过；蹦跳着走；不做（本应做的事）*n.* 跳，蹦跳

adjust *v.* 适应；调整，调节

playback *n.*（录音、录像等的）重放，回放

edit *v.* 剪辑；编辑
voila 那就是；瞧
camera-tripping 相机跳闸、触动

题目详解

Questions 27-30

解答

27. 利用细节信息“Mushroom”可以很容易地定位到段落B。原文这里讲述的是用快镜头来观察“events and movements…too slow for human perception to follow”，而且原文中也提到mushroom的生长过程是“incredibly subtle to the human eye”，对应选项C的“too slow to be visible to human eyes”。所以正确答案为C。

28. 利用细节信息“Hummingbird”也可以很容易地定位到段落C。原文这里讲的是用慢镜头来拍摄“very fast phenomena”，而且在讲到蜂鸟时，说它的翅膀振动是“80 times every second”，表示频率非常快，对应选项A的“too fast to be perceived”。所以正确答案为A。

29. 利用细节信息“Frog”定位于原文段落E。原文在这里提到的摄影技术是“adjust the playback speed, which is also called by some the film speed adjustment”。因为青蛙捕食的全过程还包括游泳部分，如果都采用慢镜头的话，就会使观看者感到无聊，所以需要调节播放速度，对应选项D的“adjust the filming speed to make it interesting”。所以正确答案为D。

30. 利用细节信息“Bat”定位于原文段落F。原文中提到“Photographers or film-makers often place camera near the bat cave, on the path of the flying bats”，该信息就直接对应选项B的“film at the place where the animal will pass”。所以正确答案为B。

Questions 31-35

解答

31. 利用细节信息“something that occurs naturally slow”定位于原文段落B第四句话“a series of photographs are taken...each frame is taken with a lapse at a time interval between each shot”，原文提到每两张照片之间（“between each shot”对应题目中的“before another picture”）都有一个时间间隔（time interval）的延迟（lapse），所以正确答案可以填lapse或者time interval。

32. 利用细节信息“finally shown on screen”和“at a normal motion picture rate”定位于原文段落B第四句话后半部分“when played back at normal speed, a continuous action is produced and it appears to speed up"，很明显可以看出观众能看到的是一个"continuous action"，而且速度也加快了，所以正确答案为 continuous action。

33. 利用顺序性原则定位于原文段落 B 的第五句话"Put simply: we are shrinking time"，所以是时间被压缩了，正确答案为 time。

34. 利用细节信息"to demonstrate how fast things move"定位于原文段落 C 的第八、九句话"The only way to truly capture this motion is with cameras that will, in effect, slow down time. To do this, a greater length of film is taken..."，文章这里都是在讲蜂鸟振翅的运动过快，要想看清楚（对应题目中的"to demonstrate how fast things move"），那么拍摄时所用的胶卷就要更长（a greater length of film is taken），对应题目中的"exposed on a ...of film"，所以正确答案为 greater length。

35. 利用顺序性原则定位于原文段落 C 的倒数第二句话"time appears to be slowed down proportionately"，所以正确答案为 slowed down proportionately。

Questions 36-40

解答

36. 根据反向思维信息"various fields"推断，原文对应段落中应该会出现具体的有关摄影术在不同领域中的应用的例子。该题对应信息出现在原文段落 A。其实该段落除了最后一句话之外，其余都是在讲摄影术在诸多领域中的应用。例如段落开头提及科学家和艺术家在摄影术诞生之初就对其产生了浓厚的兴趣，然后又提及摄影术在军事等领域中的应用，最后还提及普通人对摄影术的使用，所以正确答案为 A。

37. 根据反向思维信息"significant role in biology"推断，原文对应段落中应该提及高速摄影很重要，应该出现"significant"的同义替换或者具体的描述。该题对应信息出现在原文段落 C 的最后一句话"That is why high-speed cameras have become such a mainstay of biology"。这里的"mainstay of biology"就是题目中"significant role in biology"的同义替换表达，所以正确答案为 C。

38. 根据反向思维信息"a traditional wisdom"推断，原文对应段落中应该会出现一个具体的"traditional wisdom"。再根据"the prospects of photography（摄像术的前景）"推测该题对应信息应该出现在文章的最后一段。所以，该题对应原文段落 G 的最后一句话"No matter what future it may hold, photography will continue to develop as it has been repeatedly demonstrated in many aspects of our life that 'a picture is worth a thousand words'"。很明显可以看出，这里的"好图胜却千言万语"就是一个"traditional wisdom"，所以正确答案为 G。

39. 根据反向思维信息"processed before final release"推断，原文对应段落中应该会出现影片制作完成前的一些具体阶段等。该题对应信息位于原文段落E的倒数第二句话“but at later editing stage this high frame rate will…”。这里的“later editing stage”就对应题目中的“processed before final release”，所以正确答案为E。

40. 根据反向思维信息“without human effort”，原文对应段落应该讲的是自动照相方面的内容，而且还可能介绍到具体的设备和自动摄像原理等。题目对应信息位于原文段落F中的“To capture bats on film, one must use some type of camera-tripping device...”，这里camera-tripping就是摄像机的自我触动装置，对应“自动摄影”。当然，如果考生还看不出来，在段落最后还提及“Though highly-advanced tripping device can now allow for unmanned shooting, it still may take several nights to get a truly high quality film”，这也可以使考生意识到“unmanned shooting”就对应题目中的“filming shooting without human effort”，所以正确答案为F。

参考译文

高速摄影

A 摄影术从诞生之初就受到了诸多科学家以及艺术家的关注。科学家使用摄影来记录和研究运动，例如埃德沃德·迈布里奇在1887年对人及动物运动的研究。艺术家同样对这些方面很感兴趣，但是除了研究摄影对现实的机械展示之外，他们也尝试探索其他方面的内容，例如绘画主义摄影。军队、警察和安全部队则利用摄影进行监视、识别和数据存储。摄影术也被业余爱好者们用来记录会议、捕捉特殊时刻、讲述故事、发送信息并成为了一种娱乐方式。各种技术进步和技巧使得人们能够看见那些原本对肉眼而言过快或过慢的事物。

B 其中的一种技巧就是快镜头或者更专业一点叫做延时拍摄。延时拍摄是捕捉自然界中发生的过于缓慢的以至于人类无法察觉的事物或运动的最佳方法。例如，蘑菇的生长周期在人眼看来是极其微妙的。为了把它的生长展现在观众面前，拍摄时就要用到一个非常简单的原理：先拍摄一系列的照片，然后按照顺序播放，形成一个移动画面影像，但是由于每一帧都是在拍摄时间间隔的延迟之后拍摄的，所以当以正常速度回放时，一个连续的运动过程就产生了，而且运动的速度看起来也加快了。简单来说：我们在压缩时间。平时要花费几分钟、数天，甚至几个月的事物和事件在经过几十到几百万倍的加速后可以让我们在数秒钟内观察到它们的完整过程。

C 另外一种常用的技巧就是高速摄影，它是一种用来拍摄非常快的现象的科学方法。高速摄影可以被看做是与延时拍摄相反的摄影技术。它诸多应用的其中之一就是在生物学研究中用来观察鸟类、蝙蝠，甚至是蜘蛛丝。想象一只几乎完全静止地悬停

在空中吸食花蜜的蜂鸟。伴随着每一次振翅，它的翅膀都会弯曲、收缩并改变形状。这些细微的运动精确地控制着蜂鸟翅膀所产生的升力，使其能更出色地悬停在空中。但是一只蜂鸟振翅的频率是每秒80次。唯一能真正捕捉到这个运动的方法就是使用实际上能够使时间慢下来的摄影机。为了实现这一特技，我们要在一个高采样频率或帧速下拍摄更长的胶卷，这比胶卷实际投射在屏幕上的速率要快很多。当以正常速度重放时，时间就仿佛成比例地放慢了。这也就是为什么高速摄影机已经成为了生物学的中坚力量。

D 在通常的使用中，高速摄影也可以指使用高速摄影机拍摄能使动作看似冻结的照片，尤其是用来减少照片中的动态模糊。这就需要一个高敏感度的传感器和一个优良的快门系统或者一个非常快的闪光灯。国家地理最近拍摄的一段影片——去年夏天在辛辛那提动物园经过三天紧张拍摄的视频——具有前所未有的清晰度和细节。“我观察猎豹奔跑已经有30年了”，动物园猫科动物大使项目创立者凯瑟琳·希尔克如是说道。“但是在那超慢动作影像中我却看到了我以前从未看到过的东西。”慢镜头影像使人身心陶醉。这只快速奔跑中的猫科动物身体结构的每一部分——柔软的四肢、一条条凸起的肌肉、极具柔韧性的脊柱——在速度的交响曲下一同发挥作用，展示了世界上最快的陆地动物行云流水般的优雅。

E 但是在拍摄青蛙捕捉猎物的时候，事情并未变得更复杂。青蛙可以在几千分之一秒内用其富有弹性的舌头捕获猎物。生物学家会非常乐意观看青蛙的舌头是如何伸出，粘到猎物，再缩回口腔的。但这一切都发生得太快了，比眨一下眼睛还要快50倍。于是人们自然而然地想到利用高速摄影机以慢镜头来捕捉这个惊奇的动作。但是还有一个问题——观众如果长时间地观看青蛙在慢镜头下游泳，他们会感到厌倦。那怎样才能跳过这一段呢？解决的方法非常简单——调节回放速度，也被称为影像速度调节。影像最初是以较高的帧数拍摄的（通常每秒300帧，因为这个帧数可以被轻易地转成较低的帧数而不会产生任何大的问题），但是在之后的编辑剪切阶段只有高帧频中捕捉猎物的那部分会被保留下来，而游泳的那部分则会被转成每秒24帧的普通速度。瞧啊，科学家现在可以坐下来轻松地观看而不必再痛苦地等候了。

F 有时候拍摄一张好的照片或者一段好的影像并不完全在于技术，而在于耐心，就如在蝙蝠案例中那样。蝙蝠体型小而且颜色较暗；它们飞行速度快而且只在晚上活动。要想把蝙蝠捕捉进影像当中，就必须使用某种摄影机触发装置。摄影师或者影片制作人经常把摄影机放置在蝙蝠洞穴附近，就在蝙蝠的必经之路上。摄影机还必须与触发装置进行连接和匹配，这样只要有蝙蝠阻断了触发光束，摄影机就会自动拍摄，这个过程会在晚上一直重复直至摄影机的电池耗尽。尽管高度发达的触发装置现在允许无人操控拍摄，但是要想获得真正高质量的影像仍然需要花费好几个夜晚。

G 它究竟是科学还是艺术呢？自从大约两百年前摄影技术被人们首次使用以来，摄影已经发展到一个几乎难以辨认的状态。有些人甚至说未来的摄影术会使我们难以想象。但是不管未来如何，摄影术会继续发展因为它在我们生活的诸多方面体现了“好图胜却千言万语”的道理。

Test 6

Reading Passage 1. Thomas Young The Last True Know-It-All

词汇详解

encyclopedia *n.* 百科全书（*Encyclopedia Britannica* 就是《大英百科全书》，又称《不列颠百科全书》。网上著名的维基百科，英文就叫做 Wikipedia。）

biographical *adj.* 传记的（来自名词 biography “传记”，由前缀 bio “生命” 和 graphy “写法、记录法” 组成。）

substantial *adj.* 实质的；富有的；坚固的；可观的（来自名词 substance，意思是 “物质，实物，主旨”。）

authoritatively *adv.* 权威地；可信地

subject *n.* 主题，话题；科目；研究对象

polymath *n.* 博学的人，博学之士（由表示 “多” 的前缀 poly 和表示 “学习，学会” 的词根 math 组合构成，字面意思就是 “学会很多东西”，进一步延伸为 “博学者”。）

dilettante *n.* 业余爱好者，一知半解者，浅薄的涉猎者（同义词有：amateur、dilettante、dabbler、tyro 等，但侧重点各有不同。amateur 侧重于在艺术实践中不得要领。dilettante 更多指热爱艺术的人，而非专业从事艺术创作的人，但通常隐含着轻浮和不严谨的态度。dabbler 则含有断断续续的工作习惯，缺乏持久性的意思。tyro 通常意味着由于缺乏经验，又大胆而产生的生硬和浮躁。）

epitaph *n.* 墓志铭，碑文（由表示 “在……上面” 的前缀 epi 和表示 “坟墓” 的 taphos 构成，字面意思就是 “在坟墓的上面”，自然就延伸为 “碑文” 的意思了。）

subtitle *n.* 副标题，小标题（在电影电视中，还有 “字幕” 的意思，通常作复数。）

paleontologist *n.* 古生物学者（由 paleon “古老，古代” 和 ologist “学家，学者” 组成，所以字面意思不言自明。同类型的词汇还有：biologist 生物学家；archaeologist 考古学家；geologist 地质学家等。）

accommodation *n.* 住所；适应；调节（accommodation address 就是 “寄宿地址”。）

hypothesise *v.* 假设，假定；推测（与 suppose 的意思相当，名词形式为 hypothesis。）

correspond *v.* 相一致，符合，相当（常见的词组有 correspond to 和 correspond with。）

subsequently *adv.* 随后；后来（来自形容词 subsequent"后来的，随后的"。该词由 sub"下面"与词根 sequi "跟随"构成，所以字面意思非常清晰。与该词根相关的词汇还有：sequel 后记，后传；consequence 后果，结果；sequence 顺序，次序；obsequious 奉承的，谄媚的；sequacious 盲从的。）

instrumental *adj.* 作为手段的；仪器的（来自名词 instrument "乐器，仪器"。）

alphabet *n.* 字母表；符号系统（大家都知道英文中有 26 个字母。把什么什么按照字母表顺序排列起来，英文可以说"put...in the alphabetical order"，其中 alphabetical 是形容词形式，意思就是"in the order of the alphabet"。）

hieroglyph *n.* 象形文字（该词是由前缀 hiero "神圣的，宗教上的"和表示"雕刻"的 glyph 构成，字面意思就是"神圣的雕刻"，延伸而来就成了"象形文字"。）

demotic *adj.* 民众的，通俗的，大众的（同义词有 common、popular 等。）

coin *n.* 硬币，金属货币 *v.* 创造（新词语）；铸造（纸币就是"notes"。）

prodigy *n.* 奇才，天才；奇观（中文中要夸某个小孩是神童或天才儿童，英文就可以说"...a child/an infant prodigy"，音乐奇才就是"musical prodigy"。）

oblivion *n.* 遗忘；湮没（任何事物或技能都是这样：use it or lose it。如果长期不使用，it will go into oblivion。Tom Cruise 2013 的好莱坞大片《遗落战境》的英文名就叫做 *Oblivion*。）

maternal *adj.* 母亲的；母系的（词根 mater 就是"母亲"的意思，再加上后缀 al 表示"……的，关于……的"，所以 maternal 的意思就非常清晰了。相对应的，"父亲的"就是"paternal"。maternal grandfather 就是"外公，外祖父"的意思，paternal grandfather 则是"爷爷，祖父"了。）

devour *v.* 狼吞虎咽地吃；如饥似渴地看或读；吞没，吞噬，毁灭（前缀 de 代表"下去"，词根 vorare 表示"to swallow 吞"，所以很容易得出"吞下去"的意思。词组 be devoured by sth 的意思就是"心中充满，全部注意力为……所吸引"。）

initiative *n.* 主动性，积极性；主动权（习语 on one's own initiative 的意思就是"主动地，自发地"。）

excel *v.* 擅长，善于；胜过，超过（当代表"胜过，超过"的意思时，基本上等同于"surpass"。）

pursue *v.* 从事，进行；追赶；追求（名词形式为 pursuit，Will Smith 的著名电影《当幸福来敲门》英文片名就叫做 *The Pursuit of Happiness*。）

appoint *v.* 任命，委派；安排，确定（appoint sb as sth 就是"任命某人为某职或某种身份"，其中的 as 是可以省略的。）

professorship *n.* 教授之职，教授职位（名词 professor 本身就是"教授"的意思，再加上表示"职位，地位，身份"的后缀 ship，该词的意思就不言自明了。）

civic *adj.* 城市的，市的；公民的，市民的（研究市政和公民的权利与责任的学科，即公民学或市政学，英文就是“civics”。人们常说的“市政中心”就是“civic centre”。）

superintendent *n.* 监督人；负责人

secretary *n.* 秘书；书记；文书；部长（secretary-general 就是“秘书长，总书记”。新闻中常常听到的联合国秘书长，英文翻译就是“the United Nations Secretary-General”。）

daunting *adj.* 使人气馁的，使人畏缩的，令人生畏的（来自动词 daunt“吓到，使气馁”。习语 nothing daunted 的意思就是“毫无惧色，毫不气馁”。）

doodle *v.* 涂鸦，胡写

verse *n.* 韵文，诗句，诗体（相当于另一个单词 poetry。）

vibrant *adj.* 响亮的；精力充沛的；鲜明的（同义词有 lively、exciting、brilliant 等。）

sustain *v.* 维持；支撑，支持；遭受，忍受；供养（由前缀 sub“下面”和词根 tain“支持，hold”构成，所以该词字面意思就是“to hold/support from underneath 从下面支持”。sustainable 是形容词，中文里面常说的“可持续发展”，英文就叫做“sustainable development”。）

rancorous *adj.* 满怀恶意的；怨恨的

credit *n.* 赊购；贷款；信用，信誉；银行存款 *v.* 存入金额；认为是……的功劳，把……归功于；相信（词根 cred 的意思就是“相信”，credible 就是“可信的”，incredible 就是“难以置信的”。）

pastime *n.* 消遣，娱乐，业余活动

题目详解

Questions 1-7

解答

1. 原文对应信息出现在第一段最后两句话“…Young is a good contender(竞争者) for the epitaph(墓志铭) ‘the last man who knew everything.’ …The phrase…also serves as the subtitle of two other recent biographies…”，“最后一个无所不知的人”这个标题也是另外两位学者传记的副标题。题干中“has also been claimed to other people（同样给了其他人）”与原文意思相符，所以答案是 True。
2. 题干中的关键词为“All”，原文对应信息出现在第二段第一行“Young…did more than write encyclopedia entries. He presented(呈递) his first paper to the Royal Society of London…”，他将自己的第一篇论文自荐给伦敦皇家学会，因此并不是所有的文章都被出版在百科全书上，所以答案是 False。
3. 原文对应信息出现在第三段最后一句话“These are the landmark achievements of a man who was a child prodigy(天才儿童) and who, unlike many remarkable(卓越的) children,

did not disappear into oblivion(遗忘) as an adult”，说明了杨在小时候就已经是一个天才儿童，长大后也没有泯然众人，所以答案是 False。

4. 这一题的答案是 Not Given，原文的类似信息出现在第五段第一行“Young’s skill as a physician, however, did not equal his skill as a scholar of natural philosophy(自然哲学学者) or linguistics(语言学家)”，有些考生因此会认为这一题是 False，但注意原文中只给出了 natural philosophy 和 linguistics 两项才能，而题干中给出的是杨作为医生的天赋超过（surpassed）他其他方面的才能（other skills），“other skills”过于广泛，原文并无提及杨作为医生的才能是否超过了他其他所有方面的才能，因此答案是 Not Given。

5. 原文对应信息出现在第五段中间，“His opinions were sought on civic(市政的) and national matters…”，许多市政和国家事务都会征求他的看法。题干与原文意思相符，所以答案是 True。

6. 题干中的关键词为“various social pastimes(各种不同的社交娱乐)”，原文对应信息出现在第六段倒数第二、三句话“Young was introduced into elite society(社会名流), attended the theatre and learned to dance and play the flute(长笛). In addition, he was an accomplished horseman(精通马术)”，由此可见，杨对各种娱乐消遣都十分感兴趣，题干与原文意思相符，所以答案是 True。

7. 题干中说杨在他的晚年得了一种病，而原文中并未提及杨生病与否，因此答案是 Not Given。

Questions 8-13

8. 根据题干中的“*Encyclopedia Britannica*”找到原文第一段，根据题干中出现的“life stories(生平事迹 / 传记)”找到第一段第一句话“…including 46 biographical entries(传记条目)”，所以答案是 46。

9. 根据题干中的关键词“first academic paper”找到原文第二段，题干问杨的论文是关于科学研究的哪方面，定位到第二段第三句话“In the paper, Young explained the process of accommodation(调节) in the human eye…”，注意答案不能超过 3 个单词，因此答案是 human eye accommodation。

10. 根据题干中的关键词“a group of languages”定位于原文第三段倒数第二句话“In another entry, he coined(杜撰) the term Indo-European to describe the family of languages spoken throughout most of Europe and northern India”，因此答案是 Indo-European。

11. 根据题干中的关键词“medical studies”和“inspired(鼓舞)”找到原文中的第四段第三、四句话“After leaving school, he was greatly encouraged by his mother’s uncle, Richard

Brocklesby…Following Brocklesby's lead, Young decided to pursue(从事) a career in medicine”，因此鼓舞杨从事医学的人是 Richard Brocklesby。

12. 根据题干中的关键词“teaching position”找到原文中关于杨作为教师的部分，原文对应的信息出现在第五段第二句话“…he had been appointed to a professorship(教授职位) of natural philosophy at the Royal Institution…”因此答案是 Royal Institution。

13. 根据题干中的关键词“contribution”和“London”找到原文中出现 London 的地方，即第四段后半部分和第五段中间。第四段中只提到杨在伦敦学习，并未提及做出什么贡献,因此应定位到第五段中间“…such as the introduction of gas lighting(煤气照明) to London and methods of ship construction”，杨将煤气照明引进伦敦，因此答案是 gas lighting。

参考译文

托马斯·杨：最后一个无所不知的人

托马斯·杨（1773-1829）是《大不列颠百科全书》中 63 篇文章的作者，这些文章中包括 46 篇传记（大部分都是关于科学家和古典学者）和大量关于“桥”“色彩论”“埃及”“语言”和“潮汐”的论文。一个能够在这么多领域写出这样多有权威性文章的人应该算是一个博学者，还是一个天才，亦或是一个兴趣广泛的业余人士呢？在一篇关于他的比较激进的新传记中，安德鲁·罗宾逊认为托马斯·杨是一位强有力的竞争者，能够配得这样的墓志铭：“最后一个无所不知的人”。但是杨也要面对竞争：因为罗宾逊给他的这个传记标题，也是另外两本新传记的副标题：伦纳德·沃伦于 1998 年著的关于古生物学家约瑟夫·莱迪（1823-1891）的一生以及保拉·冯德林于 2004 年著的关于另一位博学者亚塔那修·基歇尔（1602-1680）的传记。

当然，杨的贡献远不止写了很多百科全书上的文章。他在 20 岁的时候将自己的第一篇论文自荐给伦敦皇家学会，并在 21 岁生日后的一周被选为皇家学会院士。杨在该篇论文中解释了人类眼睛的调节机制——关于眼睛如何通过不同的距离聚焦在物体上。杨推测这是通过晶状体形状的改变来达到的。他还推论到，光是以波纹的形式传播的，为了能看见颜色，眼中必须要有三个感受器对“三原色”进行感应，而视网膜能对其产生感应的三种颜色分别是红、绿、紫。所有这些假设在后来都被证明是正确的。

在他人生的晚些时候，也就是他 40 多岁的时候，杨试图用密码破译技术破解罗塞塔石碑上的未知文字，这个石碑是 1799 年在埃及被拿破仑的军队发现的。该石碑上包含了三种文字：古希腊文、不可辨识的文字以及古埃及的象形文字。其中不可辨识的文字现在被认为是世俗体文字，正如杨所推断的，是和象形文字直接相关的。他最初的有关这方面的著作出现在《大不列颠百科全书》埃及部分的词条中。在另一个条目中，他创造了术语“印欧语系”来描述在欧洲大部分地区以及北印度使用的语言群。这些都是他获得的里程碑式的成就——他从小就展露出了惊人的天赋，但不同于许多天才儿童，他长大后并没有泯然众人。

托马斯·杨于1773年出生在英国萨默塞特郡，他从小和外公一起长大，最后去了寄宿学校。他从两岁的时候就开始博览群书，并且通过自学熟练掌握了拉丁语、希腊语、数学以及自然哲学。离开学校后，他在很大程度上受到了叔祖父理查德·布罗克兹比的鼓励，他的叔祖父是一位内科医生，也是英国皇家学会的一位院士。在布罗克兹比的引导下，杨决定要在医学方面有所建树。他曾先后在伦敦大学、爱丁堡大学、格丁根大学和剑桥大学学习医学。1808年，杨在完成剑桥大学的医学学习后，在伦敦开了一家诊所。很快，他就成为皇家内科医学院的院士，并且在几年后被任命为圣乔治医院的一名内科医生。

杨作为内科医生的医术却赶不上他作为自然哲学学者或是语言学家取得的成就。早在1801年，他就已被任命为英国皇家研究所的自然哲学教授，他每年都在那里举办多达60场的讲座。这些讲座内容在1807年以两本书的形式进行出版。1804年杨就已经成为英国皇家学会的秘书，而他也担任这个职务直至去世。许多市政和国家事务都会征求他的看法，比如在伦敦引进煤气照明和造船方法。从1819年起，他就是航海天文历的主要负责人，也是经度委员会的秘书。从1824年到1829年，他担任Palladian保险公司的统计检查官和内科医生。在1816年至1825年间，他为《大不列颠百科全书》编纂了许多词条，而且穷其一生，著作、论文无数。

作为一本传记的主题人物，杨是完美的——完美而令人生畏。很少有人能够在如此多的科技领域做出如此巨大的贡献。罗宾逊的目的是向非科学研究人士介绍杨的工作和生活。他成功地将科学的实质清晰地展现了出来（尤其是关于光学和古埃及象形文字方面的内容）。这本书的有些读者会像罗宾逊一样，觉得杨的成就令人印象深刻，其他人则会像一些历史学家一样，认为他只是一知半解者。尽管这本书写了许多关于杨的事迹，但读者也无法直观了解他。我们通过杨在医学课上胡乱写的希腊文和拉丁文短语以及他将一位年轻的女士写在避暑山庄墙上的诗句翻译成希腊挽歌的举动可以看出他的幽默。他被引入社会精英阶层，参加戏剧演出，学会跳舞和吹长笛。此外，他还是一位杰出的马术师。但是，他的个人生活也因为他在事业和研究方面的耀眼成就而略显苍白和黯淡。

托马斯·杨在1804年和伊丽莎·麦克斯威尔结婚，而且据罗宾逊所述：“他们的婚姻是幸福的，因为他的夫人欣赏他的工作。”我们对于他夫人的了解几乎仅限于她在她丈夫备受一些关于光学理论方面的争议时总是坚定地支持他，并且当他的医学生涯慢慢起飞的时候，她开始担心钱的问题。关于杨和他父母之间错综复杂的关系的记述也存世极少，罗宾逊在提到杨的非凡的头脑时也并没有将其归功于他的父母或其他任何人。尽管对杨的人际关系缺少细节描述，但是，任何一位对“作为一个天才意味着什么”感兴趣的人，都该读一读这本书。

Reading Passage 2. Antarctica – in from the cold?

词汇详解

ilk *n.* 类型，种类（多指某一类型或种类的人，等同于 kind、type、sort。）

blizzard *n.* 暴风雪，大风雪；大打击

deprivation *n.* 剥夺；丧失；匮乏；贫困（来自动词 deprive "剥夺，使丧失"，其中来自拉丁语的词根 privare 本身就表示 "掠夺 to rob" 的意思，常使用的动词短语为 "deprive sb/sth of sth"。）

bleakness *n.* 严寒；苍凉；萧瑟凄凉；惨淡无望（来自形容词 bleak，意思是 "不乐观的，阴冷的，荒凉的"。）

perception *n.* 感知，知觉；洞察力，悟性；看法，见解（该词作为 "感知" 的意思时，visual perception 就是 "视觉" 的意思。当表示 "洞察力" 时，同义词有：discernment、discrimination、penetration、insight、acumen 等。）

dedication *n.* 献身，献身；落成典礼；献词（来自动词 dedicate，意思是 "把……奉献给"，等同于英文中的 devote。另外，名词形式的 dedicated 有 "专心致志的，一心一意的" 意思，相当于 "committed"。）

integral *adj.* 必需的，不可或缺的；作为组成部分的；完整的（来自拉丁语 integer，意思是 "complete"。）

occupy *v.* 占用；居住；占据（由强化前缀 ob 和代表 "拿，取" 的词根 capere 构成，当作为 "占用" 的意思是，相当于英文中的 "take up"。）

exert *v.* 行使，施加（影响）；努力，竭力

circulation *n.*（气、水等的）环流，循环；发行量；交际；流传，流通；血液循环（人们常说的 "促进血液循环"，英文就叫做 "improve blood circulation"。"货币的流通" 就是 "the circulation of money"，"消息的传播" 就是 "the circulation of information"。当我们说某人参加社交活动，英文就可以说 "sb is in circulation"，反之，没有参加社交活动就是 "out of circulation"。）

Gondwana *n.* 冈瓦纳古大陆（又称 Gondwanaland，据说是数百万年前存在于南半球的大片陆地，包括现今的印度、澳大利亚、南极洲、南美洲和阿拉伯。）

circumpolar *adj.* 极地附近的，天极附近的（前缀 circum 是 "环绕，围绕……的，在……周围" 的意思，英文就是 "around 或 about"；而 polar 则是 "极地的" 的意思，著名的北极熊就是 "polar bear"。）

current *n.* 气流；水流；电流；潮流，趋向 *adj.* 当前的，现在的；流行的（作形容词时，current prices 就是“时价”，current employer 就是“当前雇主”。）

prevailing *adj.* 普遍的，盛行的，流行的（同义词有 current、predominant 等。prevailing wind 就是指一个地区常刮的或盛行的风。）

perish *v.* 死亡，暴死；毁灭；老化（习语 perish the thought 的意思就是“没门儿，甭想了，下辈子吧”。）

katabatic wind 下降风，重力风（katabatic 就是“下降的，向下吹的”，其中前缀 kata 表示“向下，降”，batos 表示“前进，前行”，所以字面意思就是“向下走”，自然而然就有“下降的”意思了。）

reverberate *v.* 回响，回荡；震颤；产生广泛影响（同义词还有：echo、reecho、reflect、resound 等。）

rotation *n.* 旋转，转动；一周，一圈；交替，轮换（行星围绕太阳的旋转，英文就是“the planet's rotation around the sun”。庄稼的轮作或轮流种植，英文翻译就是“crop rotation”或者“rotation of crops”。）

whip *v.* 抽出，除去；使朝着某一方向快速或猛然移动；鞭打

grazier *n.* 放牧人，畜牧业者

pasture *n.* 草地，牧场；牧草 *v.* 放牧（来自拉丁语 pastus，意思是“to feed”，即“给人或动物食物，喂养，饲养”。）

degradation *n.* 毁坏，恶化；堕落；潦倒（来自动词 degrade“使退化，降低”，其中前缀 de 表示“向下”，词根 grade 或 gradus 表示“step 走”，从字面意思“向下走”延伸一下就成了“恶化，堕落”。environmental degradation 就是“环境恶化”的意思。）

prototype *n.* 原型，雏形，最初形态（前缀 proto 表示“原始的，最早的”，type 就是“类型，模式”。与 proto 相关的词汇还有：protohuman 早期原始人；protohistory 史前历史学；protoplanet 原始行星等。）

predictive *adj.* 预言的，预测的（来自动词 predict“预言，预告”，等同于 forecast。）

unravel *v.* 解开，拆散；阐释，说明；解体，瓦解（由否定前缀 un 和表示“使纠缠，使混乱”的 ravel 构成。）

krill *n.* 磷虾（是小型海洋甲壳纲动物的总称，是长须鲸的主要食物。）

staple *adj.* 主要的，基本的，重要的 *n.* 基本食物，主食；主要产品，支柱产品（值得注意的是 staple diet 也是“主食”的意思。）

hemisphere *n.*（地球的）半球；（大脑的）半球（人们常提到的南半球和北半球就分别是“southern hemisphere”和“northern hemisphere”。）

thrive *v.* 兴旺发达；繁荣；茁壮成长（同义词有：prosper、flourish、blossom 等。）

circulatory *adj.* 循环的；血液循环的

conveyor *n.* 运送者，传送者；传播者（来自动词 convey，当作为“表达，传递”的意思

时，等同于 communicate，另外，还有“传送，运输”的意思。conveyor belt 就是“传送带，输送带”的意思。）

nutrient *n.* 营养物；滋养物（相关词汇有：nutritious 有营养的；malnutrition 营养不良；nutritionist 营养学家；nutrition 营养，营养学。）

abyssal *adj.* 深海的，深渊的（来自名词 abyss “深渊”。）

scour *v.* 擦亮，擦净；搜寻，翻找；冲刷（同义词有 wipe、scrub 等。）

lagoon *n.* 泻湖；环礁湖；濒海湖；小淡水湖（其他相关词汇有：stream 溪流；lake 湖，池；pool 尤指天然形成的水塘；pond 池塘；river 江，河。）

polynya *n.* 冰间湖，冰穴，冰湖

strip *v.* 除去，剥去；使空无一物；拆开；剥夺；脱掉衣服（短语 strip sth away 的意思是“剥去，剥下”。当 strip 作为“脱光衣服”的意思时，基本上等同于英文中的“undress”。）

continental shelf 大陆架

reoxygenate *v.* 重新产生氧化，重新充氧

revitalise *v.* 使恢复生机；使新生；使再兴

productivity *n.* 生产力；生产率（相关词汇有：produce 生产，制造；producer 生产商，产地，制片人；product 产品，产物；production 生产，产量，上映；productive 多产的，生产的，有效益的。）

owe *v.* 欠，欠债，欠账，欠情（owe sth to sb/sth 或 owe sb sth 的意思是“归功于，归因于”。另外，介词 owing to 相当于“because of”和“due to”，意思是“因为，由于，因……的缘故”。其中 because of 通常用在口语中。值得一提的是，thanks to 虽然也有“因为，由于”的意思，但更强调“好的方面或事情”，中文多翻译为“幸亏，多亏”。）

题目详解

Questions 14-18

解答

14. 根据题干中的关键词“prediction for agriculture”定位于原文 D 段后半段“By receiving more accurate predictions, graziers（畜牧业者）in northern Queensland are able to…”，还有 CSIRO 正在研究新的预测系统原型，而且对将来的预测改进持有信心（…enhance and extend our predictive ability），所以答案是 D。

15. 注意题干中的“vitality”是“活力，生命力”的意思，“brings back”在此处是“补充，恢复”的意思。原文对应的信息出现在 F 段后半段“Recent research has shown that as fresh sea ice forms（随着新的海冰形成）…Cold water carries more oxygen than warm water, so when it rises, well into the northern hemisphere, it reoxygenates and revitalises the ocean（给海洋补充新鲜的氧气从而激活了海洋的活力）"，所以答案是F。

16. 根据关键词"food chain"定位于原文E段后半段"Antarctic krill（磷虾）是baleen whales（须鲸）、penguins（企鹅）、some seals、sea birds和fish的食物"，而南极洲海冰的多寡决定了这个食物链底端磷虾的丰富程度，所以答案是E。

17. 注意题干的"extreme temperature 极端寒冷"和"cold wind 冷风"指的是南极洲特有的自然现象。原文对应的信息出现在C段最后两句话"Today the ice that overlies the bedrock is up to 4km thick, and surface temperatures as low as -89.2deg C have been recorded…creating fearsome wind-chill effects"，所以答案是C。

18. 原文对应信息出现在A段最后一句话"The image was one of a place removed from everyday reality（对应题干中的"forgotten"）, of a place with no apparent value to anyone（对应题干中的"insignificant"）"，所以答案是A。

Questions 19-21

解答

19. 根据题干中的"massive size"和"influence our climate"定位于原文B段最后一句话"Scientific research during the past half century has revealed…that Antarctica's great mass（对应题干中的"massive size"）and low temperature exert a major influence（对应题干中的"influence"）on climate and ocean circulation…"，所以答案是D。

20. 根据题干中的"wind blowing from the west"找到原文中出现"西风"的段落，推测答案就是西风下生成的一个流动循环的"物体"。原文对应的信息出现在C段第二句话"…eventually created enough space around Antarctica for the development of an Antarctic Circumpolar Current (ACC), that flowed from west to east under the influence of the prevailing westerly winds"，在盛行西风的作用下流动的自然是"Antarctic Circumpolar Current (ACC)"，所以答案是A。

21. 题干关键词为"ocean temperature and index"、"predict"和"Australia"。原文对应的信息出现在D段中间"Recent work is showing that the temperature of the ocean（海洋的温度）may be a better predictor of rainfall in Australia（澳大利亚的降水）than is the pressure difference between Darwin and Tahiti—the Southern Oscillation Index（南方震荡指数）"，所以答案是C。

Questions 22-26

解答

22. 题干明确地提出是B段，原文在B段提及"…Antarctica…seen to be an integral part（整体不可分割的部分）of Planet Earth, and a key component in the Earth System"，还有

最后一句话“...that Antarctica's great mass and low temperature exert a major influence on climate and ocean circulation, factors which influence the lives of millions of people all over the globe”，符合选项 C 的基本意思。至于选项 A 中的“global warming”，在 B 段中并未出现相关信息，所以直接排除 A 选项。原文 B 段虽然提及“lives of millions of people all over the globe”，但是并未提及任何关于“sea ice brings food”的信息，所以排除选项 B。最后，选项 D“南极洲位于地球的中心”更是不符合事实，可直接排除。综上所述，正确答案为 C。

23. 根据题干关键词“Australian farmers”定位到原文 D 段中间“By receiving more accurate predictions, graziers in northern Queensland（北昆士兰的畜牧业者对应题干中的“Australian farmers”）are able to avoid overstocking in years when rainfall will be poor.（他们不会再在雨水不足的年份过度放牧）Not only does this limit their losses but it prevents serious pasture degradation that may take decades to repair.（不仅减少了他们的损失，而且可以避免草场的退化）”，所以答案是 A。

24. 根据关键词“whales and seabirds”定位到原文 E 段最后两句话“Antarctic krill... breed well in years when sea ice is extensive and poorly when it is not”，南极洲的磷虾在海冰丰富的时候繁殖良好，反之不然。而磷虾是“whales and seabirds”的主要食物，因此符合冰少磷虾就少（这里的“Antarctic krill”等同于“food source”），磷虾少就是等同食物变少，食物变少“whales and seabirds”的数量也就下降了，所以正确答案是 C。

25. 根据关键词“katabatic winds”定位到原文 F 段中部“During winter, the howling katabatics sometimes...Recent research has shown that as fresh sea ice forms（当新鲜冰层形成）, it is continuously stripped away（就会被剥离）by the wind and may be blown up to 90km in a single day...Since only fresh water freezes into ice...”，由此可见，重力风主要是促成了新鲜冰层进入海洋，所以答案是 C。

26. 根据关键词“continental shelf”定位到原文 F 段“Since only fresh water freezes into ice, the water that remains becomes increasingly salty and dense, sinking until it spills over the continental shelf”，随着淡水结成冰，那些剩余的海水盐分浓度越来越高，密度越来越大，因此才“spills over the continental shelf”，对应题目中的“move beyond the continental shelf”，所以正确答案是 A。

参考译文

南极洲——从寒冷而来？

A 一个多世纪以前，斯科特、沙克尔顿以及莫森家族的男性们与南极洲的暴风雪、严寒以及残酷的气候所带来的种种匮乏作着斗争。在英勇行为盛行的年代，他们以帝

权的名义开创了一幅南极洲的版图，而这幅版图也顺利地延续到20世纪——这是一幅遥远、艰难、苍凉和与世隔绝的景象，是一幅只属于最英勇男性的版图。南极洲的这幅景象曾使之看上去像一个远离日常现实的地方，一个对任何人来说都没有明显价值的地方。

B 进入21世纪后，我们对南极洲的看法也随之改变。虽然从理论上来说，南极洲依旧难以接近且并不温暖，生活在那里也依然需要正常生活所没有的奉献精神，但南极大陆及其周边海域越来越被认为是地球不可分割的一部分，是地球系统中的关键组件。难道是因为电视和旅游使得这个世界看起来越来越小？或是因为南极洲真的在地慢占领一个中心点？科学研究在过去的半个世纪里不断揭示南极洲的巨大质量和低温对气候和海洋环流有着重大影响，而气候和海洋环流等因素又影响了全球各地无数人的生命。

C 南极洲并不总是那么寒冷的。缓慢解体的超级古陆冈瓦纳随着非洲、南美、印度以及澳大利亚向北运动，最终创造了足够的空间，发展形成了南极洲周围的南极绕极流（ACC），在盛行西风的影响下自西向东流动。当南极洲降温后，其植被死亡，冰川时期开始，南极大陆呈现出现在的外观。如今覆盖在基岩上的冰层有4公里厚，表面的最低温记录为-89.2摄氏度。冰冷的风在冰帽和大海间呼啸——所谓的重力风——可达300公里每小时，造成可怕的风冷却效果。

D 这个极端的环境产生了一些强大的力量，在全世界回荡。随着地球的自转，南极大陆海岸耦合不断产生低压力旋，这使得宇航员用肉眼就能看到既美丽又可怕的南极洲。压力旋往东北方向旋动，并不断加强和深化，在南大洋掀起排山倒海的巨浪，连水手们看了都会感到敬畏。最近的研究显示，相对于达尔文和塔希提岛的压力差(即南方涛动指数)，海洋的温度对于澳大利亚降雨量的预测可能会更有用。通过接收更为准确的预测，昆士兰北部的放牧人能够避免在年降雨量不足的时期过度放牧。这不仅能够减少他们的损失，而且能够防止严重的、也许需要几十年才能够修复的草场退化。澳大利亚联邦科工组织（CSIRO）正将此发展为预测系统的原型，但我们可以自信地预言，随着我们对南极洲和南大洋了解的增加，我们的预测能力也能够得到提高和扩展。

E 海洋表面温度取决于深水温度、空气温度和冰层之间的相互影响。每年冬天都有400万至1900万平方公里的海冰形成，将南极大陆附近的热量锁住。直到现在，我们才开始明白南澳大利亚经历过的海冰对天气的影响。但在另一方面，海冰范围的扩展所带来的影响远远超出了南极洲本身。南极磷虾——一种小虾类的甲壳动物，是长须鲸、企鹅、一些海豹、海鸟和许多鱼类的主食——在海冰充裕的时候繁殖良好，反之则不然。许多种类的长须鲸和海鸟在南北半球之间迁徙，当磷虾匮乏时，它们的生存也会受到影响。

F 世界海洋的洋流循环系统就像一个巨大的传送带，把水、溶解的矿物质以及营养物质从一个半球传送到另一个半球，从海洋深处传送到表面。南极洲环流（ACC）是世界上最长最大的洋流。通过它，大西洋、印度洋和太平洋的深海洋流都加入了一个全球性的温盐环流。在冬天，呼啸的重力风有时会冲刷出冰片，留在海面上形成冰封的泻湖或巨大的冰穴。最近的研究结果表明，每当新的海冰形成时，它都会不断地被重力风吹走，有时一天就能被吹到90公里之外。因为只有淡水才能冻结成冰，所以残留的水会变得越来越咸，密度也会越来越大。它们不断下沉，直到从大陆架剥落而下。冷水能比热水携带更多的氧气，所以当冷流上升到北半球时，就会给那里的海洋注入氧气，同时也会重新激活海洋。北部各海洋的状态以及它们的生物生产力在很大程度上归功于发生在南极的一切。

Reading Passage 3. Source of Knowledge

词汇详解

absurd *adj.* 荒谬的，不合理的，荒唐的（同义词有 ridiculous、unreasonable、foolish、stupid、meaningless 等。）

discomfort *n.* 不舒服，不适；不便；不安，不自在 *v.* 使不舒服；使不安（由表示“否定”的前缀 dis 和表示“舒适”的 comfort 组成，所以字面意思自然就是“不舒适”。当作为“不安，不自在”的意思时，等同于英文单词“unease”。）

complex *adj.* 复杂的，费解的，难懂的；复合的 *n.* 建筑群；综合体（在数学中，complex number 是“复数”的意思。）

symptom *n.* 症状；征兆（同义词有：sign、symbol、emblem、badge、mark、token、note、indication 等。）

late stage 末期，晚期，后期

prescribe *v.* 给……开药，开处方；规定，命令，指示（由表示“在……之前”的前缀 pre 和表示“写字”的词根 scribe 共同组成。当作“规定”的意思时，等同于英文单词“stipulate”。同义词还有 dictate、decree、impose、ordain。prescription 就有“药方，处方”的意思。）

antibiotic *n.* 抗生素

diagnose *v.* 诊断，判断

pneumonia *n.* 肺炎（表示“肺，肺脏”的英文单词是“lung”。有关人体其他部位的单词还有：brain 脑；heart 心脏；kidney 肾；intestine 肠；liver 肝；stomach 胃；spleen 脾；bladder 膀胱；vein 静脉；artery 动脉等。）

scenario *n.* 设想，方案，预测；剧情梗概（当作为“剧情概要”的意思时，等同于“synopsis”，

同义词还有 outline 和 summary。）

subjective *adj.* 主观的；主语的（objective 则是“客观的，宾语的”意思。）

status *n.* 地位，身份；职位；状况，情形（status bar 就是计算机中常见的“状态栏”；status quo 就是“现状，原来的状况”的意思。）

authenticate *v.* 证明……是真实的，证实；鉴定（同义词还有：confirm、corroborate、substantiate、verify、validate 等。）

consult *v.* 咨询，请教；商议；查阅，查询，参看（当表示“查阅，参看”的意思时，等同于“refer to”。如果生病了，要请医生诊治，我们就可以说“consult a doctor”。“a consulting engineer”就是“顾问工程师”的意思。另外，名词 consultant 也有“顾问”的意思。“咨询公司”的英文说法就是“consultancy”，“咨询费”就是“consultancy fees”。）

significant *adj.* 有重大意义的，显著的；有某种意义的；别有含义的；意味深长的（“无关紧要的”英文说法就是“insignificant”，也可以说“unimportant”或者“trivial”。）

emphasis *n.* 强调，重视，重要性；加重语气，重读（等同于 stress。to place/put/lay emphasis on sth 的意思就是“强调或者重视某事”。动词形式是 emphasise，意为“强调，使突出，加强……的语气”。）

complementary *adj.* 互补的，相互补足的，补充的（complementary angle 就是“余角”的意思；complementary colour 就是“互补色，补色”或者“对比色”的意思。）

holistic *adj.* 整体的，全面的；功能整体性的（holistic medicine 就是“整体医学”的意思。名词形式 holism 的意思就是“整体论，整体观念”。）

authoritative *adj.* 专断的，命令式的；权威性的（来自名词 authority“权利，威权”。）

practitioner *n.* 从业者，从业人员；习艺者；专门人才（“牙医”除了“dentist”这种说法之外，还可以说成“dental practitioner”。）

sanction *v.* 准予，准许，许可；惩罚 *n.* 许可，批准；制裁，约束，处罚（同义词有 approve、endorse、accredit、certify 等。）

notify *v.* 通报，通知（等同于“inform”，其他同义词有 acquaint 和 apprise 等。）

astrologer *n.* 占星家（前缀 astro 表示“星的，天体的，宇宙空间的”。与它相关的词汇还有：astronaut 宇航员；astrophysics 天体物理学；astrolabe 星盘；astrology 占星术，占星学；astrometry 天体测量学；astronomer 天文学家；astronomy 天文学等。）

therapist *n.* 治疗师，治疗专家；临床医学家（来自名词 therapy“治疗，疗法”。美容院里的“美容师”的英文说法就是“beauty therapist”。）

priest *n.* 牧师，神父，教士，祭司

statutory *adj.* 法定的，法令的（我们常说的“法定假日”，英文说法就是“statutory holiday”。）

privileged *adj.* 享有特权的，受特别优待的；荣幸，幸运；特许保密的（名词或动词形式为 privilege。作名词时，意为“优惠待遇，特权，荣耀，免责特权”。作动词时，意为“给

予特权，特别优待”，等同于“favour”。）

contemporary *adj.* 同一时代的，同时期的；当代的，现代的 *n.* 同代人，同辈人，同龄人（当作“现代的”意思时，等同于英文单词“modern”。）

proceed *v.* 继续做，继续进行；接着做；进行，前往（法律中，“起诉某人”的英文说法是“proceed against sb”。）

interpret *v.* 诠释，说明；把……理解为，领会；口译；演绎（同义词有 explain、elucidate、expound、explicate、construe 等。）

drill *n.* 训练，练习；钻头，钻机；演习；操练 *v.* 钻孔；培训；作……演习

题目详解

Questions 27-34

解答

27. 根据题干中的关键词“nature”找到原文中表示自身判断和医生诊断的本质区别的地方。原文对应内容出现在 E 段第二、三句话“For example, you decide to consult the doctor in the first place because you feel unwell—this is personal knowledge about your own body（对应题目中的“the nature of personal judgement”）. However, the doctor's expert diagnosis is based on experience and training（对应题目中的“the nature of doctor's diagnosis”）, with sources of knowledge...”。由此可以看出“personal judgement”是根据个人对自己身体的了解得出来的，这是人的本能，身体不舒服了，自然就察觉出有问题了，而医生的诊断则是“based on experience and training”，是通过学习、训练和经验积累得出来的，两者“nature”的对比就显而易见，所以正确答案是 E。

28. 根据题干中的关键词“culture about pressure”定位于原文 F 段中间“...Western culture has seen a significant(重要的) emphasis(强调) on stress-related illness in the media”，西方文化见证了媒体对压力相关疾病的高度重视。后面的几个句子也都是关于“压力过大”的描述，所以正确答案是 F。

29. 题干的内容是关于请病假 (sick leave) 的，原文对应信息出现在 H 段第四句话“It would not be acceptable to notify(通知，告诉) our employer that we simply felt too unwell to turn up for work...We need an expert medical diagnosis in order to obtain the necessary certificate...”，告诉雇主我们生病了不能上班，是行不通的……我们需要专业的医疗诊断来获得相关证明。题干内容与原文此处内容相符，所以正确答案是 H。

30. 题干内容是关于社会是如何看待医生的“opinions”的，根据关键词“society”找到原文中的 H 段“Perhaps the most influential and authoritative...expect the doctor...expert knowledge. This is socially sanctioned(认可)...need an expert medical diagnosis...

to obtain…certificate…”，也许最具影响力、最权威的知识来源是全科医生的医学知识……全社会都抱着这样的希望……如果我们请病假……就必须要有专业的医疗诊断，由此不难看出社会对医生的 opinions 的态度，题干与原文此处内容相符，所以正确答案是 H。

31. 根据题干中的关键词“become part of new knowledge”找到原文 I 段最后一句话“This will then be added to the doctor's medical knowledge…”，此处的“This”指代的是前一句的“new knowledge and new experience”。题干意思与原文此处内容相符，所以正确答案是 I。

32. 题干中的关键词为“non-specialised(非专业的)”，根据题干内容“来自非专业的知识”和“other than personal knowledge”可知，这部分既不是自己的判断也不是医生的专业诊断。原文中关于判断或诊断，除了提及自己和医生，还提到了朋友及家人。因此定位到原文 G 段第二句话“Comments from friends and family such as 'you do look ill' or 'that's a bad cough'…”。题干内容与原文此处相符，所以正确答案是 G。

33. 根据题干中的关键词“an example”找到原文中 C 段第一句话“Think about this example”，C、D 两段都在描述这个例子。题干中的“collective judgment”的意思是结合了个人经验和专业医生的判断，由此定位于原文 D 段倒数第二句话“This is the result of the combination of your own subjective(主观的) experience and the diagnosis(诊断) of someone who has the status of a medical expert.”题干内容与原文此处相符，所以正确答案是 D。

34. 根据题干中的关键词“do not realise they are ill”找到原文相应内容，即 B 段倒数第二句话“…people may be suffering from a disease and fail to be aware of the illness until it has reached a late stage in its development.”题干意思与原文此处相符，所以正确答案是 B。

Questions 35-40

解答

35. 题干中的空格前是冠词 a，空格后是连接词 and，根据语法可知空格中应填入名词。首先注意题干中“symptoms”是“症状”的意思，接着根据题干中的关键词“tiredness”找到原文中相应的词“tired”，定位于 B 段中间和 C 段第一行。然而 B 段中与“tired”并列的词是“over-worked”和“hangover”，它们一个是形容词，一个是“宿醉”的意思，都不是“症状”，均不符合题干要求。因此，正确答案在 C 段，与“tired”并列的词是“bad cough”，既是名词也是一个病症，符合题干要求，所以正确答案是 bad cough。

36. 首先注意题干中的“Doctor's measurement”，说明此处是讲医生所采取的行为，接着根据关键词“temperature”定位到原文 C 段最后一句话“the doctor who listens to your chest and heart, takes your temperature and blood pressure”，所以正确答案是 blood pressure。

37. 题干中的关键词“Common judgment”说明此处并不是医生给出的诊断。从“around you”可看出答案应该是身边的人或事物。原文对应内容在 G 段第二句话“Comments from friends and family such as...”，所以正确答案是 friends and family 或 friends and families。

38. 根据题干中的关键词“medical knowledge”找到原文 H 段第一句话“...is the medical knowledge provided by the general practitioner(从业者)”，所以正确答案是 practitioner。

39. 该题与第 38 题相连接,并且是第 38 题的一个例子。因此原文对应内容应在 H 段附近。根据题干中的“doctor's medical”定位于原文 H 段中间“We need an expert medical diagnosis(诊断) in order to obtain the necessary certificate...”，所以正确答案是 diagnosis。

40. 根据题干中的关键词“hypothesis”定位于原文 I 段第二句话“Given the doctor's medical training and background, she may hypothesise...”，题干中的“drill”与原文中的“training”是同义词替换，因此答案应填与 training 并列的词，所以正确答案是 background 或者 experience。

参考译文

知识的来源

A 什么是知识？当我们说我们了解某些东西时，我们所要表达的意思是什么呢？不同种类的知识状态又是什么呢？为了回答这些问题，我们将专注于某一特定的知识领域——医学。

B 我们是怎么知道自己生病了的呢？这听起来可能是一个荒唐的问题。因为当你觉得身体不适时，你就知道自己生病了；你的身体告诉你，你生病了。但是知道自己生病，其实是比知道自己感觉不适，或身体疼痛更为复杂的。有的时候，人们觉得自己出现了某些病症，然而，事实上，他们只是太累了，或是宿醉而醒。而有一些人却对疾病的侵袭浑然不知，直到病情恶化了才察觉到自己生病了。因此，我们如何知道自己已经生病了呢？有哪些知识可以帮助我们更好地了解它呢？

C 让我们来看这样一个例子。你觉得很不舒服，咳得厉害，还易乏。这很可能是你的工作压力太大了，或者是烟抽得太凶了。接着你觉得情况还在恶化，于是去医院，医生听你的心跳，测量体温和血压后，给你开了一些抗生素的药。

D 情况并没有好转，但是你迫使自己相信，或许病情正在好转。当你再次和医生见面时，

医生的诊断令人震惊。经验丰富的医生，确诊你得了肺炎。这意味着你需要好好卧床休息和一段时间的离职调养。于是脚本改变了。尽管仍旧是相同的症状，你不再认为这些是由于工作压力造成的了。你现在有证据证明你生病了。这个结果是结合你自己的主观经验和另一个医学专家的确诊。你有一个确诊的医学认证，证实你病得很严重。你意识到你生病了，并且有证明的依据。

E 这个情况展示了不同根源的知识。举个例子，因为你感到不舒服，所以一开始你打算去咨询医生——这是因为你了解自己的身体情况。但是，医生的专业诊断是根据从医经验和培训得来的，医生还通过许多方式获取知识，比如和其他专家探讨，阅读实验报告、医学教科书和多年的经验。

F 知识的来源之一便是自身的经历：个人对于自身显著变化的认识以及一些主观的痛苦经历和生理疾病。这些经历可以通过其他形式的知识来调解，比如，一些能描绘我们经历的词、来自亲朋好友的常识以及一些从大众文化当中获得的知识。例如，在过去的十年里，西方文化见证了媒体对压力相关疾病的高度重视。“压力过大”已成为办公室日常交流的一个普遍反应，同时也成为大众常识的一部分。这也难怪我们开始寻找这样一个理由来解释身体不舒服这一症状的原因。

G 我们也会依赖那些认识我们的人的观察。来自亲朋好友的一些评论，例如，“你看起来像是病了”或“咳得厉害”也可能成为知识来源之一。一些互补的医疗实践，如整体医学，应用了一些我们用来决定不健康本质、程度以及可能的治疗方案的东西，建立起一套知识体系。

H 也许最具影响力、最权威的知识来源是全科医生的医学知识。我们希望医生能了解专业知识。全社会都抱着这样的希望。我们都知道，告诉雇主我们生病了不能上班，或是告诉他我们的信仰疗疾师、占星家、治疗师、甚至是神父说生病上班不是一个好主意是行不通的。如果我们请病假超出法定病假期，就必须要有专业的医疗诊断来获得相关证明。在这方面，医学在当代西方文明中享有特权。医生同时也被看做是拥有必备专业知识的人，这使得他们能够依法开处方和治疗方案，而这些是病人无法通过其他方式获得的。然而，当我们在判定自身健康状况时，我们还有别的知识可以引用。

I 不过，现有的知识仅是这个小故事的一部分；新的知识也要被考虑在内的。设想一个拥有医学背景和相关培训的医生，她或许会推测“是患肺炎了吗？”并且继续寻找与此有关的证据。她会通过观察和仪器来评定这些证据，并且根据她的培训和经验辩证性地阐述她的假设。这样做的结果就是产生了对个人和医生都有用的新的知识和经验。它们会成为医生的医学知识，而且还可能会对未来的肺炎诊断有所帮助。

Answer Keys

Test 1

Each question correctly answered scores 1 mark. **CORRECT SPELLING IS NEEDED IN ALL ANSWERS.**

Reading Passage 1

1 viii
2 ii
3 vi
4 v
5 i
6 x
7 iii
8 No
9 No
10 Yes
11 Not Given
12 Not Given
13 Yes

Reading Passage 2

14 B
15 D
16 E
17 H
18 wind/winds
19 swaying
20 further apart
21 footsteps
22 horizontal forces
23 upright
24 Arup
25 Imperial College
26 University of Southampton

Reading Passage 3

27 C
28 C
29 D
30 A
31 E
32 B
33 Yes
34 Yes
35 No
36 No
37 Not Given
38 No
39 Not Given
40 Yes

If you score...

0-12	13-26	27-40
you are highly unlikely to get an acceptable score under examination conditions and we recommend that you spend a lot of time improving your English before you take IELTS.	you may get an acceptable score under examination conditions but we recommend that you think about having more practice or lessons before you take IELTS.	you are likely to get an acceptable score under examination conditions but remember that different institutions will find different scores acceptable.

Test 2

Each question correctly answered scores 1 mark. **CORRECT SPELLING IS NEEDED IN ALL ANSWERS.**

Reading Passage 1

1 nests
2 tortoises
3 oaks
4 Native Americans
5 prescribed burns
6 shrubs
7 soil
8 Ants
9 eggs
10 True
11 False
12 Not Given
13 True

Reading Passage 2

14 D
15 G
16 A
17 B
18 H
19 B
20 B
21 C
22 A
23 *Poetics*
24 tragedy
25 landmarks
26 flaw/weakness

Reading Passage 3

27 iv
28 x
29 iii
30 vii
31 i
32 v
33 ix
34 Linear
35 obstacle
36 acoustic
37 barchan
38 shape
39 tone
40 minerals

If you score...

0-12	13-26	27-40
you are highly unlikely to get an acceptable score under examination conditions and we recommend that you spend a lot of time improving your English before you take IELTS.	you may get an acceptable score under examination conditions but we recommend that you think about having more practice or lessons before you take IELTS.	you are likely to get an acceptable score under examination conditions but remember that different institutions will find different scores acceptable.

Test 3

Each question correctly answered scores 1 mark. **CORRECT SPELLING IS NEEDED IN ALL ANSWERS.**

Reading Passage 1

1 True
2 Not Given
3 False
4 False
5 True
6 True
7 Not Given
8 tools
9 nomadic
10 grouped/grouped together
11 foodstuffs
12 20,000
13 craft specialists

Reading Passage 2

14 black stripes
15 12 million
16 Australia
17 European
18 A
19 D
20 C
21 B
22 A
23 D
24 B
25 D
26 A

Reading Passage 3

27 v
28 ix
29 i
30 vi
31 x
32 viii
33 C
34 B
35 D
36 D
37 A
38 Horace Walpole
39 fairy tale
40 Sri Lanka

If you score...

0-12	13-26	27-40
you are highly unlikely to get an acceptable score under examination conditions and we recommend that you spend a lot of time improving your English before you take IELTS.	you may get an acceptable score under examination conditions but we recommend that you think about having more practice or lessons before you take IELTS.	you are likely to get an acceptable score under examination conditions but remember that different institutions will find different scores acceptable.

Test 4

Each question correctly answered scores 1 mark. **CORRECT SPELLING IS NEEDED IN ALL ANSWERS.**

Reading Passage 1

1 B
2 A
3 B
4 F
5 C
6 E
7 G
8 G
9 A
10 sea water/salt water/salt
11 swimming speed
12 coastal otters
13 small mammals

Reading Passage 2

14 iii
15 vi
16 i
17 ii
18 ix
19 v
20 iv
21 yellow-fever epidemic
22 Finland
23 institutions/governments
24 Europe
25 einkorn wheat
26 Singapore

Reading Passage 3

27 B
28 C
29 A
30 A
31 Yes
32 Not Given
33 No
34 Not Given
35 Yes
36 No
37 F
38 B
39 A
40 D

If you score...

0-12	13-26	27-40
you are highly unlikely to get an acceptable score under examination conditions and we recommend that you spend a lot of time improving your English before you take IELTS.	you may get an acceptable score under examination conditions but we recommend that you think about having more practice or lessons before you take IELTS.	you are likely to get an acceptable score under examination conditions but remember that different institutions will find different scores acceptable.

Test 5

Each question correctly answered scores 1 mark. **CORRECT SPELLING IS NEEDED IN ALL ANSWERS.**

Reading Passage 1

1 x
2 xi
3 iii
4 i
5 vi
6 v
7 ix
8 vii
9 False
10 True
11 True
12 Not Given
13 Not Given

Reading Passage 2

14 guiding principles, rules
15 mentor
16 patterns of behavior/patterns
17 complex
18 knowledge
19 False
20 Not Given
21 True
22 True
23 True
24 accurate
25 human bias
26 consensus

Reading Passage 3

27 C
28 A
29 D
30 B
31 lapse/time interval
32 continuous action
33 time
34 greater length
35 slowed down proportionately
36 A
37 C
38 G
39 E
40 F

If you score...

0-12	13-26	27-40
you are highly unlikely to get an acceptable score under examination conditions and we recommend that you spend a lot of time improving your English before you take IELTS.	you may get an acceptable score under examination conditions but we recommend that you think about having more practice or lessons before you take IELTS.	you are likely to get an acceptable score under examination conditions but remember that different institutions will find different scores acceptable.

Test 6

Each question correctly answered scores 1 mark. **CORRECT SPELLING IS NEEDED IN ALL ANSWERS.**

Reading Passage 1

1 True
2 False
3 False
4 Not Given
5 True
6 True
7 Not Given
8 46
9 human eye accommodation
10 Indo-European
11 Richard Brocklesby
12 Royal Institution
13 gas lighting

Reading Passage 2

14 D
15 F
16 E
17 C
18 A
19 D
20 A
21 C
22 C
23 A
24 C
25 C
26 A

Reading Passage 3

27 E
28 F
29 H
30 H
31 I
32 G
33 D
34 B
35 bad cough
36 blood pressure
37 friends and family/friends and families
38 practitioner
39 diagnosis
40 background/experience

If you score...

0-12	13-26	27-40
you are highly unlikely to get an acceptable score under examination conditions and we recommend that you spend a lot of time improving your English before you take IELTS.	you may get an acceptable score under examination conditions but we recommend that you think about having more practice or lessons before you take IELTS.	you are likely to get an acceptable score under examination conditions but remember that different institutions will find different scores acceptable.